PASTIMES

The Context of Contemporary Leisure

Fourth Edition

Ruth V. Russell

D1509714

Sagamore Publishing, L.L.C.
Champaign, Illinois

Publishers: Joseph J. Bannon/Peter Bannon
General Manager: M. Douglas Sanders
Production Manager: Jose Barrientos/Jason Pethtel
Cover/Interior Design: Jose Barrientos

Library of Congress Catalog Card Number: 2008943290
ISBN: 978-1-57167-545-3
Printed in the United States.

Sagamore Publishing, L.L.C.
804 North Neil Street
Champaign, IL 61820
www.sagamorepub.com

For Pres and Aloise.

TABLE OF CONTENTS

Preface

The purpose of this fourth edition of *Pastimes* is to include new concepts supported by new research findings about leisure in contemporary societies. Throughout, I have tried to use the most interesting, relevant, and exciting information and approaches possible. This wasn't at all difficult. Leisure is simply a very intriguing subject.

First, as an introduction to the phenomenon of leisure, the book must be current. Momentous changes, actual and alleged, have always been the root of leisure experiences and expressions. To match, *Pastimes* again gathers together state-of-the-art practices in leisure sciences and studies, reflecting a wide range of material from the disciplines of sociology, psychology, economics, political science, anthropology, geography, the humanities, and media and cultural studies.

Second, as a teaching tool, this fourth edition teaches more. It contains more illustrations of concepts through field-based cases, biographical features, exploratory activities, and research studies. There are more definitions of terms in margins, and even new and more photographs! A new chapter has also been added for this edition, outlining leisure service delivery systems.

More than a textbook, however, *Pastimes* is very much a point of view. Leisure is presented as a human phenomenon that is individual and collective, vital and frivolous, historical and contemporary, good and bad.

Acknowledgements

This edition is the result of what I have learned from years of engagement with leisure theory, research, and personal and professional practice. Signs of my worldwide wanderings are also evident. Learning is the greatest of joys, and I am lucky to be able to devote my life to it.

Throughout these adventures I have felt grateful to many. To begin, I am indebted to my family, neighbors, friends, and colleagues for helping me learn. I wish to thank Pat Setser in particular for her constant patience and support. I also wish to acknowledge the longstanding good ideas and probing challenges provided by former doctoral students who worked with me in courses about this subject matter at Indiana University, Bloomington, and who now are distinguished colleagues in their own right. Specifically, I thank Trish Ardovino, Boyd Hegarty, Debbie Smith, Jeff Nix, and Agnes Kovacs.

PART ONE

LEISURE AS A CONDITION OF HUMANITY: PERSONAL CONTEXT

We are human in large part because of our leisure expression.

Welcome! We begin our exploration of leisure by considering its significance for us personally. Leisure helps shape us as human beings. It is expressed throughout our lives and is revealed in our growth, health, motives, feelings, and actions.

Chapter 1
Illustrates leisure's meanings for us through the humanities, and by contrasting ancient and contemporary definitions.

Chapter 2
Discusses the benefits of leisure to us: happiness, freedom, pleasure, intrinsic reward, play, and others.

Chapter 3
Offers some explanations about our leisure choices and behaviors.

Chapter 4
Traces the ways leisure helps us grow, mature, adjust, thrive, and age.

CHAPTER ONE

MEANING OF LEISURE

PREVIEW

What is leisure?
Leisure is an intricate and dynamic concept with different meanings depending on the context.

Can we find meanings of leisure through the humanities?
Perhaps leisure can be best understood through music, art, and literature. For example, individual and cultural meanings can be revealed in a story, a song, and a painting.

Are there clues to contemporary meanings of leisure in ancient history?
From the beginning of human history leisure has been a part of everyday life, and these legacies endure today.

How is leisure defined now?
Leisure is individually defined, but most common are the themes of free time, recreational activity, and a special feeling.

KEY TERMS

Skiing through a pine forest. Watching a movie. Leafing through a magazine. Winning a game of solitaire. Coaching a Little League team. Conversing with virtual pals in an electronic chat room. Playing a pick-up game of basketball. Planting geraniums. Walking the dog. These and a wide array of other experiences are our pastimes—our leisure.

To have leisure is one of the earliest dreams of human beings—to be free to pursue what we want, to spend our time meaningfully in pleasurable ways, to live in a state of grace (Godbey, 2003, p. 1). Living life on our own terms is a central idea for people, and in this chapter we set the stage for understanding the essential humanness of leisure by exploring its foundational meanings.

Figure 1.1
Leisure is a complex concept that has different meanings depending on the people, place, and time. (Shutterstock©, 2008)

Since leisure is a complex concept with different meanings depending on the people, place, and time, defining it requires journeys to different peoples, places, and times. First, we define leisure through its reflections in the humanities: literature, art, and music. Next, we examine some of the original meanings of leisure in ancient cultures. Finally, we summarize leisure's contemporary meaning according to its most common connotations. Throughout the chapter's discussion, you'll notice that leisure has multiple, and even contradictory meanings.

The Humanities of Leisure

Leisure's meanings are reflected through the *humanities*. The subjects of the humanities include the arts, such as music, paintings, and stories, that convey what it is like to be human. The word "art" itself comes from the same root as the word "artificial," meaning something made by humans.

Humanities:
human creations that describe the human experience

In creating songs, poems, and sculptures songwriters, poets, and sculptors portray their own experience. So, when we listen to a musical performance or read a poem, we understand something about the experiences of its creator. Indeed, in these expressions are the images, ideas, and words that introduce us to people we have never met, places we have never visited, and ideas that may have never crossed our minds.

Leisure's Meanings in Literature

Literature, in the broadest sense, is widely apparent in everyday life. Magazine articles, greeting card verses, hymns, and novels are all forms of literature. Reading literature in itself is an important leisure expression and to prove it, Americans spend about $25 billion a year on books (Association of American Publishers, 2008).

Fiction writers, dramatists, and poets often write about their feelings, what they believe, their times, and the daily lives they lead. Like looking into a mirror, literature offers a view of human life—including leisure.

For example, in John Updike's short story "Still of Some Use," notice how the loss of family unity is described through the loss of a favorite family pastime.

When Foster helped his ex-wife clean out the attic of the house where they had once lived and which she was now selling, they came across dozens of forgotten, broken games. Parcheesi, Monopoly, Lotto: games aping the strategies of the stock market, of crime detection, of real estate speculation, of international diplomacy and war; games with spinners, dice, lettered tiles, cardboard spacemen, and plastic battleships; games bought in five-and-tens and department stores feverish and musical with Christmas expectations; games enjoyed on the afternoon of a birthday and for a few afternoons thereafter and then allowed, shy of one or two pieces, to drift into closets and toward the attic. Yet, discovered in their bright flat boxes between trunks of outgrown clothes and defunct appliances, the games presented a forceful semblance of value: the springs of their miniature launchers still reacted, the logic of their instructions would still generate suspense, given a chance.

"What shall we do with all these games?" Foster shouted, in a kind of agony, to his scattered family as they moved up and down the attic stairs.

"Trash 'em," his younger son, a strapping 19, urged.

"Would the Goodwill want them?" asked his ex-wife, still wife enough to think that all of his questions deserved answers. "You used to be able to give things like that to orphanages. But they don't call them orphanages anymore, do they?"

His older son, now 22, with a cinnamon-colored beard, offered, "They wouldn't work anyhow; they all have something missing. That's how they got to the attic."

"Well, why didn't we throw them away at the time?" Foster asked, and had to answer himself. Cowardice, the answer was. Inertia. Clinging to the past.

His sons, with a shadow of old obedience, came and looked over his shoulder at the sad wealth of abandoned playthings, silently groping with him for the particular happy day connected to this and that pattern of coded squares and colored arrows. Their lives had touched these tokens and counters once; excitement had flowed along the paths of these stylized landscapes. But the day was gone, and scarcely a memory remained.

"Toss 'em," the younger decreed, in his manly voice.

For these days of cleaning out, the boy had borrowed a pickup truck from a friend and parked it on the lawn beneath the attic window, so the smaller items of discard could be tossed directly into it. The bigger items were lugged down the stairs and through the front hall and out; already the truck was loaded with old mattresses, broken clock radios, obsolete skis, and boots. It was a game of sorts to hit the truck bed with objects dropped from the height of the house. Foster flipped game after game at the target two stories below. When the boxes hit, they exploded, throwing a spray of

dice, tokens, counters, and cards into the air and across the lawn. A box called Mousetrap, its lid showing laughing children gathered around a Rube Goldberg device, drifted sideways, struck one side wall of the truck, and spilled its plastic components into a flowerbed. As a set of something called Drag Race! floated gently as a snowflake before coming to rest, much diminished, on a stained mattress, Foster saw in the depth of downward space the cause of his melancholy: he had not played enough with these games. Now, no one wanted to play.
(From "Trust Me" by John Updike. Copyright© 1987 by John Updike. Reprinted by permission of Alfred A. Knopf, Inc.)

Updike, whose fiction writing usually includes deep uneasiness mixed with humor over changes of relationships within a family, has used in this story "fun and games" as an explanation of family loss. Can you remember the end of a particular family leisure custom, such as playing cards on the patio in the summer or spending vacations at the same place, that symbolize a change in your family relationships?

In comparison, Maya Angelou's poem "Harlem Hopscotch," uses the rhythm of a children's street game to express a serious problem in society.

One foot down, then hop! It's hot.
        Good things for the ones that's got.
Another jump, now to the left.
        Everybody for hisself.
In the air, now both feet down.
        Since you black, don't stick around.
Food is gone, the rent is due,
        Curse and cry and then jump two.
All the people out of work,
        Hold for three, then twist and jerk.
Cross the line, they count you out.
        That's what hopping's all about.
Both feet flat, the game is done.
        They think I lost, I think I won.
(From Just Give Me a Cool Drink of Water 'Fore I Die by Maya Angelou, Copyright© 1971 by Maya Angelou. Reprinted by permission of Random House, Inc.)

In the poem Angelou uses the children's game of hopscotch to vent frustration and a sense of betrayal. Although the poem is about the injustices of race and social class, it makes light of it by putting it into a rhythm of a classic children's pastime. Or does it? What do you think is meant by the game's outcome in the last line?

Leisure's Meanings in Art

People have always had an interest in the beauty of pattern. We enjoy patterns of contrast and balance for their own sake. We doodle during class, wear jewelry, and make designs with the lawn mower in our yard. We receive an *aesthetic* experience from these activities.

Asthetic: sense of beauty

Box 1.1

 The Study Says

Dunk the Duchess

Directions: Players need two full pitchers of beer for the table and one empty glass per person, plus one extra glass. Float the extra glass in one of the pitchers. The lip of the glass should protrude about an inch above the surface of the beer. To begin, players fill their glasses from the second pitcher and take turns pouring beer from their glasses into the floating glass. Each player is responsible for an out-loud count of five while pouring beer into the floating glass. The glass then becomes the responsibility of the next player. The perfect pour is one that causes the glass to sink to the bottom in six seconds, because the player in whose turn the glass drops to the bottom of the pitcher must drink all of its contents.

In this study, a narrative analysis of the drinking game "Dunk the Duchess" reveals the game is based on a fairy tale. Fairy tales have three characteristics, as this drinking game demonstrates: character roles, binary oppositions, and archetypal narrative trajectory.

For the characters, the role of princess is played by the floating glass, the object of the action. In fact, the very name of the game refers to the floating glass as "the duchess." The floating glass also plays the role of villain. It controls the outcome of the story and has the power to bring both safety and harm to players. The beer in the pitcher containing the floating glass is like the fairy godmother: it instructs the princess/glass in what to do. Meanwhile, the role of hero is played by the individual players' glasses of beer. Yet the hero is a false one. As the game story proceeds and more beer is poured into the glass from the players' glasses, it is revealed that while appearing to nurture and care for the princess/glass, ultimately the beer is transformed into a villain.

The study also suggested drinking games are fairy tales according to their binary oppositions. Basic to any narrative is the establishment of conflict. Binary oppositions, or pairs of opposing forces, often identify the conflict. The opposition of these forces creates the excitement of the action. In "Dunk the Duchess" these competing forces are:

weak	–	strong
unskilled	–	skilled
female	–	male
chugging	–	not chugging
"winning"	–	"losing"

Finally, the narrative trajectory of the game can be analyzed. In the typical fairy tale plot, there is preparation, complication, transference, struggle, return, and rec-

Box 1.1(Cont.)

ognition. In "Dunk the Duchess" the preparation phase is the gathering of players, pitchers, beer, and glasses. The complication phase of the plot begins when the villain's (floating glass) efforts to manipulate the princess (also the floating glass) succeed, and the princess is unable to sustain the quantity of beer. There is transference in the plot's trajectory and a struggle ensues. All is ended when the "winning" player chugs, to the enthusiasm of the other players.

Russell, R.V. (1999). *Snarfing, booting, and Dunk the Duchess: A narrative tale of college drinking games.* Paper presented at the Leisure Research Symposium Nashville, TN.

Figure 1.2

The ancient Greeks were enthusiastic about sports because they greatly respected the beauty and agility of the human body. Photo of a sculpture of Nike loosening her sandal, Acropolis. (© Ruth V. Russell, 2008)

Impressionism:
an art style that achieves a vividness simulating reflected light

The use of pattern also has a commemorative function. The most important events in our religious, social, and political lives, for example, are reflected in images and icons. For example, when we take pictures of relatives at family reunions, we record the occasion in visual form to make it memorable.

In other words, art mirrors what we consider to be both beautiful and important. Since our curiosity here is about leisure's meanings, let's continue with our humanities lens. What is considered beautiful and important about leisure through sculpture and painting?

For example, the ancient Greeks admired the beauty and agility of the human body. Since it was through the perfection of their bodies that human beings most resembled the gods, sports were a spiritual as well as physical expression. The numerous ancient Greek sculptures of humans remaining today communicate that physicality was important.

Yet, perhaps one of the most readily recognized reflections of leisure in art comes from the *impressionist* period. Impressionism is a style of art that presents an immediate "impression" of an object or event. Impressionist painters try to show what the eye sees at a glance, and the composition seems spontaneous.

Although painters and other artists have created impressionistic works in several periods of history, the term is most commonly applied to the work of a group of painters exhibiting in Paris from about 1870 to 1910. What is the impression of leisure in this art?

The painting "Terrace at Sainte-Adresse" by Claude Monet depicts vacationers (figure 1.3). Painted in 1866, it is the view from a window of his aunt's villa in France where Monet stayed that summer. Out in the water are a number of ships, from the pleasure boats moored on the left to the steamers on the right. The ships represent the transition from sail to steam. In the middle-distance is a fishing boat (just above the parasol), suggesting another transition—from the local and traditional life at Sainte-Adresse before its transformation by tourists. This all mirrors what was happening at that time in most of coastal France. Fishing villages were changing into resorts, with broad avenues, sidewalks, formal gardens, and huge buildings. As many waters-edge locations have experienced in the years since and through to today, the scene depicted in Monet's painting was shortly changed by the creation of artificial spaces for the visiting tourists, changing forever the lives of the fishermen and shopkeepers who once lived there (Herbert, 1988).

Mary Cassatt's "Woman in Black at the Opera," painted in 1879, presents a woman using her upward-tilted opera glasses to scan the audience (figure 1.4). With a bit of humor, Cassatt also placed a man in the distance leaning out of his box to point his glasses in the woman's direction, emphasizing the fun of spying on one's society (Herbert, 1988). We also learn from this impressionistic painting that leisure defined the upper social class of this era.

Figure 1.3

Claude Monet. *Terrace at Sainte-Adresse*. 1866. (The Metropolitan Museum of Art, purchased with special contributions and purchase funds given or bequeathed by friends of the Museum, 1967. 67.241)

Enjoying restaurants and cafes was also an important pastime for Parisians at the time. Many paintings from the impressionist art period depict women and men enjoying each other's company over food and drink. Pierre-Auguste Renoir's painting "The Luncheon of the Boating Party," begun in the summer of 1880, shows the terrace of the Restaurant Fournaise (figure 1.5). In the painting Renoir shows us something about relationships. Notice the young man leaning over, intent on the young woman seated at the front table, while her tablemate looks away and across the table. But the object of his gaze is a woman occupied with her puppy, and the man standing behind her is gazing across the terrace at someone else. Could we say this painting reflects isolation, however relaxed, that can be part of anyone's experience at a party?

Even this brief glance at the art of the late 1800s reveals clear meanings of leisure in Paris. Indeed, idle hours and entertainment greatly expanded during this period, particularly for the upper class. As thousands of paintings by impressionist artists portray, by the end of that century, daily life there was dominated by theaters, operas, cafes, restaurants, dances, racetracks, gardens, and parks. Tourism began as well, with a focus on elegant urban culture and the peaceful beauty of the seaside.

Figure 1.4

Mary Cassatt. *Woman in Black at the Opera.* **1879.** (The Hayden Collection. Courtesy Museum of Fine Arts, Boston)

Leisure's Meanings in Music

Music is perhaps the most basic and universal activity of humankind. Beginning as the natural sound of the human voice, music over the centuries has taken many forms and reflected many ways of life. Today in Western cultures, people express themselves through jazz, rock, rhythm and blues, country, rap, gospel, classical and other musical styles. For example, U.S. recording companies in 2006 shipped over $11.5 billion in CDs, ringtones, music videos, and other musical recordings (Recording Industry Association of America, 2007).

How might music portray leisure? All forms of music reflect leisure's meanings, but just to illustrate this, we'll begin with rock and roll, and Elvis Presley, who remains rock's most indelible image worldwide. In Elvis, millions of young people found more than a new entertainer; they found themselves, or at least an idealized image of themselves that stood in stark, liberating contrast to the repressed atmosphere of the 1950s. Thus, through a popular form of leisure —rock and roll music—masses of young people found a cathartic identity.

What was this new identity? In Elvis' "Hound Dog" and the flip side's "Don't Be Cruel," the highest-selling single record of the decade, we find a summary of how Elvis' rock and roll represented young people of the time. While the straight rock of screaming guitars and drums in "Hound Dog" emphasizes a wild and raucous sound, "Don't Be Cruel" has a lighter beat and gentler accompaniment that focuses attention on a sweet melody and lyrics. This makes for a big difference between the sexually aggressive "Hound Dog" and the playfully innocent "Don't Be Cruel." And, just like the two sides of this one single record, youth of the 1950s were bumping, although timidly, against the outer edges of a sort of rebellion.

Figure 1.5

Pierre-Auguste Renoir. *The Luncheon of the Boating Party.* **1881.** (The Phillips Collection, Washington, D.C.)

While songs like those by Elvis defined the character of youth, others at that time spoke to the youth creed – having fun. One example is "All Summer Long" by The Beach Boys. Here are some of the lyrics:

> T-shirts, cut-offs, and a pair of thongs
> (T-shirts, cut-offs, and a pair of thongs)
> We've been having fun all summer long
>
> Miniature golf and Hondas in the hills
> (Miniature golf and Hondas in the hills)
> When we rode the horse we got some thrills.
> (Excerpt from "All Summer Long," by The Beach Boys – Brian Wilson, Irving Music, Inc.,
> Recorded 5/6/64 and 5/7/64)

The Beach Boys' songs were full of in-group surfing references, along with celebrations of hot rods, drag races, dance parties, going steady, and other rites of teenage life in the 1950s and 1960s. And, the purpose of that life was to have fun.

We can find meanings of leisure in musical forms other than rock and roll as well. For example, nearly two centuries before Elvis and the Beach Boys, Vivaldi's classical orchestral work "The Four Seasons" portrayed a description of the powerful emotions associated with the change of nature's seasons. The celebration in the music of things pastoral is poignant, since the composer was sickly and often housebound, yet it also reflects the eighteenth century's fashionable preoccupation with the idealization of nature.

Drawing on more contemporary forms, leisure is sometimes used as a metaphor in music. One illustration of this is country and pop singer k.d. Lang's "Wash Me Clean," where desiring someone romantically is like swimming—"you swim, swim through my veins." Meanwhile, in the rap song "People Everyday," recorded by Arrested Development, leisure is hanging out in the park, putting one's soul at ease. And Gang of Four's "Natural's Not In It" gives us a glimpse of leisure as consumption. Here are some sample lyrics from this song:

> The problem of leisure
> What to do for pleasure
> Ideal love a new purchase
> A market of the senses
> Dream of the perfect life
> Economic circumstances
> The body is good business
> Sell out, maintain the interest
>
> (Excerpt from "Natural's Not In It" recorded by Gang of Four, first recorded in 1979 in the Entertainment! album)

There are, of course, many more sculptures, paintings, stories, poems, compositions, and songs we could use to extend this excursion into the portrayal of leisure in the humanities. For example, the short stories in F. Scott Fitzgerald's *Tales of the Jazz Age* are full of leisure meanings for young Americans during the 1920s. Artist Judy Chicago's *The Dinner Party* is installation art depicting place settings for 39 mythical and historically famous women. It can be said to celebrate traditional female arts, such as weaving, embroidery, and china painting.

Classical Meanings of Leisure

It is not really known where civilization, that is settled community life, originated. The retreat of the last glaciers (about 11,000 years ago) initiated

Box 1.2

 # *In Your Own Experience*

More Leisure Meanings in the Humanities

What other examples of leisure's meaning in the humanities can you find? Here is a potpourri of experiences to help you find them:

1. Who is your favorite recording artist? Listen to samples of this music and determine how many references to leisure you can find. How is leisure defined in this music?
2. Visit your campus or community art museum. Check out any of the galleries (Western art, Eastern art, ancient art) and determine how leisure is portrayed in the paintings and sculptures.
3. Pick up a copy of your favorite magazine. By just glancing at each page from beginning to end, how many references to leisure can you find in the ads, stories, articles, and photographs? How is leisure depicted?

successive periods of cultural evolution from primitive hunting-and-gathering societies to the development of agriculture and animal husbandry, and ultimately, to the urbanization and industrialization of modern societies. As people gathered together into societies, more formalized rules of conduct naturally emerged, including governments, religions, work occupations, and, of course, leisure.

Our contemporary meanings of leisure have been shaped by the histories of these ancient societies. Let's explore some of them.

The Kingdom of Kush: Adornment in Daily Life

Africa has been called the "birthplace of the human race." And, the oldest evidence of human-like creatures found anywhere consists of bones and other fossils discovered at many sites in Africa, including in the fertile soils of the Nile Valley. Scientists have identified one such civilization and people as the kingdom of Kush, which arose in about 4,000 BC (Bayley, Baynes, & Kendall, 2004).

Based on archeological evidence, the Kushites were like their neighbors the Egyptians in their fondness for body adornment. For example, they are considered to have used strong scents. A popular form was a perfumed ointment shaped like a cone and worn on the top of the head. As the evening progressed the cone would melt and the scented oil would run down the face and neck. The cones would be renewed throughout the evening.

Eye makeup, typically green and black, was probably the most characteristic of Kushite cosmetics. And, red ochre mixed with fat was thought to be applied as lipstick. Henna was used as hair dye, and like today, tattooing was also practiced. Tattoos of the god Bes have been found on the thighs of mummified dancers, musicians and servant girls. Wigs and hairpieces were also quite popular. Other tools used in the beauty ritual that have been found include short fine-tooth combs, hairpins, and a small bronze implement with a pivoting blade thought to be a hair curler. (Pan-African Market Place, 1993; EMuseum @ Minnesota State University at Mankato, 2008)

Ancient Greece: The Leisure Ideal

One of the hallmark messages of this chapter is leisure is a paradoxical concept. Nowhere in our journey of ancient cultures is this point perhaps better made than in ancient Greece. Indeed, our leisure inheritance from this era of history is significant.

Although much has been debated about Greek concepts of leisure (see Sylvester, 1999), one constant theme from this ancient culture seems to be its focus on leisure as a means to the good life. The philosopher Plato, for example, was interested in the benefits of music and gymnastics. He believed there were spiritual and physical rewards to be gained from these expressions. Socrates believed knowledge was required in choosing the best pleasures. That is, the good life was a life of right choices and conduct.

Throughout his writings, Aristotle also conveyed ideas about the role of leisure in attaining the good life. He believed leisure was freedom from having an occupation, and was the necessary condition for happiness. He thought the goodness of anything was found in the realization of its uniqueness, and for human beings, he considered the power to think to be the most unique of human

Figure 1.6

Aristotle: Greek philosopher who shares with Plato and Socrates the distinction of being the most famous of ancient thinkers. (Shutterstock©, 2008)

qualities. Thus, Aristotle held a life of contemplation was the proper use of leisure. To him, life should be devoted to not only thinking noble thoughts, but to doing civic and productive deeds as well (Hemingway, 1988).

Leisure scholars have labeled these philosophical ideas the "leisure ideal." That is, leisure is a force that can ignoble us. This traditional historical interpretation can be exampled by the Greek concept, σχολή, which was translated as ***schole***. This translation is also connected to the Latin (licentia and licere) and associated French (loisir) and English (leisure and school) words. Extending these word associations, the ideal pastime, then, was in the pursuit of scholarship: reading, thinking, debating, discussing, and studying.

Schole: an ancient Greek term for scholarship that is translated today to the word leisure

How ancient Greek people interpreted the advice of their philosophers into their daily lives also provides a legacy for leisure today. For example, daily leisure did include such intellectual pursuits as philosophy and mathematics, as well as poetry and music. Greek children played with toys widely recognized by today's children as jacks (called knuckle bones

Box 1.3

In Profile

Aristotle

Aristotle (384-322 BC) was a Greek philosopher, educator, and scientist. He grew up in the northern Greek town of Stagira, the son of the personal physician of the king of nearby Macedonia. Some historians believe Aristotle may have lived his early years recklessly but soon made his way to Plato at the Academy in Athens and studied under this master teacher for 20 years (Simpson, 1989).

After leaving Athens, Aristotle became the tutor to Alexander, grandson of the Macedonian king. This new assignment paid off when Alexander later conquered all of Greece and ascended to the throne. With Alexander's support, Aristotle returned to Athens and founded the Lyceum. This new school immediately surpassed Plato's Academy in prestige and was particularly renown for its teaching of the natural sciences.

In spite of this, the Athenian citizenry remained at odds with Aristotle because of his friendship with Alexander, their conqueror. When Alexander unexpectedly died, the Macedonian rule in Athens quickly fell, and Aristotle was forced to leave Athens to avoid the same fate as Socrates. A few months after fleeing Athens, however, Aristotle became ill and died.

because the jacks were animal knuckle bones), kites, and marbles. Amphitheaters provided music, dance, and drama entertainment, and even proxemos, who guided fellow citizens traveling abroad, were the forerunners of today's tour guides.

The ancient Greeks also devoted much of their lives to religious expressions. For most Greeks, the pantheon of gods and goddesses were the narratives for daily decisions (Garland, 1998), including leisure choices. For example, through organized sport attention to maintaining a strong body could be practiced.

Excavation at the ancient Olympic site in western Greece shows that the first formalized Olympic Games took place in 776 BC. Originally named for the god *Olympian*, these games were later held in honor of the god Zeus. Part religious event and part sport event, the Olympic Games were held every four years, and in the first 13 Olympiads, a footrace of about 180 meters was the only event.

Olympian:
one of the ancient Greek gods; being like the god, especially in being calm and untroubled by ordinary affairs

Through the years longer running races were added, as well as other types of competition, such as horse races, weight lifting, and boxing. A savage and sometimes deadly sport called pancratium, which combined boxing and wrestling, was introduced in 648 BC. Scholars tell us that pancratium was like a form of extreme wrestling in which the only hits not allowed were gouging with the thumb and biting.

Of course, athletes in the games were the aristocratic young men who had the privilege of leisure. To point, social distinctions were prominent in all of ancient Greek leisure. What Plato, Socrates, and Aristotle taught about leisure was available only to the upper classes. In Athens at the time, native-born males who were citizens were a privileged leisure class. Their control of a system of slaves and limitations on the rights of women empowered their lives of leisure.

In the ancient Greek culture the institution of slavery was very much developed, so that there was scarcely a State in which even the poorer citizens

Box 1.4

In Focus

Are Today's Olympians Too Commercial?

These days you don't have to look far to see the connection between commercialism and sports. For example, at Olympic competitions, athletes' uniforms and equipment bear the discreet but readily identifiable trademarks of their manufacturers. After the Games we see winning Olympians endorsing all manner of products, including breakfast cereal. They become celebrities and appear on television shows, make movies, go on the talk circuit, and do many other things to cash in on their fame.

Box 1.4 (Cont.)

Is it all too much? Do you ever wish we could return to the "pure" notion of the sport competitions of the ancient Olympic games?

Maybe, though, we'd be surprised at what we'd find there! Even without Wheaties ® ancient Greeks monetarily honored and even "marketed" their athletic heroes. Although a garland of olive leaves from a tree at Zeus' shrine was the official prize awarded, an Olympic victory was also lucrative. Poets were often commissioned to celebrate these victories with odes, and sculptors were employed to render an image of the athlete to be placed in a sanctuary. Coins were minted to commemorate athletic victories, and some city-states awarded stipends to Olympic winners or allowed them to dine at public expense for life (Martin, 1996).

Questions to Consider and Discuss

1. Who is your favorite "commercial" athlete? In what ways has this person been commercialized?
2. Do you consider the treatment of favorite athletes from the ancient games to have been commercial according to today's practice? How is it similar? Different?
3. Do you think the commercialization of athletes helps or hinders the sport? Why?

did not own a male or female slave to do the rough work considered unworthy of a free man. In Attica, when the State was in its most flourishing condition, there were some 400,000 slaves, or about four times the number of free citizens (Encyclopedia Encarta, 2008).

Yet, within this contradiction to the leisure ideal, there is another contradiction. There is some evidence, for example, that women had their own games in Olympia (Pausanias, 1918). These were the Heraea Games held every four years to honor the goddess Hera, the consort of Zeus. Here unmarried women competed in foot races, with winners receiving the Olympic olive branch garland and, according to scholars, part of the cow sacrificed to Hera.

Putting all this rich complexity of leisure meaning together, then, we can conclude that for the ancient Greeks, leisure was both intellectual and physical. It was the importance of developing both the mind and the body through participation, learning, and noble actions. The good life of leisure for the Greeks was an "ideal" that maintained that knowledge and health led to virtuous choices and conduct, which in turn led to true pleasure. But, this leisure ideal was only available to the socially privileged.

Ancient Rome: Spectacle

Motion pictures and television often portray the ancient Romans as military conquerors as well as ardent pleasure seekers, and while there is some truth to these images, this civilization also shaped many other civilizations for the next

2,000 years. Even today the remains of vast building projects, including roads and bridges, enormous baths and aqueducts, temples and theaters, as well as entire towns and cities throughout Africa and Europe stand on Roman foundations.

Rome began its rise to power around 200 BC. It ruled and prospered under a policy of expansion by using both military and political methods until around 200 AD. Although ancient Romans borrowed a good deal of Greek philosophy and copied Greek art and architecture, they had a unique notion about leisure.

For example, one aspect of daily life that is comparable among these two ancient civilizations was the practice of slavery. The chief difference, according to many historians, was that the Greeks regarded slaves as laborers—an industrial necessity, while the Romans used them chiefly to minister to their personal pleasures. And, for the ancient Romans, personal pleasure had a practical purpose. Let's explore how this might have been the case.

As Rome conquered its neighbors (Greece, Syria, Egypt, Macedonia, and others), the problem of overseeing an immense empire began to require control of the social order. Discipline and careful regulation of a growing middle class of people were required. The ancient Romans accomplished this by what today we would refer to as mass leisure.

There were heated public baths, parade grounds for various ball games, and grand athletic exhibitions. Often, the middle class masses of people were spectators to such spectacles as gladiators fighting each other to the death, and political prisoners, criminals, and slaves thrown to wild animals. Based on the policy of "bread and circuses," leisure was used as a form of social control, and a means whereby rulers and officials could win popular favor.

Ludi:

a Latin word for public games and festivities

Beginning about 31 BC, such *ludi,* or public games, became annual events in the Roman calendar (Ibrahim, 1991). By the end of the Roman Empire, the year included 175 official holidays, with 101 of them for theatrical entertainments, 64 devoted to chariot races, and 10 given over to gladiatorial combats (Roberts, 1962).

Specialized facilities were provided for these events. The oldest of these, the Circus Maximus, was built for horse races, trick-riding, mock cavalry battles, and chariot races. Amphitheaters hosted gladiatorial combats, with the largest, the Colosseum, holding thousands of spectators (figure 1.7). The Colosseum also hosted the naumachiae, a ship battle requiring the flooding of the Colosseum floor. The greatest of all naumachiae was staged by Claudius outside Rome in Lake Fucine. A total of 19,000 men boarded a fleet of 50 ships and battled each other beginning at 10:00 am, and by 3:00 that afternoon, 3,000 of them were dead (Butler, 1971).

Entertainment was central to Roman life. As the games and spectacles became more popular, and more widely used by emperors to

Figure 1.7

The Colosseum in Rome today. (© Ruth V. Russell, 2008)

Box 1.5

In Profile

Gladiators

The gladiator (Latin gladius, meaning sword), was a professional fighter who performed in spectacles of armed combat in the amphitheaters of ancient Rome. This practice of fighting to the death as mass spectacle originated in Etruria, in central Italy, probably as a funeral sacrifice. The largest contest of gladiators was given by the emperor Trajan as part of a victory celebration in AD 107 and included 5000 pairs of fighters.

Mostly males, gladiators were slaves, condemned criminals, prisoners of war, and sometimes Christians. A successful gladiator not only was allowed to live, but also received great acclaim; he was praised by poets, his portrait appeared on gems and vases, and patrician ladies pampered him. A gladiator who survived many combats might be relieved from further obligation. Occasionally, freedmen, Roman citizens, and women entered the arena.

According to their arms and methods of fighting, gladiators were divided into different classes. For example, the retiarius (net man), clad in a short tunic, attempted to entangle his opponent with a net and then to kill him with a trident. Other classes fought with different weapons, or from horseback or chariots.

Though a favorite of popular film, where the spectator "thumbs down" symbol means the loser in a gladiatorial combat should be put to death, recent research suggests the meanings of the symbols have changed over the years. In 1997, Professor Anthony Philip Corbeill of the University of Kansas concluded that thumbs up actually meant "kill him," basing his assertion on a study of hundreds of ancient artworks. Thus, the "thumbs up" was an approval of the gladiator's request to kill his vanquished foe rather than a vote to allow the defeated to remain alive.

Cited in part from "Gladiator," Microsoft® Encarta® Online Encyclopedia 2007 http://encarta.msn.com © 1997-2007 Microsoft Corporation. All Rights Reserved.

gain support of the people, they also became more and more lavish and depraved as each tried to outdo his predecessor. Enormous amounts of money and human resources were spent on the games, which many conclude ultimately degraded the Roman people and their culture. Restrictions began to be imposed on these practices. For example, gladiator fights ended in the east of the empire at the end of the 4th century and in the west at the end of the 5th. The wild animal contests ceased in the 6th century.

Ancient China: Harmony

According to ancient Chinese belief, the area we call China today is situated, cosmologically, at the center of the universe. Thus, the idea of centricity has been prevalent in over 4,000 years of Chinese philosophy. For example, quests for harmony, life balance, calmness, order, and peace are central to the teachings of Confucius. Does this provide a legacy for today's leisure meanings?

The story of leisure in ancient and medieval China is framed by the histories of the imperial dynasties, in particular the Han and Tang Dynasties. With the arrival of the Han Dynasty (206 BC-220 AD), for example, China was united politically, and a lifestyle resembling that of the ancient Greek upper class evolved (Ibrahim, 1991). It was during this time that Confucianism became the official doctrine, which among other things resulted in an educated upper class devoting itself to fine arts. The goal was to prepare a broadly cultivated person in both the literary and martial arts, following an ideal of a harmonious body and mind.

Later, the Tang Dynasty (618-907) contributed another important chapter to leisure's early meanings. Culturally, this was a period of enormous vitality. China became a cosmopolitan society—one rich in music, literature, and the visual arts (Tregear, 1985). Even today, poems dating from the Tang Dynasty are regarded as unsurpassed. Interestingly, based on the idea of a square world, the Tang capital (the city of Xi'an today) was laid out like a chessboard.

The governing and merchant classes of men during these dynasty periods lived in large households with many servants, wives, concubines, children, and grandchildren. Their residences were buildings set at right angles and separated by a series of courtyards. Each building was designed to render something special, such as for admiring the moonlight, making music, painting chrysanthemums, or having banquets. Specialized servants with recreation talents were kept, such as chess players, acrobats, riddle tellers, magicians, and kite flyers (Ibrahim, 1991).

Muhammad's Early Empire: Relaxation

Muhammad, which means "praised one," was the founder of the religion of Islam and one of the most influential people of all time. Within 100 years after his death, in 632 AD, Muslims had carried his teachings into other parts of the Middle East, North Africa, Europe, and Asia. Today, Islam

Figure 1.8

Tourists at the Great Wall of China today. Built during the early dynasties periods, today the wall is maintained for tourism by the Chinese government. (© Ruth V. Russell, 2008)

is the second largest world religion, with about 1.5 billion followers, or 20% of the world's population (Central Intelligence Agency, 2008).

Included in the teachings of Muhammad is another meaning of leisure still used by people today. Early Muslims learned Muhammad's philosophy of leisure through one of his sayings: "Recreate your hearts hour after hour, for the tired hearts go blind" (from the Hadith). In the Qur'an (the Islamic holy book) paradise for the faithful is envisioned as an expression of leisure. It consists of a verdant garden where chosen men recline on beautiful carpets next to rippling water and delight in the fragrance of flowers.

The vision of these lush landscapes for relaxing were recreated by wealthy ancient Muslims and Arabs alike, who spent hours there among the pavilions, pools, and fountains. During the day they conversed with friends and played chess. At night, entertainment was provided by musicians, and dancers performed until dawn.

Ancient women from this period were segregated from men, but the wives and other female relatives and children of the wealthiest men lived similarly relaxing lives within the palace in a special place called the harem. There they received visitors, played quiet games, read, and told stories. Many of them were scholars of the Qur'an, while others learned needlework, became musicians, dancers, and singers.

Ancient New World Societies: Ceremony

Now let's consider the early societies of the Americas. In North America we can cite the ancient civilization of the Cahokia people who lived around 700 AD near what is today St. Louis. At its peak, archaeologists estimate the city's population could have been as high as 40,000 people, with more people living in outlying farming villages. Although Cahokia must have had a complex culture to maintain a sizable city and raise earthen mound monuments that still stand today, no one knows very much about this civilization. From studying the drawings on excavated pottery remains, archeologists believe Cahokia served as a ceremonial center, based on what is believed to be a highly organized ritualistic relationship between the people and the land.

Further south, meanwhile, the history of the Mayan ancient civilization offers us more complete understanding of leisure as ritual. The Maya, who around 300 AD developed a magnificent civilization in what is now parts of Mexico and Central America, are noted as having the only known fully developed written language of the time. We also know this culture for its spectacular art, monumental architecture, and sophisticated astronomical and mathematical systems.

Like the Aztec and Inca who came to power later, the Maya believed in a cyclical nature of time. Their rituals and ceremonies were very closely associated with celestial and terrestrial natural cycles, which they observed as separate calendars. Like most pre-modern societies, they believed the cosmos had three major planes – the underworld, the sky, and the earth. The Mayan priest had the job of interpreting these cycles and giving a prophetic prediction on the future as well as interpretation of the past.

Much of the Mayan religious tradition is still not understood by scholars. For example, the Maya practiced human sacrifice. In some Mayan rituals people were killed by having their arms and legs held while a priest cut their chest open and tore out the heart as an offering. It is also believed that children were offered as sacrificial victims because they were considered to be pure (Stevenson, 2005). Some of these sacrifices may have been related to sport.

For example, the Mayans built huge ball courts to play games. One popular game was pok-a-tok. The field, approximately the size of a football field, is bordered by two imposing walls 26 feet tall. Seven combatants on each team tried to get a small rubber ball to go through a small stone hoop 23 feet above the ground. While there is archeological dispute, supposedly this feat was accomplished without using their hands or feet to touch the ball. These Mayan games predate the ancient Greek Olympics by about 500 years!

Pok-a-tok is considered by archeologists to have been part of religious ceremonies. It is believed, for example, that the game losers were often sacrificed to the gods. Another interpretation is that the ball symbolized the sun and the game re-enacted its apparent orbit around the earth. The sun was worshipped as a god and by playing and winning the game, one became akin to the sun god.

Figure 1.9

Remains of a pok-a-tok court in Mexico's Yucatan region.
(© Ruth V. Russell, 2008)

Medieval Europe: The Work Ethic

The Middle Ages, or medieval period of human history, describes the era between ancient and modern times in Western Europe, extending from the end of the Roman Empire (about 400 AD) to the 1500s. The former Roman Empire was divided into large estates called kingdoms ruled by wealthy landowners. Later, this evolved into the system of *feudalism*, which altered leisure's meaning again.

Feudalism produced a social class and individual power meaning of leisure based on three characteristics: lords, vassals, and fiefs. A lord was a wealthy nobleman who owned the land, a vassal was a person who was granted possession of the land by the lord, and the land itself was known as a fief. In exchange for the fief, the vassal would provide military service to the lord. This set of mutual obligations formed the basis of feudalism. (based on the definition of Ganshof, cited by McKitterick, 1988).

Feudalism:
fragmented political power in which private ownership prevails

This meant leisure expression was personally owned and bartered. As well, leisure was never far removed from its basis in violence. The development of the castle, for example, grew from the need to fortify that which the lord owned from the hostility of rival lords. Not only did the castle provide a defensible refuge, but the center of fiefdom life as well. The lives of the lords and vassals, as might be guessed, then, centered on fighting. Thus, they were particularly interested in

Box 1.6

In Focus

Ancient Inuit Endurance Contests

One ritualistic meaning of leisure today can be found in endurance sports. Testing the limits of human endurance for the fun of it is illustrated by those who participate in the New York City and Boston marathons, the Ironman triathlons, and even endurance bicycle rides over thousands of miles. These sporting events are intended to test an athlete's physical and mental stamina. A modern idea?

In ancient civilizations, endurance sport was often used as a means to test stamina, as well. For example, in the desolate lands near and above the Arctic Circle in today's Canada, the various tribes of Inuit played in games of endurance (Craig, 2002). Some typically involved contortions of the human body, while others seem to have been more a test of pain threshold.

For instance, the ikuskikmaig has been described by anthropologists as an elbow-ear walk. Why not try it yourself! Bend down and support yourself by only your toes and elbows. Meanwhile, grasp your ears with your hands. Now, see how far you can travel before giving out or toppling over. Or, how about igiruktuk where two players stand face-to-face, wrap their arm around their opponent's head, and then insert their fingers in his mouth and pull, with the player turning his head toward the pull being declared the loser.

Questions to Consider and Discuss
1. Do you consider these ancient Inuit endurance events to be cruel and barbaric? How about the ancient Mayan sport rituals? Why or why not?
2. What legacy can you trace between these ancient meanings of leisure and such contemporary sports as boxing or wrestling?
3. Do you consider today's endurance sports to be cruel and barbaric? Why or why not?

hunting and sport contests as means to keep their fighting skills and strategies sharp (Labarge, 1965).

Hunting with hounds and falconry was the most popular, and tournaments were mock fighting events. When the events turned into wild melees, a new variation of the tournament developed—the Round Table, which was also a social occasion accompanied by jousting with blunted weapons, wrestling, darts, and even skipping contests (Labarge, 1965). The lord's castle was the setting for the Round Table. Here minstrels (musicians, acrobats, jugglers, and storytellers all in one), entertained, and guests played dice, backgammon, checkers, and chess. In fact, to be good at chess was a mark of noble distinction. Pastimes in the castle also included social drinking, gambling, and theatrical performances.

Meanwhile, the vassals, or peasants, mostly mimicked the pleasures of their lords. Dancing, vulgar singing, and general partying typically filled Sundays and church-declared saint's days (Ibrahim, 1991). Fairs featuring the antics of trained monkeys and such performers as fire-eaters and sword swallowers were also popular.

As you might already suspect, the story of leisure during the Middle Ages includes a subtext. Life was difficult for everyone. People lived only an average of 30 years. Very few people could read and write, and much superstition surrounded daily life. For example, people believed that disease was spread by bad odors.

In the midst of this hardship, the Catholic Church became the main civilizing force, and according to church doctrine, the main goal of life was abstinence from worldly pleasures. The church maintained that the way to a higher quality of life was through hard work, good deeds, and self-deprivation. Thus, officially, leisure was considered to be against church teachings because it distracted from a person's moral obligation to hard work. This is why this period of human history is often considered to be the birth of the *work ethic*. Yet, church clergy were actually wealthy noblemen and also enjoyed the pastimes of other noblemen.

Work ethic:
a cultural norm placing a positive moral value on hard work and diligence

The Renaissance: Humanism

By about 1300 medieval Europe began to give way to modern Europe, a period in history called the *Renaissance*. Renaissance is a French word meaning "rebirth," and in this 300-year period, it meant changes in ways of experiencing leisure.

Renaissance:
the transitional era between medieval and modern times in Europe, marked by a humanistic revival of the arts

As a clue to these changes, recall this was the age of Michelangelo, Leonardo da Vinci, William Shakespeare, and Cervantes. Art, music, drama, and other literary forms flourished. Under the sponsorship of nobles and royalty, theaters and opera houses were constructed, and troupes of actors, singers, musicians, and dancers were in high demand. Those with wealth arranged formal balls, exhibitions, banquets, and masquerades, while the middle classes also participated in festivities. Children's activities stressed creative pastimes, such as studies in art, music, and science (Bucher, Shiver & Bucher, 1984).

This was also the age of adventure. People were fascinated with the world and other people. They set out on dangerous voyages to explore unknown lands. Books about travel began to flood England, for example, and it became a widespread practice for young gentlemen to complement their education with lengthy travel (Hudman, 1980).

During the Renaissance people felt that art, music, and poetry should be studied using classical texts, as well as practiced in the daily celebration of life. Through the humanities they revered human worth and individual dignity. This worth was grounded in the humanist belief that everything in life has a determinate nature, and it is human privilege to be able to choose this nature.

Humanism:
a philosophy that emphasizes the importance of human beings

In short, the Renaissance was a time of renewed interest in those things human. This emphasis formed a new twentieth century philosophy known as *humanism*, which glorifies and celebrates the human being. Although today within both religious doctrine and individual beliefs there are many interpretations, humanism includes the idea of human happiness as its own justification. Like leisure, life is to include freedom of expression, awareness of beauty, and harmoniously combining personal satisfaction with self-improvement.

Today's Meanings

By tracing the meanings of leisure in the humanities and in ancient civilizations, we can see the term means many things depending on the place, the time, and the people. So, what about contemporary meanings of leisure? Our definitions today are also a matter of perspective: individual experiences and cultural biases continue to define leisure in multiple ways. As described by Kelly and Freysinger (2000), "It is an experience, but in context. It has form, but is not defined by form. It takes place in time, but defines the time rather than being defined by it" (p. 16).

Today, as it has always been, leisure means personal adornment, achieving the highest ideal, mass spectacle, harmony, relaxation, ritual, a relief from work, and humanism. It also means family traditions, civic resistance, having fun, consumerism, sport, tourism, the arts, and hanging out with friends. Leisure's meanings are complex, multiple, and even contradictory.

Therefore, as we now consider the contemporary meanings of leisure, be aware that clear boundaries are not possible. But, when taken altogether, some of the many leisure meanings can be categorized in basically three ways (table 1.1). First, leisure is free time. Next, leisure is non-work activity. Finally, leisure is a state of mind, or special attitude or feeling.

Leisure as Free Time

Discretionary time:
time that is free of obligation

Today leisure is commonly considered time available after obligations. This is not just any time, but rather leisure time is a time in which we can make personal choices. This distinction is often referred to as *discretionary time*.

According to this definition life is divided into separate spheres (e.g. work, study, sleeping, eating, leisure), which we can prioritize according to importance. Since this definition suggests that leisure is "leftover," or spare time, leisure is accorded a lower status of priority. Further, leisure as defined as free time, suggests the use of leisure is to relax or have fun—that its purpose is to entertain and fill time (Watkins & Bond, 2007).

This definition also means leisure is quantifiable and that it is possible to refer to leisure in terms of amounts possessed. We often look forward to weekends and holidays because we will have more free time. Yet, while we all have discretionary time, because we have differing obligations to take care of, we don't all have the same amount of leisure time.

Box 1.7

Definition Interviews

Why not discover the complexity of leisure meanings today for yourself! Here's one way:

1. Randomly ask at least 20 of your friends and family members what leisure means to them. Ask them to give you one-word definitions. Record every definition you are given.
2. Next, select for more formal and lengthy interviews two people you don't know very well and who are different from your friends and family. For example, you might choose someone from another country or a person quite a bit older or younger, or of a different race than you. Ask them about the role(s) of leisure in their lives. How do they experience leisure? What do they like best (and least) about leisure? How important is leisure in their life? What does leisure mean to them?
3. Compare and summarize the results from both the quick and extensive interviews in writing. Bring them to class to compare with the results of others. Discuss the multiple meanings of leisure and their context.

This quantifiable definition of leisure as free time has made comparative research possible. For example, time-budget studies that contrast leisure according to population groups demonstrate we have different amounts of it. One study by Schor (2001) compared annual paid vacations required by law and discovered wide differences. The Dutch receive nine weeks of annual paid vacation, while

Table 1.1

Contemporary Themes in Leisure's Meanings

Leisure is ...

  Free time – time free from obligations
    "To me, leisure is the weekend."

  Recreational activity – non-work kinds of experiences
    "To me, playing golf and watching TV are leisure."

  Attitude – self-actualized life perspective
    "To me, getting the most zest out of the day is leisure."

Canadians and Americans receive one to two weeks. Kelly and Freysinger (2000) have also compared free time across demographic groups in North America, and found that teens have more free time than do middle-aged adults, single men have more than married men, and employed single mothers have the least of all.

Leisure as Recreational Activity

A second definition of leisure is participation based. This refers specifically to how we use our free time in non-work activity. In this way, we define leisure by the form of our recreational activities (table 1.2).

Recreational activity experiences are of great benefit to us. According to Dumazedier (1974), for example, through leisure activities we achieve relaxation, diversion, refreshment, and re-creation of ourselves. Thus, accordingly, only those activities that satisfy these purposes can be considered leisure. Some scholars have pointed to a contradiction to this qualification, however. For example, in considering the purpose of relaxation, can't we achieve this by sleeping in on Saturday morning, competing in a triathlon, and even digging a ditch? Would you consider all these to be leisure?

Table 1.2

Adult Participation in Selected Leisure Activities, 2006

Activity	Number That Participated in Last 12 Months (in thousands)	Percent
Attend classical music / opera performances	10,567	5
Attend horse races	5,382	3
Backgammon	3,556	2
Barbecuing	74,050	34
Bird Watching	12,123	6
Board games	39,275	18
Dining out	106,180	49
Fantasy sport leagues	6,008	3
Go to bars / night clubs	39,944	18
Go to museums	25,387	12
Computer games	42,736	20
Photography	28,504	13
Play cards	47,591	22
Play musical instrument	16,852	8
Reading books	84,444	39
Woodworking	9,703	5

Mediamark Research, Inc., 2008

There is a related problem in defining leisure as recreational activity. Let's consider tennis to illustrate. Is tennis leisure when played on Saturday at the local park and something else when played in a required physical education class, or when competing in the professional tennis circuit? When might washing the dishes be a leisure activity?

As with the free time definition, leisure defined as recreational activity means it can be counted and compared across different population groups. For example, in the U.S. only 37 percent of men as compared with 57 percent of women garden as a hobby, and whereas 58 percent of people aged 18 to 24 years go to amusement parks, only 10 percent of those 75 years old and over do (U.S. Census Bureau, 2007).

Figure 1.10

According to the U.S. Census Bureau, 8% of Americans play a musical instrument for recreation. (Shutterstock©, 2008)

Leisure as Special Attitude

Defining leisure as time free after obligations and as recreation activities helps us understand leisure objectively. That is, we can observe, count, and compare leisure when considering it in the form of time and activity. But, as you can guess from our humanities and ancient culture journeys earlier in the chapter, there is more to it than this in today's connotation of leisure.

Defining leisure as a special attitude, or state of mind, although more subjective, rounds out our understanding of the contemporary meanings of leisure. This third definition asserts, in fact, that time and activity are irrelevant—that only personal feelings count. That is, leisure is defined as a psychological condition by the meaning it holds for us, as a philosophy about living. Almost poetically, Pieper (1963) observed "Leisure ... involves the capacity to soar in active celebration, to overstep the boundaries of the workaday world" (p. 78).

To investigate this definition, researchers Watkins and Bond (2007) studied leisure meanings for a sample of university students in Australia. Findings included that students described the feeling of leisure as exercising choice, escaping pressure, and achieving fulfillment. In another study (Hull, Steward, & Yi, 1992), day hikers defined their feelings as positive outlook and happiness. As these studies suggest, leisure is more than simply "feeling good." According to this state of mind definition, leisure is an entire way of being that produces meaningfulness in life, self-expression, and self-actualization.

What We Understand About Leisure's Meanings

Leisure is a complex concept. To understand its contemporary meanings, this chapter explored its definitions from three perspectives: the humanities, the histories of ancient cultures, and current connotations. After studying this chapter, you should know that:

- Leisure is contextual. That is, its meaning depends on the place, the time, and the people.
- Literature, art, and music offer interpretations of leisure as integral to the human experience.
- In ancient cultures leisure has meant many things and has varied in its importance.
- Our contemporary meanings and uses of leisure are derived in part from the legacies of ancient cultures.
- Contemporary meanings of leisure include free time, recreation activity, and a special attitude.

References

Association of American Publishers. (2008). *Industry statistics*. http://www.publishers.org/industry/index.cfm. Retrieved 1/9/08.

Bayley, R., Baynes, M., & Kendall, T. (2004). About Nubia. NubiaNet. http://www.nubianet.org/. Retrieved 1/16/04.

Bucher, C.A., Shiver, J.S., & Bucher, R. (1984). *Recreation for today's society*. Englewood Cliffs, NJ: Prentice-Hall.

Butler, J. (1971). *The theatre and drama of Greece and Rome*. San Francisco, CA: Chandler.

Central Intelligence Agency. (CIA). (2008). *World fact book*. https://www.cia.gov/library/publications/the-world-factbook/index.html. Retrieved 1/14/08.

Craig, S. (2002). *Sports and games of the ancients*. Westport, CT: Greenwood.

Dumazedier, J. (1974). *Sociology of leisure*. New York: Elsevier North – Holland.

Encylopedia Encanrta. (2008). Anciant Greece. http://encarta.msn.com/encyclopedia_1741501460 4/Ancient_Greece.html. Retrieved 1/14/08.

EMuseum @ Minnesota State University at Mankato. (2008). Ancient life in ancient Egypt. http://www.mnsu.edu/emuseum/index.shtml. Retrieved 1/14/08.

Garland, R. (1998). *Daily life of the Ancient Greeks*. Westport, CT: Greenwood Press.

Godbey, G. (2003). *Leisure in your life: An exploration* (6th edition). State College, PA: Venture.

Hemingway, J.L. (1988). Leisure and civility: Reflections on a Greek ideal. *Leisure Sciences, 10*, 179-191.

Herbert, R.L. (1988). *Impressionism: Art, leisure and Parisian society*. New Haven, CT: Yale University Press.

Hudman, L.E. (1980). *Tourism: A shrinking world*. Columbus, OH: Grid.

Hull, R.B., Steward, W.P., & Yi, Y.K. (1992). Experience patterns: Capturing the dynamic nature of a recreation experience. *Journal of Leisure Research, 23*(3), 240-252.

Ibrahim, H. (1991). *Leisure and society: A comparative approach*. Dubuque, IA: Wm. C. Brown.

Kelly, J.R., & Freysinger, V.J. (2000*). 21ˢᵗ Century leisure: Current issues*. Boston: Allyn and Bacon.

Labarge, M.W. (1965). *A baronial household of the thirteenth century*. New York: Barnes & Noble.

Martin, T.R. (1996). *Ancient Greece: From prehistoric to Hellenistic times*. New Haven, CT: Yale University Press.

MediaMark Research, Inc. (2008). *Top-line reports*. New York, NY. Available from http://mediamark.com/mri/docs/TopLineReports.html. Retrieved 1/15/08.

McKitterick, R. (1988). Ganshof, F.L. In J. Cannon (Ed.), *Blackwell Dictionary of Historians*. New York: Blackwell.

Pan-African Market Place. (September 1993). Come home to Sudan, a nation full of potential and promise! Pan-African Market Place, 1-2.

Pausanias. (1918). *Description of Greece* (vols. 1-4). (W.H.S. Jones & H.A. Ormerod, translators). Cambridge, MA: Harvard University Press.

Pieper, J. (1963). *Leisure: The basis of culture*. New York: New American Library.

Recording Industry Association of America. (2007). 2006 Year-End Shipment Statistics. Available from http://www.riaa.com. Retrieved 1/15/08.

Roberts, V.M. (1962). *On stage: A history of theatre*. New York: Harper & Row.

Schor, J. (2001). Real vacations for all. Futurenet.org. Available from http://www.futurenet.org/17work/schor.htm. Retrieved 1/26/2004.

Simpson, S. (1989). Aristotle (384-322 BC). In H. Ibrahim (Ed.), *Pioneers in leisure and recreation*. Reston, VA: The American Association of Health, Physical Education, Recreation, and Dance.

Stevenson, M. (2005). Evidence may back human sacrifice claims. Live Science. http://www.livescience.com/history/human_sacrifice_050123.html. Retrieved 1/15/08.

Sylvester, C. (1999). The classical idea of leisure: Cultural ideal or class prejudice? *Leisure Sciences, 12*, 3-16.

Tregear, M. (1985). *Chinese art*. New York: Thames and Hudson.

U.S. Census Bureau. (2007). *Statistical abstract of the United States: 2007*. Washington, D.C.: U.S. Government Printing Office.

Watkins, M., & Bond, C. (2007). Ways of experiencing leisure. *Leisure Sciences, 29*(3), 287-307.

CHAPTER TWO

THE IMPORTANCE OF HAVING FUN

PREVIEW

Is it important to have fun?
Even though we may casually think of leisure as "just having fun," philosophers and scientists have taken the matter quite seriously.

What is involved in having fun?
Leisure is fun because it gives us happiness, pleasure, freedom, intrinsic reward, play, humor, relaxation, ritual, solitude, commitment, spirituality, risk, and other benefits.

Does leisure provide all of these benefits?
For any single leisure experience some of these benefits result, yet not usually all of them. In a different leisure experience another set of benefits may result.

KEY TERMS

Are you having fun? Although this may seem a trivial question, much of our life is spent in pursuit of a good time. And, while just "fun and games" is often what we casually think of when considering leisure, almost everyone wants it. What is it that makes leisure "fun?" That is, what are the qualities, or benefits, of leisure? In this chapter, we consider the nature of leisure by characterizing its experience and expression. We go beyond the definitions of leisure explored in the previous chapter, and focus on the variety of ways we benefit from it.

Figure 2.1

Perhaps the foremost benefit from our leisure expressions is the sense of freedom. (Shutterstock©, 2008)

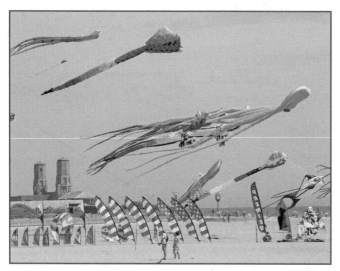

Freedom

Foremost, leisure makes us feel free. We are having fun when we choose what we're doing. In fact, scholars suggest leisure cannot exist when our perception of freedom is curtailed. Think about the last time you experienced leisure. What was the experience, and how would you describe what made it possible to label it as leisure? Most likely, your experience was leisure because you felt some freedom to choose it. No one else made you do it; it was entirely your choice.

Many leisure scholars and professionals consider the amount of perceived freedom we experience to be one of the most basic benefits of leisure. For example, as shown in figure 2.2, according to scholar John Kelly, how much freedom we perceive about the experience describes the type of leisure.

Figure 2.2

John Kelly's theory of types of leisure (Kelly. 1982)

	Freedom	
	High	Low
Intrinsic	1. Unconditional leisure	2. Recuperative leisure
Meaning		
Social	3. Relational leisure	4. Role-determined leisure

Let's focus on the first cell of the figure. When we perceive a high amount of freedom in an experience, this is considered *unconditional leisure*. This can be considered the "purest" type of leisure because it is wholly chosen by us. Unconditional leisure also is the result of another quality—intrinsic meaning, or pursuing the experience as an end in itself. We'll feature this second leisure benefit in a moment.

Unconditional leisure
leisure experiences or expressions that are freely chosen for intrinsic reasons

The idea of unconditional leisure suggests two different understandings of freedom. These are the distinctions between leisure as freedom "from" and leisure as freedom "to." First, leisure is temporary freedom "from" the necessary routine of life. That is, leisure frees us from obligations and provides a relief from work, such as in taking a vacation. Leisure as freedom "from" is considered a less satisfying experience because it carries the connotation that leisure must first be earned through work. For example, is leisure as freedom "from" possible for someone retired from a paying job?

On the other hand, leisure as freedom "to" is considered more satisfying. Here the focus is on freedom to experience a particular personal expression. This means in order to experience leisure, we must claim the possibilities of choice through our pastimes. Leisure as freedom "to" enables us to expand beyond the limits of the present to experience wonderfully fulfilling possibilities. Freedom "to" is what Kelly had in mind with the idea of unconditional leisure.

How do we acquire more leisure as freedom "to" in our lives? According to the investigations of Bregha (1991), freedom in leisure is a matter of possessing personal qualities, having the means, and receiving permission. Let's explore these three requirements.

First, freedom "to" in leisure requires having the knowledge, physical ability, personality, and other personal qualities required for a successful experience. This includes having information about what is available or permissible, as well as knowledge about oneself, including the consequences of actions. Similar to the ancient Greek ideal, this suggests leisure requires the ability to choose with intelligence and responsibility.

Second, for Bregha, leisure involves having means. Throughout history, wealth has always been considered a factor in experiencing leisure. In fact, during the 19th century in Western cultures, the wealthy were tagged "the leisure class." This link still exists today. Many forms of recreational activity require expensive fees, equipment, clothing, transportation, and instruction or training. Have you priced admission to a theme park lately?

Finally, the ability to freely choose leisure requires permission. Since few forms of leisure, except perhaps daydreaming and contemplation, can be experienced without at least the passive consent of our neighbors or civic authorities, leisure experiences and expressions require sanction from others. For example, there are city ordinances against making too much noise, restaurants are open only at specific times and days, and to jog on private property we must have prior authorization.

So, it is possible to conclude that leisure is perhaps our most precious expression of freedom. It gives us freedom to choose, but choice, in turn, requires capability, means, and authority. In other words, leisure is as much freedom to express ourselves as it is freedom to escape something.

Box 2.1

The Study Says

American and Korean Leisure Freedom Differences

As a way to understand cultural distinctions in the freedom quality of leisure, this study examined the differences between Americans and Koreans. Does nationality make a difference? Questionnaires in English were given to 116 American college students and also in Korean to 110 Korean college students. The results revealed that Koreans are more likely than Americans to focus on leisure as perceived freedom—or freedom "to." On the other hand, Americans are more likely than Koreans to understand leisure as freedom from work.

Lee, J., Oh, S., & Shim, J. (2001). *The meaning of leisure: Conceptual differences between Americans and Koreans.* In G. Klle (Ed.), Proceedings of the 2000 Northeastern Recreation Research Symposium. General Technical Report NE-276. Newtown Square, PA: U.S. Department of Agriculture, U.S. Forest Service, *Northeastern Research Station*, pp. 145-149.

Intrinsic Reward

Another, often considered basic, benefit of leisure is intrinsic reward. *Intrinsic reward* comes from doing something for its own reason. Cross-country skiers, for example, often exclaim about sensations of peacefulness while gliding along; artists typically value working with clay on the potter's wheel because of the elastic and smooth response of the clay in their hands; and dancers have described dancing as moving to a rhythm within (see Csikszentmihalyi, 1975). Having fun, then, also means experiencing something for its own sake.

Intrinsic reward
doing something
for its own reason

When an experience or expression is its own reward, the benefit is intrinsic, and we experience this as leisure. Let's return to figure 2.2 to explore more about this leisure quality. Consider again the first cell. Unconditional leisure is not only the experience of high amounts of perceived freedom, but also lots of intrinsic reward. The experience is freely chosen because it is exciting, personally expressive, and/or emotionally fulfilling.

Contrast this with the second cell in figure 2.2—recuperative leisure. This is leisure that compensates for some deficit or loss. While there is intrinsic reward, the perception of freedom is low. For example, in coming home from school and listening to music as a way to unwind, the purpose is rest and recovery. *Recuperative leisure*, according to Kelly, provides compensation for the constraining conditions of work, parenthood, school, caring for an aged parent, and even bad weather.

Recuperative leisure
leisure that makes up for
a loss or deficit

Meanwhile, relational leisure (cell three) is when our experience is freely chosen, but the reward is something other than intrinsic. That is, *relational leisure* is expressed for social reasons—for relating to the needs of others. Relational leisure is done not so much because someone else expects it, but because it is a valued way of expressing the relationship. Going camping with your family because you enjoy their companionship likely has a high amount of perceived freedom and social, rather than intrinsic, reward. This contrasts to *role-determined leisure* (cell four), which describes going camping with your family because you feel obligated to satisfy the expectations of others. Here there is low intrinsic reward and low perceived freedom.

Relational leisure leisure for sociability reasons

Role-determined leisure that helps to accomplish a social role

In figure 2.2 Kelly labels low intrinsic reward as having social meaning. Other scholars describe the opposite of intrinsic reward as extrinsic reward. *Extrinsic reward* is the consequence when we engage in a particular pastime for reasons other than its own. Our motivation is from the outside rather than from the inside. For example, we sign up for a group exercise class because we want to lose weight, not because we want to experience the exhilaration of moving our bodies (table 2.1). Both relational and role-determined leisure provide extrinsic reward.

Extrinsic reward doing something for a payoff

A particularly fascinating understanding is how intrinsic reward can turn into extrinsic reward. One example is a classic study of preschool children (Lepper, Greene, & Nisbett, 1973). Children who showed a high interest in drawing were chosen for the study, and divided into three groups. The first group was told if they would draw pictures, they would receive a "good player award." Children

Table 2.1

Types of Intrinsic and Extrinsic Rewards

Types	Definition	Example
Intrinsic Reward		
Stimulation	Engaging in a pastime for the simple reason of just doing it	"I ride a bicycle for the thrill of pedaling fast."
Accomplishment	Engaging in a pastime to feel efficient or competent	"I swim for the satisfaction I get from perfecting my strokes."
Knowledge	Engaging in a pastime to learn something new	"I play video games in order to learn new strategies for winning."
Extrinsic Reward		
Identified regulation	Engaging in a pastime because it is important	"I'm taking karate because I want to protect myself from crime."
Introjected regulation	Engaging in a pastime so as not to feel guilty for not doing it	"I play basketball because I don't want to disappoint my parents."
External regulation	Engaging in a pastime to avoid a punishment	"I hang out with these people so I'm not left out of the group."

in the second group received the same reward but were not told about it in the beginning. The third group of children was neither told they would receive an award nor did they receive an award. Two weeks later, the amount of time the children spent drawing was observed. Those children who expected the reward showed less interest in drawing than those in the other two groups. In addition, the pictures the children drew in the expected award group were judged to be poorer in quality than those drawn by children in the other two groups. In other words, the children who were offered a prize switched from intrinsically to extrinsically motivated behavior, and it was no longer as much fun to draw pictures.

Happiness

Another benefit often available to us from our leisure expressions is happiness. Also known as subjective well-being, high morale, life satisfaction, and positive life attitude, happiness generally is an indicator of the overall quality of our inner experience that typically comes from living well. How does this occur? We answer this question from two perspectives: classical philosophies and current understandings about achieving happiness.

How to achieve the quality of happiness occupied much of the thinking of Aristotle—how should the good life be lived? His answer was that the best life comes from *eudaimonia,* which most translations today interpret as happiness or personal well-being (Sylvester, 1991). Unlike today's common understanding of happiness as an inner good feeling, Aristotle meant something else, however: eudaimonia was not determined by positive feelings, but rather by good actions. Thus, for leisure to bring happiness, it must entail only moral and worthy activities, or unhappiness results.

Eudaimonia:

Aristole's idea of happiness; doing good things

Thinking about happiness by focusing on how to avoid unhappiness has been an approach for philosophers for centuries. For example, in a classic book by Bertrand Russell (1968), people who suffer from chronic unhappiness were considered, and the conclusion was the causes of unhappiness are competition, boredom, fatigue, and envy. The cure for unhappiness, Russell claimed, is zest. Happiness is the possession of a zestful attitude toward life. "The secret of happiness is this: let your interests be as wide as possible, and let your reactions to things and persons that interest you be as far as possible friendly rather than hostile" (p. 111).

Over the years there have been hundreds of studies seeking to answer the question of what makes us happy. Some have predicted age is a factor, that younger people and older people are happier than middle-aged people. Some studies suggest women are happier than men, and that having good health makes one happy. Having friends and family, enough money, a good education, a meaningful career, helpful coping strategies and life goals, a creative and nurturing personality, and even a genetic predisposition toward a positive attitude, have also been connected to happiness in research studies (Kovacs, 2007).

As well, several studies have focused on leisure's role in happiness. For example, in one study (Larson & Richards, 1998) adolescents revealed their emotional high points were on Fridays and Saturdays, with their moods dropping on Sundays

Box 2.2

 *In Focus*

The Pursuit of Happiness: Read All About It

The search for happiness makes money! Recently advice on how to find happiness has become a big seller, and a ready example is the business of publishing. Here are some samples of recent book titles.

Book	Advice
The How of Happiness: A Scientific Approach to Getting the Life You Want, by Sonja Lyubomirsky (2007, Penguin)	Uses a diagnostic quiz to help you understand your happiness "score" and then suggests ways to increase this by working at it through goal setting, learning to cope, and firming up your romantic life.
The Geography of Bliss: One Grump's Search for the Happiest Places in the World, by Eric Weiner (2008, Twelve)	Presents the happiest places in the world (i.e., Denmark, the Netherlands, and Bhutan), claiming these locations are happier because people there don't focus on physique and personal careers.
Happiness: A Guide to Developing Life's Most Important Skill, by Mathieu Ricard (2007, Little, Brown and Co.)	Suggests happiness cannot be found in fleeting experiences of pleasure, but in having compassion for others and meditation.
Stumbling on Happiness, by Daniel Gilbert (2007, Vintage)	Being happy requires a well-developed imagination and focus on the here and now. For example, our daydreams tend to be about success, rather than failure.
Happy For No Reason: 7 Steps to Being Happy from the Inside Out, by Marci Shimoff and Carol Kline (2008, Free Press)	Advises that we have a happiness set point we return to throughout life. That is, being happy is a habit of the mind, heart, and body.

Questions to Consider and Discuss
1. What does happiness mean to you? Describe what it takes to make you happy?
2. What roles do your own leisure pursuits and expressions play in making you happy?
3. After exploring some of the books listed a bit more, which advice on how to find happiness makes the most sense to you? How does your leisure apply to this advice?

Box 2.3

The Study Says

Happiness and the Enviroment

Using data in questionnaires from the British Household Panel Survey, the relationships between subjective well-being and attitudes toward ozone pollution and species extinction were studied. Results showed a negative relationship between concern about the ozone layer and happiness. This came on top of the actual pollution respondents suffered from and the region where they lived. In other words, it is not only pollution itself that negatively affects our well-being but the preoccupation with it as well. On the other hand, results demonstrated a positive relationship between concern about biodiversity loss and happiness. That is, those who cared about the loss of other species were more likely happier. This finding agrees with other studies that have found people receive positive psychological benefits from caring about others.

Ferrer-i-Carbonell, A., & Gowdy, J.M. (2007). Environment degradation and happiness. *Ecological Economics, 60*, 509–516. Available from Science Direct at www.sciencedirect.com. Retrieved 10/08.

and staying low during the rest of the week. The researchers explained this as the distinction between adult structured time (Sunday through Thursday) and teen structured time (Friday and Saturday).

In another study (Putnam, 2000), the role of specific forms of leisure in adult happiness was examined. Results demonstrated attending club meetings, volunteering to help others, entertaining at home, and attending church regularly, were related to higher levels of happiness. However, the researchers also discovered a diminishing return—that is, doing too many of these activities too often reduced happiness. Study results suggested the optimal amount of time for doing these things was slightly less than once a week.

Leisure satisfaction:
gratification and contentment with one's leisure experiences and opportunities

Perhaps the most vital link between leisure and happiness is via the concept of leisure satisfaction. *Leisure satisfaction* is our perception of how satisfying our leisure experiences and expressions are. Several studies have found, for example, that experiencing leisure with an optimistic outlook, meaningful focus and commitment, a lot of perceived freedom and intrinsic reward, and a belief in being capable determine happiness (Kovacs, 2007).

Pleasure

Leisure is pleasing. In almost all characterizations of leisure, pleasure is included. It can come from listening to your favorite music, eating a handful of popcorn, or petting your dog. What is pleasure and how does leisure bring pleasure to us?

Pleasure is difficult to distinguish from other leisure benefits. For example, pleasure has been described as a feeling of happiness resulting from an experience that is enjoyed. On the other hand, pleasure can be seen as the good feeling that comes from satisfying such needs as hunger, sex, and comfort. Further, research has demonstrated pleasure is a neurobiological phenomenon (Esch & Stefano, 2004). That is, our brains are "hard wired" to be motivated by pleasure.

To the ancient Greeks pleasure had multiple connotations as well (see Goodale & Godbey, 1988). Cynicism, for example, suggested virtue rather than pleasure was life's goal. In contrast, the ancient idea of stoicism suggested people should be indifferent to both pleasure and pain. Even today stoics accept good fortune without joy and misfortune without complaint—"You win a few, you lose a few!"

But, the two ancient ideas of epicureanism and hedonism are what we most often associate with pleasure today. Epicureanism holds that pleasure should be experienced in moderation, and that the best pleasures are intellectual—such as contemplation and appreciation. According to epicurean understanding, the inferior pleasures are those that respond to the senses, such as sexual drives and hunger. Hedonism, on the other hand, suggests pleasure is the highest goal of life. Ancient followers of hedonism included the body, fame, power, and wealth as sources of pleasure.

All four of these ancient perspectives about pleasure have influenced contemporary notions of leisure as pleasurable. For example, some consider certain forms of leisure, such as dancing, to be pleasurable because of sensations in the body (hedonism), while others consider such physical pastimes immoral because of their sensual nature (cynicism).

One more recent typology of the various kinds of pleasure resulting from our pastimes is sensory, expressive, and intellectual (Smith, 1991). **Sensory pleasures** are often found in such everyday activities as eating, listening to music, having sex, and playing sports. These expressions are pleasurable because they directly stimulate our senses. For example, by measuring people's physiological responses to musical tones using a facial electromyography technique, researchers discovered that tones of low intensity (75 dB) were more pleasing than tones of high intensity (95 dB).

Figure 2.3

Research indicates entertaining at home is related to happiness in adults. (© Ruth V. Russell, 2008)

Sensory pleasure: pleasure from direct simulation of the senses

Box 2.4

 *In Profile*

Pets

You've heard the old saying, "dogs are man's best friend?" Well, it doesn't seem to be true anymore. According to the pet census released by the American Veterinary Medical Association, cats greatly outnumber dogs as pets. Meanwhile, our total pet population has reached a record high of just over 282 million, with nearly 60% of all homes in the United States having at least one pet. Here's the census of these pleasure-providing critters:

#1	Cats:	82 million
#2	Dogs:	72 million
#3	Birds:	11 million
#4	Rabbits:	6 million
#5	Turtles:	2 million

Dale, S. (January 25-27, 2008). Animal Smart: Pet Census. USA Weekend.

Expressive pleasure:
pleasure from creativity

Intellectual pleasure:
pleasure from thinking

Expressive pleasures from leisure, on the other hand, are based on the use of creativity. As a result of an experience, something is produced, and this gives us pleasure. To distinguish, listening to rap music may trigger sensory pleasure, whereas creating a rap song more likely offers expressive pleasure. Finally, *intellectual pleasure* from leisure comes from thinking activities. These might include fantasizing, daydreaming, contemplating, and even studying.

Figure 2.4

The sculpture *The Traveler* perhaps gave expressive pleasure to its creator, Duane Hanson, and can give intellectual pleasure to travelers in the Orlando, Florida airport. In fact, giving pleasure to air passengers using the terminal is an express purpose of this airport's public art program.
(© Ruth V. Russell, 2008)

Regardless of exactly how pleasure is described, the most important conclusion about this leisure benefit is its usefulness for good health. Of course, pleasure is capable of promoting addiction and other dangerous behaviors, but in appropriate amounts and expressions, it is also healthy. Scientists have shown, for example, that moderate pleasurable experiences are able to enhance what is referred to as our biological flexibility and complexity, and thereby provide a sort of health protection. This is because feelings of pleasure are naturally occurring health processes (Esch & Stefano, 2004, p. 245).

Play

Play is human nature itself, and like all humanity, there are many different ways to express it. For example, to say we play can mean we pretend to be a cowboy, engage in a competition, wager a bet, permit a hooked fish to run with the line, or perform a musical instrument. In checking a dictionary we realize we can play along, play around, play at, play back, play down, play off, play out, play on, play up, play fair, and play possum.

Yet, while its meaning is ambiguous, variable, and paradoxical, play at its essence is a spontaneous act that elevates us to the seriousness of frivolity. As first suggested in 1938 by the Dutch anthropologist, Johan Huizinga, play is an action that is fully absorbing, includes elements of uncertainty, involves a sense of illusion or exaggeration, and most importantly, exists outside of ordinary life (Huizinga, 1955). That is, even though absorbed by the activity, players are always aware that the play is not real and that its consequences will not affect their lives outside the play.

Figure 2.5

According to Huizinga, true play exists outside of ordinary life. (© Ruth V. Russell, 2008)

We can use the playing of games to illustrate this. The English word game is related to the old German word gaman, which means glee. Thus, the original meaning of game was not far from that of play. While games vary considerably in the nature of winning, the rules, the number and roles of players, and the particular equipment and amount of time required to play, they are at heart in some way artificial. They take place as a synthetic counterpart to real life. The chess match is the artificial enactment of a medieval war. Monopoly is the counterfeit experience of capitalism.

How do we play games? In the outside-of-reality world of games, the types of play can be categorized. For example, a classic book by French intellectual Roger Caillois (1961) distinguished four types of play in games: agon, alea, mimicry, and ilinx.

Box 2.5

In Profile

Monopoly

While the founding history has been debated, the best-known story is that in the heart of the Great Depression in the United States, when the average person was either broke or about to be, unemployed Charles Darrow offered an illusion of wealth. He dreamed of escaping the summer heat of Philadelphia and going down to the cool breezes on the boardwalk at Atlantic City. One day, Darrow sat down at his kitchen table and put his fantasy on paper. He invented a board game using the street names that intersect with Atlantic City's boardwalk. Players would get $1,500 to restart life by the shore and another $200 every time they circled the neighborhood. He called the game Monopoly.

After people kept dropping in at Darrow's house to play Monopoly, he brought the game to Parker Brothers in New York. Although company executives played it all afternoon, they said it had too many design errors and rejected it. Undaunted, Darrow asked a local printer to make the games, and within a year, 17,000 orders had come from stores across the country. Parker Brothers reconsidered, and Darrow retired at age 46 to raise orchids in the countryside.

Over the years the game has added faster playing versions (Monopoly Express), at different locations (i.e. National Parks), with updated playing tokens (i.e., a Starbucks coffee cup and box of McDonald's fries), and instead of receiving $200 after a neighborhood round, newer editions award $2 million. Yet, Monopoly, the idea of amassing money and property, has remained a fun game to play, having sold over 750 million copies in 103 countries, and translated into 37 languages.

http://www.hasbro.com/games/kid-games/monopoly/default.cfm?page=worldvote/presscenter. Retrieved 3/19/08.

Agon games are competitive and require some skill. These include most sports and games. Alea games such as Bingo, on the other hand, require luck and winning is a matter of fate. Mimicry games, typically video games, involve role-playing, and ilinx games are more sensory in nature, such as in drinking games. Some games, of course, involve more than one of these forms of play. For example, playing the card game of poker likely involves both agon and alea play. This system of categorizing game playing can be useful in not only understanding the wide range of play behaviors possible, but also in considering whether some playing forms, such as mimicry in video games and ilinx in drinking games are potentially harmful to players.

While Huizinga's and Caillois' views have been actively studied and even modified since their introduction, most scholars still agree with these basic premises about the act of play. More recently scholars have also been interested in the idea of play as a quality of the action. This is the idea of playfulness. For example, Susanna Millar, in her classic *The Psychology of Play*, suggested that "perhaps play is best used as an adverb, not as a name of a class of activities … but to describe how and under what conditions an action is performed" (1968, p. 21). Playfulness is an attitude of throwing off constraints. These are the physical, emotional, social, and intellectual constraints that hold us back from high spiritedness, freedom, and creativity.

Regardless of all these attempts to describe play, we certainly know it when we feel it—a lightness of heart, a glint in the eye, alertness, enthusiasm, and readiness for surprise. We feel a sense of involvement, self-expression, whimsy, and individuality. Our defenses dissolve; we become spontaneous and expanded. We are in the moment—flexible, open, and delighted.

One enduring question for scientists and philosophers has been about why we play. Since the 18th century at least 15 different theories explaining play have been considered (Ellis, 1973), based on knowledge from biology, psychology,

Table 2.2

A Brief Comparison of Play Theories

Theory	Definition	Example	Critique
Surplus energy	Burning up excess energy	Children chasing each other around the playground	Helps justify the role of physical play for problem youth; doesn't explain non physical play
Preparation	Practice for adult life	Children playing house or doctor	Doesn't explain adult play
Relaxation	Recuperation	Playing solitaire as a study break	Doesn't explain play that is similar to work
Catharsis	Letting off emotional steam	Playing the piano after an argument	Has intuitive appeal in its field of application, yet aggressive behavior often increasing aggressive behavior
Behavioristic	A response to a pleasurable stimulus	Going out and playing basketball afer your team won the tournament	Overlooks the role of individual differences, yet has boosted play as a topic worthy of serious study
Psychoanalytic	Mastering disturbing events or thoughts	A child yelling at her stuffed animals after her school-teacher has scolded her	Initiated the practice of careful observation of play theory
Arousal seeking	Seeking optimal stimulation	Bored student counting a professor's mannerisms in class	Has more research support
Competence-effectance	Having an effect on things	Making snow angels in the yard	Requires more research testing

sociology, and anthropology. In reviewing the more common of these theories, we'll use Ellis' classification system: first the older theories, then the more recent theories, and finally the most contemporary explanations (table 2.2).

One of the oldest and most often quoted theories of play is the surplus energy theory. It claims play serves as a pressure valve for burning up stored physical energy. Another early theory viewed play as preparation for adulthood. This biologically based theory explains that children play because of instinctual urges required for survival. Finally, the relaxation theory explains play as an action that provides recuperation from fatigue and stress. Opposite the surplus energy explanation, the relaxation perspective claims play restores energy.

These and other older theories, which date back to the late 19th and early 20th centuries, are often labeled "armchair" theories because they have limited research support for humans (see box 2.6 below for research on theories of animal play). More recent theories represented attempts to make the explanation of play more scientific. For example, the catharsis theory is similar to the surplus energy theory except it focuses on pent-up emotional energy rather than physical energy. Play is viewed in this theory as a socially acceptable way to purge negative feelings.

Another more recent theory is the behaviorist explanation, which labels play as a form of learning. Based in the work of behavioral psychologists such as B.F. Skinner, play is connected with the stimulus-response mechanisms. That is, play is considered a pleasurable activity that receives praise and recognition, thus, it is learned and repeated. Finally, the psychoanalytic explanation, first discussed by Sigmund Freud, viewed many forms of play as symptoms of psychological illness. That is, play was a method of mastering disturbing events or thoughts.

While these more recent theories have been substantiated by research data they remain credible as at least partial explanations of why people play. The most contemporary explanations, in fact have often been composites of these earlier theories. For example, the arousal-seeking theory claims the main goal of play is both intellectual and physical stimulus. That is, play serves to generate

Box 2.6

 *In Focus*

Animal Play

On the African savanna, a lion cub wrestles with a young peer, first going for the kill, and then playing the victim. Young ibex race up steep rocky inclines and hurdle themselves over ridge tops, performing feats of daring that would shame the most steel-nerved skateboarders. At daybreak in Chicago's Brookfield Zoo, baby male giraffes stretch their long, strong necks, swinging and clashing them at each other like swords. Young garden warblers have been observed picking up pebbles from the ground, flying up to a branch and dropping them into a glass, producing a sharp jingling sound.

Box 2.6 (Cont.)

Numerous examples like these have popped up in the scientific record, and even to the untrained eye, animal play behavior can be quite obvious. And, as with human play, one of the most intriguing questions is why? Over the past decades a steady accumulation of research reveals some answers. For example, early research proposed the intense physical activity of play helps young mammals burn off the excess energy not needed to survive (Spencer, 1855). Other studies have suggested play helps animals, such as wolves and monkeys, form bonds with other members of their group and trains them to behave according to the norms for getting along in their social hierarchy (McDonald, 1995). As well, research has concluded animals play in order to practice patterns of behavior needed for adulthood. This later finding can be illustrated by comparing the types of animal play.

Animal play can be categorized into the types: locomotor, predatory, object, and social (Hawes, 1996). Locomotor play, for example, consists of juvenile animals carrying out movements, but with no immediate or obvious end goal. Running, leaping, pirouetting, head shaking, and heel kicking seem to function as motor skill training for animals that rely on agility and speed. Kittens demonstrate the second type of play—predatory play—when they chase a string or stalk their owner's legs. Becoming a competent predator through play does not seem to end in adulthood, however. An adult cat will play with dead prey, well after it has successfully hunted it.

Object play overlaps with predatory play in some ways, but not entirely. While playing with objects may contain predatory skill development aspects, non-predatory object play, manifested primarily by the primates, seems less goal-directed. Young chimps, for example, often toy around with sticks in the water. Finally, social play facilitates the development of cooperation, alliances, and positive behavioral patterns. Young animals from across the mammalian spectrum engage their peers in bouts of wrestling, sparring, and chasing. Chimps and gorillas have been observed playing games like hide-and-seek, follow the leader, and king of the mountain.

While most mammals outgrow play after a few years, some remain playful throughout their lives. Dolphins in captivity play with balls, toy rings, or just about any object thrown in their tanks and adult river otters have been observed to frolic year-round.

Questions to Consider and Discuss
1. How would you explain animal play? If you have a pet, have you observed its play? How would you describe what you've observed?
2. What justifications would you propose for taking research on animal play seriously? That is, why is it important?
3. How do the explanations of animal play relate to the explanations of human play? What are the similarities and what are the differences?

complexity as a guard against boredom. And, the competence-effectance theory refers to the need to produce effects—to be a cause of things taking place or being produced. Each of these contemporary theories of play, as well as others such as attribution theory, conflict-enculturation theory, and recapitulation theory, contain an element of truth, yet none fully explain all aspects of why we play. Yet, maybe this is as it should be. Perhaps play does not occur because it is useful. Perhaps it is simply an enchanted place outside ordinary life.

Humor

"Angels fly because they take themselves lightly," says an old Scottish proverb, suggesting humor is good for us. In fact, researchers at Stanford University have reported that laughter aids digestion, stimulates the heart, lowers blood pressure, strengthens muscles, improves the immune system, activates the brain's creative function, and reduces pain (Jones, 1992). Humar is a quality of issues.

For example, in a hospital near Atlanta, Georgia, there is a laughing room in which patients are encouraged to watch funny movies and read humorous books. The purpose is to help them get well. The hospital reports that the laughing room decreases patients' need for pain medication and serves as an antidepressant because it naturally stimulates endorphins in the brain. Other hospitals have instituted comedy carts and Clown Care Units.

What is humor? Jokes, cartoons, caricatures, parodies, puns, silliness, imitations, wisecracks, and tall tales provide pleasant psychological shifts. Humor usually results in an audible physiological expression of merriment, or laughter. When we laugh we experience two physiological phases: the arousal

Box 2.7

 In Your Own Experience

Checklist for Lightening Up

How many times a day do you have a good laugh? Here are some tips for returning more humor to your life. Check all those that you currently and regularly do, and then circle all those you could easily add to your daily habits.

[ ] Dress less seriously.
[ ] Keep a toy in your desk or in your car.
[ ] Share an embarrassing moment with someone else.
[ ] Pay attention to children and emulate them.
[ ] Watch comedy DVDs and TV shows.
[ ] Listen to comedy while driving.
[ ] Seek to hang out with funny people.
[ ] Ask someone, "What's the funniest thing that happened to you today? This week?"

phase—when the heart rate increases—and the resolution phase—when the heart rests. A person's heart can reach up to 120 beats per minute when laughing. On average children laugh 400 times per day while adults only laugh 15 times per day (Roach, 1996).

Various theories have been proposed as to the basis of humor (Morreall, 1983). One idea is that humor makes us feel superior, that it is self-congratulatory, involving malice toward other people, as in a practical joke. On the other hand, other scholars claim that because of its physiological nature, humor is used to vent nervous energy. We laugh as a release from denied feelings or social restrictions, such as in dark comedy films. Another explanation is that humor is an intellectual reaction to something that is unexpected, such as in the punch line of a joke.

Relaxation

For many of us, leisure is often found in doing nothing at all. A child drawing pictures in the beach sand that a wave immediately erases, a tourist wandering without an itinerary, and two friends rocking in silence on the front porch are relaxing, and through relaxation, they are experiencing being "leisurely."

Perhaps the earliest proponent of this leisure benefit was Josef Pieper, a German scholar who declared: "Leisure is not the attitude of mind of those who actively intervene but of those who are open to everything; not of those who grab hold, but of those who leave the reins loose and who are free and easy themselves" (1963, p. 41). For Pieper, leisure meant being abundantly relaxed. Doug Kleiber, a contemporary American scholar, agrees with Pieper and claims true leisure is simply being appreciative, contemplative, and peaceful. He writes, "Leisure is most essentially a position of relaxation, of faithful openness to immediate reality..." (2000, p. 83).

Figure 2.6

Relaxation is a frequently and highly desired benefit of leisure. (Courtesy of Microsoft .com. Retrieved 3/19/08)

The importance of this quality of leisure may be difficult for us to grasp because we live in societies that celebrate effort and accomplishment, and relaxation is considered nonproductive. There are at least two positions from which to argue against this perception, however. First, relaxation in leisure is of value for its ability to recharge us to be productive later. It relieves stress, improves the immune system, and generally restores us for our work or school tasks. This is the logic often used when we decide to take a vacation. But, relaxation can also be revered as an end in itself. In *Freedom and Destiny*, psychoanalyst Rollo May (1981) refers to it as "the pause," which is important because it interrupts the routine and habits of our lives with imagining, reflecting, wondering, and pondering.

The "pause" has become increasingly sought today. Doctors and therapists frequently advocate the practice of such relaxation techniques as autogenic relaxation, progressive muscle relaxation, hot stones massage, yoga, Tai chi, aromatherapy, and reflexology, and today the spa experience of herbal wraps, facials, and therapeutic massages has become popular as tourism (Walden, 2007).

Ritual

Ritual:

any customarily repeated act

How do you usually enter a swimming pool? Do you jump in off the side, dive in from the board, use the ladder, or walk down the shallow end steps? Most of us follow a consistent pattern for this, and many other leisure pursuits. Does your family celebrate Thanksgiving in much the same way year after year? Is it an absolute must that you watch the annual Super Bowl football game on television? Indeed, much of our leisure is ritualized.

In the sense we consider it a benefit of leisure, *ritual* is defined as a set of everyday acts with their sequence established by tradition. While such an everyday pattern may begin at the individual level, collective patterns may also evolve. Ritual is perhaps born from the human need for regular and mutual affirmation (Ibrahim, 1991), which explains its role in religion. But, since many forms of leisure involve ritual, leisure itself has also been ritualized.

Holidays provide rich illustrations of leisure as ritual. As in ancient societies, there are many holidays in our contemporary lives. Today, we ritualistically experience patriotic holidays (Canada Day), as well as holidays considered seasonal (New Year's Day), or religious (Hanukkah). In addition, people establish unofficial holidays that inspire specific rituals, such as Friendship Day (first Sunday in August) and Buy Nothing Day (the day after the American Thanksgiving).

Holidays in North America have evolved from a variety of cultures worldwide and have greatly changed in their meanings and how they are ritually celebrated (Godbey, 2003). In fact, for many holidays, the occasion is increasingly marked by rituals that have little relation to their origin. For example, Groundhog Day (February 2) is the American and Canadian version of Candlemas Day, an ancient European festival marking the mid-point of winter. On this day all the candles to be used in the Christian church for the coming year were brought into the church and blessed. The belief that if Candlemas Day were sunny, and thus winter would continue was somehow transferred to the groundhog's shadow when the tradition came to North America.

Many illustrations of ritual in leisure can also be found in tourism. For example, anthropologist Dean MacCannell (1999) claims modern international sightseeing possesses its own rituals that morally structure tourist behavior. His

Sight sacralization:

a tourist destination is considered sacred

point is that guided tours today are extensive ceremonial agendas involving long strings of obligatory rites. If you go to Europe, you must see Paris, and if you go to Paris, you must see the Louvre Museum, and accordingly if you go to the Louvre, you must see the Mona Lisa.

MacCannell declares this ritual attitude of the tourist originates in the act of travel itself, which in turn originated as a pilgrimage to holy places. In anthropology, a special term has been identified for the tourist ritual: *sight sacralization*. A particular destination becomes a tourist attraction because for social, historical or cultural reasons it represents something morally good. The next time you're seeing the Mona Lisa, for example, notice how reverent the other tourists are in its presence.

Decorum: socially useful behavior

Holidays and tourism are useful illustrations because ritual and leisure share certain common characteristics. For example, typically both involve intrinsic reward, having meaning in and of themselves. As well, much of the ritual of leisure is of the type labeled by Goffman (1959) as decorum. *Decorum* is nonessential, as is decoration, but is practiced because it enhances social interaction. Golf, for example, is considered one of the most decorum-rich sports. Where to stand while others are playing, how to mark the ball on the green, and whose turn it is can intimidate a new player unaware of the ritual.

Solitude

Spending time alone is an integral and important part of living. Brief periods of solitude can return us to ourselves by providing opportunities for growth and creativity (Storr, 1988). While many people fear being lonely, when voluntarily chosen, being alone provides a time and space to be ourselves, accountable only to ourselves, and free of obligations and duties. When this is the experience of solitude, we are at leisure.

May Sarton, an American poet and novelist, referred to solitude as the "richness of self." In her journal entry of September 15th, she wrote:

> I am here alone for the first time in weeks, to take up my "real" life again at last. That is what is strange – that friends, even passionate love, are not my real life unless there is time alone in which to explore and to discover what is happening.
> (Sarton, 1973, p. 3).

Figure 2.7

Some pastimes, such as reading, return us to our own world by giving us solitude. (© Ruth V. Russell, 2008)

In a sense, then, the leisure benefit of solitude is a form of narcissism. Through moments of solitude in leisure, we are allowed to return to ourselves, to "love" ourselves.

Let's illustrate this with a common leisure expression—reading. Reading is not necessarily easy; it makes demands on our skills by not only requiring literacy, but also by requiring our concentration and our attention. Have you noticed how reading isolates readers from the ordinary action around them? The fun of reading, then, like so many solitary activities, is in its escapist nature. Everyday routines are forgotten for a moment, and a special and separate sphere of privacy is provided (Davies, 1989).

Contemporary societies often make solitude difficult to attain. For example, in urban areas it is almost impossible to get away from the intrusions and noise of other people. And, most occupations require working with and around other people. Perhaps the greatest threat to the leisure benefit of solitude is personal communication devices.

Such technologies as cell phones, pagers, and personal digital assistants, are ever-present threats to privacy—both for users' and for those around the users. We receive communications almost anywhere at any time. A survey of America Online published in 2005 found that 26% of Americans say they can't go more than two or three days without checking e-mail. People are using their devices in bed (23%), in meetings (8%), in the bathroom (4%), and even in church (1%) (Shipley, 2005).

Commitment

Do you know anyone who is so committed to a particular pastime that it holds absolute primacy in his life priorities? After being asked, "How bad would it be if you were unable to downhill ski anymore?" a 57-year old man responded,

> It would be very bad. Skiing is an important part of my life. Not just of my leisure life, but of my real life. It is who I am. I cannot imagine living without skiing.

> (Russell, 2000)

For some people leisure supplies the main source of personal identity and meaning in life. For them, leisure is taken very seriously, and their commitment to developing skill and experience in a particular pastime becomes central to their lives.

There are several ways to consider this quality of leisure. For example, commitment in leisure could mean devoting energy and resources to perfecting

Box 2.8

In Focus

My Journey to the Ironman Triathlon

I floated in the deep water. Like hundreds of other swimmers around me, I wore a black wetsuit with darkened goggles, and a swim cap with my race number inked across it. The goggles and swim caps hid the features of those bobbing around me so although surrounded by over 2000 other men and women, I felt very much on my own. I tried to smile at the other swimmers but few noticed. All knew the cannon would sound in seconds and more than 8000 arms and legs would beat the water into foam as we surged toward the finish line some 141 miles away. To reach that finish line, all of us would endure a two-mile swim, 112 miles of biking, and the running of a marathon. We all knew this would be one of the most difficult days of our lives. My preparation for this event started months ago, yet I did not feel ready. Could I ever be ready for the events that were about to unfold? Even though I chose

Box 2.8 (Cont.)

this event as my leisure, at this moment it did not feel much like fun. Floating in the water, waiting to start Ironman Lake Placid, I wondered "why?" Why was I taking part in a leisure activity that seemed so daunting?
(From McCarville, 2007, p. 159)

Questions to Consider and Discuss

This excerpt is from the personal journal of Dr. Ron McCarville, a professor of leisure studies at the University of Waterloo in Ontario. In keeping this account, he was able to explore not only his own experiences, but also the community of triathletes. Here are some questions to ponder, based on Dr. McCarville's conclusions.

1. Triathletes commonly display the status of their triathlon involvement through such paraphernalia as bumper stickers, jackets, and "finisher" gear. Is this typical of serious leisure in general? Does serious leisure bring credibility that other pastimes do not?
2. Triathlons provide for a strong social world—a special community that creates a profound sense of belonging. But, what if the friends and family of a participant of serious leisure do not participate? Does serious leisure intrude into relationships? What are daily lifestyle implications of serious leisure?

the skills and knowledge needed to do it well. Also, someone who has consistently and regularly pursued a pastime from childhood through old age demonstrates a commitment. The focus of numerous research studies has recently combined these ideas into the concept of serious leisure. *Serious leisure* is the "systematic pursuit of an activity that participants find so substantial and interesting that, in the typical case, they launch themselves on a career centered on acquiring and expressing its special skills, knowledge, and experience" (Stebbins, 1992, p. 3). In other words, it is high-investment leisure.

Serious leisure:
the substantial and systematic pursuit of a pastime

Table 2.3

Characterization of Serious Leisure

- A high standard of performance
- Participation for the experience of it (intrinsic reward)
- A set of values, resources, and schedules constructed around the activity
- Involvement in groups engaged in the same activity
- Self-identification with the activity

Serious leisure is a particular type of leisure that can be contrasted with such pastimes as watching television and hanging out with friends, where little or no commitment is required to enjoy it. Commitment in leisure is a matter of degree, and in serious leisure we are referring to the highest degree of commitment. A lesser degree of commitment might be engaging in what sociologist Robert Stebbins refers to as casual leisure. That is, though immediately and intrinsically rewarding, the pursuit is a short-lived pleasurable activity, requiring little or no special training to enjoy it (2006). Another lesser degree of commitment is what Stebbins refers to as project-based leisure (2006), that is, a short-term, reasonably complicated, occasional creative undertaking. Both casual and project leisure contain fewer of the characteristics of serious leisure listed in table 2.3. That is,

Box 2.9

 # *In Your Own Experience*

Spiritual Health

		Rarely	Sometimes	Most of the time	Always
1.	I believe life is a precious gift that should be nurtured.	1	2	3	4
2.	I take time to enjoy nature and the beauty around me.	1	2	3	4
3.	I take time alone to think about what's important in life–who I am, what I value, where I fit in, and where I'm going.	1	2	3	4
4.	I engage in acts of caring and goodwill without expecting something in return.	1	2	3	4
5.	I feel confident that I have touched the lives of others in a positive way.	1	2	3	4
6.	I am content with who I am.	1	2	3	4
7.	I go for the gusto and experience life to the fullest.	1	2	3	4

Total your scores. An ideal spiritual health score is 28. Scores of 27-20 are outstanding. Your answers show you are aware of the importance of spirituality of your health. Scores of 19-10 show that although you experience some spirituality in life, there is room for growth. Study the items you answered "sometimes." What changes could you make to improve your score? For scores 9 and lower, your spiritual health is at risk. Why do you think this is so?

Adapted from: U.S. Health and Human Services, 1981. Health style; A self test. Washington, DC.: Public Health Service.

serious leisure continues over a long time, requires a great deal of effort and preparation, and provides strong personal identification.

Spirituality

Everyone's life draws on some form of spirituality. In fact, more and more, spirituality is considered a requirement for good health (Heintzman & Mannell, 2003). Not only does our belief system provide important coping resources for dealing with stress, but it also fosters a "sense of inner wholeness" (Walsh, 1999, p. 6). Living spiritually can give us hope, forgiveness, a sense of meaning, and a feeling of unity with the world around us.

Some even refer to spirituality as a kind of intelligence. For example, Zohar and Marshall (2001) consider spiritual intelligence (SQ) to reflect our capacity to vision, value, and believe. Further, spiritual intelligence is what we use to place our actions and lives into a wider, richer context. That is, when we have high spiritual intelligence, we are able to satisfy a longing for something that gives us and our actions a sense of meaning. SQ is an ability to let go of the confines of our ego and, according to Zohar and Marshall, is a necessary foundation for the effective function of both our intellectual and emotional intelligences.

How does leisure benefit us spiritually? Although our pastimes, with their connotation of pleasure, may appear to be an inappropriate context, there is perhaps no more compatible connection in our lives than leisure and spirituality.

Let's consider particular pastimes to illustrate this —skiing and snowboarding. In a study by Marsh (2007), interviews were conducted with people who had been skiing and snowboarding in the region of Teton Pass, Wyoming—a backcountry area with more than 400 inches of annual snowfall. The meanings interviewees perceived experiencing from their adventures in the backcountry were asked about. Among the findings, most frequently expressed were a transcendent experience, increased awareness, connection to others, reflection, tranquility, appreciation of beauty, and mental and physical exercise.

Thus, these leisure pursuits provided a means for participants to find an inner wholeness. Other scholars have linked leisure and spirituality in similar ways. For example, Lehman (1974) suggested a leisure state of mind is one that helps us attain enlightenment, and for Pieper (1963), leisure is a meditative state in which we discover God and the true meaning of life. Some consider the practice of such spiritual activities as prayer to be leisure-like.

Finally, leisure may be considered to have a spiritual quality because it connects us with others. Through shared leisure, we may grow to better understand and get along with each other. This can be illustrated through festivals and holidays. Pieper (1963), for example, declares that

Figure 2.8

Ice climbing is a popular pastime worldwide. It requires ascending inclined ice formations such as icefalls and frozen waterfalls. (© Amy Shellman, 2008. Used with permission)

celebration is the soul of leisure. He argues that people celebrate with each other that which is good.

Risk

Ocean cruising is an exotic way of life. Cruisers are people who sail the oceans of the world for years just for fun. They forsake the security and safety of land-based life for the formidable challenges of the high seas. Their lifestyle requires much

Box 2.10

In Focus

Is Dangerous Leisure Morally Right

"Extreme" pastimes are now popular weekend and vacation pursuits for millions of people. Accordingly, some criticism has evolved about the potential negative costs. The heart of the discussion is: as the number of people participating in risky leisure increases, so do the number of serious injuries and death.

Taking BASE jumping as an example, at least 250 conventional freefall skydives are usually recommended before attempting a BASE jump. The main reason for the danger is that initiation of the jump can be lower than the parachute opening height for conventional skydiving, with jumpers having only seconds to deploy their parachutes. Also, unpredictable side drafts can force the participant into the structure that was jumped from. Considered an "underground" activity by some, fatality statistics are accordingly difficult to confirm, as for example, the death of 58-year-old Jan Davis in 1999—the fifth such death in Yosemite National Park since 1982 (Olivier, 2006).

Other criticisms of risky leisure include the costs to rescue teams and the negative emotional impact on participants' friends and family (Olivier, 2006). Further, mass use of such natural resources as rock faces and icefalls can have a negative and often irreparable impact on the resource itself. While there are attempts to manage the risk of extreme sports, such as through training and proper equipment, there is always a possibility of great harm.

Questions to Consider and Discuss

1. Have you participated in what you'd consider to be risky leisure? For what reasons did/do you choose to participate? What benefits did/do you receive from participating?
2. What might be some reasons for you personally that taking the risk of possibly being seriously injured or even killed from risky pastimes are worth it? Also, what might be some justifications for not taking the risk?
3. Some participants have concluded that mature, rational individuals ought to have the right to pursue activities that have potentially harmful consequences for them. What do you think?

effort and expensive resources in the face of considerable danger. Are cruisers only a special case?

From formerly being viewed as "fringe" activities, high-risk leisure pursuits are now popular with millions of people throughout the world. Risky leisure has become a global phenomenon (Olivier, 2006). Examples include bungee jumping, rock climbing, surfing, whitewater kayaking, rafting, parasailing, free diving, mountaineering, storm chasing, scuba diving, and gliding.

Sometimes referred to as extreme sports, their increased popularity is mirrored by the dramatic increase in media coverage that glorifies high-risk leisure. The industries serving high-risk leisure have also grown, along with technological advances to serve them. Once the domain of esoteric enthusiasts, such as ocean cruisers, participants now encompass a wide range of age, income, and education levels (Olivier, 2006).

We are not limited, however, to consider risky leisure only on rock faces and in whitewater rapids. Other high-risk pursuits might include gambling, having a poem you've written read aloud to an audience, and baking a cake for friends using a new recipe. So, why do we do these things? What is our reward? The reward is perhaps risk itself. Risk in leisure gives us a feeling of exhilaration. We feel competent. We find an escape from the ordinary routines of our lives.

Let's consult some research to confirm this. Paxton (1998) measured gains in ability to consider oneself as able to produce intended results, labeled self-efficacy, from risky forms of leisure and concluded these gains lasted for a least one year after the experience. A study by Priest and Bunting (1993) similarly found that participation in a three-day whitewater canoeing trip resulted in increases in feelings of competence. These gains typically lasted for at least one year after the experience.

What We Understand About Leisure's Importance

There is no debating that the experience of leisure is important to us. To demonstrate this, several examples of the benefits of leisure were presented. After studying this chapter, you should know that:

- We all need leisure in our lives because it provides us with the benefits that make us human.
- These benefits include freedom, intrinsic reward, pleasure, happiness, spirituality, solitude, ritual, humor, play, commitment, risk, and relaxation.
- We don't need all of these benefits at the same time and in the same pastime, but we do need some of them at least some of the time.

References

Bregha, F.J. (1991). Leisure and freedom re-examined. In T.L. Goodale, & P.A. Witt (Eds.), *Recreation and leisure: Issues in an era of change*. State College, PA: Venture.

Caillois, R. (1961). *Man, play, and games*. Glencoe, IL: Free Press of Glencoe.

Csikszentmihalyi, M. (1975). *Beyond boredom and anxiety*. San Francisco: Jossey-Bass.

Davies, M. (1989). Another way of being: Leisure and the possibility of privacy. In T. Winnifrith, & C. Barrett (Eds.), *The philosophy of leisure*. New York: St. Martin's Press.

Ellis, M.J. (1973). *Why people play*. Englewood Cliffs, NJ: Prentice-Hall.

Esch, T., & Stefano, G.B. (2004). The neurobiology of pleasure, reward processes, addiction and their health implications. *Neuroendocrinology Letters No. 4*, August Vol. 25, 235-251.

Godbey, G. (2003). *Leisure in your life: An exploration*, 6th Ed. State College, PA: Venture.

Goffman, E. (1959). *The presentation of self in everyday life*. New York: Doubleday.

Goodale, T., & Godbey, G. (1988). *The evolution of leisure: Historical and philosophical perspectives*. State College, PA: Venture.

Hawes, A. (1996). Jungle gyms: The evolution of animal play. *ZooGoer, 25*(1), 1-5. Available from http://nationalzoo.si.edu. Retrieved 3/27/08.

Heintzman, P., & Mannell, R.C. (2003). Spiritual functions of leisure and spiritual well-being: Coping with time pressure. *Leisure Sciences, 25*, 207-230.

Huizinga, J. (1955). *Homo ludens: A study of the play element in culture*. Boston: Beacon Press.

Ibrahim, J. (1991). *Leisure and society: A comparative approach*. Dubuque, IA: Wm. C. Brown.

Jones, S.S. (1992). *Choose to live peacefully*. Berkeley, CA: Celestial Arts.

Kelly, J.R. (1982). *Leisure*. Englewood Cliffs, NJ: Prentice-Hall.

Kleiber, D.A. (2000). The neglect of relaxation. *Journal of Leisure Research, 32*(1), 82-86.

Kovacs, A. (2007). The leisure personality: Relationships between personality, leisure satisfaction, and life satisfaction. Unpublished doctoral dissertation, Indiana University, Bloomington.

Larson, R., & Richards, M. (1998). Waiting for the weekend: Friday and Saturday night as the emotional climax of the week. In A.C. Crouter, & R. Larson (Eds.), *Temporal rhythms in adolescence: Clocks, calendars, and the coordination of daily life*. San Francisco: Jossey Bass.

Lehman, H.D. (1974). *In praise of leisure*. Scottdale, PA: Herald Press.

Lepper, M.R., Greene, D., & Nisbett, R.E. (1973). Undermining children's intrinsic interest with extrinsic reward: A test of "overjustification" hypothesis. *Journal of Personality and Social Psychology, 28*(1), 129-137.

MacCannell, D. (1999). *The tourist: A new theory of the leisure class*. Berkeley: University of California Press.

Marsh, P.E. (2007). Backcountry adventure as spiritual experience: A means-end study. Unpublished doctoral dissertation, Indiana University, Bloomington.

May, R. (1981). *Freedom and destiny*. New York: W.W. Norton.

McCarville, R. (2007). From a fall in the mall to a run in the sun: One journey to ironman triathlon. *Leisure Sciences, 29(2)*, 159-173.

McDonald, K.A. (January 13, 1995). The secrets of animal play. *The Chronicle of Higher Education*, A8-A13.

Millar, S. (1968). *The psychology of play*. London: Penguin Books.

Morreall, J. (1983). *Taking laughter seriously*. Albany: State University of New York.

Olivier, S. (2006). Moral dilemmas of participation in dangerous leisure activities. *Leisure Studies, 25*(1), 95-109.

Paxton, T.S. (1998). Self-efficacy and outdoor adventure programs: A quantitative and qualitative analysis. Unpublished doctoral dissertation, University of Minnesota, Minneapolis-St. Paul.

Pelletier, L.G. (1995). Loisirs et santé mentale: Les relations entre la motivation pour la pratique des loisirs et le bien-etre psychologique. *Canadian Journal of Behavioral Sciences, 27*(2), 140-156.

Pieper, J. (1963). *Leisure: The basis of culture*. New York: The New American Library.

Priest, S., & Bunting, C. (1993). Changes in perceived risk and competence during whitewater canoeing. *Journal of Applied Recreation Research, 18*(4), 265-280.

Putnam, R.D. (2000). *Bowling alone*. New York: Simon & Schuster.

Roach, M. (September 1996). Can you laugh your stress away? *Health*, 92-96.

Russell, B. (1968). *The conquest of happiness*. New York: Bantam.

Russell, R.V. (2000). Unpublished field notes.

Sarton, M. (1973). *Journal of a solitude*. New York: W.W. Norton.

Shipley, C. (July 12, 2005). Lamenting the loss of leisure (WTN News). Available from http://wistechnology.com/articles/1981/?id=198. Retrieved 3/20/08.

Smith, S.L.J. (1991). On the biological basis of pleasure: Some implications for leisure policy. In T.L. Goodale, & P.A. Witt (Eds.), *Recreation and leisure: Issues in an era of change*. State College, PA: Venture.

Spencer, H. (1855). *Principles of psychology*. New York: Appleton.

Stebbins, R.A. (1992). *Amateurs, professionals, and serious leisure*. Montreal, Quebec: McGill-Queen's University Press.

Stebbins, R.A. (2001). *New directions in the theory and research of serious leisure*. Lampeter, Wales: The Edwin Mellen Press.

Stebbins, R.A. (2006). *Serious leisure: A perspective for our time*. Edison, NJ: Transaction Publishers.

Storr, A. (1988). *Solitude: A return to the self*. New York: Ballantine Books.

Sylvester, C. (1991). Recovering a good idea for the sake of goodness: An interpretive critique of subjective leisure. In T.L. Goodale, & P.A. Witt (Eds.), *Recreation and leisure: Issues in an era of change*. State College, PA: Venture.

Walden, K.M. (2007). Perceptions of leisure and complementary and alternative medicine among spa practitioners. Unpublished doctoral dissertation, Indiana University, Bloomington.

Walsh, F. (1999). *Spiritual resources in family therapy*. New York: Guilford.

Zohar, D., & Marshall, I. (2001). *SQ: Connecting with our spiritual intelligence*. New York: Bloomsbury.

CHAPTER THREE

EXPLAINING LEISURE

PREVIEW

What determines our pastime choices?

Because leisure behavior is complex and dynamic, there are many explanations.

What role do demographic characteristics play in determining our pastime choices?

Such factors as our age, gender, income, education level, residence, and lifestyle shape our leisure interests.

Can leisure be explained theoretically?

Many theories from such fields as psychology and anthropology attempt to explain the conditions and functions of leisure behavior and choices.

Are these theories supported by research?

Research demonstrates theories do explain some aspects of leisure behavior, but more studies are needed to develop a comprehensive explanation.

KEY TERMS

Why did you choose to take a vacation last summer? How did you choose where to go and what to do after you got there? As you begin to answer this (or the alternate question of why you chose not to have a vacation), you quickly begin to realize your reasons are numerous and interrelated.

Perhaps this is what makes studying leisure so intriguing. Indeed, leisure has been the subject of scholarship by a wide range of investigators representing a wide range of disciplines (Searle, 2000). Some of this study focuses on the causes of leisure behavior by particular life situation factors, such as age and level of education. Other explanations are derived from the development of theories that are then tested for validity through research studies. In this chapter we describe what we know about leisure behavior from both of these approaches.

Figure 3.1
Our leisure interests, needs, choices, and behaviors are determined by many interrelated factors. (Shutterstock©, 2008)

Demographic Explanations of Leisure Behavior

In explaining our leisure interests and actions, one important source of understanding is demographic information. *Demographics* refer to certain characteristics about a population of people. Commonly used demographics include age, gender, race, ethnicity, income, residential location, disabilities, availability of transportation, educational attainment, home ownership, employment status, and occupation. All of these factors play a role in determining what, why, and how we pursue our pastimes. Let's overview a few of them.

To begin, one's age affects leisure choices. This is a frequently researched demographic characteristic because age is an indication of not only maturation, but also historical experiences, abilities, social expectations, and social rights and privileges. As an example of the latter, various state and province regulations for minimum driving ages (such as 14 in South Dakota and 17 in New Jersey) have a significant impact on the leisure choices of youth, as do restrictions against driving for the elderly.

Demographics: characteristics of the population

There are many other illustrations of the effect of age on leisure. According to some research, current generations of older women experience significantly lower levels of physical activity and sports participation than do younger generations (Freysinger & Kelly, 2004). This is perhaps because older women have not had the same opportunities for physical skill development that younger generations of women have because of social restrictions against their participation in sports when of school age – the prime stage in life for learning physical skills.

As you likely also know, age as a predictor of leisure expression operates in tandem with another demographic characteristic – gender. In many societies, gender is the central focus of the structure of everyday life. Although the term *gender* is commonly used interchangeably with the term sex, within the social sciences gender more specifically refers to social differences, including social expectations and roles. This suggests that what it means to be a woman or a man is more socially than biologically ascribed.

Gender:
social expectations and roles

A great deal of research has also been done on gender as an explanation of leisure interests and behaviors, most of which has focused on describing gender differences. To summarize this literature, while gender is less limiting in some ways than it was in the past, for the most part gender still matters in leisure (McGinnis, Chun, & McQuillan, 2003).

Let's consider the leisure realm of sport as an example. In the area of sport spectatorship, men have historically dominated. Studies have indicated men and boys show greater interest in watching football, ice hockey, basketball, soccer, and baseball on television, while women and girls have greater preference for gymnastics, skiing, diving, and figure skating (Sargent, Zillman & Weaver, 1998). These differences are diminishing, however, as women have increased their interest in watching such sports as football and NASCAR . Among all NASCAR television viewers, for example, women now comprise nearly 40 percent and women make up approximately the same percentage for National Football League television audiences. (Weissman, 1999).

Gender differences are also reducing in sport participation. While men have historically dominated playing in sport activities in North America (Wiley, Shaw, & Havitz, 2000), more women are now participating in sports than ever before. Today approximately one in three women participates in organized sports (Sabo & Jansen, 1998), and young girls (ages 9 to 14) show even more interest than boys in playing sports such as basketball (Gardyn, 2001).

Figure 3.2

Typical participants in the sport of curling are well educated, professional, white, Canadian men, between the ages of 35 and 49 years. (Source: Canadian Curling Association. Shutterstock©, 2008)

Yet, such gains sometimes bring opposition. Research also suggests that when women attempt to further their sport consumption on television, they are often met with resistance by men who feel sports are their domain (Kahle, Elton, & Kambara, 1997). As well, women and men, girls and boys, remain physically separated in organized sport participation, allowing for "differentness" to be maintained (Reskin, 1998).

Our leisure is shaped not only by age and gender, but also by ethnicity and race. *Ethnicity* is a term that represents social groups with a shared history, sense of identity, geography, and cultural roots—which may occur despite racial differences. This means the leisure choices of people from various ethnic groups differ primarily because of cultural distinctions. Leisure choices according to race are also in large part socially defined. For example, many researchers have found similarities in leisure preferences between Black and White Americans who defined themselves as middle class (Shinew, Floyd, McGuire & Noe, 1996).

Ethnicity:
people who share cultural characteristics

Yet, as you rightly might wonder after reading the study in box 3.1, how much of the racial differences could be due to other demographic characteristics, such as income or residence? Let's consider each of these.

The explanatory power of income on leisure choices seems obvious, especially for those activities that must be purchased. For example, as one study in tourism demonstrated, tourists with higher incomes stay longer and spend more money

Box 3.1

 The Study Says

Race and Gender Differences in Teen Approval of Leisure Choices

This study investigated the relationship between race and gender on adolescent peer group approval of 20 leisure activities. A sample of 101 Black and 280 White adolescents drawn from the 11th and 12th grades of a southern U.S. high school were asked to rate leisure activities as appropriate for their peer group. Results indicated race was a more important factor than gender when comparing the peer group approval ratings. For example, for half of the leisure activities, significant approval differences were found between the racial groups. Specifically, Blacks indicated significantly stronger approval for playing basketball, going to the mall, singing in a choir, and dancing, while Whites indicated significantly stronger approval for playing soccer, horseback riding, water skiing, camping, fishing, and golfing.

Phillipp, S.F. (1998). Race and gender differences in adolescent peer group approval of leisure activities. *Journal of Leisure Research, 30(*2), 214-233.

per day than do those with lower incomes (Mill, 1986). Similarly, in technological cultures leisure opportunities in general are more accessible to those with higher incomes. This is why poverty is such a double tragedy. Although participation in leisure activities improves the quality of daily life, it tends to be less available to economically disadvantaged people who perhaps need it most.

There is another interesting connection between money and leisure. In some situations, leisure actually provides direct financial benefits to participants. Examples are occupations in which participants are paid for engaging in their favorite pastimes, such as being fishing guides, fitness instructors, artists, and so on.

Finally, where we live greatly affects the nature and accessibility of pastime opportunities. Some pastimes are not universally available because of climate, topography, and other elements of the demographic characteristic of residence. For

Figure 3.3

Interests in activities such as bird watching are often determined by our residential location. (© Ruth V. Russell, 2008)

Box 3.2

Noise

Since the days of Sodom and Gomorrah, cities have been singled out as bad places to be. Some of the reasons we love to hate the city include its architecture, which restricts sunlight, forms wind tunnels, and traps heat. But these troubles don't usually head most city-bashing lists. The most often-cited source of urban discomfort is noise. For example, the quietest times in New Yorkers' apartments are louder than the noisiest small towns (Gallagher, 1993).

Noise is almost entirely human-made, rarely occurring in nature. The term noise is derived from the Latin word nausea, and it causes measurable physiological and psychological problems. Changes in blood pressure, respiration rate, hormone levels, muscle tension, and digestion from noise can take a disastrous toll on well-being. Noise also lowers performance, mood, and sociability, and increases aggression (nonoise.org, 2008).

So, why not move out of the city to some peace and quiet? If you've spent even one summer's day in a suburban neighborhood, you'll quickly retort there's

Box 3.2 (Cont.)

no quiet there either! Noise from street traffic, garbage trucks, lawn mowers, leaf blowers, hedge trimmers, and weed whackers are pervasive suburban pollutants today.

So, let's head out to the lake, which, of course, turns out to be noisier than the New Jersey Turnpike, with the roar of jet skis, jet boats, cigar boats, and boom boxes. To illustrate the extent of the problem with just jet skis, according to the calculations of Komanoff (2003), Canadian beachgoers would be personally willing to pay $75 to be rid of jet ski noise at their favorite lake.

Questions to Consider and Discuss

1. How does noise affect you? How does where you choose to live affect your view about noise?
2. Would you say your own leisure interests tend to be noisy or quiet? Why? Is the noise or the quiet necessary in order to enjoy your leisure?
3. Is the noise generated by particular leisure pursuits justified? Or, does it mean that some enjoy leisure at the expense of others?

example, if you live in an urban location a wide range of commercial and cultural leisure options are available, yet activities requiring large space, such as snowmobiling, are more common in rural areas. Many people choose to live in apartments and condominiums because they typically offer swimming pools, tennis courts, and fitness rooms. And suburban locations are a good choice for organized youth sports.

The demographic characteristics we have just discussed (age, gender, race, ethnicity, income, and residence), as well as others, explain our leisure choices and behaviors directly, as well as indirectly via the concept of lifestyle. Our lifestyle can be considered the "stew pot" of these demographic factors—affecting our values, attitudes, and ultimately our interests and choices.

Lifestyles:
a quality and custom of living

Lifestyle is a pattern of living. For example, you may have heard of some of these lifestyles: retirement, healthy, couples, luxury, family, party, traditional and simple. As you can readily see these patterns of living are associated with certain demographic characteristics, such as age, income, and education level.

In fact, the numerous categories of lifestyle types are based on the mix of demographic factors. For example, the VALS (Values, Attitudes and Lifestyles) typology divides people into eight lifestyle types based mostly on age, income, and education. In the VALS, leisure is an important consequence of lifestyle type. For example, as noted in table 3.1, the innovators seek the "finer things in life" while the leisure of thinkers centers on the home.

Theory:
a plausible set of principles used to explain some behavior or event

Theories Explaining Leisure Behavior

Now we turn to theoretical ways of explaining our leisure interests and actions. What is a theory? A *theory* is a set of interrelated, testable

Table 3.1

Lifestyle Types According to the VALS

Lifestyle Type Interests	Description	Leisure
Innovators	Successful, sophisticated, take-charge people with high self-esteem and abundant resources; change leaders; receptive to new ideas	Cultivated tastes for upscale, high image, variety, and the finer things in life.
Thinkers	Mature, satisfied, comfortable, and reflective people who value order, knowledge, and responsibility; well educated; respect the status quo; open to new ideas.	Centered on the home.
Believers	Motivated by ideals; conservative, conventional people with concrete beliefs based on traditional codes of family, religion, community, and the nation.	Follow established routines, organized around home, family, community, and community organizations.
Achievers	Busy, goal-oriented, with deep commitment to career success; live conventional lives; value predictability and stability over risk, intimacy, and self-discovery.	Social lives structured around family, place of worship, and work.
Strivers	Trendy and fun loving; concerned about opinions and approval of others; don't have enough money to meet desires; feel they have a job rather than a career.	Active consumers because shopping is both a social activity and an opportunity to demonstrate to peers their ability to buy; easily bored.
Experiences	Motivated by self-expression; typically young and energetic; quickly become enthusiastic about new possibilities but are equally quick to cool.	Seek variety and excitement, savoring the new, the offbeat, and the risky; express their energy in exercise, sports, outdoor recreation, and social activities.
Makers	Experience the world by working on it - building a house, raising children, fixing a car, canning vegetables; practical people who have constructive skills and value self-sufficiency; unimpressed by material possessions other than those with a functional purpose.	Physical recreation.

Table 3.1 (Cont.)

Lifestyle Type Interests	Description	Leisure
Survivors	Live narrowly focused lives; with limited resources, they are comfortable with the familiar and primarily concerned with safety and security.	TV watching and other low-cost pursuits.

http://www.sric-bi.com/VALS/. Retrieved 8/10/08.

Philosophy:

beliefs about morals, character and behavior

propositions. Theory attempts to explain why facts are what they are—that is, giving insight into how the world works. Sometimes we confuse theory with philosophy. *Philosophy* relates to a belief system about how the world should work (Henderson, Presley & Bialeschki, 2004). As Babbie (2003) explained, "Social scientific theory has to do with what is, not what should be" (p. 26).

Numerous theories have been used to explain leisure based on propositions in sociology, psychology, anthropology, economics, and other disciplines. Some of these theories are simple—based on direct observation, whereas others are more comprehensive, involving extensive research testing. None of the theories available to us completely explain all leisure behavior for all people in all situations, however. Nonetheless, they remain useful to us, particularly for those professionals who provide leisure services, because they help predict the needs and interests of clients.

Box 3.3

 In Your Own Experience

What is your VALS type

After studying table 3.1, make an initial estimate of which lifestyle type you think you are. Then, take the actual VALS survey to see how close your estimate came. Go to the internet site: http://www.sric-bi.com/VALS/. From here, click on "VALS Survey," and then "Take the Survey." After answering all questions, click "Submit," and in a few seconds your lifestyle profile (both primary and secondary) will be reported. Read more about your profile by clicking on "The VALS Types." Were you surprised by the results? Why or why not? How does your lifestyle type relate to your leisure interests?

Compensation and Spillover

For a long time, leisure choices have been explained as a reaction to work. That is, the nature of people's work directly influences their choice of pastimes. Illustrating this approach are the theoretical ideas of spillover and compensation. Whether leisure is a spillover response to work, or a compensation response to work, depends on the nature of our work.

On the one hand, when deprivations and dissatisfactions are experienced in work, leisure makes up for them. This compensation explanation claims people participate in those activities that satisfy needs they cannot satisfy at work. As described by Wilensky (1960), a person engaged in repetitive, low-skilled, and machine-paced work, will seek the opposite for leisure. This helps explain, perhaps, why people who perform physical work choose to spend their free time resting, or why those who work indoors prefer outdoor pursuits.

In contrast, the spillover idea claims when people are satisfied and fulfilled in their work, leisure activities are chosen that mimic it. Leisure becomes an extension of the skills and attitudes used at work. Work spills over into leisure (Wilensky, 1960). This means workers are thought to participate in pastimes that have characteristics similar to their job tasks. For example, computer skills learned on the job may be used to socialize on the Internet.

Figure 3.4

Understanding why people behave in leisure as they do has been used by managers of parks to respond to the needs of visitors. (© Ruth V. Russell, 2008)

Even though compensation and spillover explain leisure in opposite ways, at their core, both propositions are based on the same premise—leisure is a response to work. Which explanation applies depends on the amount of satisfaction found in work. For work that is satisfying, work activities and interests spill over into leisure. When work is not satisfying, leisure is needed to compensate for satisfactions not derived from work.

Research testing on this theoretical approach has been limited, and with contradictory findings. As well, these principles have not been particularly helpful in explaining how people organize leisure and work in their daily lives, or the impact of work-leisure relationships on life satisfaction (Chick & Hood, 1996). Also, because the basis of the explanation is work, compensation and spillover do not explain the leisure behaviors of those who do not work, such as those who are retired and children. In spite of these criticisms, explaining leisure as spillover and compensation remains useful today.

Freedom of Choice and Intrinsic Reward

Although the ancient Greeks did not develop any leisure theories per se, they did identify two variables of explanation—intrinsic reward and personal freedom (DeGrazia, 1962). Today there are several theories that attempt to explain leisure behavior according to these two variables.

For example, leisure scholars Tinsley and Tinsley (1986, p.15) have proposed that in order for a leisure experience to occur, an individual must perceive that his or her participation is freely chosen and that the benefits of participating are derived from factors intrinsic to the activity. Another theorist, Iso-Ahola (1999, p.36), furthers the proposition by claiming a sense of freedom is the central defining characteristic of leisure, that freely choosing is a necessary condition for intrinsically motivated leisure.

One of the earliest theories to include these two variables is John Neulinger's paradigm (1981). In his theoretical work, intrinsic reward and freedom of choice were a matter of degree. He categorized the different amounts of these two variables into what he referred to as "states of mind" of leisure and work. Since this has been a popular, long-standing, and widely researched theory, we'll study Neulinger's paradigm in depth.

The theory divides freedom of choice and intrinsic reward into six states of mind according to the amount of each in the situation (Neulinger, 1976). As

Figure 3.5

Neulinger's paradigm distinguishes leisure from nonleisure by the amount of freedom of choice and intrinsic reward (Neulinger, 1981).

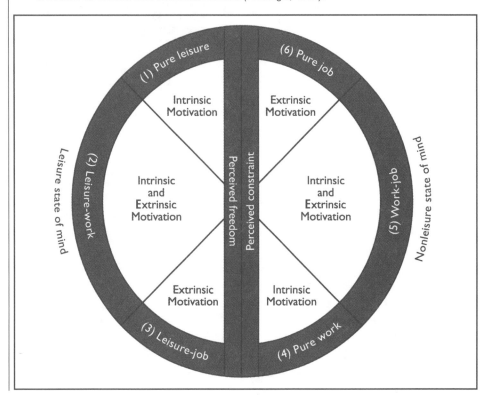

demonstrated in figure 3.5 this enables us to distinguish between leisure and nonleisure behaviors.

1. *State of Mind One*. This represents the purest form of leisure—an expression freely chosen for its own sake. Neulinger's idea of pure leisure is the same as Kelly's idea of unconditional leisure discussed in the previous chapter. That is, pure leisure requires freedom from external control, and it brings intrinsic rewards. Thus, a particular pastime can be explained as the highest form of leisure if both of these ingredients are present in your state of mind.

2. *State of Mind Two*. This leisure situation explains a wide range of experiences, all of which are freely chosen yet are both extrinsically and intrinsically rewarding. For example, perhaps you are refinishing a piece of antique furniture because you want to, and because it not only provides you with a creative feeling but also because the result will look nice in your house. Neulinger referred to this situation as leisure-work.

3. *State of Mind Three*. This situation is leisure-job according to Neulinger. It explains a type of leisure you engage in without coercion, but the satisfaction comes only from external payoffs. For some, playing cards for money (when they don't need the money) might fit this state of mind. The experience is leisure because of perceived freedom to pursue it, but like a job in that it is only extrinsically rewarding.

4. *State of Mind Four*. Neulinger's paradigm holds that the first three states of mind explain leisure behavior. The fourth through sixth states of mind are considered as nonleisure behavior. That is, without freedom of choice, we can't have leisure. Thus, the fourth state of mind is not considered to be leisure because even though it is done for intrinsic reasons, it is under

Figure 3.6

Playing with children can perhaps be considered State of Mind Three—leisure job—because a parent may willingly play with the children, but receive only the satisfaction of fulfilling an expected role as a parent. (© Ruth V. Russell, 2008)

perceived constraints. Neulinger called this condition pure work. An example might be doing your homework because you are interested and even enjoyably involved, but which you would not choose to do unless the teacher made the assignment.

5. *State of Mind Five*. This is work-job, namely, activities engaged in under constraints and having both intrinsic and extrinsic rewards. The typical employment situation may explain this state of mind. For example, in one study, the staff of a large municipal recreation and park department rated their jobs as highly meaningful and usually personally satisfying, but they did complain about low salaries. They also indicated on the survey they would quit or retire immediately if given the financial opportunity (Russell, 1993).

Box 3.4

 In Your Own Experience

What is Your Leisure State of Mind

To experience how Neulinger derived his theoretical paradigm, try out a portion of the questionnaire he and other researchers used to determine leisure and nonleisure states of mind. Follow the directions and complete the modified version of the questionnaire below.

Begin by thinking about your day yesterday (do not retrieve your appointment calendar, it is what you perceive about that day that is important). In the first column of the table, under the heading "activity," write in the main activity you recall experiencing yesterday for each of the times. Then, for the "freedom" column, enter a number from 0 to 10 reflecting how much freedom of choice you perceived for doing each activity. For the "reason" column enter a number from 0 to 10 reflecting how much intrinsic reward you perceived receiving for each activity. For both freedom and reason, a score of 0 represents no freedom of choice and no intrinsic reward, up to a score of 10, which represents the highest possible amount of choice and intrinsic reward.

Time	Activity	Freedom	Reason
10:00 am			
11:00 am			
Noon			
1:00 pm			
2:00 pm			
3:00 pm			
4:00 pm			
5:00 pm			
6:00 pm			
7:00 pm			
8:00 pm			

Box 3.4 (Cont.)

9:00 pm			
10:00 pm			

After completing the questionnaire, review your scores in the freedom and reason columns. Do you tend to have high scores (up to 10), midrange scores (4-6), or low scores (down to 0)? Accordingly, in comparing your results with Neulinger's paradigm in figure 3.5, in which state of mind did you spend your day yesterday? Why? Was it leisure or nonleisure? Why?

6. *State of Mind Six*. A state of mind in the pure job category is completely opposite pure leisure. It is an activity engaged in by necessity and under constraints. There is no reward in and of itself but only through a payoff resulting from it. Having to work at a job in its most negative connotation to earn a living only is categorized as pure job. It has no other redeeming qualities.

What is most important to realize about Neulinger's theoretical contribution to explaining leisure is that the paradigm maintains behavior is attributed solely to ourselves, rather than to external forces. Even more comprehensively, many studies have used Neulinger's paradigm to explain all of quality of life. One of these studies was of college students (Hultsman, 1984). Students majoring in business were compared with students majoring in leisure studies. The hypothesis was that as a result of their education, students pursuing a degree in leisure studies would gain an appreciation of the value of leisure for their quality of life; however, the study found no difference between the two majors. Leisure studies students did not perceive any more freedom of choice or intrinsic reward in their lives than business students.

Flow

Over more than 30 years, Mihaly Csikszentmihalyi and his colleagues have studied thousands of people who seemed to be spending time doing what they really want to. These have included rock climbers, chess players, and amateur athletes (Csikszentmihalyi, 1975), as well as surgeons, professors, clerical and assembly line workers, young mothers, retired people, and teens (Csikszentmihalyi, 1990). This research has led to one of the more popular and universally understood theories about leisure. It is called flow theory.

Flow is a word used by Csikszentmihalyi to describe becoming so involved in some activity that nothing else seems to matter. He writes, "Contrary to what happens all too often in everyday life, in moments such as these what we feel, what we wish, and what we think are in harmony" (Csikszentmihalyi, 1997, p. 29). The metaphor of flow is one many people have used to describe those moments that stand out as the best in their lives. Athletes refer to it as being "in the zone," religious mystics as being in "ecstasy," and artists and musicians as "aesthetic rapture."

Box 3.5

In Profile

Mihaly Csikszentmihalyi

Mihaly Csikszentmihalyi's interest in flow began as a very personal one. In October 1944, relatives argued with his mother that Venice, Italy, was not enjoyable at this time of year—too many mosquitoes—and the theaters would all be closed. His mother ignored their advice and left Budapest, Hungary on the early train, with 10-year-old Mihaly and his sister. Later that day, the advancing Russian army bombed the bridges, placed Budapest under siege, and within three months, more than half of Mihaly's relatives were dead. He and his family had taken the last train out (Shore, 1990). Mihaly wondered how people can be so mistaken about things.

In the winter of 1952, 18-year-old Mihaly was in Switzerland; his pockets were empty. He searched Zurich for something to do that would keep him warm and not cost anything. The solution was a free lecture given by the psychologist Carl Jung. Inspired, he began to read Jung's books, then the works of Freud, and finally, anything he could find on psychology.

To fulfill this fascination, at age 22, Mihaly arrived at Chicago's Dearborn Street Station with $1.25 in his pocket. He knew no one and spoke only the little English he had picked up from reading American comics. In five months he had passed the high school equivalency exam, and four years later earned a B.A. in psychology from the University of Chicago.

As a doctoral student, Mihaly began to feel that much of psychology was consumed with the pathological aspects of life. He was interested in the positive dimensions as he continued to reflect on his earlier war thoughts. For his Ph.D. dissertation, completed in 1965, he studied a group of art students: "I was puzzled about why they were so taken with what they were doing without any extrinsic rewards, and I realized people seek activities for their own sake—and this was generally what people in the past called happiness" (Shore, 1990, p. 34). This became the basis for a lifetime of study on the theory of flow.

Csikszentmihalyi discovered people reached this optimal experience through different activities but in similar ways. Thus, while flow may be found when people climb mountains, play on stage in a rock band, collect stamps, or give a lecture in a college classroom, the experience is the same. First, let's highlight the characteristics of the flow experience, and then we'll discuss its necessary conditions.

Flow is a subjective state we feel during an intense engagement in an activity. It is an optimal experience characterized by a (Csikszentmihalyi, Abuhamdeh & Nakamura, 2005):

Figure 3.7.

"I took my first steps onto the stage and all past memories seemed to rush past me under the darkness of the unlit lights. Behind me were three of my closest friends plugging in their instruments. In front of us, hundreds of friends were lined up, jumping up and down, and all of a sudden we hear "Ladies and gentlemen, please welcome Spread to the stage!" The next twenty minutes of my life passed in a pure bliss, every second a rush of adrenaline beyond what I had ever experienced. This was Battle of the Bands my senior year of high school and I was bewildered by this surreal experience." (Giovannoli, 2007, used with permission)

- *Loss of self-consciousness* – feeling as though the boundaries of our being have been pushed forward without self-scrutiny "My focus is always disrupted when I make a mistake and fall" – a figure skater (Jackson, 1992, p. 165).
- *Merging of action and awareness* – our attention is completely absorbed by the activity so that doing the activity becomes almost automatic "You don't feel like you're doing something as a conscious being; you're adapting to the rock and becoming part of it" – a rock climber (Csikszentmihalyi, 1975, p. 86).
- *Sense of self control* – we feel in charge of what we are doing "I felt really powerful, like I had the information in the palm of my hand and could mold it any way I wanted" – a high school student working on a paper (Larson, 1988, p. 153).
- *Altered sense of time* – time seems to pass much more quickly or we lose track of the passing of time "The next twenty minutes of my life passed in a pure bliss" – a performer in a rock band (Giovannoli, 2007).

In other words, flow is experienced as a loss of self-consciousness, a merging of action and awareness, a sense of being in control, and an altered sense of time.

In addition to these characteristics of the flow experience, specific conditions are important in enabling flow. These include (Csikszentmihalyi, Abuhamdeh & Nakamura, 2005):

- *Having a clear set of goals* – the rules of action and success are clear and feedback is immediate.
- *Autotelic* - we engage in the activity for its own reward; it is intrinsically motivating.
- *Balance between perceived challenges and perceived skills* – we are able to achieve a fine balance between what we can accomplish and what the activity requires we accomplish. In other words, flow is more likely to be experienced when the activity provides clear goals and feedback, is intrinsically rewarding, and contains a balance of challenge and skill.

Csikszentmihalyi has prepared a diagram that explains the last condition of balance between perceived challenge and perceived skill (figure 3.8). Flow tends to occur when a person's skills are fully involved in meeting a challenge that is just about manageable. If challenges are too high for our skills, we experience anxiety. If challenges are too low relative to our skills, we are bored. If both challenges and skills are perceived to be low, we feel apathetic. But, when high challenges are matched with high skills, then the deep involvement that sets flow apart from ordinary life is more likely to occur (Csikszentmihalyi, 1997).

Figure 3.8

According to flow theory, one condition for an optimal experience is a balance of challenge and skill. Flow results when high challenges are matched with high skills (Csikszentmihalyi, 2000).

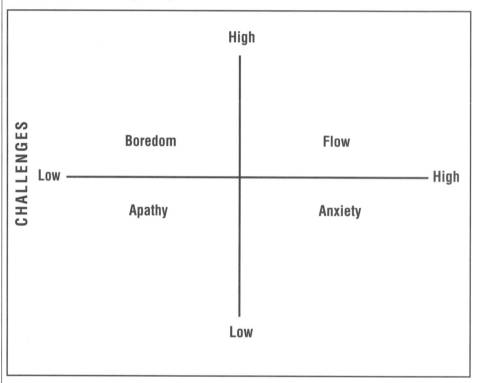

Self-As-Entertainment

Another theoretical perspective is the self-as-entertainment (S-A-E) construct developed by Roger Mannell (1984). It focuses on answering questions about leisure choices based on our personality. Self-as-entertainment reflects the capacity of people to fill their free time with activities that are personally satisfying and involving. People who are high on the S-A-E personality trait are able to fill free time satisfactorily. They do not experience time as "hanging heavily on their hands" or feel that their free time is "wasted." On the other hand, people low on this trait perceive they have "too much free time" and there is frequently "nothing to do" (Mannell, 1984, pp. 232-233).

People with the self-as-entertainment personality type are never bored in leisure. They achieve this in three possible ways: by the sheer perception that they are in control of how and what they do in their free time (self), by being able to use their mind through their own imagination and escape to fantasy to fill free time (mind play), or by going places and seeking out other people to share experiences (environment). Those who seek out their environment for entertainment, such as calling up a friend or watching television, are not relying on themselves and are thus low on the S-A-E construct.

Anti-Structure

Finally, we turn to the discipline of anthropology for a theoretical explanation of leisure. This theory is based on rituals in people's lives. Proposed by Victor Turner, and often called the theory of anti-structure, the idea is there are formal rituals that govern people's behavior both inside and outside everyday life (Turner, 1969, 1982). To Turner, leisure is the ritual that takes us outside everyday life. It does this by being antagonistic to everyday experiences. That is, they are "anti," or opposite, structure.

This is how leisure exists, according to Turner, as an anti-structure part of our lives. It's easy to see the usefulness of this theory in explaining vacations and media-based forms of entertainment as these leisure situations have their own distinct realities for the express purpose of being removed from everyday routine.

Box 3.6

The Study Says

Accounting for Leisure Preferences from Personality

There are many studies demonstrating how an individual's personality influences his/her behaviors and experiences in leisure. One study that tested the Self-As-Entertainment (S-A-E) Theory gave a battery of personality questionnaires to 999 university students and found individuals who thought they were good at entertaining themselves participated more frequently in performing arts. In contrast, those who more typically turned to their external environment preferred outdoor activities. Further, those who were unlikely to turn to their imagination and fantasies for self-entertainment enjoyed social, performing arts, outdoor, and general types of leisure. The S-A-E construct did not predict engagement in sports or water-related activities.

Barnett, L.A. (2006). Accounting for leisure preferences from within: The relative contributions of gender, race or ethnicity, personality, affective style, and motivational orientation. *Journal of Leisure Research, 38*(4), 445-474.

Figure 3.9
This interpreter at the Polynesian Cultural Center in Hawaii is using drama to help tourists transform out of their everyday lives into the world of Fiji. (© Ruth V.Russell, 2008)

Two concepts help to extend our understanding of leisure as anti-structure. These are liminality and communitas. *Liminality* is a term that comes from the Latin, meaning threshold. Turner uses it to refer to the transition from the everyday to outside the everyday. It is in this liminal stage where a more pure form of play occurs because it is free of societal norms and structures. Its transitional nature creates an environment conducive to fun (Turner, 1982, p. 40).

Liminality:
a transitional stage

People in the liminal stage tend to develop an intense comradeship with one another. Social distinctions that separated them before the ritual and that will separate them again afterward, become irrelevant. Turner called this

Box 3.7

The Study Says

Go Big Red

An excerpt from the field notes for a study of anti-structure in leisure:

Nebraska football is surrounded by ritual events. ... Inside the stadium, for example, the fans become one, jointly sharing in the ritual of the game. They move as one, highly knowledgeable of the game and the players; their responses are immediate, facilitated by radios and televisions available to approximately one in 15 fans. The fans are not passive; they express their opinions in raucous jubilation or heated anger. Jumping up and down, congratulating each other, clapping, and yelling are all typical expressions of joy. Shaking one's arm in a vengeful fashion and booing are likely displays of anger. Often they pound each other on the back or yell obscenities. They are part of one "team." Their side is "number one." (pp. 95-98)

Deegan, J.J. (1989). *American ritual dramas: Social rules and cultural meanings.* New York: Greenwood Press.

liminally produced social relationship *communitas*, by which he meant a loosely structured community of equal individuals. In thinking about the college football example in box 3.7, we can see how the actions of fans can be explained by the liminality and communitas concepts.

According to the anti-structure theory, then, leisure is very important. Deegan (1989) states, "The ability to have something in common with strangers, to sing and yell and cry in public, to root for one's team, and to publicly participate and reaffirm one's values, are strong bonds that help us tolerate and give meaning to life" (p. 87).

Communitas:
a temporary sense of social camaraderie

What We Understand About Explaining Leisure

The many ways of explaining leisure help us understand our own and others' pastime choices. In this chapter we studied this by over-viewing demographic factors that shape leisure behavior, as well as via several theoretical perspectives. After studying this chapter, you should know that:

- Leisure interests and behaviors are complex and unique, and thus difficult to explain.
- Nonetheless, leisure interests and behaviors can be explained in part by lifestyle, which is shaped by multiple demographic characteristics.
- Formal theories that explain leisure interests and behaviors come from the basic disciplines, such as psychology and anthropology.
- Beyond the excitement of knowing for the sake of knowing, explaining leisure is also useful to managers of recreation businesses, facilities, and programs.
- However, neither demographic characteristics nor the various theories are able to explain leisure behavior completely.

References

Babbie, E. (2003). *The practice of social research*. Belmont: Wadsworth.

Chick, G., & Hood, R.D. (1996). Working and recreating with machines: Outdoor recreation choices among machine-tool workers in western Pennsylvania. *Leisure Sciences, 18*, 333-354.

Csikszentmihalyi, M. (1975). *Beyond boredom and anxiety*. San Francisco: Jossey-Bass.

Csikszentmihalyi, M. (1990). *Flow: The psychology of optimal experience*. New York: Harper & Row.

Csikszentmihalyi, M. (1997). *Finding flow: The psychology of engagement with everyday life*. New York: Basic Books.

Csikszentmihalyi, M. (2000). The contribution of flow to positive psychology: Scientific essays in honor of Martin E.P. Seligman. In J.E. Gilham (Ed.), *The science of optimism and hope*. Philadelphia: Templeton Foundation.

Csikszentmihalyi, M., Abuhamdeh, S., & Nakamura, J. (2005). Flow. In A.J. Elliot, & C.S. Dweck (Eds.), *Handbook of competence and motivation.* New York: Guilford Press.

Deegan, J.J. (1989). *American ritual dramas: Social rules and cultural meanings.* New York: Greenwood Press.

DeGrazia, S. (1962). *Of time, work and leisure.* New York: Vintage Books.

Freysinger, V.J., & Kelly, J.R. (2004). *21st Century leisure: Current issues* (2nd Ed.). State College, PA: Venture.

Gallagher, W. (1993). *The power of place: How our surroundings shape our thoughts, emotions, and actions.* New York: Harper Perennial.

Gardyn, R. (2001). A league of their own. *American Demographics, 23*(3), 12-13.

Giovannoli, D. (2007). The unconscious influence. Unpublished paper for the course HPER R160, Indiana University, Bloomington.

Henderson, K.A., Presley, J., & Bialeschki, M.D. (2004). Theory in recreation and leisure research: Reflections from the editors. *Leisure Sciences, 26*(4), 411-425.

Hultsman, J. (October 1984). Leisure education as a correlate of quality of life. Proceedings: Symposium on Leisure Research, NRPA Congress for Recreation and Parks, Orlando, FL.

Iso-Ahola, S.E. (1999). Motivational foundations of leisure. In E. Jackson, & T. Burton (Eds.), *Leisure studies: Prospects for the Twenty-first Century.* State College, PA: Venture.

Jackson, S.A. (1992). Athletes in flow: A qualitative investigation of flow states in elite figure skaters. *Journal of Applied Sport Psychology, 4*(2), 161-180.

Kahle, L.R., Elton, M., & Kambara, K.M. (1997). Sports talk and the development of marketing relationships. *Sport Marketing Quarterly, 6,* 35-39.

Komanoff, C. (2003). Written Statement about Bill S-10, The Personal Watercraft Act, 6 May 2003. Available from http://www.nonoise.org/drownsum.htm. Retrieved 3/31/08.

Larson, R. (1988). Flow and writing. In M. Csikszentmihalyi & I.S. Csikszentmihalyi (Eds.), *Optimal experience: Psychological studies of flow in consciousness.* Cambridge: Cambridge University.

Mannell, R.C. (1984). Personality in leisure theory: The self as entertainment. *Society and Leisure, 7,* 229-242.

McGinnis, L., Chun, S., & McQuillan, J. (2003). A review of gendered consumption in sport and leisure. *Academy of Marketing Science Review, 5.* Available from http//.www.amsreview.org/articles/mcginnis05-2003.pdf. Retrieved 4/22/08.

Mill, R.C. (1986). Tourist characteristics and trends. In *Literature review: The President's Commission on Americans Outdoors.* Washington, D.C.: Government Printing Office.

Neulinger, J. (1976). The need for and the implications of a psychological conception of leisure. *The Ontario Psychologist, 8,* 15.

Neulinger, J. (1981). *To leisure: An introduction.* Boston: Allyn & Bacon.

Nonoise.org. (2008). *NPC: Noise Pollution Clearinghouse.* Available from http://www.nonoise.org/. Retrieved 3/31/08.

Reskin, B.F. (1998). Bringing the men back in: Sex differentiation and the devaluation of women's work. In K.A. Myers, C.D. Anderson, & B.J. Risman (Eds.), *Feminist foundations: Toward transforming sociology*. Thousand Oaks, CA: Sage.

Russell, R.V. (1993). Employee perceptions of work-place barriers to change. Technical report prepared for the Indianapolis, IN, Department of Parks and Recreation.

Sabo, D., & Jansen, S.C. (1998). Prometheus unbound: Constructions of masculinity in the sports media. In L.A. Wenner (Ed.), *MediaSport*. New York: Routledge.

Sargent, S.L., Zillman, D., & Weaver, J.B. III. (1998). The gender gap in the enjoyment of televised sports. *Journal of Sport & Social Issues, 22*(1), 46-64.

Searle, M.S. (2000). Is leisure theory needed for leisure studies? *Journal of Leisure Research, 32*, 138-142.

Shinew, K.J., Floyd, M.F., McGuire, F.A., & Noe, F.P. (1996). Class polarization and leisure activity preferences of African Americans: Intragroup comparisons. *Journal of Leisure Research, 28*, 219-232.

Shore, D. (Winter 1990). The pursuit of happiness. *University of Chicago Magazine*, 28-35.

Tinsley, H., & Tinsley, D. (1986). A theory of the attributes, benefits, and causes of leisure experience. *Leisure Sciences, 8*, 1-45.

Turner, V. (1969). *The ritual process: Structure and anti-structure*. Chicago: Aldine.

Turner, V. (1982). *From ritual to theatre: The human seriousness of play*. New York: Performing Arts Journal Publications.

Weissman, R.X. (1999). The green flag is up: High-tech companies are burning rubber to reach NASCAR fans. *American Demographics, 21*, 33-36.

Wilensky, H. (1960). Work, careers and social integration. *International Social Science Journal, 12*, 4.

.E., Shaw, S.M., & Havitz, M.E. (2000). Men's and women's involvement rts: An examination of the gendered aspects of leisure involvement. e Sciences, 22, 19-31.

CHAPTER FOUR

GROWING THROUGH LEISURE

PREVIEW

How is leisure related to life span?

Our lives are experienced both as continuous and as change. Leisure stimulates and eases the transitions of change yet remains constant throughout life.

How does leisure affect physical development?

Leisure is a tool for developing motor control when young and is an aid to staying physically vital when old.

How does leisure affect emotional development?

Leisure teaches us joy, affection, and other positive feelings and helps us cope with anger, anxiety, and other negative feelings.

How does leisure affect intellectual development?

Leisure is a prime medium for learning and keeping sharp such skills as language, intelligence, and creativity.

How does leisure affect social development?

Leisure helps us achieve and remain vibrant within a social network.

KEY TERMS

We begin young, we mature and grow older, and we die. This is the cycle of life. Attendant to this process is the benchmark of age. This chapter is about the continuities and changes of age as they relate to leisure. How do our pastimes change as we move through the life cycle? Does the significance and meaning of our pastimes stay with us our whole lives?

In the chapter we take a *life span* approach, meaning instead of studying each age group separately, we will view human life as an uninterrupted process. We use physical, emotional, intellectual, and social development across the life span as our markers for how leisure relates. But first, what is the meaning of age itself?

Life span:

the changes and continuities of life from birth to death

The Meaning of Age

To think about how and why age shapes and is shaped by leisure, it is important to begin by thinking about the meaning of age itself. On the simplest level, age is an indication of the years since birth. This is *chronological age.*

Chronological ages:

number of years since birth

Even though simple to define, chronological age is complex, because we use it as a marker of maturation, requiring matching levels of physical, intellectual, emotional, and social ability, such as "act your age." We also use chronological age to define specific responsibilities and social roles, such as "you shouldn't be running a marathon at your age."

Birth cohort:

individuals born during the same time period

Another concept of age is *birth cohort*. Here age means a group of people who share similar years of birth and subsequently share the same events in history and popular culture. Later cohorts experience different

Figure 4.1

A 75-year-old on a skateboard; his wife learning to paint in watercolors. There are individual differences to age-related role expectations. (© Ruth V. Russell, 2008)

Box 4.1

 *In Profile*

The Generations

Which of the following means the most to you?
- Elvis joins the Army
- Jimi Hendrix dies
- MTV debuts
- Kurt Cobain dies

Your answer depends on your birth cohort. Here are the current major cohorts for the United States.

Label	Born	Characteristics	Influencing Events	Leisure
Silent generation	1925-1942	Adaptive, patriotic, practical problem solvers, civically conscious, industrious, conformists when young, adherence to rules, sacrifice	Great Depression, World War II, The New Deal, Korean War	Retired from paid work, duty before pleasure, civic volunteers, snowbird lifestyle
Baby Boomers	1943-1960	Socially confident, ecology minded, well educated, global viewpoint, healthy, personal growth, involvement, driven	Vietnam War, Rock 'n Roll, television, suburbia, Cold War, civil rights	Active, wellness focus, hectic lifestyle, no free time, rejecting full-time retirement
Gen X	1961-1981	Accept diversity, individualistic, reject rules, mistrust institutions, use technology, multi-taskers, unimpressed, noncommittal	Personal computers, latch-key childhoods, MTV, AIDS	Fun, informality, friends focused, risk-takers, strive for balance between work and leisure
Millennial (Gen Y)	1982- 2000	Celebrate diversity, optimistic, individualistic, irrelevance of institutions, nurtured, team-oriented, uninterested in work, self-confident	The Internet, most child-centric time of history, school violence, World Trade Center attacks, Gulf War, Iraq	Sociability, prefer collective activities, media and technology based leisure

opportunities than earlier cohorts, which affects attitudes, interests, and behavior.

What all this amounts to is a strong relationship among leisure, our chronological age, and birth cohort. The story line of this relationship is both continuity and change. What we are in leisure today is based in part on what we were yesterday, and on how we will be different tomorrow. That is, there is both change and continuity in the types of leisure activities we choose, in our frequency of participation in these activities, and in our motivations for leisure choices across our life span (Freysinger, 1999).

Core plus balance:

there is both a persistent core and a balancing variety in our pastimes across the life span

This change and continuity relationship between age and leisure has been labeled ***core plus balance*** (Kelly, 1999). That is, there is a persistent "core" of leisure interests that occupy most people most of their lives. These represent continuity in leisure. Our core pastimes are typically those activities that are easily accessible and low cost,

Box 4.2

In Focus

Encore Careers

During her working years, Terryl Paiste supervised a group of writers and editors in the computer division of an insurance company. But at home, at night and on weekends, Terryl spent her time writing one-act comedies performed by mature actors on themes appealing to older adult audiences. Now, after retiring from her 22-year career in computing, Terryl has more time to write. So far, she's written about 20 plays that have been performed at theaters around North America.

Life has come full circle for Thomas Hovis. As a young man interested in art, he graduated from college with a degree in commercial design. He went on to spend 20 years working for a large corporation handling sales of specialty chemicals. Now, in retirement, Thomas has returned to his artistic roots as founder of Art & Frame of Tysons Corner. He sells art to corporate and government clients who need wall decorations for new or renovated offices.

Retirement is still five years away for DeVance Walker, the small-business services director in a county Department of Economic Development. But when the day comes, DeVance will be ready for a new career as a college professor. Six years ago he went back to his alma mater, Howard University, to study at night for a doctorate in political economics.

(Source: Hinden, 2000)

Questions to Consider and Discuss
1. What traces of both continuity and change in the life cycle do you see in these three cases?
2. How are their leisure interests important to their encore careers?
3. Putting yourself at about age 50, what might you plan for your retirement? What role will leisure likely play?

such as watching television, taking walks, playing cards, and reading. Such core activities usually occupy the greatest amount of our free time as well.

On the other hand, our lives also include a variety of pastimes. This is our "balance" of leisure expressions that change as we grow older. To balance out our core pastimes, we seek variety. For example, as a child you may have been involved in playing saxophone in the school band, and as a young adult, your weekends were devoted to whitewater kayaking. Then, as an older adult, you may throw yourself into flower gardening.

The core plus balance concept can be dissected more specifically by considering leisure and the major developmental tasks. These include our physical, emotional, intellectual, and social development.

Physical Development

Leisure's role in physical development remains strong throughout our life span, but the nature of its role changes. The physical benefits from leisure shift from developing motor control in children, to sustaining health during the middle years, to reducing the decline in physical capabilities in older adulthood.

Today, in the United States, the average life expectancy is 77.8 years for all races and both genders (Centers for Disease Control, 2006). How does leisure assist us physically? Well, if you live a healthy lifestyle, including regular participation in active leisure, you can expect to add up to 10 quality years to this 77.8 years.

In the beginning, the newborn's mission is to master her or his own body, and play provides an important tool for this. Early learning is the result of seemingly random movement, and an infant's individualistic play provides the platform for this learning. By two years of age, the baby has begun to develop more organized basic motor skills, such as running and jumping, and such non-motor skills as pushing, pulling, and kicking. Early play experiences are crucial for development of these skills, as well as for learning muscle control and coordination.

Between the ages of about six and 12, the amount of muscle tissue doubles and flexibility increases, thus, physical play continues to be a necessary developmental

Box 4.3

In Your Own Experience

The Longevity Game

To calculate your own life expectancy, check out this web site: http://www. nmfn.com/tn/learnctr--lifeevents--longevity. As you complete this on-line questionnaire, notice how lifestyle factors affect living longer. Also, in reflecting on your answers consider how leisure both helps and hinders.

tool, particularly for promoting normal bone growth. Playing with ropes, mastering climbing and balancing equipment, and learning to control balls give children opportunities to expand their neuromuscular coordination and strength as well.

To put it bluntly, children would not grow up without adequate play. Increased motor control does not occur automatically; the child's body develops in large part from the physical demands placed on it. Further, childhood activity levels are strong predictors of physical activity later in life (Taylor, 1999).

Yet, children in North America are not engaged in sufficient physical play experiences. According to the Surgeon General for the United States (2007), approximately 17 percent of children between the ages of two and 19 years are overweight. In addition to improving eating habits, the recommendation is that children require at least one hour of moderate physical activity every day to maintain their proper weight. Yet, about 61 percent of children do not achieve this.

Significant numbers of children today spend most of their free time watching television (about three hours per day), playing computer games, and surfing the Internet. The effect is increased body fat, but also losses to muscular strength, cardio respiratory fitness, and bone mass. Consequently blood pressure rises, and children are more susceptible to the harm of anxiety and stress, and lowered self-esteem.

So what happens to leisure and physical development in adolescence? Pinpointing the exact beginning (and end) of adolescence is very difficult, as individual human bodies mature at different rates. Yet, physical change is the major initiator of this wide-ranging passage from childhood to adulthood. In fact, the word *adolescence* is Latin and means to grow up, and the physical changes experienced (growth spurts, changing body proportions, hormone increases, etc.) are large and rapid. Thus, these changes, and the accompanying traumas, can affect concepts of self that go beyond the physical. If appropriately selected, active forms of leisure can help teens cope with their social and psychological awkwardness as well.

Adolescence:

the transition from childhood to adulthood, describing both the development to sexual maturity and to psychological and economic independence

---

Figure 4.2

Physical forms of leisure are just as important for teens as they are for children, yet studies show active leisure declines for adolescent girls. (© Ruth V. Russell, 2008)

For example, competitive sport participation by teens not only provides helpful exercise for developing strength, flexibility, height, endurance, and fine motor control, but can also improve self-confidence and social status. Unfortunately for teens, as for other age groups, the passive experience of watching TV, playing video games, text messaging, and surfing the Internet remains the most preoccupying activity. For adolescent girls, in spite of such programs as Title IX that opened doors for greater sport participation,

Box 4.4

The Study Says

Leisure and Problem Behavior of Adolescents

Even though the primary developmental process in adolescence is physical growth and sexual maturity, ramifications extend into the social, emotional, and even economic lives of youth and their parents. Therefore, teasing out leisure's role in the physicality of adolescence is difficult due to the complex interactions with other realms of human development. For example, a study examined the relationships between leisure behaviors and a variety of problem behaviors in a sample of 1,422 Hungarian adolescents (aged 14 through 19). Findings suggested some aspects of adolescent leisure, such as family or conventional activities (camping, playing a musical instrument, taking art classes, etc.), act as protective factors against problem behaviors, while peer-oriented and commercial types of leisure contribute to greater risk for problem behaviors. This relationship was the same for both males and females.

Piko, F. P., & Vazsonyi, A.T. (2004). Leisure activities and problem behaviors among Hungarian youth. *Journal of Adolescence, 27*(6), 717-730.

studies show that by age 16, 56 percent of black females and 31 percent of white females report they have no regular leisure-time physical activity in their lives (Center for Health and Health Care in Schools, 2002).

When individuals enter the workforce or attend college in late adolescence and early adulthood, their physical capabilities and energy are usually at a peak. Some then seek a wide assortment of active forms of recreation, with participation in strenuous sports continuing from youth. Interest in high-risk activities, such as skiing and rock climbing, begin to develop fully as well.

Usually by the late 20s or early 30s, leisure and physical development begin to shift their relationship. Biological maturity, when bone density is greatest and most physical skills peak, occurs at about this time (Donatelle & Davis, 1996), and participation in strenuous and high-risk sports gradually begins to decrease. As a counterforce, however, is the high-level skill development that has taken place through years of practice, which makes some physical leisure, such as golf, even more enjoyable for young adults.

For all phases in the life span, and particularly in adulthood, leisure's most basic importance is in sustaining health. Physical pastimes keep adults healthy. Indeed, the list of benefits is astounding. Active leisure provides for greater energy levels, a stronger immune system, improved cardiovascular function, an improved ability to manage stress, a more positive outlook on life, and enhanced relationships with others.

Normal physical changes that affect leisure continue through advancing age. As we age, our bodies gradually become less flexible and endurance is reduced. After about age 50, the number of muscle fibers steadily decreases. Yet, even with up to 50 percent deterioration in many organ systems, by remaining physically vigorous through leisure, life's pleasures can continue. Some surveys suggest people over 65 today are more vigorous than ever—an 8.8 percent increase since 1982.

Even people who begin a regular exercise or sport program late in life can make significant improvements in their heart and lung capacity. Nonetheless, the proportion of people starting vigorous pastimes does decline with age (Iso-Ahola, Jackson, & Dunn, 1994), even though older adults identify physical exercise as one of the important needs satisfied by leisure (Donatelle & Davis, 1996).

Emotional Development

All people go through the process of learning how to deal with their feelings. Some are very good feelings, such as joy, affection, thankfulness, and sensuality. Others, such as anger, fear, anxiety, and frustration, are not pleasant at all. Leisure itself is often considered a type of emotion, a positive state of mind, thus, its role in the development of emotional health is particularly intriguing. Let's begin with children.

Young children have all the basic emotions of adults, but their expression is typically immediate, impulsive, and direct. Most children grow up learning to manage their emotions by using coping strategies so their expression is more controlled and socially appropriate. Play is an important ingredient in this emotional development.

For example, two of the emotions children must learn to manage are fear and anxiety. As an early proponent, Freud (1955) argued play helps children master fear and anxiety, and children not allowed to deal with these emotions through play can become psychopathic adults. Later studies by Barnett (1984) similarly supported the importance of fantasy play to neutralize the anxieties children feel. Researchers observed that children use fantasy play to reenact sources of emotional distress, often by changing the outcome of the stressful event or by reversing roles to achieve a more pleasant result.

Locus of control:
the perception of the factors responsible for the outcome of an event

Another way leisure aids in the emotional development of children is through a concept called locus of control. *Locus of control* is our own perception about the source of power in our life. When we have an external locus of control, we perceive that we have no control, that we are merely pawns moved by forces outside of us. With internal locus of control, we perceive we are the origin of our own life events. Internal locus of control is related to emotional maturity.

As for the role of leisure, we know the more time children spend in a supervised, child-centered play program, the more internal their locus of control becomes. An example of this is the "playwork" or adventure playground (Brown, 2002). The concept originated in Europe after World War II when a playground designer studied children playing in asphalt and cement playgrounds. He found they preferred playing in the dirt and lumber from the post war rubble. He realized children have the most fun designing and building their own equipment and manipulating their environment. On an adventure playground this means children are encouraged to play and build creatively. They climb on the forts, boats, and towers they themselves have built. They ride a zip line or hammer, saw and paint.

In growing from childhood to young adulthood, adolescents often display a curious combination of emotional maturity and childishness. This is often an awkward mixture, but it serves an important developmental function, as the emotional task to be

Figure 4.3

The formula for adventure playgrounds includes earth, fire, water, and lots of creative materials. (© Berkeley California Parks and Recreation Department, 2008)

Box 4.5

In Focus

Kids and the Mall

According to the market research group Teenage Research Unlimited (2004), 68 percent of teens ages 12-19 spend an average of 3.5 hours and $103 at the mall in any given week. In 2003 in the U.S. this totaled to $175 billion. Some malls have taken steps to cater to their young customers, and certainly a glimpse at the types of stores in malls these days indicates retailers' understanding of their economic importance. In fact, some view their mission as one of training teens for a life of hard-core shopping.

On the other hand, according to the International Council of Shopping Centers (2001), teens have become such a problem that many malls now have policies requiring them to be accompanied by an adult after a set curfew. For example, two malls in the Detroit area, Fairlane Town Center and Eastland Mall, prohibit kids under the age of 17 from being in the mall past 5 p.m. unless with an adult over 21. Security guards check teens' IDs at the entrances, and patrol courtyards and corridors for lone youths.

Sociologists (cf. Lewis, 1989) have suggested kids who spend a lot of time at the mall are exhibiting a good deal of alienation from both family and school. They use the mall as neutral ground on which to create a fragile but mutually supportive

Box 4.5 (Cont.)

community. "Structure is the dominant idea, since true 'mall rats' lack just that in their home lives, and adolescents about to make the big leap into growing up crave more structure than our modern society cares to acknowledge" (Kowinski, 1989, p. 351).

Questions to Consider and Discuss

1. Were you a "mall rat" when you were younger? Did you know anyone from your school or neighborhood who spent a lot of time at the mall? How would you describe the situation?
2. What is your opinion of the two issues presented in this case? That is, should malls be training teens for a life of hard-core shopping or setting curfews that limit their independence? Why?
3. Considering the concept of locus of control as a developmental emotional task for teens, might the mall be helping them achieve this? If teens learn about themselves through the mall, what developmental emotional tasks might they face as adults?

Identity:

individuality, distinct uniqueness

accomplished is the formation of *identity*. The fundamental question of "who am I?" characterizes the early teen period, and assisting in the answer is a main function of leisure. Leisure provides a context for experimenting with one's identity. The more relaxed setting of the playing field, band room, Scout meeting, and even the mall is a safe haven in which teens can try things out.

College students are also engaged in discovering their identity. At this stage in the life span, leisure provides a vital context for breaking with the personal identities associated with family and home community. Several emotional transitions occur, such as the emergence of a focused sexuality and confidence in greater social and economic independence from parents (Kelly, 1982). In fact, the college years are a final time to try out new possibilities for an adult identity.

Universities and colleges aid in this process by providing real-world simulations. Students can participate in politics through student government and in a profession through practicums and internships. Social events, intramural sports, spring break trips, activity clubs, and other campus experiences are crucial for the development of a future selfhood. They provide ways of experimenting with attitudes of influence, dissent, and cooperation. They also play a role in reducing the stress some college students experience. For example, researchers Ragheb and McKinney (1992) found the more students participated in campus recreation activities, the less academic stress they experienced.

The years from 35 to 45 have been called the "deadline decade," or the era of the "midlife crisis." Divorce and career changes occur with increasing frequency. Predictable at this point in life is a feeling of stagnation. Some people experience tumultuous struggles within themselves and with others. Married persons with children often find their recreation patterns disrupted and restricted. Some resent the change from the lifestyle they enjoyed at earlier life stages. Others welcome the stable, noncompetitive, and predictable leisure patterns of family life.

Meanwhile, the decade of our fifties has been labeled the reintegration period (Rapoport & Rapoport, 1975). Emotionally, this is when we reevaluate ourselves, and the meaning and worth of our life commitments. This includes questioning whether our pastimes are producing the fulfillment they once promised. As we approach the retirement years the free-choice nature of leisure makes it a prime medium for life evaluation. Often

Figure 4.4

Campus organizations provide ways of experimenting with influence, dissent, and cooperation. (© Ruth V. Russell, 2008)

new pastimes can be tried with minimal changes to family and work. As well, with increased free time and money, people in this life stage can bring former leisure interests back into their lives. Particularly interesting is that just before retirement there can occur an increase in experiences chosen primarily for their own sake. That is, leisure is more intrinsically motivated.

In retirement itself leisure undergoes changes again. Anticipation of life without employment can be positive or negative. Some look forward to this life phase exactly because they will have more time for leisure. Others worry they'll feel at loose ends without the structure of employment. Should I buy a motor home so I can travel? Maybe I should move into a retirement community?

Alongside these uncertainties is continuity as well. In this time, people generally continue the pastimes of previous years. If they have had fulfilling life patterns outside of work, this will be a time of joy. Without leisure interests that are personally meaningful, the adjustments of retirement may be difficult, including feelings of loneliness and apathy. Expanding their favorite leisure interests can aid in these emotional adjustments. In fact, leisure should be part of retirement preparation decisions.

Eventually, the death of a partner or spouse becomes a reality for many. One's companion in leisure is gone. Not only does this loss create loneliness, but it also changes the context of leisure, requiring a rebuilding of leisure roles. For most people, grief does not allow them to accept their new freedom until the process of working through the loss has been accomplished, but once begun, leisure can help with the emotional healing.

Intellectual Development

It has long been understood that one of the main contributions of a child's play is the development of cognitive skills. Specifically, play has been linked to

Box 4.6

The Study Says

Types of Retirement Leisure Behaviors

This study examined patterns of continuity and change in the leisure behavior of recently retired individuals in Israel. It explored the life satisfaction differences among four post retirement leisure patterns: reducers, concentrators, diffusers, and expanders. Expanders were people who reported participation in a larger number of activities and at higher frequency after retirement. Reducers were people who reported participation in the same or in fewer activities at the same or at a lower frequency; concentrators reported participation in the same, or in fewer activities, but at a higher frequency; and, diffusers reported participation in a larger number of activities, but at the same or at a lower frequency. Results indicated the expanders and the concentrators enjoyed a significantly higher life satisfaction.

Nimrod, G. (2007). Expanding, reducing, concentrating and diffusing: Post retirement leisure behavior and life satisfaction. *Leisure Science, 29*, 91-111.

Convergent thinking:

using information to find one right answer. For example, which tool is best for driving a nail into wood?

Divergent thinking:

thinking in different directions. For example, how many uses for a hammer are there?

the development of two modes of thought: convergent and divergent (Fromberg & Bergen, 1998; Vandenberg, 1980). On the one hand, an important function of play and games for children is enhanced *convergent thinking* ability. This is because a child's playful experience with objects and processes can be applied to real-life issues. By exploring objects in play, children not only learn the properties of those objects but also their possible application to various other situations (Barnett, 1990).

In addition, games and play contribute to *divergent thinking* ability. This is due to both the spontaneous and symbolic nature of these activities. Play provides the child with a broad repertoire of skills that can be applied creatively. Also, play enhances the child's transition from concrete to abstract thought because of the way children's play frequently uses unreal things to represent real ones. Make-believe play is the key link. The role of imagination is so important to intellectual development that it prompted Albert Einstein to note, "imagination is more important than knowledge."

Another intellectual skill to which leisure contributes is language. Sounds, syllables, words, and phrases provide children with a rich source of play material. Infants discover the joy of vocal play when starting to babble. By the time they are uttering their first words and sentences, preschool children are playfully manipulating grammar, rhyme, nonsense words, and multiple meanings. School-age children have an underground oral tradition of rhymes, jokes, and incantations they have passed on to each other for generations. Do you remember "1, 2, 3, 4,

I declare a thumb war; 5, 6, 7, 8, try to keep your thumb straight" that begins a thumb-wrestling match?

The idea that play and language are interrelated is not surprising, since both serve several common functions in the child's life: (a) both involve a communicative function, and (b) children use both play and language to experiment and learn about themselves and others (Barnett, 1990). Whereas play clearly comes before language in the growth of a child, play is, in a sense, a form of language itself because it incorporates symbolic as well as social interactions.

Figure 4.5

Make-believe play helps children develop divergent thinking ability. (© Jane Duffy, 2008, used with permission)

For example, it was Piaget (1936) who discovered that playing out a story forces a child to use mental skills. In order to re-create the events of a story, the child must create a mental representation of the events and then engage in social interaction to coordinate the playing. A number of studies have demonstrated this relationship between symbolic play and language during the early stages of

 *In Profile*

Jean Piaget

Jean Piaget (1896-1980), a Swiss psychologist, won fame for his studies on the development of thought in children. The research consumed most of his life, including constant study of his own three children.

Piaget's goal was to define children's increasingly effective intellectual abilities. His work led him to conclude children pass through four stages of development. First, during the sensorimotor stage from birth to two years, they obtain a basic knowledge of objects they play with through their senses. By 15 to 18 months of age, children try to use objects as they were intended, and the play becomes still more realistic by 24 months. For example, toddlers take dolls out for walks and line up toy trucks in the right direction.

Next, children enter the preoperational stage. From about ages two to seven years, they use language and imagination skills to help build some facsimile of the outside world. They develop the ability to see adult action at one point in time, store that information in memory without performing the act, and imitate the act at a later time.

Box 4.7 (Cont.)

From about seven to 11 years of age children begin to think logically. Essentially, this concrete operational stage is when children begin to use symbols. For example, whereas younger children require props to be similar to the real object for pretend play, older children can play with only abstract representations, such as a stick for a gun.

Finally, in Piaget's fourth stage of intellectual development, formal operations, which lasts from about 11 to 15 years of age, children begin to reason realistically by imaging all the possibilities. Their thought is richer, broader, and more flexible.

language acquisition in children both with and without language disabilities.

What happens next? Stereotypes about inevitable intellectual decline as we grow older have been largely refuted. "We used to think that the adult brain couldn't grow," says neurologist Jay Lombard (as cited in Merrell, 2003, p. 143). Given an appropriate length of time, middle and older adults may learn and develop mental skills in a manner similar to younger people, and some mental abilities improve well into the middle years.

Researchers have also determined that what many older people lack in speed of learning is made up for in practical knowledge. For example, longitudinal studies suggest those intellectual abilities requiring experience, knowledge, and judgment are retained into the 60s and beyond. According to one study, when compared with people between the ages of 20 and 40, those age 55 and over needed more time to complete tasks but were just as accurate (Goldman, 1996).

The best of it is that as you age, you can actually encourage brain growth and regeneration, and several studies have confirmed the contribution of leisure to this process (cf. Riddick, 1993; Riddick & Daniels, 1984; Rothschadl, 1993). For example, keeping mentally sharp can be aided by engaging in intellectually challenging pastimes, such as playing board and card games, joining book clubs, attending lectures, and learning new hobbies. In fact, recent studies (cf. Verghese, et. al., 2003; Lyketosos, 2005) are demonstrating participation in a variety of leisure activities lowers the risk of dementia.

Social Development

Human infants are born into an environment rich with social expectations, norms, and traditions. A full social heritage with standards of behavior awaits them. However, infants have no sense of their relationship with others around them. Thus, a rather dramatic series of changes takes place during their first two years as they become aware of their surroundings and the ways they relate to them. Play, of course, is a prime teacher in a child's social development. From it they become aware of family relationships, themselves as girls or boys, and what is good behavior and bad behavior.

Peer:

one who is of equal standing, usually based on age and economic status

The importance of the *peer* group in teaching social skills has been well documented. As children become increasingly

Box 4.8

 In Your Own Experience

Smartening-Up Strategies

Age is undeniably a factor in mental functioning, but people of any age can benefit from these leisure-based ways of keeping sharp. The brain is like a muscle: it can always use a little exercise. The following checklist will help you determine if you're getting enough brain exercise.

Strategy	Description	Frequency Needed to Reduce Risks of Dementia	Check if you do
1. Play games often.	Classic games such as chess, checkers, bridge, and backgammon encourage you to think ahead, see the big picture, and consider options.	At least once a week	
2. Work crossword puzzles.	Crossword puzzling is to the brain as running on a treadmill is to the heart.	Four days a week	
3. Choose right-brain hobbies.	Activities that force you to think before acting, such as pinball, juggling, some video games, doodling, looking at art, listening to music.	Daily	
4. Spend more time with favorite hobbies.	Doing what you enjoy creates more synapses, especially hobbies that use your fingers (needlework or playing an instrument), keeping a journal, and doing balancing things (tai chi, yoga).	Daily	
5. Be active.	Cardiovascular exercise increases brain power by pumping more blood to the brain, bringing vitalizing oxygen and nutrients to cells, and slowing the rate of normal brain-cell death.	20 minutes, four days a week	

based on Merrell, 2003.

more effective at communicating and better at understanding the thoughts and feelings of others, the amount and quality of peer interaction increases greatly. This is particularly evident in play. For example, studies of peer relations in children have charted the development of six different levels of social interaction in play (table 4.1).

These levels of interactive play predominate at certain ages, yet what matters most is children are given opportunities to experience them all. Through them they are able to perfect such skills as empathy, role taking, self-control, and sharing. As they continue to grow, and their social play involves more ritual, they are better able to make decisions about taking turns, setting boundaries, and stipulating rules about what is and what is not permitted.

Gender identity:

a person's internal self-awareness of being either masculine or feminine, or something in-between

Gender identity is a particular example of the role of play in social development. Scientists suggest that much of the basis for an individual's gender identity is acquired by age three and is primarily

Table 4.1

Levels of Play According to Peer Interactions

Level of play	Age	Interaction
Nonsocial play	Infant to one year	Unoccupied, unfocused. No peer interaction
Solitary play	infant to one yar	Child plays alone. No peer interaction.
Onlooker play	two years	Child's interaction with peers is limited to just observing other children.
Parallel play	two to three years	Children play alongside each other but not interact with each other.
Associative play	four to five years	Some interaction; children engage in separate activities but interact by exchanging toys and commenting on another's behavior.
Cooperative play	six to seven years	Fully interactive with peers; children's actions are directed towards a common goal.

Conger & Peter, 1984.

a result of the different ways parents interact with male and female babies (Craig & Baucum, 2001). For example, fathers' play with male babies tends to be physical and arousing rather than intellectual, as is the case with mothers' play with female babies (Berk, 2003). Parents allow boys more freedom to display aggressive behavior and to engage in more vigorous activities with toys. Boys also receive more gross motor stimulation from parents, whereas girls receive more verbal stimulation.

For older children, parents, teachers, peers, and even television characters reinforce gender stereotypes. These stereotypes can be problematic for development because they provide arbitrary scripts for behavior. For example, whereas older boys usually stick to masculine pursuits, such as weapon-based fantasy play, girls experiment with a wider range of options. Besides playing with dolls, they join organized sport teams and build forts in the backyard.

For adolescents, difficult changes in social interactions join those in emotional and physical development. If an adolescent is to become truly adult and not just physically mature, he or she must fit into a social world, achieve independence from parents, and establish enduring relationships with others. This means the development of *autonomy* is central. The teen must become adjusted to the demands and privileges of independence, and an important context for developing autonomy is in social leisure experiences.

Autonomy:
emotional, social, and physical independence from others; the ability to self-govern

Most teens are attached to social groups that have considerable power over their interests and behavior. Whereas, during middle and late childhood, peer relationships center around informal neighborhood play groups, for the teenager, the world widens, and social groups become more highly organized with special membership requirements and rituals.

In general, the teen's peer relationships fall into three broad categories: the *crowd*, the *clique*, and individual friendships (Conger & Petersen, 1984). Teens experience a great deal of their leisure within these relationships. In fact, such social recreation pursuits as parties, movies, dances, concerts, driving, and just "hanging out" with a friend, clique, or crowd provide the setting for adolescent social development. At their best, these forms of peer relationships can help teens accomplish positive social development. At their worst, worries over social acceptance and rejection are potent at these ages, thus peer relationships can be painful and peer influences negative.

Crowd:
a large, loosely organized peer group in which membership is based on reputation and stereotype

Clique:
a small group of about five to seven peers who are friends

What influences the sorting of teens into cliques and crowds? In addition to personality and interests, family factors are surprisingly important. For example, a study (te Poel Zeijl, et.al., 2000) of Dutch youth focused on the degree to which teens associate with parents and peers in their free time. To the surprise of the researchers, much of what was discovered was based on social class differences. It was found that 10- to 12-year-old children from wealthier families spent a substantial part of their leisure with parents and siblings. Fourteen- and 15-year-old boys from wealthier backgrounds focused on peer groups, whereas girls of the same age and background had a preference for friendships with one another. As well, teens from higher socioeconomic families encountered the most parental attention to peer-based leisure expressions.

Figure 4.6

Most teens are attached to a social group that has considerable power to shape pastime interests and behaviors, including those of a sexual nature. (© Ruth V. Russell, 2008).

Peer groups also serve as the platform for the development of sexuality. "Romantic" leisure is important for testing sexuality and for establishing ways of relating lovingly to others. In fact, sexuality is a preoccupation in the development of social selfhood for many adolescents, and sexual activity itself can be a major pastime.

Upon leaving school, young adults are propelled into more adult social roles related to the social institutions of family, the economy, and community. For many, these can be exciting times of exploring and filling new social identities. For example, some young adults get married, and the impact of this transition on leisure depends on whether residence, employment, and family size change as well. Most likely their leisure will be expressed primarily with a partner, and becomes an important context for building the relationship. This may also mean involvement in some pastimes formerly experienced separately will decrease. Young adults are also taking on more work roles, thus leisure is predominantly commercial, taking place in bars, clubs, restaurants, and apartment complexes.

If children are added to the family, the time and money spent for leisure tend to be restricted. Typically, the first change in leisure new parents realize is that engaging in spur-of-the-moment pastimes outside the home becomes more difficult. As well, at-home pastimes become more interrupted and crowded.

Despite the old adage "the family that plays together stays together," research suggests this may not necessarily be so. For example, a study by Freysinger (1994) found leisure experienced between children and their parents was satisfying only for the fathers. This may be because leisure with their children is an important way fathers interact with them, hence, it may be more valued by them. For mothers, on the other hand, experiencing leisure with children may be perceived as just another duty of daily care giving.

As children leave the family and assume their own lives more completely, their middle-aged parents change, although exactly how varies. Three different leisure patterns seem to be the main options for "empty nest" adults. First, some use their new freedom to turn back to the marriage or partnership for leisure. For them, leisure may become more important as some of the pursuits laid aside during parenting are taken up again. Others turn outward and seek new and separate social groups and activities. This can also be a renaissance time for middle-aged adults who have not reared children, as their careers stabilize and become financially rewarding. Finally, some pour themselves into greater work engagement by launching new careers or increasing civic responsibilities, thus continuing the restrictions on their leisure time.

As we grow into old age, the nature of our social roles and relationships changes again. Spouses and partners may die, and socializing with coworkers on the job disappears with retirement. The way older people interact in their social worlds of family, friends, and neighbors is affected by physical, situational, and even economic changes. Sometimes circumstances can mean former social involvements diminish, requiring the making of new friends. Keeping socially connected is important, however, because older adults who are part of well-defined friendship groups tend to have higher morale (Searle, et.al., 1995).

Figure 4.7

The "empty nest" adult sometimes seeks new social groups and activities. (© Ruth V. Russell, 2008)

In fact, some research has demonstrated friends are more important than family for life satisfaction in old age (cf. Adams, 1986). The explanation for this might be given from a leisure perspective. That is, friendship is more rewarding because it is not obligatory, and leisure often provides the context for friendship. One of the primary benefits of living in age-segregated retirement communities, for example, is the availability of potential friends.

What We Understand About Human Development and Leisure

The cycle of life is both certain and uncertain, constant and changing. In this chapter we emphasized that leisure is necessary for growing, maturing, and reaching old age. Though the nature of its role may change, leisure is constantly helping us develop. From studying this chapter, you should know that:

- The role of leisure in human development is both constant and changing.
- Leisure helps children develop motor skills, and in the middle and later years it helps sustain physical capabilities.
- For children, leisure is a tool for learning; for adults, leisure is important in maintaining previously acquired mental abilities, as well as developing others more fully.
- Although leisure itself is often considered an emotional state, it also plays a role in the development of positive emotions for children and in the maintenance of emotional health for adults.
- Through leisure, children are able to acquire skills for social interaction, and when people grow into older adulthood, leisure is often their sole connection to the social world.

References

Adams, R.G. (1986). A look at friendship and aging. *Generations, 10*, 40-43.

Barnett, L.A. (1984). Young children's resolution of distress through play. *Journal of Child Psychology and Psychiatry, 25*, 477-483.

Barnett, L.A. (1990). Developmental benefits of play for children. *Journal of Leisure Research, 22*, 138-153.

Berk, L.E. (2003). *Child development* (6th ed.). Boston: Allyn & Bacon.

Brown, F. (2002). *Playwork: Theory and practice.* Buckingham, U.K.: Open University.

Centers for Disease Control (CDC) (2006). *Chartbook on Trends in the Health of Americans.* Available from http://www.cdc.gov/nchs/data/hus/hus06.pdf#027. Retrieved 4/4/08.

Center for Health and Health Care in Schools (September 5, 2002). Study finds adolescent girls have little physical activity. Available from http://www.healthinschools.org/static/newsalerts/2002/sep05b_alerts.aspx. Retrieved 4/8/08.

Conger, J.J., & Petersen, A.C. (1984). *Adolescence and youth: Psychological development in a changing world.* New York: Harper & Row.

Craig, G.J., & Baucum, D. (2001). *Human development.* Englewood Cliffs, NJ: Prentice-Hall.

Donatelle, R.J., & Davis, L.G. (1996). *Access to health* (4th ed.). Boston: Allyn & Bacon.

Freud, S. (1955). Beyond the pleasure principle. In J. Strachey (Ed.), *The standard edition of the complete psychological works of Sigmund Freud* (Vol. 18). London: Hogarth.

Freysinger, V.J. (1994). Leisure with children and parental satisfaction: Further evidence of a sex difference in the experience of adult roles and leisure. *Journal of Leisure Research, 26*, 212-226.

Freysinger, V.J. (1999). Life span and life course perspectives on leisure. In E.L. Jackson, & T.L. Burton (Eds.), *Leisure studies: Prospects for the Twenty-first century.* State College, PA: Venture.

Fromberg, D.P., & Bergen, D. (Eds). (1998). *Play from birth to twelve: Contexts, perspectives, and meanings.* New York: Van Nostrand Reinhold.

Goldman, D. (1996). Good news about the aging brain. In *Global aging report: What's happening in aging everywhere* (pp. 8-20). Washington, D.C.: American Association of Retired Persons.

Hinden, C. (October 1, 2000). Second careers: Four who planned for a retirement of personal fulfillment. *The Washington Post*, pp. H1-H6.

International Council of Shopping Centers (October 2001). Centers turn to curfews as last resort to cope with teens. *Shopping Center News.* Available from http://icsc.org/srch/sct/current/sct1001/page1b.php. Retrieved 4/8/08.

Iso-Ahola, S.E., Jackson, E., & Dunn, E. (1994). Starting, ceasing, and replacing leisure activities over the life-span. *Journal of Leisure Research, 26*, 227-249.

Kelly, J.R. (1982). *Leisure.* Englewood Cliffs, NJ: Prentice-Hall.

Kelly, J.R. (1999). Leisure and society: A dialectical analysis. In E.L. Jackson, & T.L. Burton (Eds.), *Leisure studies: Prospects for the Twenty-first Century.* State College, PA: Venture.

Kowinski, W.S. (1989). Kids in the mall: growing up controlled. In D. Cavitch (Ed.), *Life studies: A thematic reader* (pp. 192-206). New York: St. Martin's Press.

Lewis, G.J. (1989). Rats and bunnies: Core kids in the American mall. *Adolescence, 24,* 881-889.

Lyketosis, C. (April 27, 2005). Variety may be spice of life for warding off dementia, study finds. *The Herald-Times,* Bloomington, Indiana, p. A7.

Merrell, K. (November 2003). Get smart: Science has found new strategies to help our sharp minds keep their edge. *Real Simple.* 143-147.

Piaget, J. (1936). *The origins of intelligence in children.* New York: W.W. Norton.

Ragheb, M.G., & McKinney, J. (1992). Campus recreation and perceived academic stress. Paper presented at the Leisure Research Symposium, National Recreation and Park Association, Cincinnati, OH.

Rapoport, R., & Rapoport, R.N. (1975). *Leisure and the family life cycle.* London: Routledge & Kegan Paul.

Riddick, C.C. (1993). Older women's leisure and the quality of life. In J.R. Kelly (Ed.), *Activity and aging* (pp. 105-119). Thousand Oaks, CA: Sage.

Riddick, C.C., & Daniels, S. (1984). The relative contribution of leisure activities and other factors to the mental health of older women. *Journal of Leisure Research, 16,* 136-148.

Rothschadl, A. M. (1993). The meaning and nature of creativity in the everyday lives of older women. Unpublished doctoral dissertation, Indiana University, Bloomington.

Searle, M.S., Mahon, J.J., Iso-Ahola, S.E., Sdrolias, H.A., & vanDyck, J. (1995). Enhancing a sense of independence and psychological well-being among the elderly: A field experiment. *Journal of Leisure Research, 27,* 107-124.

Surgeon General for the United States (2007). Childhood obesity prevention. Available from http://www.surgeongeneral.cov/topics/obesity. Retrieved 4/8/08.

Taylor, W.C. (1999). Childhood and adolescent physical activity patterns and adult physical activity. *Medicine and Science in Sports and Exercise, 31,* 118-123.

te Poel Zeijl, E., du Bois-Reymond, Y., Ravesloot, M. & Meulman, J.J. (2000). The role of parents and peers in the leisure activities of young adolescents. *Journal of Leisure Research, 32,* 281-302.

Teenage Research Unlimited (January 9, 2004). Press Release. Available from http://www.teenresearch.com/PRview.cfm?edit_id=168. Retrieved 4/8/08.

Vandenberg, B. (1980). Play: A causal agent in problem solving? Paper presented at the meeting of the American Psychological Association, Montreal, Quebec.

Verghese, J., Lipton, R.B., Katz, M.J., Hall, C.B., Derby, C.A., Kuslansky, G., Ambrose, A.F., Sliwinski, M. & Buschke, H. (June 19, 2003). Leisure activities and the risk of dementia in the elderly. *New England Journal of Medicine, 348*(25), 2508-2516.

PART TWO

LEISURE AS A CULTURAL MIRROR: SOCIETAL CONTEXT

Leisure also helps define who we are as a culture.

Leisure is significant to us not only individually, but also collectively. How we express ourselves through our pastimes helps define who we are as a community, a society, and a world. And like a mirror, our pastimes are likewise shaped by who we are collectively.

Chapter 5
Discusses leisure's cultural significance according to anthropology.

Chapter 6
Presents the expression of leisure as geographically determined.

Chapter 7
Debates the boon and bane of a technological society and leisure.

Chapter 8
Explores common culture—the most typical pastimes of a majority of people.

Chapter 9
Portrays cultural leisure expressions that due to law, custom, or belief are considered taboo.

CHAPTER FIVE

LEISURE'S ANTHROPOLOGY

PREVIEW

What is leisure's cultural significance?

Leisure is so much a part of the patterns of our collective life that it can describe how cultures are characterized, changed, and compared.

Did the earliest human cultures have leisure?

Leisure was a part of human culture before civilization itself.

How is leisure unique in developing cultures?

Leisure can be used as a tool for cultural development. As such, leisure is also typically changed by development.

How does modernity affect a culture's leisure?

Leisure in modern societies is more commercial, diverse, sped up, and technologically oriented. Is it better?

KEY TERMS

Before the massive urbanization of black South Africans into white South African areas, which began in the 1930s, few parents of black children had money to buy toys. The result was all sorts of play inventions. For example, the boys, sometimes eagerly assisted by their fathers and elder brothers, made elaborate wire cars, complete with wheels that could turn and a functioning steering system. With urbanization and increased foreign influences, cheap plastic toys became available, which brought an end to this ingenuity. (Grobler, 1985).

As the story illustrates, in this chapter we consider leisure according to culture—how leisure is shaped by and in turn helps to shape culture. Our focus is on the anthropology of leisure. *Anthropology* is a discipline that incorporates ideas from the social sciences, the humanities, and the biological sciences to study human society. So, when we consider leisure anthropologically, we are interested in how leisure both influences and is influenced by human societies.

Anthropology:
the study of humanity

We explore the anthropology of leisure first in terms of basic concepts about culture. Then we trace the likely role of leisure for humans in the earliest cultures. Finally, we contrast leisure's expression today in relation to cultural development and modernity.

Figure 5.1

A day at the beach on Bali, Indonesia. From an anthropological perspective we would be interested in understanding the cultural meanings of going to the beach in Indonesia and how this compares to the cultural meanings of going to the beach in other cultures. (© Ruth V. Russell, 2008)

Leisure and Culture

Culture is the central idea in anthropology. *Culture* is a complex and flexible concept, so there are many definitions for it. Usually the term denotes the set of distinctive features of a social group, including its art, literature, lifestyles, ways of living together, value systems, traditions, and beliefs (UNESCO, 2002). Culture, then, includes the collective expression of leisure. This means our individual leisure expressions fit within what our culture considers appropriate.

Culture:
a set of traditions and ideas shared by members of a society

Characteristics of Culture

Through the comparative study of many different cultures, anthropologists are able to understand the basic characteristics of all cultures (table 5.1). By understanding these characteristics, we can see that leisure functions as a cultural mirror.

Table 5.1

Characteristics of Culture

Characteristics	Defined	Leisure example	Related concept
Shared	Values and standards of behavior are held in common.	Sepak takraw is a favorite sport in Malaysia	Subcultures based on leisure
Learned	We learn our culture by growing up in it.	The appropriate time to eat is learned from the culture.	Enculturation
Symbols	Cultural "currency" is based on such symbols as language	Symbols include the visual image in art and the scoring system in bowling.	Whorfian hypothesis
Intergrated	All parts of a culture are interrelated	After communism in Poland, changes occurred in leisure resources.	Cultural changes

The first characteristic is that culture is shared (Haviland, 1990). As its definition suggests, culture is a set of shared ideas and standards of behavior. Because they share a common culture, the actions of individuals are understandable and people can predict how others are most likely to behave in given circumstances. For example, in the United States children are likely to participate in basketball, whereas children in Chile will consider soccer their more popular sport, and children in Malaysia more likely will grow up learning sepak takraw.

Just because culture is shared, doesn't mean everyone in a culture is the same, however. Within American culture, for example, people listen to a wide variety of music, including country, jazz, classical, rap, and rock. In fact, we can categorize people into subgroups, or *subcultures*, based on their specific musical tastes. This demonstrates that while subcultures can be based on such demographic factors as race, geographic region, or

Subcultures:

smaller cultures within a dominant culture

social class, they can also be based on leisure interests. Examples of leisure-based subcultures include riding motorcycles, long-distance running, gospel singing, and the Wednesday night poker club.

A second characteristic of culture is that it is learned (Haviland, 1990). The idea that culture is learned, rather than biologically inherited, prompted anthropologist Ralph Linton (1936) to refer to it as our social heredity. We usually learn our culture by growing up with it, but this learning process is needed for

Box 5.1

 *In Profile*

Sepak Takraw

Sepak takraw is a popular sport in Southeast Asia. It resembles volleyball, except that it uses a rattan ball and only allows players to use their feet, knee, chest, and head to touch and move the ball over a high net.

Figure 5.2

The sepak takraw ball is made of woven rattan. The aim of the game is to keep the ball off the ground using any part of the body except the hands. (© Christopher B. Stage.)

The game is likely based on the Chinese game of cuju, a term that means "kick ball." By the early 1400s the game had been brought into Malaysia and Thailand through trade. Back then the game was played mainly by men and boys standing in a circle, kicking the ball back and forth between them. The game remained in its circle form for hundreds of years, and the modern version of sepak takraw began taking shape sometime during the early 1800s. By 1829 the Siam Sports Association had drafted the first rules and introduced the volleyball-style net.

Within a few years, takraw was introduced to the curriculum in Thai and Malaysian schools, and the game became such a cherished local custom that exhibitions were staged as part of the celebrations of independence for both countries. By the 1940s, the game had spread throughout Southeast Asia, and today play is governed by the International Sepak Takraw Federation.

anyone new to a culture. For example, Tsai (2000) studied Chinese immigrants in Australia and found that only after the immigrants sufficiently learned their new culture, were they able to participate in the leisure expressions of the culture.

The process whereby culture is transmitted is called *enculturation*. An established culture teaches an individual new to the culture accepted norms and values by repetition so that the individual can become an accepted member of the group and find a suitable role. Most importantly, it establishes a context of boundaries and correctness that dictates what is and is not permissible within that group's framework. For example, the appropriate times of day to eat vary from culture to culture, and through enculturation we learn what time this is. When we eat may not have anything to do with when we're hungry, but rather we eat when our culture tells us it's time.

Figure 5.3

Snowmobiling is a pastime that forms the basis for a subculture of participants. In North America leisure subcultures based on engines that require fuel and large tracks of land are in jeopardy as both become more costly. (Microsoft, 2008)

Enculturation:
the process by which cultural understanding is transmitted to new members

Box 5.2

The Study Says

Cross-Cultural Differences in Eating Motivation

This exploratory study compared motivation for eating between individuals from the United States and Japan. Questionnaires were administered to 1,218 college-aged people in both cultures. Findings concluded that women in the U.S. were more likely to initiate eating for emotional reasons, while women in Japan were more likely to eat for physical reasons. (There were no differences for men.) Both women and men in the U.S., however, were more likely than the Japanese respondents to eat in response to watching TV or movies.

Hawks, S.R., Madanat, H.N., Merrill, R.M., Goudy, M.B. & Miyagawa, T. (2003). A cross-cultural analysis of "motivation for eating" as a potential factor in the emergence of global obesity: Japan and the United States. *Health Promotion International, 18*(2), 153-167.

The third characteristic of culture is that it is based on symbols. The anthropologist Leslie White (1959) insisted all human behavior originates in the use of symbols. For example, art, religion, and money all involve the use of symbols—the visual image in art, the icon in religion, and the coin in money. The most important symbolic aspect of culture is language—the substitution of words for objects (Haviland, 1990).

One way of thinking about leisure relative to this characteristic is to consider the word leisure itself. According to deGrazia (1962) "leisure cannot exist where people don't know what it is" (p. 3). That is, one must have a symbol (language) for leisure in order to have it. For example, while conducting research with the Sherpa people of the Khumbu region of Nepal, I realized many people were unable to understand my question "What do you do for leisure?" because they did not have a readily translatable word for the English word leisure.

This idea is labeled the Whorfian hypothesis. Named for the anthropologist who first formed a full-fledged theory about it (Benjamin Lee Whorf in 1956), the idea argues that language not only provides a way of communicating among people, but it also becomes the entire definition of the culture itself.

What do you think? Does the absence of a word such as leisure mean the absence of that experience? The Whorfian hypothesis has received only limited and confusing research support, even though many commonly agree with it (Chick, 1995). For example, as I discovered in my own study, the Sherpa people indeed have a life experience characterized by many of the qualities we identify with leisure, even though their word for it does not translate into the English word leisure. Thus, we must be careful in thinking that leisure differs among cultural groups because of language differences.

Finally, culture is integrated. This characteristic means all aspects of a culture relate to one another, so that changes to one seemingly unimportant part of a particular culture can reverberate throughout the entire culture and affect all other aspects.

An example of this characteristic as related to leisure is what occurred in Poland with the demise of communism. Formerly, under the communist system, government-owned companies in Poland were required to generate cultural funds to be used to subsidize holidays and trips for employees, recreational services for employees' children, book purchases for company libraries, and tickets for the theater, cinema, and concerts. When the country shifted away from a communist political system in 1989 by implementing market-oriented economics, one essential feature was the privatization of these government funds (Jung, 1992).

This meant not only that some establishments formerly used for recreation had shifted to other uses, but also that, with the commercialization of recreation, recreational services were now available only to more wealthy consumers. Thus, with one change in the political system, changes were also felt in the economic system, which in turn had an impact on leisure resources and how leisure services were made available in Polish culture. This process is labeled cultural change, which we next explore more in depth.

Cultural Change

An outcome we realize from the characteristics of culture we've just discussed is that cultures change. All cultures change over a period of time, sometimes gently and gradually, without altering any of the fundamental ways underlying the core of the culture. At other times, the pace of change may be dramatically fast, causing radical cultural alternation in a short period of time, sometimes to the disadvantage of the culture. Regardless, certain mechanisms are at work in cultural change having implications for leisure. These mechanisms of cultural change are innovation, diffusion, loss, and acculturation (Haviland, 1990).

Innovation as a mechanism of cultural change refers to any new practice, tool, or principle that gains widespread acceptance within a culture. A significant example of how innovation changes cultural expressions of leisure is the invention of television. Television has changed just about everything—almost everywhere. When television was introduced (in 1936 in Great Britain and in 1945 in the United States) very few homes could afford the "box." By 1950, nine percent of American homes had it; but its popularity grew quickly and five years later TV was in 65 percent of households. Today, 99 percent of American households have a television and 66 percent have three or more (Nielsen Media Research, 2006).

Innovation:
a chance discovery that gains widespread acceptance

Initially, the impact of this innovation was felt in the role of TV as an advertising medium. As well, it was nearly a perfect expression of suburban leisure as it celebrated domesticity in the "sit-com" programming format, and warned of urban dangers in the action-adventure shows (Cross, 1990). From nearly its beginning, American critics argued television was a good example of Gresham's Law about culture: bad stuff drives out the good, since it is more easily understood and enjoyed (Cross, 1990, p. 184). Since then the impact of television has been widely and thoroughly studied and commented about. Table 5.2 summarizes some of the changes to leisure resulting from the innovation of TV.

Table 5.2

Summary of Cultural Changes from the Invention of Television

- People stay home more.
- Household timetables changed, with "prime time" now devoted to entertainment rather than to family, religion, and education.
- Less socializing in the family, neighborhood, and community and increased social isolation.
- Television characters used as role models.
- Freakishness and sensation treated with solemn importance.
- Expansion of such forms of leisure as the arts, cooking, travel, and sports.
- Development of new forms of leisure, such as extreme sports.
- A more homogenized expression of leisure across all members of the culture.

Diffusion is another mechanism of cultural change. Diffusion is the spread or borrowing of customs or practices from one culture to another. So common is diffusion that anthropologist Linton suggested that borrowing accounts for as much as 90 percent of any culture's content (Haviland, 1990). One major example of cultural change brought about by diffusion is McDonald's restaurants. What began as a single establishment in Des Plaines, Illinois in 1955 has now expanded to more than 31,000 restaurants in over 119 countries (McDonald's, 2007). Yet, while global in its market, the company also encourages local operators to tailor menu items to local tastes, such as the Ebi Filet-O (shrimp burger) in Japan and the McLaks, a sandwich made of grilled salmon and dill sauce in Norway.

Diffusion:
the spread of customs from one culture to another

This demonstrates that as with the mechanism of innovation, the mechanism of diffusion doesn't always cause cultural change. This is because people are choosy about their borrowing and pick only those that are compatible with their existing culture. In leisure, for example, particular games, songs, sports, dances, and art forms introduced in one culture spread to others and are often changed in accordance with the dominant values of the receiving culture. Heider (1977) described a game of physical skill developed in Java, Indonesia, and later introduced in a highland New Guinea tribe. New Guinean culture valued noncompetitiveness, so when they played the Javanese game, they disregarded scorekeeping and rules to be more in keeping with their own cultural values (Chick, 1995).

Figure 5.4

Gridlock of tourist jeeps in Cancun, Mexico. The diffusion of customs from one culture to another is not always compatible. (© Ruth V. Russell, 2008)

As our discussion has led us so far, most often we think of cultural change as an accumulation of innovations and borrowings; new things are added to those already in a culture. This is not always the case, of course, and frequently the acceptance of an innovation or borrowing leads to loss in a culture. This is *cultural loss* (Haviland, 1990).

To turn again to the innovation of television for an example, when cultures changed from primarily radio home entertainment to television, several pleasurable qualities of leisure were lost. With television we were no longer able to use our imaginations to fill in the picture of the action, and the family no longer sat in a circle facing each other while being entertained. With television, someone else's visualization of the action is provided for us, and the family sits shoulder to shoulder in a straight line without eye contact.

Cultural loss:
change resulting in the loss of a cultural tradition

Box 5.3

In Focus

Torrent of Tourists in the Khumbu

Nepal packs more geographical diversity into fewer square miles than any other country in the world. The people who inhabit this land mirror this diversity. In Nepal, no majority culture exists —all are minorities. One of the most famous of these cultures is the Sherpa.

The Sherpa live in the high valleys in the southern shadow of Mt. Everest in the region known as the Khumbu. They are Buddhists, culturally Tibetan, and a numerically insignificant portion of the population (Fisher, 1990). Their villages are situated mostly on rock, ice, and snow at altitudes between 10,000 and 13,000 feet, and are connected by narrow mountain footpaths. Sherpas have traditionally operated at a very low level of technology, farming potatoes, turnips, and cauliflower, weaving woolen cloth by hand, and following their yak herds to higher pastures in the summer. Community celebrations follow a pattern set mostly by the passage of the seasons and center around local monasteries.

Figure 5.5

Figure 5.5. The airstrip in Lukla brings tourists into Nepal's Khumbu region.
(© Ruth V. Russell, 2008)

Box 5.3 (Cont.)

Beginning in 1961, life began to change for the Sherpa of the Khumbu. Inducing the most cultural change was the construction of an airstrip at Lukla, which shortened travel time from Kathmandu (the capital) to the Khumbu from 14 days to 40 minutes. This single development brings more than 18,000 tourists per year to the region today.

What has this meant for the Sherpa culture? Those who observe and comment on the impact of tourism generally divide into two camps. One view is that tourism ultimately destroys the cultural integrity of the host area. Tourism is considered to place "the whole of the visited culture on sale, distorting its imagery and symbolism, ... transforming a way of life into an industry" (Smith, 1980, p. 60). As one Khumbu tourist wrote in a visitor's log book, "A hot shower, steaks, and 500-foot viewing tower with central heating would definitely be in order' (Fisher, 1990).

The other view is that tourism is good because of the economic benefit it brings to local people, not only by bringing in outside money, but also by increasing employment. Residents of the Khumbu now work as guides, cooks, and porters for trekking and mountain-climbing trips. In fact, the word Sherpa has come to describe the particular job of assisting the trekking party by setting up tents and managing loads. And, although most tourist spending goes to the trekking companies that arrange the trips headquartered outside the Khumbu, Sherpa income has still increased by about 730 percent (Fisher, 1990).

Which perspective is true for the Khumbu? Has tourism created cultural change resulting in a gain or loss for the Sherpa?

In the region, one popular way to spend increased income has been on jewelry, especially watches. Yet, some traditional crafts are dying out; with so much ready cash, people now tend to buy manufactured items instead of making it themselves. Class differences are also emerging as a new "tourist Sherpa" class develops. Formerly, land and yak herds were the sources of wealth and status. Now, an almost nouveau-riche subculture can be distinguished by their imported hiking boots, down parkas, baseball caps, and American university-labeled sweatshirts. For those Sherpa who are trekking guides or porters, daily life has shifted dramatically as they spend roughly 10 months a year away from their villages. This has meant women have taken on greater farming and domestic responsibilities as tourism has employed mostly men. Yet, studies have demonstrated families involved in tourism are more likely to achieve more education.

Other impacts from mass tourism to the Khumbu have resulted in a degraded environment, which has changed cultural practices as well. Over the past 40 years, it is estimated the culture has had to cope with over 18 tons of garbage left behind by tourists, and sewage management is also a new concern. Massive deforestation (for heating and cooking) and soil erosion have created resource management problems formerly unknown to the Sherpa.

Questions to Consider and Discuss

1. Which perspective do you think best portrays the effect of tourism in the Khumbu? Has it been good or bad? Why?

Box 5.3 (Cont.)

2. Is the torrent of tourists in the Khumbu an example of the mechanisms of diffusion or acculturation? Has it meant cultural loss? Why or why not?
3. As a project, select an undeveloped area near you that has recently promoted itself as a tourist destination. This could be a small town, county, or specific facility. Interview local people to learn about the impact of tourism on them. Has this been good or bad?

A final mechanism of cultural change is acculturation. *Acculturation* occurs when different cultures come into intensive firsthand contact, with subsequent changes in the original cultural patterns of one or both (Haviland, 1990). Acculturation implies a mutual influence in which elements of the two cultures mingle and merge. It has been hypothesized that in order for acculturation to occur, some relative cultural equality has to exist between the giving and the receiving cultures.

Acculturation: exchange of cultural features as a result of prolonged contact between groups

Acculturation is a complex cultural change concept, with different anthropologists suggesting different outcomes. For example, J. W. Berry (1986) has suggested there are four possible outcomes of the acculturation process: assimilation, integration, rejection, or marginalization.

Assimilation is the first outcome from acculturation. While assimilation can happen at the individual level, here we are referring to the process whereby a minority group gradually adopts the customs and attitudes of the prevailing dominant group. For example, in considering the acculturation of immigrants, the goal is typically that they will become more like their new country. The term Americanization reflects this perspective—to become more like other Americans in values, behaviors and traditions.

Assimilation: to adopt the ways of the main culture

Integration is another way a culture can change as a result of acculturation. When integration results, there is a merging of the two cultures. This is the "melting pot" idea. We usually refer to integration as the bringing of people of different racial or ethnic groups into unrestricted and equal association, such as in an organization. For an example, consider the leisure organizations to which you belong. Are they integrated? The word integration comes from the Latin integer, meaning whole or entire, thus another way of thinking about integration of cultures is to describe them as becoming whole and unified.

Integration: combining parts so they form a whole

Rejection, on the other hand, is directly opposite of integration. When rejection results from the prolonged contact between two cultures, each individual culture reaffirms its own traditions and ways, rejecting those of the other culture. One example might be the Amish. Members of the Amish movement are a conservative Christian group in North America that maintain a principled rejection of modernity.

Rejection: denial and avoidance of others

Finally, *marginalization* is the label applied to relegating or confining a group to a lower or outer edge. Common examples of marginalized groups in our societies have been persons living with

Marginalization: to relagate to an unimportant or powerless position wihin a group

Box 5.4

 The Study Says

Mexican-American Assimilation and Leisure

The purpose of this study was to examine the relationship between assimilation and family leisure involvement from Mexican-American parent, youth, and family perspectives. Is there an impact on leisure participation and interests from the assimilation resulting from acculturation? Questionnaires were administered to members of 74 families that had immigrated to the United States from Mexico. There were many findings from the study, but researchers considered the most important to be the role leisure played in the assimilation of youth. In agreement with other studies, it was found that highly assimilated youth participated in more water or snow based outdoor recreation activities, urban pursuits, and travel than youth with low assimilation.

Christenson, O.D., Zabriskie, R.B., Eggett, D.L., & Freeman, P.A. (2006). Family acculturation, family leisure involvement, and family functioning among Mexican-Americans. *Journal of Leisure Research, 38*(4), 475-495.

disabilities, women, racial minorities, Aboriginal communities, the elderly, single mothers, and homosexuals (Mullaly, 2007).

Marginalization does not only refer to groups of people. We can also find examples in other types of groups. Let's consider the arts. If you visit galleries and museums in North America you'll notice an illustration of marginalized art. The Metropolitan Museum of Art (2008) in New York City, for instance, is having difficulties with its considerable yet under-cataloged holdings of Islamic art. This collection is closed at the museum until 2011, as the exhibition space is renovated to try to correct this marginalization. Of course this is not only the museum's fault, as Western audiences also hold a cultural bias against appreciating the aesthetic of traditional Islamic art forms like ceramics, textiles and calligraphy. Western museum visitors see these as decorative arts, and prefer the high-art of three-dimensional sculpture and easel painting.

Hunches About the Earliest Human Cultures

One of the most illuminating ways to understand present human culture is to view it from its distant origins. Leisure was a part of culture before human civilization developed, even before our ancestors learned how to speak (Shivers & deLisle, 1997). All this makes for a fascinating story.

Humans are classified by biologists as belonging to the primate order, and some evidence suggests humans evolved from the small, apelike ramapithecines, which lived about 15 million years ago. By four million years ago, this apelike creature became fully adapted to moving about on its hind legs, and by 2.5 million years ago, the appearance of the earliest stone tools, along with the gradual enlarging of the brain, set the stage for the human of the present (Haviland, 1990).

These early tools were choppers, scrapers, gougers, and hammer-stones for cutting meat, scraping hides, and cracking bones to extract marrow. Their invention marks the beginning of the *Paleolithic era* of human culture. During the Paleolithic era humans in mostly what today is Africa and Asia were grouped together in small-scale societies called bands and gained their subsistence from gathering plants and hunting or scavenging wild animals. They ate what was available and then moved on, building shelters only if there was enough food in an area to last awhile. The Paleolithic period covers the greatest proportion of humanity's time—roughly 99 percent.

Paleothic era:
a period of prehistory characterized by the use of rough stone implements

What we know about the leisure expressions of Paleolithic people is, of course, very limited, but we do have surviving cave paintings to offer clues. In fact, during the last 50 years, archeologists have discovered thousands of paintings and carvings on the walls of caves and on the surfaces of rocks at sites in Europe, Africa, Australia, and North America. Some discovered as recently as 1996 in southeastern France contain images of animals, birds, fish, and other symbols, all of which reveal a high degree of artistic sophistication (Fiero, 1998).

Box 5.5

In Your Own Experience

The Human

Humans are bipedal primates belonging to the mammalian species Homo sapiens (Latin for knowing man). Compared to other species, humans have a highly developed brain capable of abstract reasoning, language, and introspection. This mental capability, combined with an erect body that frees their upper limbs for manipulating objects, has allowed humans to make far greater use of tools than any other species. Scientists estimate that during the Paleolithic era there were roughly 10,000 humans in the world, mostly in Africa.

What has become of the human since? Go to the web site for a "world clock." For example, try: http://www.poodwaddle.com/worldclock.swf.

Select several categories of statistics in the clock and watch the counts as they progress. What do you conclude? In your opinion, how well are humans fulfilling their potential as a species?

These artistic artifacts document a great deal about the culture of Paleolithic people. For example, the cave paintings found in France reveal a culture of hunting people. Realistically depicted bison, horses, and reindeer are shown standing, running, and wounded by spears. Because they are located in the most inaccessible regions of the caves, and frequently drawn one over another, it is unlikely the paintings were intended as decorations. According to the interpretations of some scholars (Fiero, 1998), the cave art reflects a kind of prayer, a means of engaging superhuman forces to advance human needs and efforts. Further, scholars believe the prayer not only included the drawings, but also song and dance. In other words, perhaps this represents the very earliest use of leisure as ritual.

Beyond these cave drawings, we don't know much more about the leisure of the Paleolithic era. There are conjectures, of course. For example, the standard anthropological view is that because they were constantly on the move in search of food for subsistence survival, these people must have lacked free time. Yet, there is also an alternative view. Marshall Sahlins (1988), an American anthropologist, has suggested prehistoric people were in fact the original leisure society. Sahlins based his claim on two suppositions. First, Paleolithic people may not have spent as much time hunting and gathering food as formerly assumed. Second, Paleolithic people had comparatively few material goods and thus were free from the effort of protecting and maintaining them. Let's ponder each suggestion in turn.

First, Sahlins cited research about two hunter-gatherer groups living in Australia in the 1960s as examples of what life could have been like for Paleolithic

Figure 5.6

The hours per day spent in hunting and gathering activities by one of Sahlins' groups.

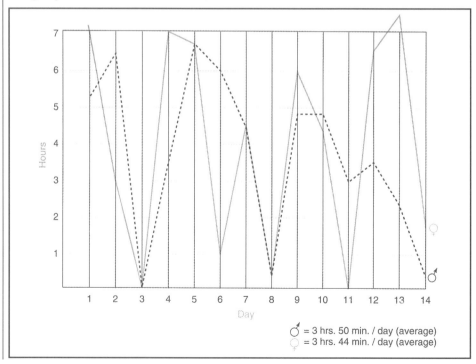

♂ = 3 hrs. 50 min. / day (average)
♀ = 3 hrs. 44 min. / day (average)

Figure 5.7

Amount of daytime devoted to sleep. According to Sahlins's hyothesis, free-time activities could have also included rest, chatting, and general sociability.

Day	◯→ Average	◯+ Average
1	2'15"	2'45"
2	1'30"	1'0"
3	Most of the day	
4	Intermittent	
5	Intermittent and most of late afternoon	
6	Most of the day	
7	Several hours	
8	2'0"	2'0"
9	50"	50"
10	Afternoon	
11	Afternoon	
12	Intermittent, afternoon	
13	–	–
14	3'15"	3'15"

people. The results are surprising. As shown in figure 5.6, the number of hours per day spent by one of the groups in hunting and gathering activities was not that much. The most obvious conclusion Sahlins drew from these data was the people did not have to work hard to survive, particularly by modern standards. The average length of time each person spent per day collecting and preparing food was three to four hours.

What might they have done in their spare time? As indicated in figure 5.7 much of the time freed from the necessities of survival could have been spent in rest and sleep. According to Sahlins, other free-time activities may have included chatting, gossiping, and general sociability.

Sahlins' second supposition about the leisure of Paleolithic cultures has to do with what today we call materialism. In contrast to the many affluent societies of today, with their focus on the acquisition of stuff, early people possessed very little. Most likely their possessions included a few pieces of clothing, portable housing materials, a few ornaments, spare flints, some medicinal quartz, a few tools and weapons, and a skin bag to hold it all. In contrast to the possessions we have today, and the time we spend purchasing, repairing, cleaning, putting away, transporting, sorting, finding, protecting, and storing it all, Sahlins reasoned Paleolithic people were comparatively free. Although some might consider this prehistoric culture poor because they didn't have anything, another view is to think of them as rich in free time.

Cultural Development and Leisure

The story of humankind after these prehistoric times is one of cultural development. *Development* simply means the extent to which the resources of an area have been brought into full productivity. In common usage it refers to the amount of economic growth and modernization, and to the production and consumption of goods. Today, countries can be identified according to the extent of their development. In this section of the chapter we discuss what cultural development means to the expression of leisure. The conclusion is that with development there are both advantages and disadvantages for leisure.

Development:
the process of improving the material conditions of people through the use of knowledge and technology

"Developing" was the term U.S. President Harry S. Truman introduced in 1949 as a replacement for "backward," the unflattering reference then in use. This new term implies that ultimately all portions of the world will reach a high level of development. Yet, since development is a fluid condition, while the standard of living in most cultures of the world has improved, one serious trend is the widening of the development gap. Rich countries have grown richer, and poor countries have become relatively poorer (table 5.3). Thus, such organizations as

Table 5.3

Gross Domestic Product (GDP) per Capita for Selected Countries, 2003

More than $37,000	Less than $10,000	Less than $1,000
Denmark	Czech Republic	Afghanistan
Ireland	Greece	Bangladesh
Luxembourg	Mexico	Ethiopia
Norway	Poland	Haiti
Switzerland	Slovak Republic	Liberia
United States	Turkey	Rwanda

The Clearinghouse on International Developments in Child, Youth and Family Policies at Columbia Universitiy. Retrieved 4/17/08 from http://www.childpolicyintl.org.

the Peace Corps and the World Bank attempt to marshal some of the resources of more-developed areas to help less-developed ones.

Well-Being

However, a country's level of development can be determined by more than economic factors. According to the United Nations, development is measured as a combination of three factors: economic, social, and demographic. That is, development is a multifaceted concept with interrelated conditions. The World

Box 5.6

The Study Says

The Material World

In 1994 a research team headed by Peter Menzel set out to learn about the material well-being of families of the world. Using country statistics and photographs, Menzel provided a comparative analysis of the material goods of typical families from 30 nations.

Data experts at the United Nations and World Bank helped determine what an average family was in a country according to location (rural, urban), type of dwelling, family size, annual income, occupation, and religion. To find an actual family that represented what was average, researchers knocked on doors of typical houses looking for families that fit the statistics. Then, for all 30 families, their precious belongings were moved outside to the front of the house for the photographs, to provide a visual means of analyzing the material well-being of the family.

In studying the photographs, many things can be understood about the material condition of families in various cultures. For example, the researchers noted the possessions of the family in Uzbekistan overwhelmingly consisted of carpets, and those of the average Icelandic family were focused on playing music, whereas the photo of the typical family in Kuwait was crowded with four shiny new automobiles, including a Mercedes.

Figure 5.8

The Regzen family outside their ger with all of their possessions. Ulaanbaatar, Mongolia. (From *Material World*, pp. 40-41 © Peter Menzel/menselphoto.com. Used with permission.)

Box 5.6 (Cont.)

Most visible, however, was the common denominator of the television in typical households across the globe. In the photo of the typical family in Mongolia (figure 5.8), the television is located in the front center of the photograph with the family positioned behind it. The South African, Albanian and Vietnamese families are also pictured with a television nearby, and the family from Cuba is shown with two televisions, as are families from the United States, Russia, Italy, and Great Britain. In fact, in all but the very poorest countries (Mali and Haiti), the television is located in the photograph in such a way as to suggest its primacy among the material wealth of the world's families.

Menzel, P. (1994). *Material world: A global family portrait.* San Francisco: Sierra Club Books.

Bank (2008), for example, includes such indicators as prevalence of HIV, school enrollments, forest area, CO_2 emissions, energy use, inflation, cash surplus, time required to start a business, military expenditure, and Internet users.

Another way to comprehend all this is to notice how leisure relates to development. For example, in developing countries such as Indonesia, Slovakia and Tunisia, leisure is richly laced with the traditions and folkways of the culture. Music, dance, and art forms are woven into the fabric of society in ways uncommon in developed countries such as Singapore and Canada.

As any underdeveloped area seeks to develop, it embraces new income-generating efforts that sometimes mean the ruin of traditions and folkways. On the other hand, traditional arts and crafts are possibly updated and exported as a result of development. As illustration, today, perhaps the single largest use of leisure as a development tool is tourism. In such developing countries as Malaysia, tourism is a leading foreign exchange earner and thus a prime motivator for enhancing the country's infrastructure.

Leisure relates to development in other ways as well. Basically, leisure can be an important source of growth as it widens a culture's relationship to the environment, builds social identity and harmony, and contributes other provisions of well-being. For example, research by Ryff and Keyes (1995) found individual self-acceptance, positive relationships with others, autonomy, purpose in life, and personal growth to be associated with a culture's well-being. On the other hand, Diener and Diener (1995) showed that high income, individualism, human rights and social equality were also decisive factors.

Modernization:

a process involving the implementation of recent techniques, methods, or ideas

Leisure and Modernity

Those cultures considered to be developed are also considered modern. The concept of *modernization* relates to developing and using current techniques, methods, or ideas. Basically, modernization results in the multiplying of institutions as the simple structures of traditional societies are transformed into complex ones.

The concept of modernization actually has several different connotations. To many people, modernization is what happens when undeveloped societies acquire some of the characteristics common to developed societies. That is, becoming modern really means "becoming like us." Accordingly, there is a clear implication that not being like us is to be antiquated and obsolete. We realize this perspective is an *ethnocentric* one, because it insists these other societies must be changed to be more like us, irrespective of other considerations, including traditional ways of life.

Ethnocentric:

tendency to look at the world primarily from the perspective of one's own culture

Although people in every culture, developed and undeveloped, have at least some feelings of ethnocentricity, it seems Western cultures are particularly good examples. Let's consider baseball in Japan to illustrate. Even though the traditional sports of judo and sumo continue to be popular, baseball has grown to such an extent that the Japanese are now providing strong competition with major league teams in the United States. An ethnocentric response to this trend would be to assume the Japanese version of baseball is inferior to the American version. After all, since baseball was invented in the United States, and is considered the "national pastime," it follows that it is played there the best.

Since an ethnocentric view of modernization is less useful, then, let's explore a more anthropologically sound one. The process of modernization may be best understood as made up of four sub-processes: technological development, agricultural development, industrialization, and urbanization (Haviland, 1990). These elements are interrelated and occur simultaneously. First, with modernization, traditional knowledge and techniques are replaced by scientific knowledge and techniques. Likewise, the culture shifts from an emphasis on subsistence farming to commercial farming. Industrialization occurs when work is done by machines rather than by humans and animals, and the population becomes urbanized by moving from rural settlements into cities.

Figure 5.9

Art/graffiti on the Berlin Wall before reunification of East and West Germany in 1990. One consequence of the wall that separated East and West Germany was the expression of ethnocentric views. (© Ruth V. Russell, 2008)

In other words, modernization is the ultimate goal of cultural development. Yet, there are other changes likely to follow with modernization. For example, political parties and some sort of electoral system likely appears, along with a bureaucracy. There is also usually an expansion of learning opportunities and literacy increases. Typically, there are major improvements in health care, yet the environment usually becomes more precious as industrial pollution renders the air and water quality and supplies more fragile. The mobility of people also increases, as does the diversity of roles they assume in the culture. People's daily lives change as a result of modernization too. With modernity we become busier

Box 5.7

In Your Own Experience

Ethnocentricity Quiz

Check those statements you think indicate an ethnocentric perspective:

[ ] When reading it is natural to read from left to right and from top to bottom.
[ ] On a toggle switch the universal position for "on" is up.
[ ] Placing an "X" in a box indicates acceptance of the item.
[ ] Using chopsticks at every meal to eat is silly.
[ ] In Britain drivers drive on the wrong side of the road.

Answers: All statements reflect ethnocentricity. For example, many other languages read from right to left and bottom to top. In some countries the switch position for "on" is down. In Japan placing an "X" in a box indicates non-acceptance. Using chopsticks is the normal way to eat for millions of people, and why not just say drivers from Britain drive on the left hand side?

as time efficiency becomes more important. In fact, one of the most noticeable signs of modernity is that efficiency becomes a very important cultural value (Godbey, 1997).

Because the impact of modernity can be so extreme and dramatic, a special concept has been adopted by anthropologists and other scientists. This is *postmodernism*. The term is very slippery to define because it can mean different things when applied to literature, art, philosophy, and architecture.

Postmodernism: skeptical reation to moderism

Postmodernism is largely a reaction to the assumed certainty of modernity. That is, it is skeptical of the presumed truth of science, religion, and technology, as it claims to understand all groups, cultures, traditions, and races. Instead the postmodern perspective focuses on the relative truths of each person. Postmodernism interprets what the world means to us individually.

We can all readily observe that in the last few decades the nature of modern societies has changed dramatically. Social theorists have commented about these changes through such labels as a "media society," a "society of spectacle," and a "consumer society." Today, modern cultures are indeed dominated by consumption, media, and new technologies. From a postmodern perspective this means we live in a fragmented way. Old identities and common interests have become diffused.

Much is being written today about postmodernism, and much of it that applies to leisure carries a negative tone, as though leisure has lost something as a result of modernism. In essence, leisure in modern societies is more commercial, diverse, and sped up. It is thus more cherished, as it has to compete with the busyness of work and family responsibilities. Modern leisure is more of a competition to collect fun experiences and recreational equipment. As well, modern leisure is expected to be more concerned with individual self-fulfillment, self-reliance, and on image. For example, according to some leisure scholars, our modern "day-to-day lives have been reduced to sedentary, boring routines, largely devoid of excitement, challenge, and personal growth" (Kernan & Domzal, 2000, p. 79).

Not everyone agrees the condition of leisure in modern cultures is as described by the perspective of postmodernism. Some continue to argue that leisure is largely unchanged by economic and social progress. For example, Crouch and Tomlinson (1994) suggest leisure is still lived in communities and in family and social groups, and is not dependent on commodities and media. Similarly, Kelly (1999) contends most leisure still takes place in and around the home and serves to integrate communities and personal relationships.

What We Understand About Leisure's Cultural Meaning

From the perspective of anthropology, leisure can be understood as a significant cultural phenomenon. That is, leisure helps shape a culture, and like a reflection in the mirror, leisure is a result of a culture's shape. After studying this chapter, you should know that:

- As a cultural phenomenon, leisure is characterized as shared, learned, based on symbols, and integrated.
- Leisure contributes to and is affected by the cultural change mechanisms of innovation, diffusion, loss, and acculturation.
- Contrary to the standard view, new data suggest prehistoric people had abundant free time and spent it relaxing.
- Leisure can contribute to cultural development.
- Leisure is subject to the processes of modernization. The result may be both good and bad.

References

Berry, J. W. (1986). The acculturation process and refugee behavior. In C.I. Williams, & J. Westermeyer (Eds.), *Refugee mental health in resettlement countries*. New York: Hemisphere.

Chick, G.E. (1995). The anthropology of leisure: Past, present, and future research. In L.A. Barnett (Ed.), *Research about leisure: Past, present, and future*. Champaign, IL: Sagamore.

Cross, G. (1990). *A social history of leisure since 1600*. State College, PA: Venture.

Crouch, D., & Tomlinson, A. (1994). Collective self-generated consumption: Leisure, space, and cultural identity in late modernity. In I. Henry (Ed.), *Leisure: Modernity, postmodernity, and lifestyles* (Publication No. 48, pp. 309-321). Brighton, UK: Leisure Studies Association.

deGrazia, S. (1962). *Of time, work, and leisure*. New York: Twentieth Century Fund.

Diener, E., & Diener, M. (1995). Cross-cultural correlates of life satisfaction and self-esteem. *Journal of Personality and Social Psychology, 68*, 653-663.

Fiero, G.K. (1998). *The humanistic tradition: The first civilizations and the classical legacy*. New York: McGraw-Hill.

Fisher, J.F. (1990). *Sherpas: Reflections on change in Himalayan Nepal*. Berkeley: University of California Press.

Godbey, G. (1997). *Leisure and leisure services in the 21st century*. State College, PA: Venture.

Grobler, J.E.H. (April 1985). The developing patterns of leisure time activities in South Africa's black cities since ca. 1930. *World Leisure and Recreation Association Magazine*, 35-41.

Haviland, W.A. (1990). *Cultural anthropology*. Orlando, FL: Holt, Rinehart, and Winston.

Heider, K. (1977). From Javanese to Dani: The translation of a game. In P. Stevens (Ed.), *Studies in the anthropology of play*. West Point, NY: Leisure Press.

Jung, B. (Winter 1992). Economic, social and political conditions for enjoyment of leisure in Central and Eastern Europe of 1992 – The Polish perspective. *World Leisure and Recreation Association Magazine*, 8-12.

Kelly, J. (1999). Leisure and society: A dialectical analysis. In E.L. Jackson, & T.L. Burton (Eds.), *Leisure studies: Prospects for the Twenty-first Century*. State College, PA: Venture.

Kernan, J.B., & Domzal, T.J. (2000). Getting a life: Homo ludens as postmodern identity. *Journal of Travel & Tourism Marketing, 8*(4), 79-84.

Linton, R. (1936). *The study of man: An introduction*. New York: Appleton.

McDonald's (2007). *Home Page*. Available from http://www.mcdonalds.ca/en/aboutus/faq.aspx. Retrieved 4/16/08.

Metropolitan Museum of Art. (2008). *Introduction to Islamic Art*. Available from http://www.metmuseum.org/Works_of_Art/islamic_art. Retrieved 4/16/08.

Mullaly, B. (2007). Oppression: The focus of structural social work. In B. Mullaly (Ed.), *The new structural social work* (pp. 252-286). Don Mills: Oxford University Press.

Nielsen Media Research. (2006). *Statistics*. Available from http://www.nielsenmedia.com. Retrieved 4/21/08.

Ryff, C.D., & Keyes, C.L.M. (1995). The structure of psychological well-being revisited. *Journal of Personality and Social Psychology, 69*, 719-727.

Sahlins, M. (1988). The original affluent society. In J.B. Cole (Ed.), *Anthropology for the nineties*. New York: The Free Press.

Shivers, J.S., & deLisle, L.J. (1997). *The story of leisure: Context, concepts, and current controversy*. Champaign, IL: Human Kinetics.

Smith, A. (1980). *The geopolitics of information: How western culture dominates the world*. New York: Oxford University Press.

Tsai, E.H. (2000). The influence of acculturation on perception of leisure constraints of Chinese immigrants. *World Leisure, 3,* 33-41.

United Nations Educational, Scientific and Cultural Organization (UNESCO). (2002). *Universal Declaration on Cultural Diversity.* Available from http://www.unesco.org/education/imld_200/unversal–decla.shtml.Retrieve 4/10/08.

White, L. (1959). *The evolution of culture: The development of civilization to the fall of Rome.* New York: McGraw-Hill.

World Bank. (2008). *United States Data Profile.* Available from http://devdata.worldbank.org/external/CPProfile.asp?Ptype=CP&CCode=USA. Retrieved on 4/20/08.

CHAPTER SIX

LEISURE'S GEOGRAPHY

PREVIEW

What is the geographical significance of leisure?

Leisure is expressed in both space and place, which are the basic concepts of geography.

How is leisure expressed in space?

Leisure participation is distributed according to spatial pattern, density, and concentration.

How is leisure expressed in place?

People have a strong attachment to specific leisure places.

What is the future of leisure's geography?

Without wise management many leisure expressions will be lost due to the demise of leisure space and place resources.

KEY TERMS

Recent world events lend a sense of urgency to understanding geography. Do we face an overpopulation crisis? Will the planet have adequate energy supplies? Why are world refugee flows at unprecedentedly high levels? Is it too late to do something about global warming? At even a more personal level you may be right now asking, "Where shall I live?" Answers to all of these questions require we pay attention to geography.

Geography is the scientific study of where things are located on the earth's surface and why (Rubenstein, 2003). Specifically, geographers investigate the way people respond to place and how space is shaped by human behavior (Smale, 1999). This means leisure's expression is based in geography. For example, we know that the home is a more satisfying place for leisure for men than it is for women (Henderson, et al., 1996). We also know we need a flat, large space for playing croquet. As well, we know how differently we feel when we are in a large crowd at a football game versus in a large crowd along a wilderness trail.

Geography:
the study of earth and its life

Let's set the stage by considering climate. Climate determines not only those pastimes we choose in different seasons of the year, but also where we choose

Figure 6.1

While actual numbers are difficult to determine, participation in backyard pursuits is perhaps the most predominant example of the relationship between leisure and geography. (Microsoft, 2008)

to travel for vacations. Climate is determined by location; thus, pastime choices are also location related. That is, the beaches in the northeastern United States are among the finest in the world. However, the area's climate

Box 6.1

In Your Own Experience

Find Your Spot!

Take an online quiz to determine where you should live. Log onto http://www.findyourspot.com. From the home page, in the upper right corner, click "take our quiz." As you complete the survey notice the role of climate as well as the role of your leisure interests in determining the best places for you to live. When you've finished the quiz, a list of your top spots will be given. Explore the descriptions of them, and then choose your own top five. What are these? What is the relationship between your climate and leisure needs? What other factors did the quiz use to determine your best place to live?

limits their use for sunning and swimming only to the summer months. In contrast, the climate of Hawaii makes it attractive for beach activities throughout the year.

What is climate? *Climate* refers to the average conditions of temperature, barometric pressure, wind and precipitation in a locale over a long period of time (Davidoff, Davidoff & Eyre, 1988). It is different from weather, which refers to current conditions. Climate is primarily determined by latitude and altitude. The earth is divided into five basic climatic zones: tropical, dry, temperate, cold, and polar (Koppen Climate Classification System), and expressions of leisure are determined accordingly. For example, these basic climatic zones have been broken down even further into hardiness zones for gardening activities. If you live in hardiness zone 5b you can successfully grow Shasta daisies, but you can't if you live in zone 4a. (See http://www.garden.org/zipzone/#zone_info for more information.)

Climate: meteorological elements, including temperature, precipitation, and wind, that characterize a region over a period of time

In this chapter we explore some additional ways we can understand leisure as a geographical concept. These are organized according to the concepts of space and place. We conclude the chapter by reviewing a particularly relevant geographic leisure concern: environmental impact.

Leisure as Space

The famous German philosopher Immanuel Kant (1724—1804) compared the concern of geography for space with the concern of history for time. Whereas historians identify the dates of important events and explain why human activities follow one another across time, geographers identify the location of important places and explain why human activities are located beside one another in space. That is, historians ask when and why; geographers ask where and why (Rubenstein, 2003).

To do this, the basic principles of density, concentration, and pattern are important to leisure space. First, the frequency with which something occurs in space is its *density*. This frequency of something in space could be people, houses, cars, parks, green open spaces, or almost anything. The space could be measured in square kilometers, square miles, hectares, acres, or any other unit of measurement. *Concentration* is the extent of a feature's spread over space. If the objects in an area are close together, they are clustered, or if they are relatively far apart, they are dispersed.

Density: the frequency with which something occurs in space

Concentration: the extent of a feature's spread over space

It can be difficult to distinguish density and concentration, but they are not the same concepts. For example, in North America the distribution of major-league baseball teams changed in the second half of the 20th century (figure 6.2). That is, the number of teams expanded from 16 to 30 between 1952 and 2000, thus increasing the density. While, at the same time, six of the 16 original teams moved to other locations, thus dispersing their concentration. In 1952 all teams were clustered in the northeastern United States, but after some teams moved, they were dispersed to the west coast, the southeast, and Canada as well.

Table 6.1

Amount of Space Needed By Selected Pastimes in the United States

Recreational Space	Number
Golf courses	17 billion
Ski Resorts	492 million
Cruise Ships	192
Amusement Parks	3,196
Motion Picture Screens	39,000
National Park Areas	79 million acres
State Park Areas in Rhode Island	9,000 acres
Vehicle Trips for Fun	11 million miles daily

U.S. Census Bureau (2007). Tables 1214, 1226, 1229, 1239, 1240, 1241, 1245. Statistical Abstract of the United States: 2007. Washington, D.C.: U.S. Government Printing Office.

Figure 6.2

Density and concentration of major-league baseball teams in 1952 and 2000.
(Adapted from Rubenstein, 2003, p. 6. Used with permission.)

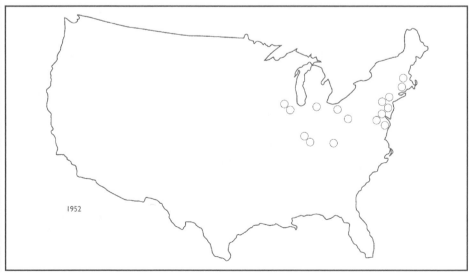

Figure 6.2 (Cont.)

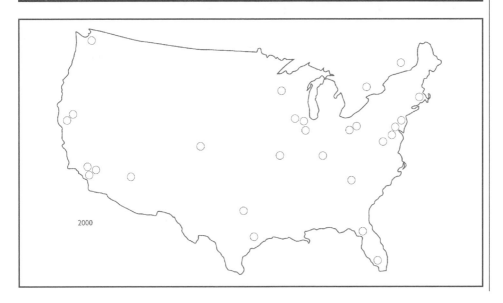

2000

The third property of leisure space is pattern. *Pattern* is the geometric arrangement of objects. Objects such as boat slips at a marina and campsites at a campground can be arranged linearly, in squares, in circles, and so on. For example, figure 6.3 shows the campground map for the Kentucky Horse Park in Lexington. Notice the pattern of campsites is two sets of concentric circles.

Pattern:
geometric arrangement of objects in space

There are many ways to demonstrate the concepts of density, concentration, and pattern of leisure in space. We'll next consider two: crowding and distance.

Crowding

All of us have probably already noticed that parks are becoming more crowded. In U.S. national park areas, for example, the number of visits in 1990 was approximately 57 million, compared to over 63 million in 2005 (U.S. Census Bureau, 2007). Fortunately, this means more people are enjoying these important leisure resources, but unfortunately, this also means they may be experiencing traffic congestion, full parking lots, cramped campgrounds, long lines for services, overtaxed rangers, more stringent rules, higher fees, conflict among visitors, and degraded facilities (Lime, 1996).

At Mount Rainier National Park in Washington, park rangers have become "parking rangers" as they regularly try to cram up to 600 cars into a 250-space parking area for the daily sunrise. At Gettysburg National Military Park in Pennsylvania, monuments are being hit and knocked down by motorists seeking a parking spot. Such urban-style congestion has spawned urban-style solutions. For instance, at Yosemite National Park in California, a shuttle service has been put into place to transport people from their cars in parking lots outside the park (as many as 7,000 cars daily during peak season) into the park's central valley (Foster, 2001).

Figure 6.3

Campground map of the Kentucky Horse Park, Lexington, Kentucky. (http://www. kyhorsepark.com/kpp/campground/campmap.asap. Retrieved 2004)

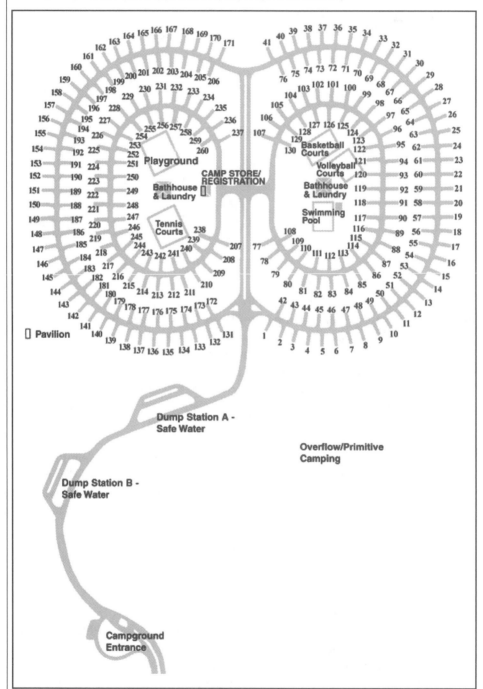

Of course, determining what is crowded is a value judgment. That is, when the number of visitors to parks (density) increases to a point where visitors and managers perceive its use is interfered with, the result is crowding. Whereas density is a neutral concept, crowding is a negative evaluation of density. For example, visitors to the Great Smoky Mountains National Park in Tennessee and North Carolina are advised how to avoid crowds by visiting during the off-season and in less popular places within the park. This advice presumes that crowded mountains are undesirable.

Researchers in outdoor recreation have studied how we determine perceptions of *crowding*. For example, studies have found perceptions of crowding can result from the personal characteristics of visitors, the characteristics of other visitors encountered, and the nature of the outdoor setting. Let's discuss each of these determinants in turn.

Crowding:
a subjective and negative judgment about the number of people in a given space

Several studies have demonstrated differences in visitor motivations are the source of perceptions of crowding. For example, a study of visitors to the Buffalo National River in Arkansas (Ditton, Fedler & Graef, 1983) found wide diversity in perceived crowding among a sample of river floaters. Those visitors who felt crowded reported significantly higher ratings on the motivation "to get away from other people." Other visitors, who did not feel crowded while floating down the river, rated the motivation "to be part of a group" higher.

In terms of the characteristics of other visitors encountered, it seems only reasonable to think that tolerance for being with lots of other people in a leisure setting would depend on what these other people were like. For example, studies in the Boundary Waters Canoe Area Wilderness found paddling canoeists sharply disliked encountering motorboats, were less resentful of encountering motorized canoes, and were relatively tolerant of at least some other paddled canoes (Manning, 1999). Thus, canoeists tolerated crowding at much lower levels when motorboats were present.

The third factor determining perceptions of crowding is situation specific. From my own interests in camping, I know I have a sliding scale for feeling crowded depending on whether I'm in a highly developed RV campground or a primitive campground reached by walking. Certain design aspects of a site, such as trees or hedges between sites, can also affect one's sense of crowding. As well, research has shown the level of disturbance of a leisure site also determines the perception of crowding. That is, those trails, campsites, and rivers trashed from overuse are perceived as more crowded (Vaske, Graef & Dempster, 1982).

Distance

In addition to crowding, distance is another application of geographic space and leisure. Are we likely to work out at the gym every day if it is across the street from our house, across town, or across the region? How fantastic does the gym need to be for us to be

Figure 6.4

Campgrounds are able to manage the perception of crowding by way of natural plantings between sites. (Shutterstock©, 2008)

willing to travel across our region to use it? Distance is important in influencing our behavior, including our leisure behavior. Notice in figure 6.5 how distance affects participation rates for different types of recreational sites.

Figure 6.5

Impact of the distance from a residence on the number of participants. (Adapted from Smale, 1999.)

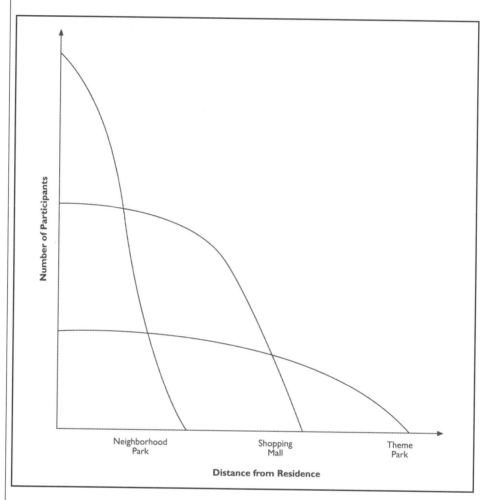

As the figure illustrates, a neighborhood park will likely attract large numbers of users from nearby, but participation drops off as distance to a shopping center or theme park increases. This means participation results from a combination of the distance from the participant's residence and the type of recreation facility. As a site's appeal becomes more specialized, smaller proportions of people are willing to travel farther distances. Geographers call this *distance decay*.

The basic principle of distance decay is different recreational sites have varying abilities to draw participants to them according to distance (Smale, 1999). But, of course, it is not always so simple. In today's world, more rapid connections among places

Distance decay: increases in distance that bring about decreases in most forms of behavior

have reduced the distance between them, not literally, of course, but in the effort needed to get there. Geographers call this *space-time compression*. Thanks to advances in transportation and communication, distant places seem less remote and more accessible to us. Thus, distances to recreational sites might be perceived in terms of time (or cost) rather than by miles or kilometers.

Space-time compression: processes that accelerate the experience of time and thus reduce the significance of distance

The basic principle of space-time compression is if the distance to a recreation site is perceived to be less (or greater) than its actual physical distance, the perception may have more influence on potential participation in the leisure pursuit than does the actual distance. Even though many recreation sites, such as parks (table 6.2) are designed according to distance from expected users, the perception of distance is what actually controls leisure behavior. For example, a park that is many miles away from potential users might be heavily used if rapid and inexpensive transportation is available to get there.

Table 6.2

Types of Parks

Park Type	Definition	Purpose	Example
Mini-park	Small - up to 1 acre.	To be within a 10-minute walk	Park Ridge Park, Bloomington, Indiana
Neighborhood park	Serves up to 5,000 people in an immediate locale.	To serve a single residential area	Huber Village Park, Westerville, Ohio
Community / City park	Serves an entire town.	To serve multiple neighborhoods	Balboa Park, San Diego, California
Regional park	Serves users from several communities and rural areas. Often governed by coalitions of governments.	To serve users from a wide area	Fort De Soto Island Park, Tampa Bay area, Florida
State / Provincial park	Serves an even broader jurisdiction, with historic or natural significance. Governed by state or provincial governments.	More remote from population centers	Amherst Shore Provincial Park, Nova Scotia
National park	An area of special scenic, historic, or scientific importance set aside and maintained by a national government.	To protect an important resource and provide enjoyment for users	Yosemite National Park, California
Linear park	Area designated for walking, biking, skiing, horseback riding, driving.	To provide for travel-related, self-propelled leisure	Cape Cod Rail Trail, Massachusetts

Leisure as Place

In addition to the importance of space, we have a strong sense of place. That is, we have feelings for particular places. The Golden Gate Bridge in San Francisco, Graceland in Memphis, Yankee Stadium in New York City, Vieux-Quebec in Quebec City, and Horseshoe Falls at Niagara are all particular places to which many people attach strong feelings:

> *Imagine red and brown sandstone towers rising out of the desert floor. Imagine the sun setting with black silhouettes of ocotillo cacti vertically slicing the horizon. This describes Juniper Canyon in Texas' Big Bend National Park, which is a special place to me.*

> (Presley, 2003, p. 22)

Box 6.2

In Your Own Experience

Campus Places

An easy demonstration of how people attach feelings to places can be made on your own campus. Interview alumni of your college or university and ask them to recall the places on campus that hold special significance to them. What is the meaning of these places to them? How did these places become meaningful for them? When they return to campus, must they always visit these places? How do these visits make them feel? After the interviews, think about your own place attachments on campus. What places will you think about after you've gone?

Box 6.3

In Profile

Yi-Fu Tuan

Until his retirement in 1998, Yi-Fu Tuan was professor of geography at the University of Wisconsin-Madison. His many essays and 10 books published over the past 30 years have been pivotal in the establishment of the discipline of human geography, and influential in such diverse fields as theater, literature, anthropology, psychology, and theology.

Yi-Fu Tuan is also probably the most idiosyncratic geographer of our time. His distinguished career has been far from awed contemplation of rocks and trees. Rather his determination to grandly describe how humans inhabit and shape the earth, not just with their bodies, but with their emotions, minds, and spirits, has rarely been attempted by others (Monaghan, 2001).

Box 6.3 (Cont.)

Born in China, by the age of 10 his father was determined to lift his family out of their food-scarce existence, and so in 1941 accepted a consular position in Australia. At 17, after a time in the Philippines and London, Mr. Tuan went to the University of Oxford and then headed to Berkeley for his graduate work before beginning his academic career at Indiana University, and later the Universities of New Mexico and Minnesota (Monaghan, 2001).

Throughout this career Yi-Fu has strained the habits of his discipline, determined to lead it toward accepting what makes the earth so much more than a physical setting for human endeavors. He wants geography to extend itself to understanding emotional,

According to eminent geographer Yi-Fu Tuan both space and place are imbued with human emotions. To distinguish, he suggests while space represents freedom to us, place is our security; we long for the one and are attached to the other. To Tuan, our sense of place is not only for obvious built environments such as neighborhoods or natural environments such as a park, but also such artifacts as fireplaces and favorite armchairs, or ships at sea. For Tuan, the most significant place for his emotions is the desert. Upon awakening on a camping trip in Death Valley, he recalls, "I awoke to lunar beauty," to "a phantasmagoria of shimmering mauves, purples, and bright golds, theatrically illuminated" (as cited in Monaghan, 2001, A14).

Smellscape: smells are place related

We are not limited only to the visual for our sense of place. The sense of smell is also important. Scholars refer to this as *smellscape*, a concept suggesting, "like visual impressions, smells may be spatially ordered or place related" (Porteous, 1985, p. 359). Smells give character to places, making them distinctive and thus easier to identify and remember (Tuan, 1977). Think of the community gym you knew as a youth. Do you associate this memory with a smell?

There is perhaps no better illustration of smellscape than its calculated management at the Magic Kingdom in Disney theme parks. Frontierland smells like leather and gun smoke and the attraction *Pirates of the Caribbean* smells of musty spices—all this in an effort to enhance visitors' experiences. Indeed, many promoters of tourism fill their marketing with the aromatic framing of places, such as an

Figure 6.6

We have created parks and gardens reflecting our natural preference for open vistas, with meadows punctuated by trees, bushes, and meandering streams. (Shutterstock©, 2008)

advertisement for a suite in Los Angeles' Hotel Bel Air describing "a fire roaring with scented avocado wood, and the French windows open onto a private herb garden" (Mather, 2001, p. 1).

This is a tricky subject to discuss, of course, because just as beauty is in the eye of the beholder, so too are aromas. Nonetheless, a study by Dann and Jacobsen (2003) examined the association of smell with tourist sites by studying classical and contemporary travel diaries and essays. In all, they analyzed 65 accounts, 20 that referred to rural settings and 45 that described urban settings. The findings suggested a definite trend toward romantically portraying the countryside as smelling more pleasurable than the city.

In addition to sight and smell, our emotional attachment to specific places is based on a kinesthetic sense. For example, the vast number of mountain resorts is testimony to the fact that many of us feel emotionally elevated at moderately high altitudes —a kind of mountain high. When you ask people who love mountains to explain what is so special there, the reply is likely to be "just something in the air." This is perhaps why we associate certain spiritual practices, such as meditation, with high mountains.

Some intriguing studies have been reported explaining our preferences in nature according to our evolution as human beings. For example, findings maintain during our long evolution as hunters and gatherers on the East African savannah, we developed a preference for that kind of terrain. We therefore like natural scenes with a meandering creek and a thundering waterfall; we prefer open vistas, such as a meadow punctuated by trees and bushes (Orians, 1986). Sure enough, around the world people have created open parkland and gardens reflecting this same sensibility.

So, we do have places that are special to us, and perhaps it is this association with a particular place that is so vital to leisure's geography. In studying the role of place in leisure, two primary concepts are place attachment and place identity. Let's explore both of these.

Place Attachment

The concept of *place attachment* holds that people bond with places. Some writers refer to this as "sense of place," "rootedness," or "insideness," yet many

Place attachment:

an emotional bond between a person and a certain place

agree it is the natural environment that is most likely associated with our emotional attachments to place (Kyle, Mowen, & Tarrant, 2004). To understand this, researchers have begun to investigate the complex and differing meanings recreation participants attach to outdoor recreation sites.

For example, Bricker and Kerstetter (2000) investigated how place attachment varied with levels of specialization among whitewater boaters. They found more specialized whitewater boaters had stronger place attachments. Why is this so? A later study by Bricker and Kerstetter (2002) concluded whitewater river place meanings included repose, peace, beauty, wildness, an appreciation of nature, reverence, and a need to protect the river—ideas perhaps only possible after intense and long-term experiences with the river.

What causes place attachment? Studies have shown the development of place attachment is influenced by a number of factors. For example, several scholars

The Study Says

Place Attachment and Fishing

Many things affect how recreationists choose sites for their pastimes. One study investigated place attachment as a factor as applied to fishing on Thunder Bay in Northern Ontario. Anglers (N = 142) kept diaries for five months as they fished their favorite fishing areas. The diaries included a total of 845 fishing trips, or an average of 5.9 trips per angler. Results indicated anglers take many more trips to the same fishing sites than expected by chance and also that anglers take their fishing trips in closer proximity to past trips than expected by chance. Thus, the investigator concluded anglers view themselves as dependent on a specific fishing area.

Hunt, L.M. (2008). Examining state dependence and place attachment within a recreational fishing site choice model. *Journal of Leisure Research, 40*(1), 110-127.

suggest place bonds develop over time in response to individual interactions with a place (Milligan, 1998). As well, other writings have illustrated that memories of these individual interactions contribute to place bonding (Vorkinn & Riese, 2001). Finally, studies imply social ties with significant others within an environment help develop attachments to it (Uzzell, Pol & Badenas, 2002). Thus, it seems our memories of individual interactions with a place along with other people who are important to us, creates place attachment.

Of course there are differences in the reasons we become emotionally attached to particular places. Different people and cultures prioritize place meanings differently. For example, white Americans attach the highest priority to an individually expressive meaning of place, followed by an instrumental goal-directed meaning, and then a cultural symbolic meaning. For many Native Americans the priority given to the meaning of a place is just the opposite, with a cultural symbolic meaning first and an individually expressive meaning last (McAvoy, 2002).

These differences in the meanings applied to places help explain why there are conflicts over places. Different users of a recreation facility or resource hold different reasons for appreciating it. This helps us understand, for example, why cross-country skiers and snowmobilers often are at odds when trying to share the same trails. Recently, this realization has been useful to natural resource managers, who, by helping competing users of a resource negotiate and appreciate each others' place attachments, can promote a sharing of the contested landscape (Clark & Stein, 2003).

Box 6.5

In Profile

The Motor Home

It is hard to say exactly when the motor home began. In the 1880s a horse-drawn replica Gypsy wagon was a favorite vacation vehicle in England. Americans did not own camping vehicles in large numbers, however, until automobiles were mass-produced in the early 20th century. By 1920 millions of campers were sleeping in cars or in tents attached to their cars, and hundreds had purchased trailers with built-in folding tents.

Hundreds more built wooden house bodies and placed them on an automobile chassis. Called a "housecar," they offered a portable parlor and bedroom, and a picture window on America. But it wasn't until the 1960s that Americans chose factory-built motor homes. Nationwide sales of housecars began when a small manufacturer of house bodies in Michigan linked up with the Dodge Division of Chrysler Corporation to manufacture the Frank Motor Home. It sold for $7,000.

Since then, with Winnebago in the lead, between 1961 and 1973 output soared from 200 to 65,300 motor homes per year. In 1992 Winnebago rolled out its 250,000th motor home, and today, with 87 different floor plans, Winnebago has come to symbolize and reaffirm the conflicted American identity of both staying home and wandering away (White, 2000).

Figure 6.7

Mr. and Mrs. Kinnear with their housecar, Yellowstone National Park, 1925. (Courtesy of Yellowstone National Park, National Park Service Historic Photograph Collection.)

Place Identity

In fact, people value their relationships to places just as much as they might value their relationships with other people. In applying this to leisure places, and according to Williams (2002), "we choose leisure places not merely because they are useful for leisure, but to convey the very sense of who we are" (p. 353). So, we might consider place identity as a specific case of place attachment.

As we've explored in earlier chapters, leisure provides opportunities for people to create and develop personal and group identities. In leisure in particular, place meanings help translate individual values. This is the concept of *place identity*. Leisure places have meaning to us because of who they affirm us to be: "I'm a mountain person" or "Only a Winnebago for me."

Place identity:
a place provides the source of self-identification for a person

Box 6.6

City as Theme Park

As the leading purely tourist destination on the planet, welcoming close to 30 million guests a year who spend nearly $31 billion, Disney World in Orlando, Florida is the world's utopia of leisure. But, the empire of Disney transcends the actual physical sites; its aura is all-pervasive (Sorkin, 1992). It is literally a place maker. Beginning with Disneyland in Anaheim, California and also spreading to Tokyo Disneyland and Euro Disneyland in France, Disney World's place power has also spread to urban design. And, architect Michael Sorkin considers this a bad thing.

America's cities, according to Sorkin (1992), are being rapidly transformed by a sinister and homogenous design that is manipulative, dispersed, and hostile to traditional uses of public space. The evidence is in megamalls, hermetically sealed atrium hotels, corporate enclaves, gentrified community zones, and pseudo-historic marketplaces. Like a theme park, these apparently benign public places, in which all is structured to achieve maximum control of people, dictate via pedestrian and vehicular traffic flow design, the juxtaposition of commerce and housing, and a false fantasy of pleasure.

As in the Disney theme parks, for example, downtown Atlanta and the Opus office complex in Minneapolis are sited for convenient access by commuters. Radiating from a strong center—occupied by the castle of fantasy—the design is arranged in thematic regions (like Tomorrowland, Frontierland, etc.), which flow into one another. While the inside is designed for pedestrian circulation, the perimeters are the domain of transportation systems: trains, cars, monorails. In fact it is this keep-them-moving idea that, Sorkin argues, is the centerpiece of the design's control over people. We are in constant movement to get there, through there, and out. There is no option to linger and enjoy.

Box 6.6 (Cont.)

Questions to Consider and Discuss

1. What is your initial reaction to Sorkin's critique? Can you think of any places near you that might fit his description of "city as theme park"?
2. In his book of essays on the topic, writers illustrate this critique in such actual locales as Silicon Valley, South Street Seaport in New York City, downtown Los Angeles, the West Edmonton Mall in Canada, and the skyways of Minneapolis. Do some investigation of one or some of these destinations to test Sorkin's critique? What do you conclude?
3. Have urban designs based on leisure characteristics become a problem? What are some of the advantages? The disadvantages? What is your conclusion?

Indeed, some scholars argue that because of the process of modernization in society, leisure places have become an increasingly important source of our identity. As modernity sweeps away tradition, our sense of self is no longer passively awarded to us by our original homes and neighborhoods. No longer do things automatically stay the same from generation to generation, where hometowns create and anchor our sense of identity.

As Godbey (2003) declared, while we have become nomads, we still need a sense of self that is associated with a place. Perhaps leisure places provide for this. Perhaps this is what youth are seeking when they hang out at the mall, or what explains the allure of leisure-based villages for retirees, or why the neighborhood sports bar is "home" for many.

Table 6.3

Sailboats Versus Power Boats in Canada

Type of Boat	Estimated Number of Boats	Fuel Consumed Per Boat (liters)	Total Fuel Consumed (liters, in millions)	
			Diesel	Gasoline
Sailboats	124,000	80.7	3.6	6.4
Motor boats	693,500	1,373.90	77.8	875.0

Environment Canada (1996). The State of Canada's Environment – 1996. Available from http://www.ec.gc.ca/soer-ree/English/SOER/1996report/Doc. Retrieved 4/24/08.

Oldenburg (1989) calls these the "great good places." Accordingly, these great good places represent "third places," a term he uses to describe the many public places that host "regular, voluntary, informal, and happily anticipated gatherings of individuals" (p. 16) beyond the home (the first place) and work and school (the second place). Third places may take many forms, such as cafes, coffee shops, bars, beauty shops, community centers, and street-corner hangouts. Oldenburg sees them as providing identity. That is, the third place provides an accessible, socially neutral ground that encourages a playful mood for regulars to engage in their main activity: conversation (Wenner, 1998).

Environmental Impact

Growth in especially outdoor recreation and tourism has fueled global concern for a special case of leisure's geography, namely, pressures on the environment. For example, scientists at Breda University of Professional Education in the Netherlands (Peeters, 2005) estimate greenhouse gas emissions from tourism transportation will increase from 33% of the total in 2000 to 44% by 2020. But, there's more. Ecological threats from mass tourism also lie in the sprawl development of resorts, consumption of fuel by buildings, overuse of local water resources, extra sewage and litter, and other often irreversible environmental degradation.

As well, outdoor sports that may seem environmentally friendly require considerable outfitting in clothing and equipment and use often more fragile natural resources, such as the land for ski areas and golf courses. The chlorofluorocarbons (CFCs) often used in the refrigeration systems of indoor skating rinks, the chemicals needed to purify the water in swimming pools, and the emissions and spills from powered equipment such as snowmobiles and jet skis also represent environmental health threats.

In Canada, for example, the impact of human use on the country's most visited national park, Banff, has been the focus of particular attention. Park officials have called for a re-greening of national parks; that is, their reinstatement as models of ecological harmony (Sellers, 1997). In many respects, the future of leisure depends on such efforts. With the destruction of soil, water, forest, energy, and animal resources, many pastimes would no longer be possible.

At the root of the solution are the concepts of conservation and preservation. *Conservation* involves the scientific and rational planning of natural resources for their best use. Conservation implies the renewal of resources as they become damaged. In contrast, the *preservation* of natural resources means they are protected from human influence. Preservation applies mainly to nonrenewable resources. For example, whereas conservation refers to managing deer populations through hunting, preservation is keeping recreationists out of bald eagle habitat completely.

Conservation: efficient use of natural resources over long term

Preservation: protection of natural resources from human damage

Many management strategies are available to achieve both the conservation and preservation of natural resources for and from leisure. These include multiple use, dispersed use, single use, carrying capacity, and wilderness designation (Jensen, 1995).

The idea of multiple use encourages managers to make resources in a region available for a variety of uses, such as using land and water for timbering, watershed protection, as well as outdoor recreation. In contrast, the idea of single use stipulates some resources have restricted use, such as in a national park where historical, archaeological, cultural, and scenic features are managed solely for the enjoyment of people.

The concept of dispersed use encourages spreading out the use of a particular area over a wide swath, rather than concentrating it in a particular area. For example, a deer herd habitat that extends over an entire region also disperses hunting activities. Determinations of carrying capacity have also been a useful management strategy for outdoor recreation. Accordingly, standards are determined for the saturation point for the impact of people on soil compaction, altered stream flows, and the destruction of vegetation.

Figure 6.8

Backroads is an adventure travel company offering luxury accommodations, fine dining, and tours to some of the world's most beautiful regions. But what makes Backroads special is its attention to sustainable tourism. Small groups of tourists travel to their destinations via their own efforts—walking, biking, and kayaking. They abide by the "leave no trace" philosophy and directly support the wildlife and natural resources of the areas visited. (Courtesy of Backroads.)

Finally, conservation and preservation can be achieved through the establishment of wilderness areas. A wilderness designation can apply to desert, forest, water, and coastal resources. The point is that minimal human intervention is allowed. In the United States, with the passing of the 1964 Wilderness Act, areas legally classified as wilderness prohibit motorized equipment, signage, built recreation facilities, and commercial use.

One of the best illustrations of the usefulness of these conservation and preservation measures is *sustainable tourism*. Sustainable tourism implies not consuming natural resources at a higher rate than they can be protected or replaced. Mass tourism, for example, is usually not sustainable. Sustainable tourism promotes low-impact forms, including small tour groups and low energy-consuming modes of transportation.

Sustainable tourism: controlling visitation to tourist sites so that impacts are neither permanent nor irreversible

What We Understand About Leisure's Geographical Significance

From the perspective of geography, leisure can be understood as having meaning in space and place. As a result of reading this chapter, you should know that:

- The distribution of leisure in space differs according to density, concentration, and pattern.
- Crowding in leisure is a contemporary problem of density.
- Distance is a concentration and pattern phenomenon that affects participation rates for different types of leisure sites.
- Attaching strong sentiment to leisure places comes from our visual, olfactory, and kinesthetic senses.
- Strong leisure place attachments contribute to our self-identity.
- Considerable attention must be applied to the conservation and preservation of leisure resources.

References

Bricker, K.S., & Kerstetter, D.L. (2000). Level of specialization and place attachment: An exploratory study of whitewater recreationists. *Leisure Sciences, 22,* 233-257.

Bricker, K.S., & Kerstetter, D.L. (2002). An interpretation of special place meanings whitewater recreationists attach to the South Fork of the American River. *Tourism Geographies, 4,* 396-425.

Clark, J.K., & Stein, T.V. (2003). Incorporating the natural landscape within an assessment of community attachment. *Forest Science, 49,* 867-876.

Dann, G.M.S., & Jacobsen, J.K.S. (2003).Tourism smellscapes. *Tourism Geographies, 5,* 3-25.

Davidoff, P.G., Davidoff, D.S., & Eyre, J.D. (1988). *Tourism geography*. Englewood Cliffs, NJ: Prentice Hall.

Ditton, R.B., Fedler, A.J, & Graef, A.R. (1983). Factors contributing to perceptions of recreational crowding. *Leisure Sciences, 5*, 273-288.

Foster, G. (May 29, 2001). Park ranger now "parking ranger." *Seattle Post-Intelligencer*. Available from http://seattlepi.nwsource.com/local/25049_parks29.shtml. Retrieved 2/16/04.

Godbey, G. (2003). *Leisure in your life: An exploration (6th edition)*. State College, PA: Venture.

Henderson, K.A., Bialeschki, M.D., Shaw, S.M., & Freysinger, V.J. (1996). *Both gains and gaps: Feminist perspectives on women's leisure*. State College, PA: Venture.

Kyle, G.T., Mowen, A.J., & Tarrant, M. (2004). Linking place preferences with place meaning: An examination of the relationship between place motivation and place attachment. *Journal of Environmental Psychology, 24*, 439-454.

Jensen, C.R. (1995). *Outdoor recreation in America*. Champaign, IL: Human Kinetics.

Lime, D.W. (Ed.). (1996). Congestion and crowding in the national park system. *Minnesota Agricultural Experiment Station Miscellaneous Publication 86-1996*. St. Paul: University of Minnesota.

Manning, R.E. (1999). Crowding and carrying capacity in outdoor recreation: From normative standards to standards of quality. In E.L. Jackson, & T.L. Burton (Eds.), *Leisure studies: Prospects for the Twenty-first Century*. State College, PA: Venture.

Mather, V. (December 9, 2001). Heaven on earth. *Sunday Telegraph Travel*, pp. 1-2.

McAvoy, L. (2002). American Indians, place meanings and the old/new West. *Journal of Leisure Research, 34*, 383-396.

Milligan, M.J. (1998). Interactional past and potential: The social construction of place attachment. *Symbolic Interaction, 21*, 1-33.

Monaghan, P. (March 16, 2001). Lost in Place: Yi-Fu Tuan may be the most influential scholar you've never heard of. *The Chronicle of Higher Education, 47*(27), A14.

Oldenburg, R. (1989). *The great good place: Cafes, coffee shops, community centers, beauty parlors, general stores, bars, hangouts, and how they get you through the day*. New York: Paragon House.

Orians, G.H. (1986). An ecological and evolutionary approach to landscape aesthetics. In P. Rousell, & D. Lowenthal (Eds.), *Landscape meanings and values*. London: Allen & Unwin.

Peeters, P. (2005). Climate change, leisure-related tourism and global transport. In C.M. Hall, & J. Higham (Eds.), *Tourism, recreation and climate change*. Clevedon, UK: Channel View Publications.

Porteous, J. (1985). Smellscape. *Progress in Human Geography, 9*, 356-378.

Presley, J. (July 2003). In praise of special places. *Parks & Recreation*, 22-29.

Rubenstein, J.M. (2003). *The cultural landscape: An introduction to human geography*. Upper Saddle River, NJ: Pearson Education.

Sellers, R.W. (1997). *Preserving nature in the national parks: A history*. New Haven, CT: Yale University Press.

Smale, B.J.A. (1999). Spatial analysis of leisure and recreation. In E.L. Jackson, & T.L. Burton (Eds.*), Leisure studies: Prospects for the Twenty-first Century*. State College, PA: Venture.

Sorkin, M. (1992). *Variations on a theme park: The new American city and the end of public space*. New York: Hill and Wang.

Tuan, Y. (1977). *Space and place: The perspective of experience*. Minneapolis, MN: University of Minnesota Press.

U.S. Census Bureau (2007). Table 1239. *Statistical Abstract of the United States: 2007*. Washington, D.C.: U.S. Government Printing Office.

Uzzell, D., Pol, E., & Badenas, D. (2002). Place identification, social cohesion, and environmental sustainability. *Environment and Behavior, 34*, 26-53.

Vaske, J.J., Graef, A.R., & Dempster, A. (1982). Social and environmental influences on perceived crowding. In *Proceedings of the Wilderness Psychology Group Conference* (pp. 35-41), Morgantown: West Virginia University.

Vorkinn, M., & Riese, H. (2001). Environmental concern in a local context: The significance of place attachment. *Environment and Behavior, 33*, 249-263.

Wenner, L.A. (1998). In search of the sports bar: Masculinity, alcohol, sports, and the mediation of public space. In G. Rail (Ed.), *Sport and postmodern times* (pp. 210-231). Albany: State University of New York Press.

White, R. (2000). *Home on the road: The motor home in America*. Washington, D.C.: Smithsonian Institution Press.

Williams, D.R. (2002). Leisure identities, globalization, and the politics of place. *Journal of Leisure Research, 34*, 351-367.

TECHNOLOGY ASSISTED LEISURE

PREVIEW

Is technology important to leisure?
Absolutely! And its importance is increasing exponentially.

In what ways is technology important to leisure?
Technology has both enhanced traditional pastimes and invented completely new ones.

Has technology been good for leisure?
The role of technology in leisure has received both accolades and criticisms. The answer most likely lies in individual values.

KEY TERMS

From the invention of the wheel in ancient cultures to the perfection of robotics today, technology *has always affected leisure.* For example, in ancient Persia (now Iran) trick vessels were popular. To amuse dinner guests there were pitchers from which pouring could not resume after it had been interrupted even though the vessel still contained liquid. Inventions such as conical valves, siphons, balances, pulleys, gears, floats and cranks made them work. In the 1830s, the vulcanization of rubber by Charles Goodyear led to the development of elastic and resilient rubber balls for tennis and golf. And, over the past 25 years technology has helped spur a tripling in the number of people who sport fish, as the invention of fiberglass rods made it possible for amateurs to match professionals (Hammel & Foster, 1986).

Technology:
how people modify the natural world to suit their own purpose

Just as the technological development of the television and computer clearly changed people's leisure in the past, technology continues to create entirely new kinds of play possibilities. Thanks to technology, we can ice skate year-round, our bowling pins are automatically reset, snow is manufactured and blown onto our ski slopes, and we can see every player's hand in televised poker tournaments. How could we go for a walk without our iPod?

Advances in technology have given people physically and virtually innovative places to play, better equipment and clothing to aid their adventures, and new activities to pursue. The influences of technology in our pastimes also include access to information about leisure options, new horizons in leisure for people with disabilities, and tourism as an easy and global enterprise. The efficiencies of technology have also been a boon to professionals working in the leisure fields.

Information Technology (IT) Revolution:
the rapid changes brought about by all forms of technology used to create, store, exchange, and use information

Even though technology has changed our lives for thousands of years, many consider the rapid changes brought about today by particularly information technology to signify a revolution. The *Information Technology (IT) Revolution* is probably the most important force shaping communities and individuals today. For some this drastic and far-reaching change in ways of thinking and behaving is considered to be total—affecting all aspects of our lives. Whereas the Industrial Revolution was slower and localized, the IT Revolution is faster and global (Castells, 2000, p. 30).

Figure 7.1

Information technology is pervasive in every aspect of our lives.
(Shutterstock©, 2008)

And, the prospects for the future of this revolution are even more exciting, as predictions for the next quarter-century suggest the fastest technological change the world has ever known (Forrester, 2004). In fact, some observers consider the leisure fields to be among the first to be affected by technological change. One day soon you could be participating in plane zorbing (jumping out of airplanes in an inflatable), playing a hologram version of your opponent in a web game, and visiting an earth-orbiting resort.

In this chapter we first discuss examples of leisure that are invented, assisted, and changed by technology. Then, we debate the issues surrounding technology's impact on our leisure and thus our lives.

Technology Assisted Leisure (TAL)

We begin with a consideration of leisure that has been assisted, improved, expanded, or invented by technology. The distinctions are blurry, however. Technology Assisted Leisure (TAL) could include just about all leisure as examples. So pervasive has technology been in leisure in most societies, that even a presentation about such long-standing pastimes as stamp collecting or knitting would include revelations on how technology has affected them. In this section of the chapter we overview computer and video games, artificial surfaces and equipment, simulated leisure, and social networking as examples.

Box 7.1

In Your Own Experience

Geocaching

Geocaching is an outdoor treasure-hunting game for global positioning system (GPS) users. In a traditional geocache, a geocacher will place a waterproof container housing a log book with pen or pencil and trinkets or some sort of treasures, then post the cache's coordinates on a website. Other geocachers obtain the coordinates from the web site and seek out the cache using their GPS handheld receivers. The rules stipulate when you take something from a cache, you also leave something for the next person to find. Today, well over 800,000 geocaches placed in over 100 countries, and all seven continents, are registered on various websites.

Here's how to get started.
1. Buy a GPS unit. About the size of a bulky cell phone, and at a cost of around $100, you'll find these at stores selling outdoor gear.

2. Look up nearby caches. Visit www.geocaching.com, sign up for a free account, and type in a ZIP code. The site will list all nearby caches.

3. Enter the coordinates. Choose caches to look for then enter their latitude and longitude coordinates into your GPS unit.

4. Go find them. Drive as close as you want to the cache, then get out, turn on your GPS and follow the arrow.

Computer and video games have been part of leisure for over 30 years (Bryce & Rutter, 2003). The black-and-white block graphics of the tennis game Pong first made their way onto people's television screens in the mid-1970s, and since then their popularity has created an industry projected to be worth $22.1 billion by 2011 (Business Communications Company, 2006).

In common usage computer / video games refer to a media form involving a player interacting with a personal computer connected to a video monitor. There are various platforms supporting these games, including console games played on specialized electronic devices connected to a television set, handheld gaming devices that are self-contained, arcade games, and devices with screens not dedicated to video playing, such as mobile phones, PDAs, MP3 players, watches, and digital cameras. Most video games are meant for entertainment, however other types are represented, such as educational games and training games. Regardless, video games are a pervasive and significant form of expression in today's culture (Jones, 2008).

Surveys of regular users (cf. Nielsen Entertainment, 2006) indicate the U.S. video games market is diversifying. These games are no longer only for young males. For example, the age group among male players has expanded significantly into the 25-40 ages, and for casual online puzzle-style and simple cell phone games, the gender divide is about equal. As well, females are now more significantly attracted to playing certain online multi-user video games that offer a more sociable experience.

In fact, video gaming has traditionally been a social experience. From its early beginnings these games have typically been playable by more than one person. Today multiplayer video games can be played either competitively or cooperatively by using either multiple input devices on the computer or via the Internet, such as MMOs (massively multiplayer online games). MMOs are receiving increasingly enthusiastic participation as they can support extremely high numbers of simultaneous players. For example, EVEonline (a role-playing space game) hosted over 42,000 players on a single server one March evening in 2008 (EVEonline, 2008).

As you know, computer and video games have always been the subject of frequent controversy, especially due to the depiction of graphic violence, sexual themes, the consumption of drugs and alcohol, profanity, and advertising and propagandizing in some games. Critics include parents' associations, politicians, organized religious groups, and other special interest organizations. Even though all of these characteristics can be found in other forms of entertainment and media as well, particular video games have been accused of "causing" addiction and violent behavior.

This is the conclusion drawn from a summary examination (called a meta-analysis) of 32 independent samples involving 5,240 research participants (Anderson, 2004). Based on experimental studies investigating violent video game effects, results for the variables of aggressive behavior, aggressive thoughts, aggressive feelings, helping behavior, and physiological arousal were summarized. The analysis revealed exposure to violent video games is significantly linked to increases in aggressive behavior, aggressive thoughts, aggressive feelings, and cardiovascular arousal, and decreases in helping behavior.

Another category of examples of Technology Assisted Leisure (TAL) is artificial and "smart" leisure surfaces, equipment, and clothing. We use technology to make our equipment stronger and lighter, our playing surfaces more dependable, and our clothing warmer or cooler. We use sonar to locate fish, we fall off the playground equipment onto soft rubber, and we can lay a patch of artificial grass in our living room to practice our golf putt. Night vision goggles enable us to hunt at night. Without the trouble of traveling we can stay at Gaylord Palms Hotel in Orlando, under a biosphrere-type dome, and experience Florida's St.

Box 7.2

 *In Focus*

The Video Games Debate

Eleven-year-old Randy locked his eyes on the target, and with arms straight and steady, raised the gun and fired. His victim screamed and staggered to the ground, but he wasn't dead. The bullet had only grazed his arm. As he was trying to crawl to safety, Randy finished him off with a single bullet to the head. While the victim's body bled and convulsed, Randy had already shifted his attention to a new threat entering through the doorway. Randy has been shooting people for the past two years.

There are arguments on both sides about video games. Some can be contrasted as a debate of pros and cons:

Pros	Cons
The games are entertaining. As a form of multimedia entertainment, video games contain a unique synthesis of 3D art, sound effects, dramatic performances, music, and storytelling. At least they're better than staring at the TV.	**Too much entertainment is bad for us. A lot of things are more entertaining than TV**. Further, like TV and other forms of passive entertainment, video games promote inactivity. People sit for long periods of time, and in one position, thus there is a potential for long-term obesity. Exceptions are fitness video games (i.e.Wii) that have the user perform lower-body balance and weight-shifting activities.
They develop good visual-motor skills. This includes good eye-hand coordination both because of the requirement of responding quickly and the use of peripheral vision. Also the games help develop a greater attention span and resistance to distractions.	**They develop physical ailments and complaints**. Doctors have found the possibility of eye strains, as well as wrist, neck and back pain to frequent gamers. Photosensitive epilepsy, headaches, hallucinations, and nerve and muscle damage have also been reported.
The games encourage social interactions. All games are playable for two or more people. In particular, MMOs encourage socializing among thousands of people world-wide.	**The social interaction is shallow**. In particular those games played with virtual others, studies have shown participants are less engaged and less sincere with the virtual human. This likely comes from the virtual human's limited expressive behavior. In all forms of video games the level of social interaction communicates lower interest and empathy for others.

Box 7.2 (Cont.)

They are intellectually demanding. Video games are based on the player navigating (and eventually mastering) a highly complex system with many variables. This requires a strong analytical ability, as well as flexibility and adaptability.

The abilities needed for life are not as simple. Even though the games have demonstrated the potential for developing good spatial analytical skills, they are not a good replacement for the wide range of intellectual development afforded by reading, writing, conversation, and puzzles. For one, the games greatly misrepresent problem solving as simply triggering a lever.

The games are a safe form of fantasy. The interactivity in the games enables players to explore environments that range from simulated reality to stylized, artistic expressions where the actions of the player will play out a slightly different way every time. Even if the game is highly scripted, this can still feel like a large amount of freedom to the person who is playing the game.

Too much fantasy blurs reality. When your life revolves around fantasy, it becomes reality in your eyes. This of course refers to school shootings, inappropriate sexual conduct, and aggression in general that have been blamed on video games. Instead of encouraging mature behavior, video games cause children to lash out at their problems instead of handling them properly.

Questions to Consider and Discuss

1. Which side of the debate do you think wins? What do your classmates think? Why do you support the side you chose?
2. Do some library and Internet investigations to locate research articles on video games. What evidence do these studies offer in support of either the pros or cons of the debate?
3. Take a field trip to your local toy and/or computer store. As you study the kinds of video games available, how would you characterize their play value? Are there games that go beyond blasting and zapping moving targets? Are there games designed to encourage cooperative play? How would you characterize the gaming market these days?

Augustine, Key West, and Everglades swamp. Indeed, one of the fastest growing leisure pursuits is indoor rock climbing on artificial walls (Kalaygian, 2002). Available to us now are wallets that beep whenever a plastic card is removed and continue to beep every 20 seconds to remind us to replace it. There are clothing lines (i.e., the SmartShirt) that are not only fashionable and comfortable, but also provide a constant monitoring of heart rate, respiration, and body temperature.

The technology that is enabling much of this is called *nanotechnology*. In manufacturing it involves developing materials at the atomic and molecular level, giving them special electrical and chemical properties. Since nanotechnology can make most products lighter, stronger, cleaner, less expensive, and more precise, in leisure its greatest impact is expected in the areas of sport and outdoor recreation.

Nanotechnology:
a field of applied science involving the control of matter on the atomic and molecular level

There are, of course, worries about this application of technology. Some of the recently developed nanoparticle products may have unintended consequences. For example, researchers have discovered the nanoparticles used in socks to reduce foot odor are being released in the wash, and possibly into the environment as solid waste (Lubick, 2008). Other unintended complications arise when considering the use of such artificial products as prosthetic legs that enable faster performance in track and distance running competition. In the 2008 Olympic Games in Beijing swimsuits with ultrasonically bonded seams fit swimmers like a true second skin. With low-drag panels embedded within the fabric, the design also led to a controversy over whether the mix of polyurethane layers enabled illegal levels of buoyancy. Performance enhancement, legal or illegal, already is no longer limited to doping. For instance, laser surgical procedures to improve eyesight are common among top athletes.

This brings us to another area of leisure assisted by technology: *simulated leisure* experiences. Not only are leisure settings and equipment being simulated, but also leisure activities themselves. Leisure experiences, in fact, are being simulated at an unprecedented rate (Priest & Gass, 2000). There are numerous examples of this. For example, the attraction *Mission:*

Figure 7.2

Stone Age Climbing Gym, Albuquerque, New Mexico. (© Eric Hewitt Photo, 2008, used with permission)

Simulated leisure: an imitation of the reality of leisure expressions

Box 7.3

In Your Own Experience

Let's Ride Some Thrill Rides

Go to the Internet and visit sites that have simulated experiences available. For example, you could visit Cedar Point Amusement Park in Sandusky, Ohio, by going to http://www.cedarpoint.com. You can "ride" some of the roller coasters, including Top Thrill Dragster. Or ride The Giant Dipper at http://www.beachboardwalk.com/03_giant_dipper_ride.html. Or, check out some virtual attractions at theme parks. For example, go to Epcot at Walt Disney World (http://disneyworld.disney.go.com/wdw/parks/parkLanding?id=EPLandingPage) Check out the attractions Sourin and Mission:SPACE. Afterward, reflect on what kind of fun you had in these simulated leisure experiences. Is the nature of this fun any different from actually riding a roller coaster, hang gliding, or going into outer space? How or how not?

SPACE at Epcot in Walt Disney World in Florida promotes "as close as you can get to blasting off into space without leaving earth."

Virtually you can play baseball, swim with dolphins, golf, ride roller coasters, and hang glide. Some leisure scholars envision a day when technology will allow the simulation of any human experience (Forrester, 2004). One of the major questions about simulated leisure experience, however, is what is called *fidelity*. How authentic is the simulation compared with the "natural" or original activity? For example, when playing a game of simulated golf at your neighborhood pub, are your actions, thoughts, and attitudes the same as when you are outside at a real course?

Fidelity:

in simulated leisure, refers to the accuracy of reproducing of the expereince

In studies investigating this question, simulated golfers have agreed the simulator did not reproduce a very realistic experience when compared with outdoor golf (Beggs, 2002; Forrester, 2004). Everything, from the teeing and putting surfaces, to the screen images, to the portrayal of shots on the screen, to how people choose to play certain shots, to what they wear and what they do between shots combine to produce a very low-fidelity experience. Other simulated pursuits, such as roller coaster rides, seem to have higher fidelity.

Of course, as with all matters of technology, simulated leisure has its critics, and this question of fidelity is at the heart of it. Most likely it is an individual

Box 7.4

 The Study Says

The Experience of Apathy in Simulated Leisure

To measure fidelity in simulated leisure, two simulated leisure experiences were chosen for this study: an indoor golf simulator and an indoor rock-climbing wall. Data were collected by analyzing operations and policies documents, observing people participating, and group and individual interviews. Results indicated overall participants experienced a less challenging, easier leisure activity in the simulated situation. In particular, the simulated leisure experience produced a more static episode in which participants were more apathetic. Several of the qualities producing this apathy were analyzed to include little anticipation or build-up for the experience (lack of experiencing the height, the scenery and camaraderie with other people as in outdoor rock climbing), and instant feedback and gratification (instantaneous results for golf shots posted on a diagnostics screen).

Forrester, S.A., Russell, R.V., & Ross, C. (May 2005). The experience of apathy in simulated leisure environments. Paper presented at the Eleventh Canadian Congress on Leisure Research. Malaspina University-College, Nanaimo, BC.

question of values and preferences. For example, which would you rather see, a robotic crocodile at Disneyland or a real crocodile in the River Gambia? The Disney version rolls its eyes, moves from side to side, and disappears beneath the water surface just like a real crocodile, which actually also spends most of its time sleeping. Some of you may prefer the Disney crocodile because it's easier to get to Disneyland than to Africa, but others of you may prefer the crocodile in the River Gambia, primarily because it is harder to get to.

This example also points to another criticism of simulated leisure, which is that the fake sometimes seems more compelling than the real. That is, Disney's crocodile might seem a more fulfilling experience because you are able to experience its full range of behaviors. As overheard at the Brooklyn Botanical Gardens, a child asked the attendant to make the flowers open fast—just as she'd seen in the time-lapse photography of Disney films (Turkle, 2004, p. 373).

A final example of technology's application to leisure is *social networking*. Within recent years services available via the Internet have become popular ways for people who share interests to get together. Users can join networks organized by locale, workplace, profession, school, and specific hobbies to connect and interact with other people via chat rooms, messaging, email, video, voice chat, file sharing, blogging, and discussion groups.

Social networking: linking people to each other in some way

For example, millions of people worldwide use more than 125 online network services everyday. Popular sites in North America include MySpace (110 million registered users) and Facebook (80 million registered users), which primarily use self-description pages. Bebo, MySpace, Skyrock Blog, Facebook and Hi5 are widely used in Europe, while Orkut and Hi5 are popular in South America and Central America. Frienster and Orkut are widely used in Asia and the Pacific Islands.

In fact, these social network sites have revolutionized the way we communicate and share information with one another in today's society. For example, Facebook has been named the second most popular thing among North American undergraduate college students, tied with beer and only ranked lower than the iPod (Associated Press, 2006). As you can imagine, this has resulted in an increasing number of academic researchers interested in studying social networking technology applications.

Typically, studies have examined such worrisome online social networking issues as identity, privacy, and predators. From a leisure perspective, however, other studies focused on the concept and experience of friendship. For example, a study by Golder, Wilkinson, and Huberman (2006) examined the patterns among 362 million messages and "pokes" sent by 4.2 million college student Facebook users. Among the findings were that messages are mostly sent to friends, but most friends do not receive messages, suggesting it's easier to have lots of friends than lots of message partners. The researchers explained this as it still requires an investment of time and energy to keep friendships going.

Box 7.5

 *In Profile*

Most Unwanted Inventions

Marilyn vos Savant writes the popular newspaper column, "Ask Marilyn" and in 2007 she asked readers what item they would most like to uninvent. About 2,000 wrote in and here are the top 10 most unwanted inventions:

1. High heels
2. Jet skis
3. Leaf-blowers
4. Automated telephone assistance
5. Television
6. Video games
7. Bass amplifiers
8. Neckties
9. Car alarms
10. Cell phones

The Goodness of Technology Assisted Leisure

Midst the fast changing world of technology, it is clear people both love and hate it. For example, YouTube, created in February 2005, is a video sharing website where users can upload, view and share video clips. In January 2008 alone, nearly 79 million users worldwide watched over 3 billion videos on YouTube. (Yen, 2008). Yet, some governments and school systems around the world are banning YouTube for students and citizens. Why? Perhaps it is as Goodale and Godbey (1988) once noted: the large amount of leisure afforded us today by technology is trivial at best—a "sordid route to human happiness" (p. 127).

What exactly has technology meant for the quality of our leisure? There are both positive and negative answers, of course. For example, although many people get tremendous enjoyment from such vehicles as jet skis and snowmobiles, other people see them as incompatible with leisure because of the noise, pollution, resource depletion, and habitat destruction they cause (Henderson et al., 2001). However, technology has also made many environmental conservation improvements possible, such as using recycled plastic to make polar fleece.

Other concerns center on the changes in leisure expressions themselves. For example, the application of titanium to golf clubs has made it necessary to remodel golf courses to allow for longer hit balls. And, the use of titanium rather than wood bats in youth baseball and softball has resulted in harder hit balls and the possibility of serious injuries. Pitchers are now required in many programs to wear protective chest pads. Injuring children is certainly a bad thing, but is hitting golf balls farther and baseballs harder in and of themselves bad?

Violence also seems to accompany the use of technology in leisure. Although violence has certainly been a part of leisure for centuries, there is concern today that some technology-based leisure pursuits create too much violence in our lives. For example, such activities as paintball, where camouflaged participants hunt each other down and shoot other players with gel bullets from realistic-looking guns, have been criticized as going too far. Yet, technology has also enabled us to better apprehend and punish those who use the Internet for pornography and the perpetuation of violence against women and children.

Box 7.6

The Study Says

Cell Phone and Teen Girls

In Australia, where it is claimed that teens currently lead the world in cell phone use, a study evaluated the role of these phones as a form of leisure. Through in-depth interviews with 42 female teenage cell phone users it was found that not only does the phone become a fashionable clothing accessory but as a leisure activity occurring in public places, cell phone use can also impart a sense of self-confidence, sexuality, and autonomy. The researchers concluded the cell phone allows adolescent women to safely reject traditional images of femininity.

Foley, C., Holzman, C., & Wearing, S. (2007). Moving beyond conspicuous leisure consumption: Adolescent women, mobile phones and public space. *Leisure Studies, 26*(2), 179-192.

Increased consumerism is also strongly tied to technology. As more activities and equipment are developed at faster rates, the discarding of old activities and equipment, and the purchasing of new ones, often occurs at breakneck speed. Having the latest and greatest in technological advancements symbolizes our expertise, wealth, and status (Henderson et al., 2001). Is this necessarily negative?

Another example of both the positive and negative impact of technology on leisure is what technological development was supposed to have meant for saving labor. People, it was predicted, would be set free from the drudgeries of work and be able to pursue more enjoyable lives. Although some would argue that we are actually working harder, thanks to technology, the technology that has saved labor has also made us less active. For example, even though some data suggest television watching may be declining slightly, the difference is being picked up by an increased use of computer-based entertainment (Kaufman, 2000), which still features inactivity.

Box 7.7

In Profile

Unvacations

After months, maybe years, it's official: you get a vacation! So, where shall you go? An island? The mountains? A resort? It doesn't really matter, because what you'll be having is an unvacation. Through your laptop computer, cell phone, beeper, and fax machine you won't be leaving work at all.

According to the Steelcase Workplace Index, a semiannual survey that gauges workplace trends in the United States, while on vacation

- 40% catch up on work-related reading
- 28% catch up on work-related paper work
- 27% put out fires in client and/or employee relations
- 27% stay in touch with the office
- 18% learned a new work skill

Steelcase Workplace Index: The Nature of Work (2006). Available from http://www.steelcase.com/na/workplace_index_survey_reveals_News.aspx?f=25748. Retrieved 6/10/08

Cyberculture:
collection of cultures and cultural products (such as stories) that exist on and are made possible by the internet

Perhaps the prime example of technology's positive and negative impact on our lives is the cyberculture. *Cyberculture* exists in the global, computer-based "network of networks." Although originally made possible by computer wires, cables, servers, and terminals, cyberculture now thrives where users meet within the wires and also without the wires. These on-line social interactions are as broad as they are diverse and take place within email, newsgroups, listservs, bulletin board systems (BBSs), MOOs and MUDs, Internet Relay Chat (RC), and interactive sites on the Internet.

Internet:
a global, publicly accessible, network of computer networks (such as the World Wide Web)

Please don't misunderstand. It is difficult to exaggerate the importance of the *Internet* in the way people access information, communicate with others, and do business. (See table 7.1.) It has also become the "superhighway" of leisure. In fact, for many, it is an entertaining way to spend most of their free time. And, this is expected to increase in popularity even more. However, as with anything this powerful, the Internet receives both accolades and criticisms.

One of the earliest critiques of cyberculture was the book *Escape Velocity: Cyberculture at the End of the Century*, published in 1996 by Mark Dery. The book takes us on a journey into the dark heart of high-tech subcultures: cyberpunks, cyberhippies, cyberpornographers, and technopagans, to name a few. Dery's point was that such fringe computer countercultures use technology in ways never

Table 7.1

Internet Users in the World. March 2008 (in millions) (Miniwatts Marketing Group, 2008. http://www.internetworldstats.com. Retrieved 7/24/08.)

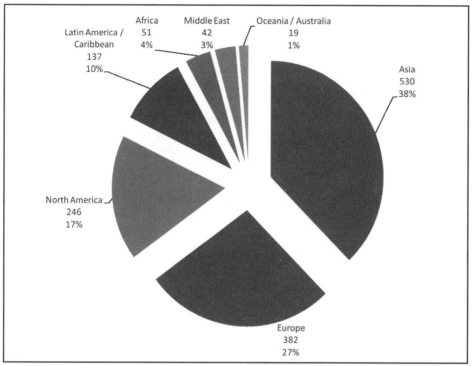

intended by manufacturers, which ultimately means technology will enslave us in the coming millennium.

Another critique of cyberculture is offered by Barlow (2004). Referring to the virtual communities formed in chat rooms, mailing lists, and discussion groups on the Internet as *cyberhoods*, Barlow asks how well they reproduce a real neighborhood. Barlow claims a lot is missing from the cyberhood. To his thinking, foremost, is prana. Prana is the Hindu term for both breath and spirit. Barlow uses the term to mean that even though the cyberhood offers information, it does not offer experience. When we're in a chat room, for example, we cannot really sense the others—their smell, tone of voice, the breeze from their bodies—the qualities that Barlow claims make an experience.

Cyberhood: virtual neighborhoods formed in cyberculture

There is something else missing in the cyberhood, claims Barlow: diversity. Indeed, as enthusiasm for computers and the Internet in particular runs wide and deep, across all regions of much of the world, all races, all political ideologies, and both genders, there are still people who find themselves on the other side of the digital divide: those with lower incomes, with less education, and who are over the age of 75. For example, according to a 2008 study by the Illinois Tech Policy Bank, 70 percent of households in Illinois earning less than $15,000 annually do not own a computer, and nearly 80 percent have never used the Internet (Williams-Harris, 2008). As Barlow (2004) writes, "There is not much human diversity in cyberspace, which is populated, as near as I can tell, by white males under 50 with plenty of computer terminal time, great typing skills, high math SATs, strongly held opinions on just about everything, and an excruciating face-to-face shyness, especially with the opposite sex" (p. 364).

Figure 7.3
What kind of neighborhood is the cyberhood? (© Ruth V. Russell, 2008)

In contrast, a study by Steinkuehler and Williams (2006) drew a more constructive conclusion about the goodness of cyberculture. In examining the form and function of massively multiplayer online games (MMSs) in terms of social engagement, they concluded the virtual worlds of the Internet are structurally similar to third places. (See Chapter 5 for a review of this anthropological concept.) That is, MMOs provide spaces for social interaction and relationships beyond the workplace and home. Like the neighborhood bar, these social relationships, while not usually providing deep emotional support, typically function as sources of informal sociability.

This and other studies focus on the impact of cyberculture on social capital. *Social capital* refers to the connections within and between social networks. As distinguished from physical capital (a tennis racquet) and human capital (a college education), leisure activities typically rely on human connections for expression. Yet, as some leisure scientists (cf. Putnam, 2000) argue, such activities as television watching and computer use lower the social capital available in our lives.

Social capital:

features of community life, such as interpersonal network, volunteering, and participation in self-governance

Box 7.8

 *In Focus*

Social Capital

Technologically based leisure is increasingly important, but some worry about its goodness. Primary is a fear of losing social capital: the interpersonal networks that make a community cohesive. It is the decreasing participation in Parent Teacher Associations, League of Women Voters, and Canadian Red Cross. It is volunteering less in the Boy Scouts or not belonging to the community garden club.

Research by Putnam (1995) documented a decline in social capital in North American communities. He claimed people are not participating as much as they used to in making their communities good places to live, citing a roughly 25-percent decline in the time spent in informal socializing and face-to-face visiting since 1965, and a nearly 50-percent decline in memberships in clubs and organizations. Some social critics disagree with Putnam, however. They argue Putnam's research ignored grassroots political groups, religious organizations, and youth sports leagues. Also, Stengel (1996) proposed people may be redefining the forms and nature of their participation with the community. For example, more of the efforts of social capital may now be done on home computers and therefore not be as visible.

Regardless, social capital is necessary, and possible declines in it are ominous for our communities. Consequences include a lack of participation in democratic governance, increased alienation and loneliness, and a decreasing ability to solve problems in groups. It may also mean a decline in a sense of caring about one's neighborhood and community (Godbey, 1997).

Figure 7.4

Even while camping in her motor home, this person is virtually participating in the social capital of her community back home. (© Ruth V. Russell, 2008)

Box 7.8 (Cont.)

Questions to Consider and Discuss

1.   Have you observed a decline in social capital in your hometown? College? Family? Do you consider Putnam's claim to have validity? Why or why not?
2.   Putnam's research was published in a book titled *Bowling Alone*, suggesting people no longer even participate in leisure in groups. For example, what would your community be like if there were no community-wide celebrations? Or, what if basketball games were only played by one player, on one computer, with a virtual court and opponents? What if we bowled alone?
3.   What do you think is the relationship between technology and social capital?

What We Understand About Technology Assisted Leisure

The use of technology in leisure is as old as leisure itself, yet the current revolution of particularly information technology has assisted, invented, and changed contemporary leisure in significant ways. From studying this chapter you should know that:

- Advances in technology have given people innovative places to play, better equipment to aid their adventures, and new activities to pursue.
- Specific examples include computer/video games, artificial surfaces and equipment, simulated leisure, and social networking.
- The positive influences of technology on our pastimes include access to information about leisure options, the creation of new leisure pursuits, new horizons in leisure for people with disabilities, and tourism as a global focus.
- Negative consequences from technological advances in leisure include environmental damage, passivity, violence, and consumerism.
- Particular debates have centered on the goodness/badness of the cyberculture.

References

Anderson, C.A. (2004). An update on the effects of playing violent video games. *Journal of Adolescence, 27,* 113-122.

Associated Press. (June 8, 2006). Survey: College kids like iPods better than beer. *FoxNews.com.* Available from: http://www.foxnews.com/story/0,2933,198632,00.html. Retrieved 6/15/08.

Barlow, J.P. (2004). Cyberhood vs. neighborhood. In M. Petracca & M. Sorapure (Eds.), *Common culture: Reading and writing about American popular culture* (pp. 211-236). Upper Saddle River, NJ: Prentice Hall.

Beggs, B. (2002). Activity satisfaction in golf and simulated golf. Unpublished doctoral dissertation. Indiana University, Bloomington.

Bryce, J., & Rutter, J. (2003). Gender dynamics and the social and spatial organization of computer gaming. *Leisure Studies, 22,* 1-15.

Business Communications Company (2006). *Research Report: Electronic Games and Gaming.* Available from http://www.bccresearch.com/report/treport. php?rcode=IFT052A. Retrieved 6/12/08.

Castells, M. (2000). *The rise of the network society* (2nd Ed.). New York: Wiley-Blackwell.

Dery, M. (1996). *Escape velocity: Cyberculture at the end of the century.* New York: Grove Press.

EVEonline. (June, 2008). *Tranquility Server Status.* Available from: http://eve. coldfront.net/status/tranquility. Retrieved 6/11/08.

Forrester, S.A. (2004). The grounded theory of the leisure experience in simulated environments. Unpublished doctoral dissertation, Indiana University, Bloomington.

Godbey, G. (1997). *Leisure and leisure services in the 21st Century.* State College, PA: Venture.

Golder, S., Wilkinson, D., & Huberman, B. (November 27, 2006). Rhythms of social interaction: Messaging within a massive online network. Available from http://arxiv.org/PS_cache/cs/pdf/0611/0611137v1.pdf. Retrieved 6/15/08.

Goodale, T., & Godbey, G. (1988). *The evolution of leisure: Historical and philosophical perspectives.* State College, PA: Venture.

Hammel, R., & Foster, C. (1986). A sporting chance: Relationships between technological change and the concept of fair play in fishing. *Journal of Leisure Research, 18,* 40-52.

Henderson, K.A., Bialeschki, M.D., Hemingway, J.L, Hodges, J.S., Kivel, B.D., & Sessoms, H.D. (2001). *Introduction to recreation and leisure services* (8th Ed.). State College, PA: Venture.

Jones, S.E. (2008). *The meaning of video games: Gaming and textual strategies.* New York: Routledge.

Kalaygian, M. (January 2002). Advice from the pros: The climbing wall industry sounds off. *Government Recreation and Fitness, 9,* 18-20, 41-42.

Kaufman, W. (June 26, 2000). The way we play: The changing face of America (Radio broadcast). *National Public Radio Morning Edition.* Available from http://www.npr.org/programs/morning. Retrieved 3/3/04.

Lubick, N. (April 9, 2008). Silver socks have cloudy lining. *Journal of Environmental Science and Technology.* Available from http://pubs.acs.org/subscribe/ journals/esthag-w/2008/apr/science/nl_nanosocks.html. Retrieved 6/13/08.

Nielsen Entertainment (2006). *Active Gamer Benchmark Study.* Available from http://www.prnewswire.com/cgi-bin/stories.pl?ACCT=109&STORY=/ www/story/10-05-2006/0004446115&EDATE=. Retrieved 6/16/08.

Priest, S., & Gass, M. (2000). Future trends and issues in adventure programming. In J.C. Miles & S. Priest (Eds.), *Adventure programming* (pp. 416-432). State College, PA: Venture.

Putnam, R. (January 1995). Bowling alone: America's declining social capital. *Journal of Democracy, 6*(1), 65-78.

Putnam, R. (2000). *Bowling alone: The collapse and revival of American community.* New York: Simon & Schuster.

Steinkuehler, C.A., & Williams, D. (2006). Where everybody knows your (screen) name: Online games as "Third Places." *Journal of Computer-Mediated Communication, 11*(4), 885-909.

Stengel, R. (July 22, 1996). Bowling together. *Time*, 35.

Turkle, S. (2004). Virtuality and its discontents. In M. Petracca & M. Sorapure (Eds.), *Common culture: Reading and writing about American popular culture* (pp. 181-205). Upper Saddle River, NJ: Prentice Hall.

Vos Savant, M. (March 11, 2007). Ask Marilyn: The most unwanted inventions. *Parade Magazine.* Available from http://www.parade.com/articles/editions/2007/edition_03-11-2007/Ask_Marilyn. Retrieved 6/10/08.

Williams-Harris, D. (June 1, 2008). For the poor, a gaping digital divide. *Chicago Tribune.* Available from http://www.chicagotribune.com/business/chi-sun-digital-divide-jun01,0,7129925.story. Retrieved 6/10/98.

Yen, Y-W. (March 25, 2008). YouTube looks for the money clip. *Fortune.* Available from http://techland.blogs.fortune.cnn.com/2008/03/25/youtube-looks-for-the-money-clip/. Retrieved 7/10/08.

CHAPTER EIGHT

COMMON CULTURE

PREVIEW

What is common culture?

Common culture refers to the everyday pastimes of the majority of people in a society. It is the leisure of the masses.

What are examples of common culture?

In Western technologically oriented societies examples of common culture are typically the media-based forms of entertainment, including television, popular music, and films.

Why is understanding common culture important?

Mediated entertainment as a form of leisure is perhaps the most obvious reflection of who we are as a society.

KEY TERMS

What did you do yesterday? Did you listen to music? Did you go to a movie, watch television, read a newspaper, shop at Aeropostale, or eat at McDonald's? You most likely did at least one of these activities, perhaps all of them. In fact, you probably do at least one of these activities every day. If so, you are not unusual at all, because these are the sorts of things most people in modern societies do with most of their free time. These are examples of common culture.

Figure 8.1

Eating at McDonald's is an example of common culture in many societies. This restaurant is located in Beijing, China. (© Ruth V. Russell, 2008)

Common culture encompasses the most immediate and contemporary activities of our lives. Common culture is not so much defined by its content; it could be music, literature, drama, food, or sport. Rather, common culture is defined by its typicality. It is labeled "common" because it offers a common ground for the most visible and pervasive level of culture in a society. Other terms for common culture include *popular culture*, pop culture, mass culture, and mass leisure.

Popular culture:

cultural communication including newspapers, television, advertising, comics, pop music, radio, novels, movies, etc.

Why study common culture? What can we learn by studying images in music videos, the language of Starbucks, or the endurance of Star Trek? Because these forms of common culture serve as a kind of mirror in which we can see ourselves, we understand who we are, what we are, and why. We see reflected in common culture certain standards and commonly held beliefs about beauty, success, love, or justice. We also see reflected there important social contradictions—the tension between races, genders, generations, and even societies. As Lipsitz (1990) suggested, "perhaps the most important facts about people have always been encoded within the ordinary and commonplace" (p. 5).

Another argument for studying common culture is the important influence it exerts on us (Petracca & Sorapure, 2004). Today, for many societies, common culture is driven by media. The media, therefore, is the primary fund of ideas that inform our daily activities, sometimes exerting a more compelling influence than family, friends, school, or work. When we play sports, for example, we mimic the gestures and movements of the professional athletes we see on TV. We learn to dance from the MTV music videos. Even if we consider common culture as merely low-quality amusement, it delivers messages that we internalize and act on later. This means we should examine common culture in order to assess, and perhaps also resist, its influences.

This chapter focuses first on the characteristics of common culture. Then, examples are presented of the most pervasive forms of common culture in modern

Box 8.1

In Profile

Auto Culture

The automobile has had an immense influence on our lives. Indeed, Henry Ford has been credited with the creation of leisure for the working class with the mass production of the car. The automobile has also been accused of being a primary factor in altering the American family structure. Its presence in our daily lives is so pervasive that the car itself perhaps represents common culture. Popular music has often used the car as a cultural theme of status. For example, there was "In My Merry Oldsmobile" in 1909, "Rocket 88" in 1949, "Mustang Sally" in 1966, and "Little Red Corvette" in 1999. Television shows have also paid homage to the glory and wonder of the car. In fact, there is a channel, "Speed," devoted to automobiles and racing. Movies have portrayed hot rods in connection with social outcasts, and sport cars with wealth and success. According to some scientists, the automobile culture reveals our essential cultural character—individual independence.

societies, beginning, of course with television. Other examples include popular music, print, film, and theme parks. Finally, we critique the thread weaving these examples together: the role of mediated entertainment.

Characterizing Common Culture

How do we know what pastimes to put on the common culture list? Why is *The Simpsons* on the list, and ballet not? In characterizing common culture, we refer to it as: popular, commercial, trendy, and specific to age groups. Let's discuss each of these characteristics of common culture more fully.

Beginning with its popularity, common culture refers to those pastimes we engage in most often. It is the way we use free time that has the most in common with others in our society. It is popular because it is a fundamental leisure expression of a culture.

This means common culture can be distinguished from both folk culture and high culture. *High culture* refers to the typical pastimes of a society's elite, such as intellectuals or the upper socioeconomic classes of people. Examples of high culture might include classical music by composers such as Beethoven, fine art from impressionist painter Manet, the plays of Shakespeare, and the literature of Sartre. In some societies, high culture can also be very popular. For example, classical ballet is one of Russia's most popular pastimes.

Folk culture, on the other hand, refers to the local pastimes that are shared through direct, oral communication by a specific community or

High culture:
typical pastimes of the social elite of a society

Folk culture:
local or regional traditional pastimes shared through direct, oral communication

ethnic group. Examples of American folk culture include handmade quilts, Creole cuisine, bluegrass music, and urban legends. Sometimes folk culture can become common culture when a particular pursuit becomes so widespread that it crosses subcultural boundaries and becomes commercial. Wearing blue jeans is certainly an illustration of this.

Therefore, a second characteristic of common culture is that it is commercial. It is leisure that is marketed and sold as a product. For example, in 2004 visitors to U.S. amusement and theme parks spent $9,344 million. That same year Americans spent $38.7 billion on magazines and newspapers. They also spend about $788 per consumer per year on television, radio, and sound equipment (U.S. Census Bureau, 2008). And, you may be surprised by the top grossing female musician for 2007—Madonna at $72 million (Pomerantz, 2008). Thus, common culture is for sale.

You are probably wondering which examples from the common

Figure 8.2

Performers at the 42nd Annual Bill Monroe Bluegrass Festival, Bean Blossom, Indiana. (© Ruth V. Russell, 2008)

Box 8.2

In Your Own Experience

Urban Legends

An urban legend is a form of oral folklore, consisting of stories thought to be factual by those circulating them. Like all folklore, urban legends are not necessarily false, but they are often distorted, exaggerated, or sensationalized over time. Some urban legends, however, have passed through the years with only minor changes to match regional themes. One example of a story that hasn't changed much is of a woman killed by spiders nesting in her bouffant hairdo. A story that reflects more contemporary societal circumstances is the one of people being ambushed at bars, secretly anesthetized with a drink, and waking up minus a kidney that was removed. In recent years, urban legends have been typically distributed by e-mail, with the sender frequently alleging such tales happened to a "friend of a friend."

What has been your experience with urban legends? What ones can you tell your classmates? Since e-mail has become a common way to pass along urban legends, explore some sites focused on these stories. For example, try http://www.urbanlegendsonline.com and http://www.snopes.com. At this writing a fun site that offers a quiz on whether common e-mail distributed photos are real or fake is http://www.urbanlegends.about.com.

culture list are this year's top money-makers. What are the "hot" music groups, films, TV shows, and restaurants? This question introduces a third characteristic of common culture: it is trendy. Common culture typically does not last long (The Rolling Stones and Madonna are exceptions!) Although television, magazines, and films as categories of common culture are generally enduring, particular programs or titles are not. Recently someone new took the place of Hillary, who took the place of Beyonce, who took the place of Britney, who supposedly took the place of Madonna, who took the place of Gidget. Thus, what is common responds to what is actually contemporary in people's lives. This means things once popular are inevitably unpopular later.

This also suggests the final characteristic of common culture: it is specific to age groups. For example, kids are watching *Hannah Montana*, college students are watching reality TV, middle-aged adults enjoy *Everybody Loves Raymond* re-runs, and some elderly people are still faithfully watching *The Lawrence Welk Show*. Further, popular culture that is common among all age groups is usually dependent on the tastes of youth. That is, a culture's best-selling music, movies, foods, etc. is largely determined by the interests of its young people.

The Example of Television

At the hub of common culture is undoubtedly television. Not only does it hold a central place in our use of free time, but it also has become a primary means of communicating and validating what is popular (Kelly, 1982). Television tells us what music to listen to, what history to believe, what is funny, what clothing to

Box 8.3

The Study Says

Barbie's Lesson

In an experimental study the Barbie doll was examined as a possible cause for young girls' body dissatisfaction. A total of 162 girls, from age 5 to age 8, were exposed to images of either Barbie dolls, Emme dolls (U.S. size 16), or no dolls (baseline control) and then completed questionnaires about body image. Girls exposed to Barbie reported lower body esteem and greater desire for a thinner body shape than the other two groups of girls. The researchers concluded that even if dolls cease to function as role models for older girls, early exposure to dolls depicting unrealistically thin bodies may damage girls' body image, which could contribute to an increased risk of disordered eating and weight loss.

Dittmar, H., Halliwell, E., & Ive, S. (2006). Does Barbie make girls want to be thin? The effect of experimental exposure to images of dolls on the body image of 5- to 8-year-old girls. *Developmental Psychology, 42*(2), 283-292.

wear, and what to eat for breakfast. Television has the power to bring together the population of a nation and even the world (Kelly & Freysinger, 2000).

Indeed, the amount of time people spend watching television is astounding (table 8.1). According to a Nielsen Media Research report (2008), in the average American household the television is on for eight hours and 15 minutes in a 24-hour period. The average daily amount of viewing time per individual (over the age of two) is about four and a half hours. At this rate, someone who lives to age 75 would spend more than nine full years in front of the tube (Kubey & Csikszentmihalyi,

Table 8.1

TV Watching in the United States

8 hours and 15 minutes – total average time a household has a TV set turned on per day
4 hours and 34 minutes – average amount of television watched by individual viewers per day
111.4 million – number of TV households
20.5% - households with digital video recorders
90 million – viewers of the *Super Bowl*
1 – rank of the primetime program *American Idol*

Nielsen Media Research. (2007). Nielsen Reports Television Tuning Remains at Record Levels. Available from http://nielsenmedia.com. Retrieved 6/17/08.

2004). Further, almost all of the gain in free time we've experienced in recent years has been given over to television (Robinson & Godbey, 1997).

Who watches television? Almost everyone, of course, but studies indicate women watch more than men, persons aged 25-54 watch the most, and African Americans watch more than other ethnic groups (Nielsen Media Research, 2008). According to the surveys of Kubey & Csikszentmihalyi (2004), people who are married and single by choice seem to watch television about the same proportions of time, whereas divorced and widowed people report less TV viewing. Viewing for all adults living with children is slightly higher, while more educated people tend to watch less. Finally, studies indicate most people do not watch television exclusively. Typical accompanying activities are talking on the telephone, eating meals, getting dressed, doing chores, caring for children, and studying.

Since its beginnings more than 50 years ago, television's hold on us has been of keen interest to scientists. Although television can teach and train, allow us to reach aesthetic heights, and provide a healing distraction, most of the research literature has focused on its problematic consequences. In fact, some scholars liken television watching to substance addiction. The idea of a TV addiction is imprecise and laden with value judgments, of course, but psychologists and psychiatrists characterize addiction as spending more time with something than intended, thinking about reducing the use of something, and reporting withdrawal symptoms when stopping it. All these criteria can apply to people who watch a lot of television.

To determine if watching television is harmful, researchers have undertaken a wide variety of studies, including laboratory experiments monitoring the brain waves (using an electroencephalograph, or EEG), skin resistance, and heart rate of people watching television. From the EEG studies, as you might expect, people show less

Box 8.4

In Your Own Experience

Are You Addicted to TV?

There are many quizzes that help you assess your addiction to television. Try this one: http://www.trashyourtv.com/survey (Retrieved 6/18/08). Based on your results, would you say you do or do not have a television addiction? Why do some scientists refer to a television-watching problem as an addiction?

mental stimulation while watching TV (Kubey & Csikszentmihalyi, 2002).

Other studies have focused on the effects of the experience of television watching. For example, Kubey and Csikszentmihalyi (1990) sampled people's feelings while they were engaged in various activities, including television watching. Foremost, and in agreement with the EEG studies, they found television viewing to be a passive, relaxing, low-concentration activity. Consequently, in contrasting this with other activities (table 8.2), television watching was found to be less challenging, less social, and less active.

Because television watching is so easy to do, results from the same study also showed loneliness and negative feelings often drive the motivation to watch TV. Heavy viewers wish to escape something or avoid negative feelings. In addition, television seems to become less rewarding the longer it is watched. That is, although it is relaxing, as we increase the amount of time spent watching TV, our satisfaction and enjoyment in the experience tend to drop off. Ironically, this means even though people often choose to watch TV to escape bad feelings, they can feel worse as a result. Long TV hours are also linked to higher material aspirations and anxiety (Frey, Benesch, & Stutzer, 2007).

What is it about TV, then, that has such a hold on us? In part, the attraction seems to spring from our biological orienting response. First described by Ivan Pavlov in 1927, the *orienting response* is our instinctive visual or auditory reaction to any sudden or new stimulus (Kubey & Csiksczentmihalyi, 2004). It is part of our evolutionary heritage, a built-in sensitivity to movement from potential threats.

Orienting response: the instinctive visual or auditory reaction to any novel stimulus

Table 8.2

Rank Ordering (1=strongest to 5=weakest) of the Experience Qualities for Television Viewing and Other Activities

Experience qualities	TV viewing	Public leisure (parties, sports, dining out, cultural events)	Working outside the home
Concentration	3	2	1
Challenge	5	2	1
Skill	5	2	1
Cheerful	3	1	4
Relaxed	1	2	5
Sociable	4	1	3
Alert	4	1	2
Strong	4	1	2
Active	4	2	1

Note. From Kubey and Csikszentmihaylyi (1990)

Typical orienting responses include dilation of the blood vessels to the brain, slowing of the heart, and constriction of blood vessels to major muscle groups. The brain focuses its attention on gathering more information while the rest of the body quiets. This is why it is very difficult not to watch television when it is on. The stylistic features of television, such as cuts, edits, zooms, pans, and sudden noises, activate the orienting response, thereby keeping our attention on the screen.

Producers of educational television for children have found these features help learning by increasing kids' attention. But, increasing the rate of cuts and edits eventually overloads the brain. For example, music videos and commercials that use rapid intercutting of unrelated scenes are designed more to hold our attention than to convey information. The orienting response is overworked. Because viewers are paying full attention, they may remember the name of the product, but feel tired and worn out afterward (Kubey & Csikszentmihalyi, 2004).

Another answer to how television is able to have such a strong hold on us comes from the leisure quality of pleasure (as discussed in Chapter 2). British cultural studies scientist John Corner (1999) maintains we watch television simply because it is pleasurable. Specifically, it provides four types of pleasure: knowledge, comedy, fantasy, and distraction (table 8.3).

In other words, this suggests the pleasure of television is in the act of viewing itself. This is labeled *scopophilia*—being the onlooker to unfolding events. As noticed early by psychologist Sigmund Freud (1999/1915), watching other people is considered a way to objectify them, both in order to gain control and out of curiosity. In watching television, the enjoyment of being present at a distant and interesting event as it happens can be a powerful one. Although the concept of scopophilia is applicable to films, photographs, and other visual common culture forms as well, it is a particularly powerful pleasure in television viewing because of how much time we spend at this pastime.

Commenting on the trend of reality television in particular, Mark Andrejevic, in the book *Reality TV: The Work of Being Watched* (2003), explained scopophilia democratizes celebrity. In doing this, reality television paves the way for what he refers to as the coming interactive economy—relinquishing control of the media to consumers and viewers. That is, being watched is doing economic work.

Scopophilia:
pleasure in viewing, particularly of attractive people

Figure 8.3

An average child sees 30,000 TV commercials in a year. (© Ruth V. Russell, 2008)

Table 8.3

Types of Pleasure from Watching Television

Type of Pleasure	Definition	Sources
Knowledge	Gaining information and understanding	Quiz shows; history, science, and nature programs; news
Comedy	Teaches what society considers to be funny	Situation comedy; stand-up comedy
Fantasy	Portrays scenarios that are highly improbable in real life	Soap opera; reality shows
Distraction	Easily available and familiar relaxant – a break that is always available throughout the day	The customized pattern of the regularity and repetition of the viewing week

Corner, 1999.

Other Common Culture Examples

In addition to television, there are other examples of common culture worthy of mention. These include popular music, popular print, films, and theme parks.

Because of its popularity, music has been a tremendously important barometer of the character of a culture throughout history. As we think back over the 20th century, for example, every decade has a melody or rhythm that characterizes it. The years and the sounds blend together.

In the United States the century started off blue: Robert Johnson selling his soul to the devil at the crossroads. Then the Jazz Age: Louis Armstrong and Duke Ellington. By mid-century things started to rock: in the beginning, a confused collage of Buddy Holly's hillbilly style, Little Richard's frenzy, and Elvis Presley's blend of country and African American rhythms. Later, the boy and girl groups, such as The Coasters and The Shirelles, relayed the trials and joys of young love. By the mid-1960s, Bob Dylan and Joan Baez combined folk lyrics with the beat and instrumentation of rock to produce folk music, while Led Zeppelin and Frank Zappa pinned their antiestablishment tone to hard rock. Then on to the Beatles, Aretha Franklin, Bob Marley, and Stevie Wonder. (Are you humming along?) Eventually the memorable sounds of R.E.M., U2, and Prince drowned out the thumping sounds of disco in the 80s.

Box 8.5

 *In Focus*

Hip-Hop: Engine or Mirror?

Hip-hop music has been portrayed as a vivid illustration of the experience of urban youth. During the 1970s, when hip-hop music began its climb in popularity, the inner city was reeling with drugs, poverty, and unemployment. Hip-hop had the ability to motivate Black and Latino youth living in these circumstances; both its lyrics and rhythms spoke of outrage and power (Clay, 2003).

Almost as soon as it was born, hip-hop was criticized by parents and politicians as an evil influence on impressionable youth. Critics dismissed the violent, protesting, and misogynistic lyrics as a fad, yet today a great deal of scholarship now supports the view of hip-hop as an important social movement that harnessed the energy of disenfranchised, primarily African American, youth (Ogbar, 1999). However, the full cultural importance of hip-hop is not yet fully explored.

For example, one unanswered question is whether the hip-hop movement is the cause or the effect of changing political systems and mainstream culture (Trapp, 2005). Hip-hop artists often adopt a hostile stance toward White-controlled commerce, government, and media, seeking to draw attention to racial injustice and social neglect. Does this stance reflect what exists in the lives of urban youth or does it

Box 8.5 (Cont.)

seek to change this; is it the mirror or the engine? Hip-hop exploded out of an era of poverty and racial inequality, so perhaps hip-hop has both shaped and been shaped by this culture – in a cyclic fashion.

Questions to Consider and Discuss

1. What do you think has been the significance of hip-hop on its host culture? Has it been an engine for social change or a mirror of social condition? Why do you take this position?
2. Between 2000 and 2006, sales of hip-hop music decreased 44 percent (Nielsen SoundScan, 2007). Do these data demonstrate one way or the other the answer to whether the hip-hop movement has been the cause or the effect of changing political systems and mainstream culture? How?
3. Two early star icons of hip-hop were Queen Latifah and Tupac Shakur. Do some investigation about their early lives. For example, Queen Latifah's autobiography is *Ladies First*, published in 2000, and a good biography of Tupac Shakur is Jamal Joseph's *Tupac Shakur Legacy* published in 2006. Are there any clues from their lives for answering the question of the meaning of the hip-hop movement?
4. Also study the early lyrics of Queen Latifah and Tupac Shakur in terms of their positions about women. Then, using women as a case, do you feel hip-hop is the cause or effect of the circumstances of African American women today?

So powerful have been all these musical legacies they can still be heard on the radio today. But, how will we remember the end of that century and the beginning of this one? Added to blues, jazz, country, rock, folk, and disco music is *hip-hop*. "Rock is old," said Russell Simmons, head of a hip-hop label that took in nearly $200 million in 1998. "The creative people who are great, who are talking about youth culture in a way that makes sense, happen to be rappers" (as cited in August, et al., 2004, p. 301).

Hip-hop: a genre of music typically consisting of a rhythmic style of speaking called rap over backing beats performed on a turntable by a DJ

Hip-hop music is part of an entire hip-hop subculture (which also include dance movements, clothing, and films), that began in the Bronx in New York City in the early 1970s. Founded by young African Americans and Latinos who just wanted to get a party going, the music quickly gained in popularity and widespread acceptance, to the point it appears regularly on television and has been adopted by major recording labels. By 2000, for example, album sales had reached over $800 million annually (Nielsen SoundScan, 2007). Today, more than 70 percent of hip-hop recordings are purchased by whites—a fact some feel means that hip-hop has been appropriated.

As the first decade of the new century progressed, hip-hop has transformed from an edgy rhythmic rap to a more melodic sound that contains elements of jazz, classical, pop, and reggae. In fact, this is the main point about popular music

Pluralistic:

ethnically, religiously, racially, and socially diverse

as an example of common culture. North American popular music (or any other culture's for that matter) is not just of one form. It is at heart *pluralistic.*

Although different music forms appeal to different social and ethnic groups, foremost it is always an interwoven reflection of the whole culture. Rock, jazz, blues, country, and hip-hop do not remain pure forms as they become popular; they become amalgamations of all ethnic strands and social group values. In directly interpreting the emotional language of a culture, popular music picks up influences as it goes, much like a snowball rolling downhill.

Next, let's consider the example of popular print. Reading has been a popular pastime since printing was first possible. For example, since the invention of the printing press in the 1400s, today 272.2 million North American subscribers can now choose from more than 550 magazine titles. In addition, currently there are hundreds of daily newspapers in the world. The top daily newspaper in the United States is *USA Today* with a circulation of 2.2 million (Audit Bureau of Circulations, 2007), while the top daily newspaper in the world is *Yomiuri Shimbun* from Japan, with a circulation of over 14.5 million (World Association of Newspapers, 2005). Reading books remains popular as well. According to the U.S. Census Bureau (2008), about 35% of Americans regularly read books.

Box 8.6

 In Your Own Experience

Magazine Ads – What Does Your Analysis Conclude?

It is not unusual to be exposed to an average of 3,000 ads every day as we watch television, listen to the radio, and read magazines (Pozner, 2004), which makes advertising a dominant force in society. Thus, advertising has been an important way to study how common culture relates to its society. Ads carry powerful messages about appropriate modes of behavior, standards of beauty and status, gender roles, and other markers for normalcy and success. Do these ads reflect or create society?

Try a little investigation yourself. First, select a copy of your favorite magazine. It can be any title that interests you as long as it includes advertising. Study the content and visual images of only the ads in the magazine. Think about what these ads are instructing you to do to be cool, successful, or happy. Why do you need the product? How is the product used to market lifestyle, relationships, beauty, and even leisure? Who are the messages targeted toward? How do these ads make you feel?

With your magazine sample in hand, discuss your findings with classmates. Together, what do you conclude?

Although publishing remains a major industry, annually consuming 10 million tons of paper (Freysinger & Kelly, 2004), it is no longer considered a growth industry. Yet, this does not necessarily reflect a decrease in the popularity of reading. For example, even though newspaper subscriptions have dropped overall, the number of people who regularly read electronic versions of newspapers has increased. And, even though many general-interest magazines have failed, there is a growth market

Box 8.7

 *In Profile*

Slasher Films

The Texas Chainsaw Massacre (1974), *Friday the 13th* (1980), *and I Know What You Did Last Summer* (1997) have been popular films. So popular, that even their sequels (*A Nightmare on Elm Street* had seven sequels), parodies (*Scream*, 1996), and pooled remakes (*Freddy vs Jason*, 2003) have also been widely viewed.

These are labeled slasher films—a sub-genre of the horror film. They typically involve a psychopathic killer who stalks and vividly murders a series of teen victims. The victims are usually in an isolated setting doing something they shouldn't (sex, drugs, etc.). Slasher films typically open with the murder of a young woman and end with a lone woman survivor who manages to subdue the killer—but not permanently. Although Alfred Hitchcock's *Psycho* (1960) provided an early inspiration, the first authentic slasher film is considered to be *Black Christmas* (1974).

What does the popularity of these films tell us about the nature of the culture that loves them? Based on several content analyses of this sub-genre of film, we find some clues to the answer. One interpretation is that many of these films are an assault on all that society is supposed to cherish: youth, home, and school (*Modleski*, 1986). The individual, the family, and the institution are dismembered in gruesome ways. For example, *The Texas Chainsaw Massacre* has been analyzed as a critique of capitalism, since it shows the horror of people quite literally living off other people. Another analysis pertains to how women are viewed. In slasher films, an attractive young woman is always threatened by a maniac. This is claimed to be because she embodies sexual pleasure and also a great many aspects of the "specious good" (*Modleski*, 1986).

Studies have pointed out the camera location in slasher films typically offers the audience the perspective of the often unseen and nameless presence that annihilates. This delights audiences as they cheer and applaud each outrage from their own vantage point as the slasher. Does this mean the audience revels in the demise of their own culture—the very culture they also enthusiastically support? In *Dawn of the Dead* (1978), for example, zombies take over a shopping center. This has become a midnight favorite at shopping malls all over the U.S. As well, film analysts claim the audiences' expectations for non-closure by the end of the film reflects the impermanent nature of the culture.

for specialized publications based on specific leisure interests, such as cooking, sports, fitness, travel, etc. For example, for ocean surfing alone, 16 different titles are available.

How does popular print relate to society? As with the point of the focus on hip-hop in box 8.5, the question is always whether common culture reflects its society or creates it, or both. According to a study of advertising in *Vogue* magazine (United Kingdom edition) between 1916 and 1999, displaying skin and tight clothing in images of women increases as economic conditions decline (Hill, Donovan & Koyama, 2005). The researchers concluded that in this case common culture is used as a tool in society; in times of economic downturn, women use their bodies as an economic strategy to attract eligible marriage partners.

On the other hand, another study (Sullivan & O'Connor, 1988) analyzed advertisements appearing in eight general interest magazines in 1983 and compared the data with similar studies of magazines published in 1958 and 1970. Results suggested the more recent advertisements more accurately reflected the diversity of women's social and occupational roles than did those of earlier time periods. Thus, the ads mirrored society.

Figure 8.4

Perhaps surprisingly, the blockbuster film *Titanic* had a positive economic impact on the cruise industry. (© Ruth V. Russell, 2008)

As with popular print, in the face of television's growing popularity, movies have also experienced declines in theater attendance in many societies since the 1950s. For example, an average of 80 million Americans went to the movies every week in 1946 (Chubb & Chubb, 1981) compared with the average moviegoer of today who attends a film at the theater less than once per month (Motion Picture Association of America, 2008). Although some predict movie theaters will disappear as technology continues to offer visual media alternatives, this is doubtful because going to the movies means more than seeing the entertainment on the screen. The movie experience (both in and out of theaters) reflects, defines, and redefines society.

Genre:

a kind or type, usually applied to films, books and plays

Blockbuster:

lavishly produced, having wide popular financial success

Movies are categorized in terms of *genre*—drama, action, comedy, disaster, crime, horror, documentary, etc., and as such use different plot, characterization, imagery, and symbolism conventions to relate to society. Psychologically, for example, viewers of the drama film genre can identify with the characters and project their own feelings into the plot, giving them a deep emotional tension and, ultimately, a release. Economically, such action films as the *blockbuster* can have significant financial importance for the marketplace. For example, worldwide the highest grossing film of all time is the blockbuster *Titanic* (1997) at more than $1.8 billion. And, from a sociological perspective, movies of all genre instruct and reflect social norms and depict urgent social problems.

The movie industry now uses multiple avenues to gain popularity. In addition to playing in theaters, films are also marketed on videos and DVDs, and via television and the Internet. Film production is also now a worldwide enterprise. Prior to the 1970s, the major American film companies dominated. Now, other countries (such as Japan, France, and Sweden) generate more than half of annual film revenues. Some film critics argue the film industries in Asia and Europe have produced the majority of socially and artistically worthwhile works as well.

This has also meant movie audiences have become more diverse. Thanks to multiple media options for viewing, as well as wide-ranging production sources, all cultures, ages, socioeconomic classes, genders, ethnicities, occupational groups, and educational levels enjoy movies. Although today's movie viewer in the U.S. is more likely young, more affluent, better educated and urban, film as a common culture example is universally popular.

In addition to television, popular music, popular print, and films, expressions of common culture could also include radio (especially considering the emerging popularity of talk radio), comics, and even spectator sports. But, our final illustration of common culture is theme parks because they provide a fascinating reflection of culture.

Figure 8.5

Beginning in the early 1990s, roller coasters began a growth spurt that shows no signs of letting up. The Millennium Force, Cedar Point, Sandusky, Ohio. (© Cedar Point. Used with permission.)

Figure 8.6

Figure 8.6. A view of the Magic Kingdom from The Swiss Family Robinson Treehouse in Adventureland, Disneyland, California. (© Ruth V. Russell, 2008)

The roots of the amusement park go back to the Middle Ages, with pleasure gardens located on the outskirts of major European cities. These gardens featured live entertainment, fireworks, dancing, games, and even rides. One of these, Bakken, north of Copenhagen, Denmark, which opened in 1583, continues to operate today. Early history also points to the ice slides in Russia during the 17th century. Structures were built out of lumber with a sheet of ice several inches thick covering the surface. Riders climbed the stairs attached to the back of the slide, sped down the 50-degree drop on a sled, and then swooped up the slide that lay opposite to the first one.

Amusement parks entered their golden era with the 1893 World's Columbian Exposition in Chicago, which introduced the Ferris wheel and the midway. Under full swing by the 1930s, the center of this growing worldwide industry was Coney Island in New York City, where the world's most well-known roller coaster—*The Cyclone*—opened in 1927. Innovations provided greater and more intense thrills to the growing crowds, but following the Great Depression of the mid-1930s, the world's amusement park census had gone from 1,500 to about 400. With the advent of television in the 1950s, the industry was again in distress as people stayed home for entertainment. What was needed was a new concept.

That new concept was Disneyland. When Disneyland opened in 1955 many people were skeptical that an amusement park without any of the traditional attractions would succeed. Instead of a midway, Disneyland offered five distinct themed areas, providing "guests" with the fantasy of travel to different lands and times. But, as you know, Disneyland was an immediate success, and the theme park era was born.

Whereas the attraction of earlier amusement parks was allowing visitors to break with accustomed social norms and mock the established social order, the new theme parks sought to emphasize wholesomeness. As Walt Disney envisioned it:

Disneyland will be based upon and dedicated to the ideals, the dreams and the hard facts that have created America. And it will be uniquely equipped to dramatize these dreams and facts and send them forth as a source of courage and inspiration to all the world.

(as quoted in Mosley, 1985, p. 221)

Today numerous theme parks are thriving. Sesame Place, a children's water park featuring the characters from the television program, and Knott's Berry Farm, which draws on a western theme, are also representative of the coordinated package of attractions around a single theme. So is Sea World, which uses marine life to educate and entertain, and Universal Studios, a park celebrating another form of common culture—the movies. But, the Disney theme parks remain the industry standard-bearers. In addition to the California Disneyland park, Disney theme parks are located in central Florida, Hong Kong, Tokyo, and Paris. The company also owns a cruise line, restaurant chains (e.g. ESPN Zone), and resort hotels and vacation clubs.

Recently, critiques have emerged about what the Disney properties, the theme parks in particular, reveal about the culture. First, Rojek (1993) has written that Disney theme parks present a moralistic and idealized version of the "American Way." Here's how he described it. The moral order of the parks is based on a nostalgic picture of American society: the barbershop quartet, the streets of a small town, shiny-faced youth dressed in red, white, and blue, and the ever-smiling characters from Disney films—and, throughout, a narrative of the moral and economic superiority of the American way of life.

For example, in Adventureland, the armchair traveler goes to far-off and mysterious destinations, such as the Caribbean. When they encounter "ferocious" wild animals and "barbaric" pirates, the dangers are always defeated by the "superiority of white, middle-class power" (p. 128). Next stop is Frontierland, which "symbolizes the triumph of white, male culture over nature" (p. 128), and then Tomorrowland, where a "sense of eternal progress" is conveyed (p. 128). Essentially, Rojek's criticism is the Disney theme parks overstep their entertainment role. They are underpinned by powerful political and social values. They distort history and present American society as free of conflict.

Another criticism of the Disney parks comes from Bryman (1995). His critique is directed at the nature of control. Control, says Bryman, is in evidence in a variety of ways. It operates at the level of how the visitor is handled while in the parks to the way in which the parks relate to their surrounding environment. For example,

Box 8.8

In Focus

The End of Common Culture?

As you know the rise of the "blogosphere" continues to change the face of culture. According to observers, the Internet is now home to millions of web-logs (or blogs), and something like eleven million Americans claim to have started blogs themselves (Mohler, 2005). Does this popularity qualify blogging as an example of common culture?

Art critic Terry Teachout (2005), whose writings are primarily about high culture —the art, museum, theatre, classical music scene—leapfrogs that question altgether. He believes that because of blogging America's common culture actually no longer exists. Commenting on the change that produced the blogging phenomenon, Teachout offers this observation: "The simplest description of this change is also the starkest one: the common culture of widely shared values and knowledge that once helped to unite Americans of all creeds, colors, and classes no longer exists. In its place we now have a 'balkanized' group of subcultures whose members pursue their separate, unshared interests in an unprecedented variety of ways" (p. 40).

Questions to Consider and Discuss

1. What do you think of Teachout's prognosis? As a result of rapid technological change are we no longer reading the same books, hearing the same popular songs on the radio, and watching the same movies and TV programs? Upon what bases do you agree or disagree with Teachout?
2. What might be some examples of change in common culture today that can be attributed to technology? For example, many people no longer access the news via the morning newspaper. Instead, they want their news on demand, when it works for them. What other examples can you describe?
3. What are some of the disadvantages of the examples you've described? For example, to many, newspapers are more than reading the news. They are part of the dawn, with coffee. This suggests the big question here is whether leisure is harmed by mediated entertainment.

there is control over the imagination of visitors. One way this is done is through selecting out undesirable elements in stories told in the attractions. Also, Bryman cites how visitors' movements are controlled, both overtly and covertly, by the park's physical layout and by its built-in narratives. For example, the distinction between a ride and its queue has been eroded. Also, all staff are trained to behave in the Disney way, including control over language (customers are guests), and rules about physical appearance (the Disney look).

The Role of Entertainment

So, what do television, popular print, popular music, films and theme parks suggest is the character of the society that loves them? We have explored many things common culture reveals about culture, but in industrialized societies perhaps the overarching reflection is that we crave entertainment.

Entertainment comes from a variety of sources, but its goal is to have someone else or something else amuse us. Entertainment is the basis for the common culture of contemporary societies. Further, today's common culture delivers entertainment primarily through the media. Television, film, magazines, CDs, and even theme parks are forms of *mediated entertainment*. This hasn't always been the case.

Entertainment: amusement provided by someone or something else that divert and hold attention

Current popular pastimes can be traced to the mid-18th century when opportunities for the masses began to increase. Urban living made entertainments possible in cheap forms. Seaside amusement centers for music and dancing, as well as bowling occupied much of people's free time. Industrialization in the 19th century produced such public amusements as penny theaters with 30-second pantomimed melodramas viewed on kinescopes, weekly newspapers (later to become magazines), and chapbooks (paper-covered booklets). By the 1920s radio provided a major form of entertainment. Finally, with the collision of advancing technology and the rise of a consumer-based market, the availability of the television in the 1950s sealed the connection between media and popular pastimes.

Mediated entertainment: entertainment provided via media

Box 8.9

What We Know From *The Simpsons*

Since its premiere in 1989, *The Simpsons* has repeatedly ranked in the Nielsen top ten for prime-time television shows, as it has become "an industry trendsetter, cultural template, and a viewing experience verging on the religious for its most fanatical followers" (Waters, 1990, p. 58). A literary content analysis of this notoriously popular television show provides insight into how a sophisticated satire is able to comment on the American culture.

Week after week, this television show continues to offer scathing critiques of America's faults and flaws. According to the study, among other things, The Simpsons operates from a leftist political position as it mercilessly exposes the hypocrisy and ineptitude of pop psychology, corporate greed, commercialism, consumerism, and modern child-rearing, as well as the potential dangers of fundamental religion, homophobia, racism, and sexism. The study's analysis concludes, however, that the program has not yet given a clear interpretation of feminism—as it presents women with a great deal of ideological confusion and contradiction.

Henry, M. (2007). "Don't ask me, I'm just a girl": Feminism, female identity, and The Simpsons. *The Journal of Popular Culture, 40*(2), 272-303.

Is a mediated, entertainment based common culture a good thing? Some, like Neil Postman, say no. In the book *Amusing Ourselves to Death* (1986), Postman argued our common culture, particularly television, does not merely reflect our culture, but rather has become our culture. Generations reared on mediated entertainment, he asserts, view the world, and ideas, differently. We come to expect life to be presented in small, disconnected, and amusing chunks. As a result, we can no longer think critically or behave rationally. He feels our ability to live a meaningful life, both individually and communally, is compromised by a medium that "must suppress the content of ideas in order to accommodate the requirements of visual interest" (p. 92). The result of such ignorance is a culture addicted to "fluff."

David Bianculli (2000) also wrote about mediated entertainment, especially television. In contrast to Postman's view, Bianculli believes television serves critically important educational and social functions. He asserts TV is actually opening the American mind because it provides positive role models, good storytelling, and likable characters.

Similarly, Steven Johnson (2005) defends mediated entertainment by claiming it is actually making us smarter. In the mid-1980s, Johnson claims, roughly starting with the television show *Hillstreet Blues*, programming of all sorts became more complicated and nonlinear. Since then viewers have been required to remember bits of information, fill in gaps in plots, and make learned guesses to understand what is going on. Although highly controversial and unproven, Johnson even makes the claim IQ scores have increased steadily over the past few decades. Just compare the sort of brain that was happy watching *Dragnet* in the 1960s, he points out, to the brain that watches *The Apprentice* today.

What is your position on the goodness of contemporary common culture? Probably somewhere in the middle? There is a lot of trash in everything. The point is, perhaps, that we must all learn to discern for ourselves what we will consume and why. Television, movies, popular music, magazines, and theme parks in and of themselves cannot make or break us as a culture. It is up to us to decide what entertainment forms make "good" culture.

What We Understand About Common Culture

Common culture, or mass leisure, is an important reflection of society. Because of its pervasive expression of the society itself, it also can shape and instruct society. From studying this chapter, you should know that:

- Common culture is characterized as popular, commercial, trendy, and youth-directed.
- Television is by far the pastime we participate in most frequently, and thus a central example of common culture.
- Yet, research suggests even though television viewing is freely chosen and provides relaxation and escape, it is the least enjoyable and invigorating of all pastimes.
- Such print media as magazines and newspapers, as well as popular music, films, and theme parks are all typical expressions of common culture in many societies.
- Since most common culture in modern societies is media-based entertainment, its positive or negative role in shaping and reflecting the values of society is worthy of debate.

References

Andrejevic, M. (2003). *Reality TV: The work of being watched*. Lanham, MD: Roman & Littlefield.

Audit Bureau of Circulations. (2007). *Reports*. Available from http://www.accessabc.com/. Retrieved 6/18/08.

August, M., Brice, L.E., Harrison, L., Murphy, T., & Thigpen, D.E. (2004). Hip-hop nation: There's more to rap than just rhythms and rhymes. In M. Petracca & M. Soropure (Eds.), *Common culture: Reading and writing about American popular culture* (pp. 311-328). Upper Saddle River, NJ: Prentice Hall.

Bianculli, D. (2000). *Teleliteracy: Taking television seriously*. Syracuse, NY: Syracuse University Press.

Bryman, A. (1995). *Disney and his worlds*. London: Routledge.

Chubb, M., & Chubb, H.R. (1981). *One third of our time? An introduction to recreation behavior and resources*. New York: John Wiley & Sons.

Clay, A. (2003). Keepin' it real: Black youth, hip-hop culture, and black identity. *American Behavioral Scientist, 46*(10), 1346-1358.

Corner, J. (1999). *Critical ideas in television studies*. Oxford: Clarendon.

Frey, B.S., Benesch, C., & Stutzer, A. (2007). Does watching TV make us happy? *Journal of Economic Psychology, 28*(3), 283-313.

Freud, S. (1999 – originally published in 1915). Triebe und Triebschicksale. *Sigmund Freud Gesammelte Werke*. Frankfurt am Main: Fisher Taschenbuch Verlag.

Freysinger, V.J., & Kelly, J.R. (2004). *21st Century leisure: Current issues* (2nd Ed.). State College, PA: Venture.

Hill, R.A., Donovan, S., & Koyama, N.F. (September, 2005). Female sexual advertisement reflects resource availability in twentieth-century UK society. *Human Nature, 16*(3), 266-277.

Johnson, S. (2005). *Everything bad is good for you: How today's popular culture is actually making us smarter*. New York: Riverhead Books.

Kelly, J.R. (1982). *Leisure*. Englewood Cliffs, NJ: Prentice Hall.

Kubey, R., & Csikszentmihalyi, M. (1990). *Television and the quality of life: How viewing shapes everyday experience*. Hillsdale, NJ: Lawrence Erlbaum.

Kubey, R., & Csikszentmihalyi, M. (February 2002). Television addiction is no mere metaphor. *Scientific American, 286*(2), 74-80.

Kubey, R., & Csikszentmihalyi, M. (2004). Television addiction is no mere metaphor. In M. Petracca, & M. Sorapure (Eds.), *Common culture: Reading and writing about American popular culture* (pp. 251-272). Upper Saddle River, NJ: Prentice Hall.

Lipsitz, G. (1990). *Time passages: Collective memory and American popular culture*. Minneapolis: University of Minnesota Press.

Modleski, T. (1986). The terror of pleasure: The contemporary horror film and postmodern theory. In T. Modleski (Ed.), *Studies in entertainment: Critical approaches to mass culture* (pp. 76-89). Bloomington: Indiana University Press.

Mohler, R.A. (May 26, 2005). A common culture in the age of blogging? *Commentary*. Available from http://www.albertmohler.com. Retrieved 6/16/08.

Mosley, L. (1985). *The real Walt Disney*. London: Futura.

Motion Picture Association of America (2008). *Movie Attendance Study: 2007*. Available from http://www.mpaa.org/MovieAttendanceStudy.pdf. Retrieved 6/20/08.

Nielsen Media Research. (2008). *Reports*. Available from http://www.nielsenmedia.com. Retrieved 6/14/08.

Nielsen SoundScan. (2007). *Reports*. Available from http://www.soundscan.com. Retrieved 6/20/08.

Ogbar, J. (1999). Slouching toward Bork. *Journal of Black Studies, 30*, 164-183.

Pavlov, I.P. (1927). *Conditioned reflexes: An investigation of the physiological activity of the cerebral cortex*. London: Oxford University Press.

Petracca, M., & Sorapure, M. (2004). *Common culture: Reading and writing about American popular culture*. Upper Saddle River, NJ: Prentice Hall.

Pomerantz, D. (January 29, 2008). The top-earning women in music. *Forbes.com*. Available from http://www.forbes.com/2008/01/28/music-madonna0holywood-biz-cz_dp_0129music.html. Retrieved 6/19/08.

Postman, N. (1986). *Amusing ourselves to death*. New York: Viking.

Pozner, J.L. (2004). You're soaking in it. In M. Petracca & M. Sorapure (Eds.), *Common culture: Reading and writing about American popular culture* (pp. 319-341). Upper Saddle River, NJ: Prentice Hall.

Robinson, J.P., & Godbey, G. (1997). *Time for life: The surprising ways Americans use their time*. University Park: The Pennsylvania State University.

Rojek, C. (1993). Disney culture. *Leisure Studies, 12*, 121-135.

Sullivan, G.L., & O'Connor, P.J. (February, 1988). Women's role portrayals in magazine advertising: 1958-1983. *Sex Roles Journal, 18*(3-4), 181-188.

Teachout, T. (June 2005). Culture in the age of blogging. *Commentary, 119*(6), 39-48.

Trapp, E. (2005). The push and pull of hip-hop: A social movement analysis. *American Behavioral Scientist, 48*(11), 1482-1495.

U.S. Census Bureau. (2008). Tables 1213, 1217 and 1218. *Statistical Abstract of the United States: 2007*. Washington, D.C.: Government Printing Office.

Waters, J. (April 23, 1990). Family feuds. *Newsweek*, 58-62.

World Association of Newspapers (2005). *World Press Trends*. Available from http://www.wan-press.org/article2825.html. Retrieved 6/19/08.

TABOO RECREATION

PREVIEW

Is leisure always wholesome?

No. In spite of leisure's vital importance to the health and well-being of individuals and societies, our pastimes can also produce harmful outcomes.

What is taboo recreation?

Pastimes that are forbidden by law, custom, or belief are taboo. Examples are gambling, substance abuse, and vandalism.

Why does taboo recreation occur?

There are many explanations. The theories we explore in this chapter are anomie, differential association, and retreatism.

Is taboo recreation leisure?

This question is at the crux of the dilemma. If leisure is a condition of personal attitudes, preferences, and values, labeling leisure as harmful is useless. On the other hand, if leisure is a matter of making good choices, labeling certain pastimes as unworthy is possible.

KEY TERMS

As we've already explored, leisure is a major factor in the well-being of people and their communities. Leisure can help relieve tensions, maintain physical fitness, enhance mental equilibrium, and teach us how to get along with others. It is one of the best methods of health insurance, builds unified communities, yields a productive workforce, and can serve as a catalyst for protecting and rehabilitating the environment. Specially trained professionals working in treatment centers use leisure to help ill and injured patients return to health. Leisure is, in simple fact, one of the more positive and wholesome aspects of contemporary life.

However, leisure also has a negative side. Unpleasant results, as well as pleasant ones, are possible through our pastimes. People can be injured, or even killed, while participating in leisure pursuits. Teens can develop bad habits as a result of experimenting with harmful recreation activities. Exhaustion, apprehension, nervousness, disappointment, and frustration can be experienced through participation in outdoor pastimes and sports in particular (Lee, Howard & Datillo, 1992).

The focus of this chapter is the negative outcomes of engaging in pastimes society considers deviant. We label this taboo recreation. Our distinction lies in society's perspective about the pastimes. For example, in the United States only certain forms of gambling are legal, and in certain locations. Buying sexual pleasure is considered a problem in several countries of the world, but not in others. Vandalism can be a lot of fun for participants, but it costs property owners billions of dollars each year. Binge drinking is increasingly popular for college students, but administrators spend significant amounts of energy and money to curb it.

Pursuits such as these are considered *taboo* in many societies. The word taboo comes from the Polynesian word tapu, which usually refers to a negative supernatural force. We use the term here to signify behaviors restricted by social custom. In all societies there are strong social prohibitions against certain words, objects, and actions. Breaking a taboo can be punishable by law, or by embarrassment or shame.

Taboo:

restriction of a behavior based on social tradition

All groups of people have taboos, but the same taboos are not universal. For example, some religious groups have dietary restrictions (i.e. kosher diets). Such bodily functions as burping, spitting and nose-picking are

Figure 9.1

What is considered good leisure and bad leisure is largely determined by the values and beliefs of society. For example, the pursuit of running is given both a good and bad label by society depending on how extensively it is pursued. Running that consumes extensive time, causes feelings of strain and anxiety, and interferes with work and school responsibilities is labeled bad by some societies. (Shutterstock©, 2008)

considered either funny or taboo according to age groups. And in India it is considered desirable to eat with your fingers, while in some Western cultures this is frowned upon. What is considered taboo also changes within the same society or group across time. For example, tattooing did not become accepted in North America, Europe, and Japan until the early 2000s, when it became a popular culture expression.

Taboo is a useful descriptor of the pastimes we consider in this chapter because they are typically forbidden by custom or belief, as well as often by law. We begin our discussion of taboo recreation by describing its core concept—deviance. Then, we consider examples of taboo recreation, followed by possible explanations for them. Finally, the dilemma of taboo recreation's goodness is debated.

Box 9.1

The Study Says

Cyberslacking

Cyberslacking, or cyberloafing, refers to employees who use their work Internet access for personal reasons, while maintaining the appearance of working. Some estimate cyberslacking steals from employers about $1 billion a year in computer resources. Is personal Internet use while at work common for certain employees? Using data collected in a national telephone survey (N = 1,024), findings indicated that contrary to conventional wisdom, higher-status employees, as measured by occupational status, job autonomy, income, and education, engage in significantly more personal Internet use at work.

Garrett, R.K., & Danziger, J.N. (June 1, 2008). On cyberslacking: Workplace status and personal Internet use at work. *CyberPsychology & Behavior, 11*(3), 287-292.

Leisure and Deviance

Taboo recreation is a particular case of deviance—any behavior that violates a group's norms. In some cases the norms have been codified into laws. For example, in many cultures robbery, theft, rape, murder, and assault are considered acts of deviance that are against the law. This is referred to as *formal deviance*. In other cases, the group's norms do not have legal authority over people's behavior; in this case the deviant behaviors and consequences are more casual, or *informal deviance*. Smoking in a nonsmoking area might be an example of informal deviance.

Formal deviance:
behavior that violates formal cultural norms, such as laws

Informal deviance:
behavior that violates informal cultural norms, such as customs

Yet, from a leisure perspective, even with this clarification, what is deviant is much more complex and ambiguous. Going for a jog may build fitness levels, but so might hooking hubcaps. Joining a Scout troop may provide outlets for socialization and building self-esteem, but so could hanging out with a street gang. In truth, everyone is involved at least occasionally in deviant behavior. We've all bent a rule, taken a shortcut, and told a white lie. This is because the rules governing social life are inherently ambiguous and thus open to different interpretations. To some extent, deviance is nothing but the activity that exploits this ambivalence (Rojek, 1999a), and to some this is leisure.

We can also understand the complexity and ambiguity within deviance in terms of the sanctions applied (Becker, 1963). That is, reactions to behavior are value laden and cannot be understood in absolute terms. So instead of being a matter of seeing right and wrong in specific actions, deviance is a matter of who or what has the power to shape our judgments about social acts. Differences in power mean that if an action is considered wrong by those in power, then it is labeled deviant (Foucault, 1981). No-running-on-the-pool-deck is a rule against a deviant behavior at the community swimming pool. Running in a bathing suit in and of itself may not be considered bad, except that when it occurs where authorities (i.e., lifeguards) deem it a problem, then it is considered deviant.

Box 9.2

 *In Profile*

Forensic Leisure Science

While the field of forensic leisure science has yet to be recognized as an area of study, it may prove to yield substantial contributions toward solving societal problems involving crime (Williams, 2006).

One way to envision this is through the long-standing relationship between leisure and crime present in correctional institutions. Despite some attitudes holding that criminals shouldn't be allowed to enjoy themselves, providing particular recreation services for offenders in prison can make important rehabilitative contributions. For example, leisure has been found to offer a means for self-discovery and self-awareness (Rucker, 2005; Hood, 2003), which may be useful in the eventual release of inmates.

Another way to envision the field of forensic leisure science is via studying the lifestyles and daily behaviors of people who commit crimes (Williams, 2006). For example, although we don't usually think of serial killing as leisure [although Rojek (1999b) refers to it as mephitic leisure, or leisure that destroys life], leisure likely functions in different and complex ways at various times for the killer, including the development of the murder fantasy, techniques of capturing the victim, and techniques for avoiding detection. A better understanding of serial killers' leisure patterns might help solve cases more quickly, and perhaps even prevent them.

The incidence of deviance in leisure is not only documented in police records and social work files, but in research as well. For example, in one study (Agnew, 1990), a sample of teens indicated the reasons for their participation in 14 illegal activities. These included personal pleasure, thrill seeking, social pressure, and boredom—all qualities associated with leisure. Further, Aguilar (1987) provided rationale for considering delinquent behavior a game: "In theft or vandalism activities, the object of the game is to complete the task without getting caught" (p. 5).

Box 9.3

The Study Says

Taking Risks by College Students

Researchers have suggested experimentation with forms of taboo recreation may be a necessary and constructive component to growing up. An investigation of this explored the personal meaning of taboo recreation for college students. A sample of 12 community college students and 20 university students was interviewed. Students described a deliberate and functional process of experimenting with a variety of risk behaviors, including substance and alcohol abuse, vandalism, date rape, and unprotected consensual sex. In fact, interviewees maintained the college culture itself promotes participation in these behaviors as developmentally appropriate. For example, as one of the interviewees described it

You stick 36,000 students who are basically between the ages of 18 and 25 together, without parents ... they're on their own for the first time...shoved into a small area. I think it's gonna develop a culture of its own, and I think that would be the weekend ritual of getting dressed up and going out and getting blitzed or going dancing or finding a guy to sleep with. (p. 232).

Dworkin, J. (2005). Risk taking as developmentally appropriate experimentation for college students. *Journal of Adolescent Research, 20(*2), 219-241.

In fact, some studies refer to the concept of playful deviance. As typically applied to the behaviors of attendees of Mardi Gras in New Orleans and college students at the beach for Spring Break, playful deviance is defined as unseemly ways of performing for others (Rojek, 2000). These performances often include public nudity, raucous dancing, and drinking alcoholic beverages. Playful deviance is usually considered harmless, entertaining, and fun because it is concentrated in leisure spaces that are structured for such, and in front of an audience who encourages it.

Examples of Taboo Recreation

To illustrate the concepts discussed so far, we now consider substance abuse, gambling, and vandalism. Although there are many examples we might label as taboo recreation, these offer a breadth of behaviors most likely found in a leisure setting. That is, some of these activities are punishable by law in some circumstances or if extended too far. Some harm only those who participate, while others are harmful to others who do not participate and the society as a whole.

Substance Abuse

First, we consider *substance abuse*. Narcotics are essential in the practice of medicine; they are often effective for the relief of particular diseases and pains. Alcohol is also useful. In modest amounts it provides a means of relaxation from hectic pressures, providing both physical and psychological benefits. However, when drugs and alcohol are overused, problems can result.

Substance abuse:

over indulging in and depending on a drug, alcohol or other chemical, to the detriment of physical and mental health

Substance abuse is perhaps the most prevalent type of taboo recreation. Experience-enhancing drugs are in every region of the world, and every society has alcoholics. No society is too poor and none too knowledgeable about the consequences (Freysinger & Kelly, 2004). Nor is the abuse of alcohol and drugs for recreation a new phenomenon. In fact, the invention of agriculture seems to have been motivated not only by a need for a constant food supply, but also by the discovery of the use of cultivated grains for beer (Lazare, 1989).

Drugs and alcohol are often used in a leisure context, and themselves have many leisure qualities. They warm up a social group and cheer on a sport team. They also provide temporary escape from everyday life. Interestingly, a euphemism for using drugs is "taking a trip"—meaning to enjoy a change of pace, just as we do when we go on vacation. Cocktails are served at parties; beer is sold at baseball games; pills are popped at concerts. Marijuana is on the menu in some coffee shops in the Netherlands.

Figure 9.2

Substance abuse sometimes begins with recreational uses and settings. (© Ruth V. Russell, 2008)

How prevalent is recreational substance use? Sixty-one percent of American adults drink alcohol (Centers for Disease Control and Prevention, 2008), and the primary reason for Canadians is companionship, followed by entertainment (Cosper, Okraku & Neuman, 1985). Some authorities have declared social drinking is second only to television watching as America's favorite pastime (Gross, 1983).

Unfortunately, alcohol and other substances provide only short trips, and overuse to make the trip longer can lead to insurmountable personal and social problems. Witness the more than two million members of Alcoholics Anonymous, an organization that helps people with alcohol-related problems. As well, according to the National Institute on Drug Abuse (2007), approximately 10 percent of 8th through 12th graders abuse club drugs (such as Ecstasy, GHB, and methamphetamines).

Leisure experiences enrich the participant, and although the use of drugs and alcohol may provide momentary sociability and relaxation, their abuse ultimately prevents enrichment and leads to harm. In fact, the relationship between dysfunctional substance use and leisure is a reciprocal one. Although substance use typically begins as a leisure expression, as the use of the substance increases, the individual's leisure becomes secondary to the substance.

Box 9.4

In Focus

College Binge Drinking

Who binges?
About 44 percent of U.S. college students engage in binge drinking: 51 percent of men drink five or more drinks in a row and 40 percent of women do so. Students more likely to binge are white, age 23 or younger, and residents of a fraternity or sorority. If they were binge drinkers in high school, they are three times more likely to binge in college. The proportion of students who binge drink is nearly uniform across freshman to senior years. Almost one in four students binge drink three or more times in a two-week period. More than 2.8 million students report driving under the influence of alcohol.

Why?
To get drunk, have fun with friends, achieve the status associated with drinking, and fit in the college campus culture.

Effects?
Frequent binge drinkers are 21 times more likely than other drinkers to: miss class, fall behind in school or work, be injured, and engage in unplanned sexual activity. Each year more than 1,700 college students suffer alcohol-related deaths.

Impacts on other students?
Three of four students report experiencing at least one adverse consequence of another student's binge drinking, including: sleep or study interrupted, having to

Box 9.4 (Cont.)

take care of an intoxicated student, been insulted, experienced unwanted sex, and had a serious argument.

(adapted from Wechsler, 2005; Hingson, et al., 2005)

Questions to Consider and Discuss
1. What is your reaction to the facts on binge drinking? How prevalent is binge drinking on your campus? Do you talk with your friends about binge drinking? In what ways?
2. From your perspective, is binge drinking leisure? For example, does it help social interactions? Is binge drinking part of specific celebrations on your campus (such as 21 for 21 birthday events)?
3. If college students wanted to have leisure options other than binge drinking, what sorts of experiences would be viable alternatives? Why?

Gambling

Next, we consider gambling as an illustration of taboo recreation. How can gambling provide many of the qualities of leisure but also be harmful?

Nevada is the driest state in the United States, with an average annual rainfall of only about seven inches. As a result, much of Nevada is uninhabited, sage brush-covered desert. In 1931 the state created a new industry: gambling. Today in almost every public place, visitors and residents can enjoy slot machines, and the casinos of Reno, Tahoe, and Las Vegas are legendary. Today, gambling taxes account for about 43 percent of state revenues (Butterfield, 2005).

Dedicated gamblers in many parts of North America who were once satisfied to visit Las Vegas once or twice a year now scarcely have to leave home to play the slots, bet on the horses and dogs, buy a lottery ticket, or visit a casino. Today there are over 95 casinos in North America. They are located in resorts, Native American reservations, cruise ships, riverboats, and dog and horse tracks. Slot machines account for about 70 percent of a casino's income, and about

Figure 9.3
Las Vegas is considered the gambling capital of the world. On the strip and downtown the streets are lined with casino-gambling resorts, nightlife, shopping, and world-class tourism.
(© Ruth V. Russell, 2008)

26 percent (51.2 million) of Americans gamble in casinos—on average, once every two months. Nationally sponsored lotteries are available in six continents. Sponsors of Internet gambling are said to net $14 billion in annual profits, and about 80% of bets on horse racing are not placed in person at the track.

Gamblers are a varied demographic. For example, according to a survey conducted by Harrah's Entertainment (2006) U.S. casino gamblers range from 21 years (about 3%) to retirees (14%). Incomes range from under $35,000 (20%) to over $95,000 (31%). Thirty-three percent of gamblers are in the West, while 18 percent are in the South. Beyond casinos, and based on findings from 20 studies surveying middle and high school youth in North America (Jacobs, 2000), two out of three legally underage youth have gambled for money. Most of this underage gambling is in lotteries.

Gambling is betting on the outcome of a future event. Although people bet on almost anything with an unpredictable outcome, they bet most often on games of chance and skill. Indeed, the basis of gambling in games is reflected in its other label: gaming. As a pastime, gambling awards the player with the thrill of competition and winning. For most gamblers, it is a form of leisure. Psychologists believe the real attraction of gambling lies in the thrill of uncertainty, the daring involved in taking chances, and the challenge of testing one's skill. For example, in a study examining gambling motives among college students (Neighbors, et al., 2002), primary reasons were to win money, for fun, for social reasons, for excitement and just to have something to do.

Box 9.5

 In Your Own Experience

Gambling More Than You Want?

French Lick Casino in Indiana actively tries to help those with gambling problems. To determine who needs the help, people are encouraged to ask themselves the following questions. Try them yourself.

1. Do you lose time from work (school) due to gambling?
2. Does gambling make your home life unhappy?
3. Does gambling affect your reputation?
4. Do you ever feel remorse after gambling?
5. Do you ever gamble to get money with which to pay debts or to otherwise solve financial difficulties?
6. Does gambling cause a decrease in your ambition or efficiency?
7. After losing, do you feel you must return as soon as possible and win back your losses?
8. After a win, do you have a strong urge to return and win more?
9. Do you often gamble until your last dollar is gone?

Box 9.5 (Cont.)

10. Do you ever borrow to finance your gambling?
11. Do you ever sell anything to finance gambling?
12. Are you reluctant to use "gambling money" for normal expenditures?
13. Does gambling make you careless about the welfare of yourself and your family?
14. Do you ever gamble longer than you planned?
15. Do you ever gamble to escape worry or trouble?
16. Do you ever commit, or consider committing, an illegal act to finance your gambling?
17. Does gambling cause you to have difficulty sleeping?
18. Do arguments, disappointments or frustrations create within you an urge to gamble?
19. Do you have an urge to celebrate good fortune by a few hours of gambling?
20. Do you ever consider self-destruction as a result of your gambling?

If you answer yes to at least seven of these questions, the casino says you may have a gambling problem.

Brochure, 2008, French Lick Resort / Casino, French Lick, Indiana

Unfortunately, some gamble because they also believe it is a quick way to make money, and others gamble despite a desire to stop. This is referred to as *problem gambling.* Problem gambling often is considered in terms of the harm experienced by the gambler or others, rather than by the gambler's behavior. For example, people with problems gambling tend to have lost significant amounts of money, use gambling as a way to escape and withdraw from family and jobs, are preoccupied with thoughts of gambling, and are more likely to engage in illegal activities. A study by the United Kingdom Gambling Commission (2007) found that approximately 0.6% of the adult population had problem gambling issues, and, according to a University of Buffalo (2008) study of American gamblers, 2.1 percent of youth between ages 14 and 21 have problems with gambling.

Problem gambling:
an urge to gamble despite harmful negative consequences

With the pastime of gambling it is perhaps easiest to understand the application of the term taboo. Some gambling is legal—indeed government sponsored and sanctioned. Other gambling events are illegal. The distinction between is quite hazy. When state laws continue to maintain that gambling is immoral and prosecute people for engaging in it (about 20,000 each year), yet increasingly sponsor state lotteries and receive tax receipts from casinos, tracks, etc., there appears a contradiction. We might be tempted to conclude all gambling from which a government doesn't earn money is illegal!

In Profile

Sport Betting: Legal or Illegal?

Sports betting is the pastime of predicting sporting event results by making a wager. Perhaps more so than any other form of gambling, the legality and general acceptance of sports betting varies widely worldwide. For example, in the United States, the Professional and Amateur Sports Protection Act of 1994 makes it illegal to operate a betting or gambling scheme except for in a few states, such as Montana, Delaware, and Nevada where certain forms of sport betting are legal. Meanwhile, the FBI estimates that $3.8 billion is bet illegally each year on the NCAA basketball tournament alone.

In many European countries bookmaking (the profession of accepting sports wagers) is highly regulated, but not criminalized. For Americans, the legality of sports betting on the Internet is even more confusing. It is relatively safe to conclude it is illegal, yet no arrests have been made as a result of any of the millions of daily bets placed online on sporting events. Proponents of legalizing sports betting regard it as a hobby for sport fans that increases their interest in particular sporting events. Opponents fear it threatens the integrity of amateur and professional sports, as exampled in the history of attempts by sports gamblers to fix matches and games.

Vandalism

Finally, we cite vandalism as an example of taboo recreation. Defined as damaging or defacing private or public property, vandalism takes many forms: covering walls with graffiti, breaking streetlights, salting lawns, cutting trees without permission, egg throwing, tire slashing, draping toilet paper in trees, keying, writing on the pages of library books, and even creating crop circles. In many cultures, vandalism per se is often considered one of the least serious crimes, but in Singapore, a person who commits an act of vandalism may be liable for up to three years in prison.

Regardless, vandalism is usually expensive to correct. For example, vandalism to parks alone annually cost taxpayers in King County, Washington $21,000, in Boise, Idaho $60,000, and in Colorado Springs, Colorado $100,000. According to the National Crime Prevention Council (2008), some vandals work in groups, and most vandals are young people—from children to teens to young adults, who vandalize out of boredom, anger, revenge, defiance, and in association with friends.

These motives vary, actually, according to the category of vandalism. For example, slovenly vandalism is an expression of bad manners and carelessness, such as littering. Although the least destructive, it is so pervasive that this form of vandalism is the most expensive to solve. No-other-way-to-do-it vandalism results from such actions as sitting on a fence because there is no bench, or leaning a bicycle against a tree because there is no bike rack. In addition, conflict vandalism occurs from doing what is most logical and natural, regardless of the intent of a facility's design, such as paths resulting from people choosing the most direct route through an open space. Malicious vandalism usually results from people feeling mistreated and wanting to get back at society, or a particular agency or person, such as by defacing a park sign. This form of vandalism can also feel threatening and frightening to the victim.

Some people declare that for them vandalism is a form of leisure, and ironically, places of leisure, such as parks and playgrounds, suffer the most. Indeed, the most common forms of vandalism are the ones that can be considered the most recreational. For example, self-expression vandalism, such as graffiti, is

---

Figure 9.4

Outdoor art – or is it graffiti? Graffiti – or is it outdoor art? (© Ruth V. Russell, 2008)

usually an attempt to be noticed, and thrill vandalism arises from the goading or daring of friends, or from an individual's desire for excitement, such as the damage to private property from swimming in limestone quarries. Indeed, it is self-expression vandalism that is perhaps at the heart of the taboo dilemma. Is graffiti, for example, pop art or is it deviance?

Explanations of Taboo Recreation

Why do people participate in leisure pursuits considered harmful, immoral, wrong, or a crime? What explains the popularity of substance abuse, gambling, and vandalism? As with most dilemmas in society, explanations for taboo recreation have been sought in order to reduce its incidence. But, as with deviant behavior in general, available explanations do not fully settle the matter. As a result, there are many theoretical positions currently available. We'll consider three that are perhaps most applicable to taboo recreation behaviors: anomie, differential association, and retreatism.

The first explanation for taboo recreation is the concept of anomie. *Anomie* is a state of isolation that occurs when once-viable social norms no longer work for people (Merton, 1968). Anomie can be traced to an imbalance between a goal and the means to attain it.

Anomie:
a lack of purpose resulting in the demise of formerly useful social norms

Simmel (1971) blames the changes and disruptions of life in modern society in general as creating ripe conditions for the development of anomie. Although the point is not that modern stress causes deviant forms of leisure, perhaps it does provide an environment in which taboo pastime choices are nurtured (Moore, 1982). In fact, this may not only describe individual normlessness, but also that in groups and entire societies.

An example of such social instability caused by the erosion of norms is sport spectating. Around the world, watching sport competitions is a major pursuit. Television has a constant stream of sports programming 24 hours a day. Universities have multimillion-dollar sport programs with stadiums seating up to 100,000 spectators. Sporting events are a daily topic of conversation wherever people gather, and attachments to particular teams and athletes seem to provide social and personal identity for many of us. A wonderful vicarious pleasure results from watching top athletes perform.

Yet, something has gone wrong! With greater frequency we read about rioting and violence in the crowds at sporting events. Fires have been started in the stands and property destroyed. Fans have crossed barricades to attack and sometimes kill the fans for the other team. Athletes have been attacked in parking lots after the event. Referees have been assaulted. It seems the attitude has gone from "It doesn't matter whether you win or lose, but how you play the game" to being "In your face."

There are numerous estimates as to why sport spectator violence occurs, many having to do with the conditions of the sport event environment itself. For example, alcohol consumption is usually associated with eruptions of fan violence. Also, the media is believed to encourage "hooliganism" at sporting events by way of sensationalizing its occurrence. As well, certain sport types seem to be more conducive to spectator disruptions. For example, an examination of newspaper accounts by Eitzen (1984) demonstrated that in 75 percent of the cases, the precipitating event of spectator sport violence was violence in the game. This is perhaps why football, soccer, and ice hockey are often cited in sport spectator violence examples.

Figure 9.5

Thoroughbred horseracing is one of the most popular live spectator sports in the world, yet is usually not an example of spectator violence. Why? (© Ruth V. Russell, 2008)

Boredom may provide another environment conducive to the creation of deviant leisure choices. Boredom is a human emotion that occurs when one's life experience is not meaningful enough. Boredom usually results from too little stimulation, motivation, and interest. Although we typically consider leisure as an antidote to boredom, it commonly occurs in those who regularly perform monotonous exercise routines, and it is one of the main reasons participants drop out of sports.

For example, Iso-Ahola and Weisinger (1990) have proposed that boredom is a common consequence of our pastimes. They called this *leisure boredom*. How true for you are the following questions?

- For me, leisure time just drags on and on.
- In my leisure time, I usually don't like what I'm doing, but I don't know what else to do.
- I waste too much of my leisure time sleeping.
- Leisure-time activities do not excite me.

Leisure boredom:

when people feel they cannot escape a meaningless leisure routine

These and other questions in the study (p. 10) helped Iso-Ahola and Weisinger discover that boredom can indeed occur in leisure. If you agreed with these questions, your perception is likely to be that leisure can be boring. Leisure boredom is the perception that leisure is a meaningless routine that does not satisfy the need for optimal arousal. Many consider leisure boredom a special case of anomie that can lead to destructive choices in many aspects of life. For example, in a study of school drop-outs, while adjusting for the effects of age, gender, and race, leisure boredom was a significant predictor of dropping out of school (Wegner, et al., 2007).

In addition to anomie, other explanations for taboo recreation are plausible. For example, the theory of *differential association* simply claims that delinquent behavior, including taboo recreation, is learned through interaction with others. If a person's social group is delinquent, deviant forms of leisure may be learned

Differential association:

delinquent behavior learned from others

from it. Such social groups as peers on sports teams, housemates at college, classmates at school, and friends in the neighborhood affect young people in particular.

Box 9.7

The Study Says

High School Sports Participation and Deviance

Despite its long-standing popular appeal, the idea that athletic activity for youth is a deterrent to delinquency is not empirically supported. A study testing the relationship between high school sports participation and deviance concluded it depends on both the type of deviant behavior and the level of athletic involvement. For example, it was found that shoplifting decreases with sports participation, while drunken driving increases. Perhaps this is an illustration of the theory of differential association, whereas peers are a more constant companion for athletes.

Hartmann, D., & Massoglia, M. (2007). Reassessing the relationship between high school sports participation and deviance: Evidence of enduring, bifurcated effects. *The Sociological Quarterly, 48*(3), 485-505.

An obvious example of this is youth gangs. In the United States there are an estimated 24,000 gangs with 760,000 members, and internationally youth gangs have been documented in both developed and developing countries in North and South America, Europe, Asia, and Africa. Youth gangs are located in urban, suburban, small-town, and rural areas, and are often organized along ethnic, racial, and gender lines. Their activities include robbery, vandalism, drug sales, and aggravated assault.

Because youth gangs typically offer opportunities for power, recognition, excitement, and independence (Manson, 1990), they create pleasurable ~~...~~ tentially lead to antisocial actions. Lo (2000) highlighted ~~...~~ sociation that controls this. That is, the influence ~~...~~ depending on how frequently they assemble, ~~...~~ the level of priority the friendship is to ~~...~~ ndship group.

~~...~~ taboo recreation may be the idea of ~~...~~ yle that pulls away from dominant social norms ~~...~~ pression (Rojek, 1999a). Dropping out, taking drugs, ~~...~~ n, and engaging in other pastimes that are antithetical to ~~...~~ rder of life may be considered an expression ~~...~~ nich a lifestyle centered around an alternative ~~...~~ identity is created. Merton (1968) provided the classic ~~...~~ cription of retreatism as those who have "relinquished ~~...~~ ulturally prescribed goals, and their behavior does not accord with institution norms" (p. 207).

Retreatism: differences from the dominant social norms as a matter of personal expression

Box 9.8

 *In Focus*

Freaks Talk Back

Nobody wants to watch anything that's smarmy or tabloid or silly or unseemly – except the audience.

(talk show host Sally Jessy Raphael, 1990)

Tabloid talk shows are a genre of American television that achieved peak viewership during the late 20th century. Airing mostly during the day, the genre originated with the *Phil Donahue Show* and was popularized by the personal confession-filled *Oprah Winfrey Show*. Sometimes described as the freak shows of the late 20th century, guests were encouraged to reveal nasty personal secrets on national television. The hosts riled them up and then scolded them for being so malicious. Cheating spouses, drag queen makeovers, Christian pornographers, a black man who wants to join the Ku Klux Klan, and all manner of different lifestyles were paraded before the television audience.

Critics observed that *Geraldo, Montel Williams, The Jerry Springer Show, Sally Jessy Raphael, Jenny Jones* and many others blurred the lines between what is bizarre and alarming, and what is typical and inconsequential (Abt & Mustazza, 1997). They boosted abnormality by exaggerating its frequency and embellishing its consequences. Yale sociology professor Joshua Gamson (1998) argued that the genre's focus on alternative lifestyles provided a great deal of media visibility for people formerly invisible to the rest of society.

By the early 2000s, the tabloid talk show began to decline in popularity with viewing audiences. One explanation is the audience shifted over to the new reality TV genre that rose to prominence around the same time.

Questions to Consider and Discuss

1. If you can, watch an episode of a tabloid talk show, particularly *The Jerry Springer Show.* As you watch, ask yourself what are the appropriate boundaries between public and private, classy and trashy, normal and abnormal, deviant and not deviant.
2. These shows have been labeled "paradoxes of visibility." That is, with dramatic fury they democratize through exploitation, tell truth wrapped in a lie, and normalize through a freak show. Do you think this is a correct interpretation? Why or why not?
3. What are some similarities between the tabloid talk show and the reality TV genre? Would you consider today's reality television to be "paradoxes of visibility?"

One of the more interesting studies of a retreatist lifestyle is Willis' (1978) account of motorcycle subcultures. He found lifestyle disengagement constituted their basis for existence. They violated certain dominant social norms because of their passion for engine technology, not because they rejected dominant society. Simply, the motorcycle culture was felt by its members to be superior—where real life happened to them. Other studies (cf. Maynard, 2008) point to the celebration of masculinity in many motorcycle subcultures as the basis for the retreatist lifestyle.

The Dilemma of Goodness

We close this chapter where we began. There is widespread undeniable proof that leisure is good for us. Theoretical, empirical, and anecdotal testimony abounds demonstrating the economic, physiological, environmental, social, and psychological benefits of leisure. Indeed, according to Mannell and Kleiber (1997), for leisure to be of genuine benefit, it must be responsible for at least the maintenance of a desired condition, and preferably an improvement of what would have otherwise occurred.

This, of course, is not always possible in all situations. Some leisure expressions harm participants as well as other people, including societies as a whole. Indeed, as pointed out by Rojek (1999a), "an obvious and indisputable fact about leisure in modern society is that many of the most popular activities are illegal" (p. 82).

Can we conclude, then, that leisure is only leisure when it is healthy, moral, legal, and productive? This is the *dilemma of goodness*. Let's discuss the two sides of the dilemma.

Dilemma of goodness: the question of whether leisure is only leisure when it is good

Aristotle wrote in *Politics* that the cultivated ability to use leisure properly is the basis of a person's and a society's worth. Making good and healthy free-time choices is leisure, not simply doing anything one pleases. Leisure is a matter of social responsibility. To Aristotle, leisure meant making the right choices among life's many alternatives, and also doing them well (Sylvester, 1991). Today, we call this idea of positive life choices *wellness*.

Wellness: making choices that lead to social, mental, physical, and spiritual health

Indeed, wellness is the premise of professionals who work in leisure agencies. Helping people achieve healthy free-time choices is why the YMCA, Girl Scouts, municipal parks and recreation departments, camps, and other organizations and services exist. Professionals in leisure services consider leisure to be a force of good that allows us the space and time to develop our healthy selves—to be well.

There is another side to the dilemma of goodness, of course. Contrary to the teachings of Aristotle and the goals of leisure services agencies, an alternative perspective maintains leisure is derived from personal feelings alone. According to this distinction, leisure is in the heart and mind of the individual and has nothing to do with outside factors, such as what other people think. Leisure is considered a private choice based on intrinsically motivated joy and freedom and is not a matter of morality.

Figure 9.6

Leisure services provide opportunities for creating wellness for people and society. (© Ruth V. Russell, 2008)

Ideational mentality:
something is bad based on our own ideas

Sensate mentality:
something is bad based on your own experience

Prole leisure:
the pastimes of the lowest social or economic classes of people

What do you think? Of course, this dilemma is not as simple as it may appear. In fact, the label taboo recreation itself suggests complications. For example, another concept that attempts to explain deviant leisure pursuits is *ideational mentality* (Heise, 1988). Laws and beliefs against substance abuse, vandalism, and gambling based on ideational mentality are primarily morally derived. That is, people have an "idea" that something is bad. Even though they do not wish to participate in it themselves, they feel the need to prohibit others from being involved because they believe such a restriction is for the public good. For example, some people morally know experiencing a mood uplift from walking through an inspiring natural landscape is leisure, while experiencing a mood uplift induced by a hallucinogenic drug is not.

Another concept that makes the dilemma of goodness complex is *sensate mentality*. This explanation focuses on the more tangible and physical aspects of laws, such as antisocial acts of crimes with victims (Heise, 1988). When we consider substance abuse, vandalism, and gambling as deviant leisure activities it is because our own senses tell us through our own experiences that they are harmful. For example, some people also experientially know that experiencing a mood uplift from walking through an inspiring natural landscape is leisure, while experiencing a mood uplift induced by a hallucinogenic drug is not.

Still yet, even though it may be rather straightforward either way to distinguish mood uplifts from landscape and from drugs, other distinctions in goodness are not so simple. For example, is attending the opera better than attending a rock concert? Is paintball bad and finger painting good?

This introduces another concept—*prole leisure*. Prole leisure expressions include motorcycling, demolition derbies, rock concerts, bar hopping, roller derby, street racing, paintball, mudding, and professional wrestling. While some might argue leisure in modern society is becoming more prole and thus more debased, the idea that leisure is a matter of personal definition, makes this argument seem elitist. Therefore, is taboo recreation simply prole leisure?

Regardless of your position on the dilemma of goodness, one thing is certain: leisure is both the problem and the remedy for deviance. Leisure produces socially productive behavior as well as socially unproductive behavior.

What We Understand About Taboo Recreation

Leisure holds tremendous potential for people's well-being, but at times leisure can have negative outcomes. As a result of studying this chapter you should understand that:

- Taboo recreations are those pastimes typically forbidden by law, custom, or belief.
- Examples of taboo recreation include substance abuse, vandalism, and gambling.
- As an explanation of taboo recreation, anomie occurs when once viable social norms no longer control people's actions.
- As another explanation of taboo recreation, differential association is the idea that delinquent behavior is learned through our social groups.
- As a third attempt to explain taboo recreation, retreatism claims deviance is simply a matter of personal expression.
- Determining good from bad leisure is a dilemma. If leisure is a matter of personal preferences, distinctions of worth for specific pastimes are useless. Or, if leisure requires social responsibility in making free-time choices, certain pursuits are unworthy.
- This dilemma of goodness is further complicated by the concepts of ideational mentality, sensate mentality, and prole leisure.

References

Abt, V., & Mustazza, L. (1997). *Coming after Oprah: Cultural fallout in the age of the TV talk show*. Bowling Green, Ohio: Bowling Green University Popular Press.

Agnew, R. (1990). The origins of delinquent events: An examination of offender accounts. *Journal of Research in Crime and Delinquency, 27*, 267-294.

Aguilar, T.E. (1987). A leisure perspective of delinquent behavior. Paper presented at the Fifth Canadian Congress of Leisure Research, Halifax, Nova Scotia.

Alcoholics Anonymous. (2008). *A. A. Fact File*. Available from http://www.alcoholics-anonymous.org/en_information_aa.cfm. Retrieved 6/24/08.

Becker, H. (1963). *Outsiders*. New York: Free Press.

Butterfield, F. (March 31, 2005). As gambling grows, states depend on their cut. *New York Times*. Available from http://www.nytimes.com/2005/03/31/national/31gamble.html?pagewanted=print&position=. Retrieved 6/25/08.

Centers for Disease Control and Prevention. (2008). *Data and Statistics*. Available from http://www.cdc.gov/datastatistics/. Retrieved 6/24/08.

Cosper, R., Okraku, I., & Neuman, B. (1985). Public drinking in Canada: A national study of a leisure activity. *Society and Leisure, 8*, 709-715.

Eitzen, D.S. (1984). *Sport in contemporary society*. New York: St. Martin's Press.

Foucault, M. (1981). *The history of sexuality (Vol. 1)*. Harmondsworth, United Kingdom: Penguin.

Freysinger, V.J., & Kelly, J.R. (2004). *21st Century leisure: Current issues* (2nd Ed.). State College, PA: Venture.

Gamson, J. (1998). *Freaks talk back: Tabloid talk shows and sexual nonconformity.* Chicago: The University of Chicago Press.

Gross, L. (1983). *How much is too much: The effects of social drinking.* New York: Random House.

Harrah's Entertainment, Inc. (2006). *Gambler Survey.* Available from http://www. harrahs.com/harrahs-corporte/about-us-profile-of-gambler.html. Retrieved 6/25/08.

Heise, D.R. (1988). Delusions and the construction of reality. In T.F. Oltmanns & B.A Maher (Eds.), *Delusional beliefs (Wiley Series on Personality Processes).* (pp. 45-69). New York: John Wiley & Sons.

Hingson, R., Heeren, T., Winter, M., & Wechsler, H. (2005). Magnitude of alcohol-related mortality and morbidity among U.S. college students ages 18-24: Changes from 1998 to 2001. *Annual Review of Public Health, 26,* 259-279.

Hood, C.D. (2003). Women in recovery from alcoholism: The place of leisure. *Leisure Sciences, 25,* 51-79.

Iso-Ahola, S.E., & Weisinger, E. (1990). Perceptions of boredom in leisure: Conceptualization, reliability and validity of the leisure boredom scale. *Journal of Leisure Research, 22*(1), 1-17.

Jacobs, D.F. (2000). Juvenile gambling in North America: An analysis of long-term trends and future prospects. *Journal of Gambling Studies, 16*(2-3), 119-152.

Lazare, D. (1989). Drugs 'r' us. In *Drugs, Society, and Behavior.* (pp. 26-39), *91/92.*

Lee, Y., Howard, D., & Dattilo, J. (1992). The negative side of leisure experience. Paper presented at the Leisure Research Symposium, National Recreation and Park Association Congress, Cincinnati, OH.

Lo, C.D. (2000). The impact of first drinking and differential association on collegiate drinking. *Sociological Focus, 33,* 265-280.

Mannell, R.C., & Kleiber, D.A. (1997). *A social psychology of leisure.* State College, PA: Venture.

Manson, G.W. (1990). *Why join a gang?* Burnaby, British Columbia: Burnaby Parks and Recreation Department.

Maynard, J.R.A. (2008). *Between man and machine: A socio-historical analysis of masculinity in North America motorcycle culture.* Unpublished masters thesis, Queen's University.

Merton, R.K. (1968). *Social theory and social structure.* Glencoe, IL: Free Press.

Moore, T.J. (1982). A study of leisure choices of young offenders and young non-offenders and the impact of social structure and anomie on these choices. Unpublished masters thesis, Acadia University, Wolfville, Nova Scotia.

National Institute on Drug Abuse. (2007). *Drugs of Abuse / Related Topics.* Available from http://www.nida.nih.gov/DrugPages/Clubdrugs.html. Retrieved 6/24/08.

Neighbors, C., Lostutter, T.W., Cronce, J.M., & Larimer, M.E. (2002). Exploring college student gambling motivation. *Journal of Gambling Studies, 18*(4), 361-370.

National Crime Prevention Council (2008). *The Scoop on Vandalism* (brochure). Available from http://www.ncpc.org/publications/brochures/teens-1/vandalism.pdf. Retrieved 6/24/08.

Raphael, S.J. (1990). *Sally: Unconventional success*. New York: Morrow.

Rojek, C. (1999a). Deviant leisure: The dark side of free-time activity. In E.L. Jackson, & T.L. Burton (Eds.), *Leisure studies: Prospects for the Twenty-first Century* (pp. 81-96). State College, PA: Venture.

Rojek, C. (1999b). Abnormal leisure: Invasive, mephitic and wild forms. *Society and Leisure, 22*, 21-37.

Rojek, C. (2000). *Leisure and culture*. New York: St. Martin's Press.

Rucker, L. (2005). Yoga and restorative justice in prison: An experience of 'response-ability to harms.' *Contemporary Justice Review, 8*, 107-120.

Simmel, G. (1971). *On individuality and social forms*. Chicago: Chicago University Press.

Sylvester, C. (1991). Recovering a good idea for the sake of goodness: An interpretive critique of subjective leisure. In T.L. Goodale & P.A. Witt (Eds.), *Recreation and leisure: Issues in an era of change* (pp. 83-96). State College, PA: Venture.

United Kingdom Gambling Commission. (2007). *British Gambling Prevalence Study 2007*. Available from http://www.gamblingcommission.gov.uk/Client/detail.asp?ContentId=288. Retrieved 6/30/08.

University of Buffalo (May 7, 2008). Estimated 750,000 problem gamblers among America's youth. *ScienceDaily*. Available from http://www.sciencedaily.com/releases/2008/05/080506163918.htm. Retrieved 6/25/08.

Wechsler, H. (2005). Harvard School of Public Health College Alcohol Study, 2001 [Computer file]. ICPSR04291-v2. Boston, MA: Harvard School of Public Health [producer], Ann Arbor, MI: Inter-university Consortium for Political and Social Research [distributor], 2008-02-05.

Wegner, L., Flisher, A.J., Chikoubvu, P., Lombard, C., & King, G. (2007). Leisure boredom and high school dropouts in Cape Town, South Africa. *Journal of Adolescence, 31*(3), 421-431.

Williams, D.J. (2006). Forensic leisure science: A new frontier for leisure scholars. *Leisure Sciences, 28*, 91-95.

Willis, P. (1978). *Profane culture*. London: Routledge & Kegan Paul.

PART THREE

LEISURE AS INSTRUMENT: SYSTEMS CONTEXT

Leisure is a powerful system that both helps and harms the social order.

In this final section, we turn our attention to the functional side of leisure: its ability to be a tool for accomplishing other things beyond itself.

Chapter 10
Explores leisure's use as an instrument of social good by tracing its history in the U.S.

Chapter 11
Considers how leisure mirrors a nation's level of economic development and drives its economy.

Chapter 12
Demonstrates how an instrumental web among leisure, time, and work dictates our lives.

Chapter 13
Focuses on leisure as a means to both achieving and resisting human equity.

Chapter 14
Concludes our explorations by overviewing today's leisure services system.

CHAPTER TEN

USING LEISURE

PREVIEW

Can leisure be functional?

Yes. Today leisure is viewed as an important force for achieving goals beyond itself.

How does leisure become functional?

As societies become more complex, they become more reliant on leisure as a tool for solving problems.

How did leisure's functionality come about?

One example is the history of leisure's use as a social problem-solving tool in the United States.

KEY TERMS

As societies become more complex, they also become more reliant on leisure as a tool for solving problems and creating social good. That is, leisure has a *utilitarian* role. This chapter uses history to set the stage for making this point, while later chapters in this final part of the book further illustrate the point through specific contemporary examples.

Utilitarian:

something useful

Even in ancient societies leisure served purposes greater than its own expression. That is, leisure served a specific and needed function. Today we also recognize leisure for its ability to solve problems and be a *public good*. It plays a key role in not only civic celebrations and family vitality, but also in counteracting deprivation, and improving social communication and cooperation. Leisure is useful in creating higher quality lives for individuals and societies.

Public good:

resources that benefit everyone

Although leisure is far from being a perfect solution to social difficulties, it is a major contemporary problem solver. It accomplishes this by creating community. That is, communities take life-sustaining actions, as community members work together because they care for each other. It is through community that we demonstrate leisure's ability to accomplish so much. In this chapter we use the United States to demonstrate leisure's utilitarian role in creating public good by creating community.

Figure 10.1

Leisure develops public good by creating community.
(© Ruth V. Russell, 2008)

Colonial America

As late as the 1400s, native people were the only inhabitants of the western hemisphere, but following Columbus' voyage of 1492, for the next 400 years, large waves of non-native people mostly from European countries sailed across the Atlantic Ocean to North and South America. Among them were British colonists, who settled on the East Coast of North America between what are now the states of Maine and Georgia. They came in search of opportunities for wealth, power, freedom, and adventure.

However, those who settled in the northern regions of this area did not find great riches at first; instead, they found rugged wilderness. These dangers and difficulties in the early 1600s meant the earliest colonists suffered from starvation and disease. America's abundant resources of fertile soils, abundant water supplies, and plentiful minerals had to be harnessed. Little time and energy could be squandered when there was so much work to be done just to survive. In some cases this view about idleness led to strict governmental policies. For example, the Virginia Assembly declared in 1619 that any person found idle would be condemned to prison.

As well, since many of the new settlers were motivated to cross the Atlantic because of a belief in a "divine mission," a calling that rebelled against the conspicuous pleasures of the privileged classes of the English aristocracy, leisure's role was doubly questioned. For example, the Puritans of England and the American colonies represented a broad movement of radical Protestants that emerged within the Church of England in the 1590s. Their objectives were both to purify worship (eliminating remnants of Catholicism from church doctrine and practice) and to purge society of godlessness, or sinfulness (Cross, 1990). Indeed, the Puritan calendar of the late 1640s abolished all Catholic holy days, including Christmas, and replaced them with both secular and religious holidays based on fasting, humiliation, and thanksgiving (Borsay, 2006).

Over the years, history has incorporated evidence such as this as the basis for concluding the Puritans did not enjoy themselves, associating them instead with dour prudery. The popular analysis about this era and people is that their strict religious principles are actually what prevent Americans from truly enjoying themselves—that the Puritan past of the early colonies renders contemporary American pleasure chained to guilt, sanctimony, and hypocrisy (Daniels, 1995).

Yet, as you know, everyone plays. The need for relaxation, joy, and happiness is built into the biology and psychology of every human being. It is the forms of play, however, that are not universal but rather a social construction shaped by specific circumstances. Thus, a few historians publishing recently have begun to develop a new view of Puritanism that is in opposition to the popularly held view. According to them, the Puritans did enjoy themselves.

Therefore, in spite of the hard work to be done and religious reforms, early European colonial life provides numerous examples of common pastime practices. Colonial recreations included reading, socializing, singing, dancing, archery, shooting, hunting, fishing, fowling, football, wrestling, nine-pins, tennis, horse racing, gambling, billiards, card games, and an early version of shuffleboard (O'Keefe, 2002). Typical of people of the 17th century, they liked to drink, eat well, and play games. The wealthy also enjoyed private pastimes, including theatrical amusements.

What is distinctive about colonial leisure is that it was expected that people's pastimes serve a purpose. Their recreation ethic is best understood as utilitarian. Celebrations while making a quilt or building a barn, for example, made it possible for many hands to help with the task. Therefore, the northern colonists took great pains to distinguish "lawful" recreation as that contributing to the greater good from "unlawful" recreation, or idleness.

Social activities were favorite pastimes of the settlers in the southern East Coast colonies as well, but for different reasons. Unlike their northern counterparts, the lifestyle of the southern colonies more closely resembled that of the British aristocracy—they shared in their tastes for lavish entertainment and hospitality.

Weddings and funerals, as well as horse races, cockfights, and bowling matches brought people together for festivities. Dances, parties, barbecues, and little plays were popular forms of home entertainment. Gambling was celebrated with cards, dice, coin tossing, and lotto. A notable southerner, Thomas Jefferson, was an avid reader, writer, and gourmet cook!

Some scholars have drawn a similarity between the nature of leisure in the southern colonies and that of the ancient Greeks. That is, what made all this devotion to pastimes possible for the antebellum South was a system of slavery for people brought from Africa beginning in the 1600s. By the Civil War, about four million slaves supported a privileged leisure lifestyle for about one fourth of southern white people.

Although American folklore portrays cheerful slaves dancing to banjo music, in reality they experienced very little leisure. Only during the Christmas season did owners allow a few days for feasting, dancing, music, and games. Those who worked in the fields labored daily from sunrise to sunset. If there was a full moon during the cotton-picking season, the field slaves worked until late at night. Even when there was free time, slaves did not experience the freedom of leisure.

It is symbolic, then, that many of the musical and dance forms prevalent in the slave culture featured the theme of freedom. For example, although still debated among scholars, some claim the early songs sung by slaves contained words that were codes for seeking freedom. In "Wade in the Water," one of the most common slave songs and still a gospel standard, some interpreters claim there are literal escape instructions provided, such as in the song "Drinking Gourd" where the lyrics suggest following the big dipper star constellation to flee:

> *When the sun comes up and the first quail calls, follow the drinking gourd.*
> *For the old man is a-waiting to carry you to freedom,*
> *If you follow the drinking gourd.*

Box 10.1

 *In Profile*

Nicodemus

Soon after the end of the Civil War in 1865, slavery was outlawed with the adoption of the Thirteenth Amendment to the Constitution. Soon after that Nicodemus in north-central Kansas witnessed great arrivals of African Americans escaping the horrors of Reconstruction in the south. They were known as "exodusters." As former slaves they came to begin a new life.

At first Nicodemus settlers had to cope with many hardships on the Kansas frontier. Their early shelters were burrows dug in the sides of dirt banks. Wooden structures eventually replaced the burrows, but finding food was a far more difficult problem. Few of the settlers had any money, as most had spent all their funds just to get there. But, by the 1880s the Nicodemus Town Company was established to secure food from across the state.

By now 35 residential and commercial structures had also been erected, a school district was initiated, with most of the classes taught in people's homes, and Nicodemus had a baseball team, a literary society, social lodges, and an ice cream

Box 10.1 (Cont.)

parlor. But, by 1910 Nicodemus began a gradual decline in population, and with the closing of the post office in 1953, the importance of this African American settlement ended.

In 1996 Nicodemus was established as a national historic site, and stands today as a symbol of the pioneer spirit of the African Americans who dared leave the only region they had known to seek personal freedom and the opportunity to develop their talents and capabilities (National Park Service, 2002).

Transitions of the 1800s

During the early 1800s, European settlers moved westward by the thousands over the Appalachian Mountains into the new states and territories. As before, these hardy people were searching for a better life, and through hard work and sacrifice, settled the western wilderness as earlier settlers had done in the East. As native residents of these lands were forced out, they also endured the hardships of sickness and death.

The economic value of expansion into the rich interior of the continent enabled the United States to become a leading agricultural nation. Developments in transportation also contributed to major economic growth as new roads and about 9,000 miles of railroad lines enabled the shipping of goods by land. Accompanying these economic and industrial changes were, of course, changes in how people lived, that eventually meant a more utilitarian role for leisure.

For example, because city populations were growing so rapidly the need for mass entertainments became useful. City people flocked to plays performed in theaters. Groups of entertainers and magicians toured the countryside performing for small town audiences. P.T. Barnum, the most famous showman of the time, fascinated the public with unusual attractions, including tightrope walkers, pantomimes, and tumblers. The variety musical show also became popular, and by the 1860s, entrepreneurs such as New Yorker Tony Pastor enticed men, women, and children to his "opera house" on the Bowery for a program of singers, comedians, and animal and acrobatic acts. By 1879 more than 10 large traveling circuses toured the country.

This was also the era of taking a spa treatment at a resort. With roots in ancient Greek and Roman times, and a rich tradition in Western Europe, American spa tourism originally focused on the curative powers of spring water. Each year the affluent from the urban north and the southern gentry made a migration to summer at Newport, winter at Palm Beach, and spring and autumn at one of the inland spas such as the Greenbrier Hotel in White Sulphur Springs, West Virginia. These socially exclusive resorts were preeminent until the late 1800s, when a wider social base began to be served by such seaside resorts as Atlantic City in New Jersey and Coney Island in New York (Towner, 1996).

Figure 10.2

P.T. Barnum and Charles Sherwood Stratton (Tom Thumb) c. 1850. (Courtesy of the National Portrait Gallery, Smithsonian Institute, Washington, D.C.)

Another transition in the pastime patterns of the 1800s was the increasing respectability of sports. Previously associated with gambling, drunkenness, and violence, sports gradually gained legitimacy (Cross, 1990). A new attitude toward the human body helped, as it became a symbol of physical courage and disciplined will. New sports were also introduced from other countries. For example, German immigrants introduced gymnastics and Scottish immigrants imported track-and-field events.

It also helped that a concern for the nation's health increased and public schools began to promote the idea of fitness and sports for youth. Although colleges initially offered little leadership in the growth of other sporting activities, they did introduce and promote football. The first intercollegiate game was played between Princeton and Rutgers in 1869, arousing spectator enthusiasm from the start.

Private athletic clubs were also founded to provide indoor exercise primarily for businessmen. The American country club, originating in 1882 near Boston, first provided cricket and tennis, and later golf, to its exclusive membership. By 1891, with the invention of basketball by James Naismith of Springfield, Massachusetts, American sports became based on a kind of gentleman's amateur athleticism. Indeed, because the player in basketball had to throw the ball softly in an arc, the sport was considered more "civilized" (Cross, 1990).

Figure 10.3

The Greenbrier Hotel, founded in 1778 at White Sulphur Springs, West Virginia, continues to be a popular resort today. Still noted for its curative spa, it has also gained distinction in gourmet cuisine and golf. (© Ruth V. Russell, 2008)

Thus sports of the late 1800s were militantly male, reaffirming the view that the vulnerable female was unsuited for vigorous physical activity. In the 1860s women were allowed to play croquet, and in the 1870s an easy form of lawn tennis was introduced for women. However, so powerful was the lure of sports that women gradually entered into all of them in spite of social constraints.

Finally, the continuing growth of leisure's utilitarian role in society can be glimpsed in the 1800s through concerns for preservation of the natural heritage, intellectual capacity, and health care. First, in terms of preserving natural heritage, as the European settlers moved west in the early 1800s, their relationship with wilderness shifted. As it became less

Figure 10.4

Ina Gittings pole vaulting in the late 1800s at the University of Nebraska – Lincoln. A little ahead of her time? (© University of Nebraska-Lincoln Photography. Used with permission.)

hostile, in their collective minds it began to represent the unique value of their new country. Assisted by the artists and writers of the time, a new reverence for nature emerged. The novels of James Fenimore Cooper, for example, described those who lived on the frontier as pure of heart and noble in deed. Such poets as Ralph Waldo Emerson swore undying love to nature, and artists Thomas Cole and Thomas Moran made forays into the thick woods to paint their majestic beauty.

As the century progressed, such romanticizing of nature led to concern for its destruction. In the face of increasing industrialization and urbanization in the later decades, one solution seemed to be parks. The need for open spaces for leisure was felt first in the larger cities. Following the example of William Penn, who set aside five undeveloped squares for a park in Philadelphia in 1682, and James Oglethorpe, who designed public gardens and squares in Savannah, Georgia in 1733, New York City planners provided the grandest example of the park solution at the time: Central Park.

Using a design by Frederick Law Olmsted and Calvert Vaux, beginning in 1853 New York city planners created the 850-acre park. Designed to provide relief from the cramped, concrete conditions of the city with the joys of the countryside, this model was followed by other cities. By the turn of that century, over 750 cities had set aside land for public parks. Unlike the formal gardens of Europe, Olmsted's vision was winding paths, scenic views and large open areas for people to relax in.

Figure 10.5

Frederick Law Olmsted was America's best known landscape architect. Writer, engineer, and visionary, he became a driving force behind many of America's urban parks. In this photo of the gardens of the George Vanderbilt estate, The Biltmore, in Asheville, North Carolina, an example of Olmsted's work can still be enjoyed today. (© Ruth V. Russell, 2008)

Concern for the care of the natural heritage also began to be answered by the federal government. In 1865 Congress set aside Mariposa Big Tree Park for the state of California. The intention was to preserve significant natural resources for the enjoyment of future generations. New York, Michigan, Minnesota, and New Jersey followed this lead and claimed open spaces for the benefit of their citizens as well. Later, the Mariposa Big Tree Park in California became Yosemite National Park. The establishment of Yellowstone National Park in 1872, however, marked the real beginning of the national park movement in the United States.

Considerable civic concern also developed for improving the intellectual capacity of Americans. One solution was universal public education, where there was a growing conviction that leisure, properly used, could contribute to an elevated intellectual character of the people. An example of this was the *Lyceum* movement. During its peak, Lyceum was a national organization with more than 900 local chapters. To reflect its program of lectures, readings,

Lyceum:
the 19th century American association for popular instruction of adults by public lectures and concerts

and other educational and cultural events, the name was borrowed from the name lyceum of the ancient Athenian gymnasium and garden where Aristotle taught. The idea that all citizens should be educated to improve their quality of life was also promoted by the Chautauqua organization, which took lectures and other programs on the road.

The prevalence of this humanistic philosophy evident in the 1800s also led to the use of leisure in health care. The utility of chess, gardening, reading, needlecraft, and walking as treatments became most prevalent in the psychiatric hospitals of the time (Carter, vanAndel & Robb, 1985). Florence Nightingale, the pioneer of modern nursing, recommended in *Notes on Nursing*, published in 1873, the use of music and pets to improve the hospital environment.

Birth of Organized Leisure Systems

Along with transitions in entertainment, tourism, sport, education, health care and preservation of the natural environment that evolved during the 1800s, later decades in the century witnessed even more specific illustrations of the idea of using leisure as a tool. As the nation continued to expand, there were new challenges. Many of these resulted from the development of industrialization. So significant were these challenges that historians refer to this period as the *Industrial Revolution*.

Industrial Revolution:
a rapid and major change in society brought about by the introduction of power-driven machinery

Beginning in Great Britain during the 1700s, industrialization spread to other parts of Europe and to North America in the early 1800s. Widespread by midcentury, industrialization created an enormous increase in the production of many kinds of goods because of the introduction of power-driven machinery. Obviously this revolution had significant impact on society's work: the spinning wheel was replaced by the spinning mule and the hand loom by the power loom.

Perhaps not so obvious were the radical changes in just about every other area of life as well. Foremost, industrialization changed the nature of work itself by taking it out of the rural home and workshop and into the urban factory, which accordingly enabled distinctions between those who work (as in gainfully

Box 10.2

 *In Focus*

Tragedy of the Commons

The actual beginnings of the city park in the United States are obscure. Some historians assert the plaza in St. Augustine, set aside in 1565, should be considered the first city park, whereas others refer to the Boston Common, established in 1634, as the first city park. The common was originally a British tradition, and the plaza a Spanish one. Both had similar uses: people had unlimited access to the commonly held land for whatever they wanted, including grazing their livestock. As cities grew and open space was lost, the common or plaza became an important commonly held recreation resource.

Recently, the consequences of this idea have been destructive, so claims an essay published in 1968 by Garrett Hardin. Hardin explained this as tragedy of the commons, presenting the following logic. Imagine a pasture, fixed in size, and accessible to all the livestock owners of a village. Each herdsman naturally wants to maximize his use of the pasture by grazing as many cattle as possible. Therefore, he expands the size of his herd, recognizing the benefits from this will be his alone, whereas any costs for the increased grazing will be shared among all the village members. What each herdsman fails to recognize, however, is that every other herdsman in the village is following the same logic, and the cumulative effect of their independently rational action ultimately destroys the pasture.

Later, in their own essay, Dustin, McAvoy and Schultz (1982) asked us to imagine this tragedy of the commons another way. Consider an urban resident who wishes to escape the heat, congestion, and noise of the city on a summer weekend. She gathers the family, packs the car, and heads for one of the public beaches (or mountains or lakes). In fact, thousands of other city dwellers are making the same logical decision. So, instead of a cool, quiet, and refreshing leisure experience, they are treated to traffic jams, noise, and crime – the very problems they attempted to escape, and to the ultimate destruction of the recreation resource itself.

Questions to Consider and Discuss
1. What is meant by the tragedy of the commons concept? Can you explain it in your own words?
2. Is Hardin's logic applicable to recreation settings as Dustin et al. suggest? What other examples can you cite of this?
3. Visit a public recreation area in your community or campus. Can you find traces of the tragedy of the commons there? What are these?

employed outside the home) and those who don't work (as in those who work inside the home). These changes in work also changed thinking about time. The clock was now important as it ordered the pace of industrial work. Also, women and men were now separated for most of the day, the importance of community traditions diminished as no one was there much anymore, and it helped to divide even more the upper class from the middle class.

For example, some people were able to amass huge fortunes through industrialization. In 1900 there were about 3,000 millionaires, compared to only 20 in 1850. American author Mark Twain called this era the Gilded Age, describing the leisure-based culture of the newly rich. Attending operas and horse races, holding balls and parties in large mansions for over 1,000 guests, yachting, and relaxing at luxurious resorts represented the pursuit of lavish pleasure not known at any other time in American history.

For the middle and lower classes there were major changes in how leisure was experienced as well. While some historians consider these changes in negative terms as a breakdown in leisure traditions, others have pointed to significant leisure legacies from the Industrial Revolution, which remain with us today. Table 10.1 outlines some of these.

Table 10.1

Leisure Legacies of the Industrial Revolution

- Work and leisure increasingly experienced as opposites
- Less time available for leisure
- New blocks of time for leisure created: evening, weekend, summer vacation, childhood, and old age
- Home as the focus of family-based recreations
- Child-centered leisure
- Commercial leisure forms replaced community-based traditions
- Attitudes about leisure as a basic right of citizenship extended to the lower classes, youth, and others

Indeed, the main story of leisure's utilitarian role is rooted in how particularly the lower classes of people experienced daily life at the onset of the Industrial Revolution. Most of those who tended the machines lived and worked under harsh conditions. In the factories the machines forced workers to work faster and without rest. Jobs became specialized, so the work was monotonous. Factory wages were low; workers worked at least 60 hours a week for an average of 20 cents an hour (Fourastie, 1951). Women and children worked as unskilled laborers and made only a small fraction of men's low wages. Children, many under age 10, worked up to 14 hours a day. Housing in the growing industrial cities of New York, Chicago, and others could not keep up with the migration of workers from rural areas and other countries. Severe overcrowding resulted, along with poor sanitation and inadequate diets, making people vulnerable to disease.

As an obvious consequence, some Americans came to believe that social reforms were needed to correct these inequalities of condition. Churches and social welfare groups set up charities to aid the poor. Horace Mann demanded better schools and Dorothea Dix tried to improve the dismal conditions in the prisons and asylums. Workers' strikes for better wages and shorter work schedules erupted. Even though little progress was made during the late 1800s, by 1917 the reformers had many successes.

Most meaningful from our perspective were those reforms that used leisure. Some reformers believed wholesome and enriching leisure experiences would solve the problematic consequences of the Industrial Revolution. We will use as examples two turn-of-the-century *social movements*: settlement houses and playgrounds.

Copying the British model of Toynbee Hall in London, *settlement houses* were established in the United States as a way to help the urban poor. Stanton Coit established the first settlement house in 1886 in New York City, and three years later Jane Addams and Ellen Starr established a settlement house in Chicago that became famous as the Hull House.

Social movements:

a significant change in the social conditions and patterns of behavior in a society

Settlement houses:

an institution providing various community services

Box 10.3

Jane Addams, Ellen Starr and Hull House

In 1889 Jane Addams and Ellen Starr, college-educated, upper-middle class women, using their own money, founded the Hull House and quickly made it a model for nationwide efforts to improve the lives of people coping with urban poverty. When the heir of Charles Hull granted Jane and Ellen a rent-free, four-year lease on his large, dilapidated old home that had become surrounded by the sprawling, densely packed, and deteriorating immigrant slums of Chicago's 19th ward, they took it. A few days after Jane's 29th birthday, the two former college roommates moved in. They intended to share their gifts of culture with the poor.

From the beginning, Hull House was the center of activity. A day-care center and kindergarten were available in the morning. In the afternoon, classes and clubs for teens were provided, and adult education programs were held in the evening. Nearby buildings were acquired and converted into a coffeehouse, gymnasium, and playground. Carefully supervised recreation in these facilities was central to their efforts to help children resist the negative effects of the city (McBride, 1989).

Box 10.3 (Cont.)

Hull House made a special reputation for itself, however, not so much for its efforts to correct social ills, but in the methods used. Classes were offered in pottery, rhythm and dance, photography, and chorus. Its specialty was "the exaltation of art for the benefit of the masses" (Smith, 1890, p. 10). Concerts, dramatic readings, and lectures were weekly events; the audience was always packed. There were art history classes, literary reading groups, and art exhibits.

During Addams' tenure, Hull House grew from a large house to a 13-building complex. And, in 1911, Addams and Louise deKoven Bowen purchased 72 acres of land outside Waukegan, Illinois and developed the Bowen Country Club—a year-round outdoor camp for Hull House youth and families (Dieser, et al., 2004). Although it has different organizational and physical structures, Hull House still provides numerous leisure and human service programs to impoverished youth and families in Chicago today.

The objective of settlement houses was to improve living conditions in city neighborhoods, particularly for new immigrants. To accomplish this, they offered educational classes, nurseries, civil rights and fair employment advocacy, and recreational services. The recreational services—typically play apparatus for young children, sport activities and social clubs for older children, and cultural arts programs for adults—not only provided a more positive balance in desperate lives but also taught the skills needed to create productive lives.

Meanwhile, the first organized use of play specifically as a tool is traced to Friedrich Froebel, who founded the first kindergarten in Germany in 1837. He believed children should be schooled early in a gentle manner that allowed them to develop freely. Thus, using free play as a tool in child development led the way for another social movement.

In the United States, the insight of public-spirited members of the New England Woman's Club led to the establishment of children's play areas in Boston. The Boston Sand Garden, established in 1885, is considered by many historians to be the first actual playground in the U.S. The idea was borrowed from the public parks of Berlin, Germany, where huge piles of sand were given to the city's children for playing.

Later, additional strides for promoting playgrounds in Boston were made by Joseph Lee, who helped create a model playground that included an area for small children, a boys' section, a sports field, and individual sand gardens. In 1889 the Charlesbank Outdoor Gymnasium opened; it provided apparatus for gymnastics, a running track, and space for games for older boys and men, and a section for women and girls was added two years later. By 1899 Boston had 21 playgrounds.

Other playgrounds sprang up elsewhere. For example, Jacob Riis initiated the movement for publicly sponsored playgrounds in New York City. School buildings began to be used as community centers in Pittsburgh, and Philadelphia moved ahead with full playground programs in the summer. Unfortunately, most of these playgrounds were segregated. In general, playgrounds for African American children were "less numerous, smaller, poorer in equipment and less adequately supervised than playgrounds for white children in the same city" (H.J. McGuinn, as cited in Johnson, 1930, p. 91).

These early, scattered efforts to provide space, leadership, and facilities for playgrounds began to come together when, in 1906, Jane Addams, Joseph Lee and others met at the White House. Their goal was to establish a way of connecting their individual efforts (MacLean et al., 1985), which resulted in the 1911 creation of the Playground and Recreation Association of America,

Figure 10.6

A turn-of-the-century Boston playground. (© Joseph Lee Memorial Archives, National Recreation and Park Association. Used by permission)

Box 10.4

In Profile

Joseph Lee

Although he received a law degree from Harvard Law School in 1888, Joseph Lee never pursued that career. Instead, he chose a life dedicated to promoting playgrounds. It began with his participation in a 10-year study of child delinquency in Boston. He researched play in Boston playgrounds, sand gardens, and streets. He made observations, drew descriptive maps, compiled statistics, and studied the relationships among play, population density, and lawbreaking (Sapora, 1989).

To the confusion of Lee, and in spite of setting aside special places for play, activities in the new Boston playgrounds did not differ much from those on the streets. Fights frequently broke out, often over card games. Older boys and men monopolized the game areas, and gangs prevented the smaller children from playing. Lee's solution was planning and leadership.

In 1900 he proposed a model playground be developed. He chose for the experiment the North End playground, and supervised the installation of play equipment. He had areas marked off for different age groups, and with his own money, hired two Harvard students as paid play leaders, and recruited others as volunteers. Before the playground opened, the staff had completely planned the program. All this organization for play was a new idea at the time, and despite the lack of understanding by the local neighborhood, the program attracted over 300 children per week (Sapora, 1989).

Box 10.5

Janie Porter Barrett

Janie Porter was born in 1865 to former slaves in Athens, Georgia. She grew up in a white household because her mother was a nurse to the children. Upon graduating from Hampton Institute in Virginia, she felt her role as an educated African American was to help all African Americans improve their lives, so she began teaching.

In 1889 she married Harris Barrett, also a Hampton graduate, and while raising four children, started a school to teach life skills to other neighborhood children. What began as a sewing class for a few girls in her home on Tuesday afternoons soon became a club. The response was so enthusiastic that two years later it became known as the Locust Street Social Settlement. Like other settlement houses of the time, Locust Street activities included handicrafts, homemaking, gardening, and reading classes. Athletic programs and a playground were also established. One of Janie's most appreciated programs was the summer excursion on Chesapeake Bay for mothers without their children.

Figure 10.7

Janie Porter Barrett works with girls at the Locust Street Settlement. (Courtesy of Hampton University Archives)

which later became the National Recreation Association in 1930, and ultimately the National Recreation and Park Association in 1965. This laid the foundation for today's organized use of leisure for social good.

There were other initiatives using leisure as a problem solver at this time as well. For example, agencies serving youth also organized to help the cause. Sir Robert Baden-Powell of Great Britain started the Boy Scout movement in 1907 when he formed a camp for 20 boys. Baden-Powell was convinced after his experiences in the Boer War that training in citizenship and outdoor skills was essential for young men.

As a result of a British Boy Scout helping him find his way in a thick London fog, William Boyce, an American businessman, brought the idea to the United States in 1909. The movement spread throughout the world, and today approximately 28 million boys, girls, and adult leaders in 156 countries are members (World Organization of the Scout Movement, 2008).

When Baden-Powell began the Boy Scouts in Great Britain, 6,000 girls registered too. As he "could not have girls traipsing about over the country after his Boy Scouts," he got his sister, Agnes Baden-Powell, to help. They formed the Girl Guides program in 1909 (Schultz & Lawrence, 1958). Their first law was that they must not even speak to a Boy Scout if they saw him in uniform!

A few years later, while visiting Britain, Juliette Gordon Low met the Baden-Powells and became fascinated with their organizations. When she returned to her home in Savannah, Georgia, she brought the idea with her. Changing the name to Girl Scouts, Daisy, as her friends knew her, held the first troop meeting in her home on March 12, 1912. Today, Girl Guides and Girl Scouts involve about 10 million girls and adult leaders in 144 countries (World Association of Girl Guides and Girl Scouts, 2008).

Other initiatives of the time included the establishment of therapeutic recreation services in state hospitals, expansion of the national park system, the beginnings of the organized camping movement with the first private camp set up to offer healthy outdoor experiences to boys in poor health, and the offering of college-level professional training for recreation leaders.

Figure 10.8

Juliette Gordon Low with Girl Scouts. (Courtesy of the Girl Scouts of the USA Archives)

What began as a simple play initiative shifted to a far-reaching social movement. Sports, games, music, dance, and enjoying the outdoors became means to create better communities. The result was so sweeping that it involved cities, states, and the federal government. Hospitals, clinics, social work agencies, and voluntary welfare efforts relied more and more on leisure as a tool. People formed organizations, raised funds, held interminable meetings, wrote volumes of handbooks, and conducted numerous training sessions to discover better ways to teach people how to use their leisure productively. This "leisure movement" continues today.

Box 10.6

 *In Profile*

The History of Professional Preparation in Leisure

One of the earliest leadership training programs specifically for leisure professionals was a summer school program conducted in the 1880s by Luther Gulick, then a professor of physical education for the School of Christian Workers (now Springfield College) in Massachusetts (Butler, 1965). In 1905, Gulick joined the faculty of New York University and offered the first university course on play, which included units on sports and games, the theory of toys, and play and the exceptional child (Sessoms, 1993).

Later, the awareness of the need for special training for recreation leaders increased, resulting in the start of a one-year graduate curriculum sponsored by the National Recreation Association. Known as the National Recreation School, its founding in 1926 confirmed the desirability of educating professionals in the use of leisure as a tool. Its curriculum included the construction and planning of play facilities and administering city and county recreation departments. It graduated over 295 students in its nine years of operation.

Soon professional preparation programs in leisure began to appear within the curricula of forestry, landscape architecture, education, social work, and physical education at colleges and universities across North America. Among the first were those at the University of Minnesota (1937) and the University of North Carolina (1939). Quickly other colleges and universities began to offer specialized and separate undergraduate degrees in leisure, and by 1945, 37 such degree programs were available, and by the 1960s the number had nearly doubled (Kraus & Bates, 1975).

Today, professional preparation programs in leisure, awarding associates through doctoral degrees, are provided in more than 600 colleges and universities. The predominant subjects of study include recreation management, programming and leadership; outdoor recreation and resource management; commercial and tourism services; therapeutic recreation; and sport management.

The Movement's Zenith

The time period following World War I continued to bring monumental changes to the people of the United States. Initially, the economy entered a period of spectacular growth. Spurred on by the good times and a desire to be "modern," large numbers of Americans adopted new attitudes and lifestyles. There was greater acceptance of the pursuit of pleasure as people both young and old visited supposedly secret nightclubs called speakeasies, where they danced the Charleston and listened to jazz. Labeled the Roaring Twenties, this fun decade ended with the stock market crash and a long economic depression.

The Great Depression of the 1930s in the United States (and in much of the industrialized world) resulted in mass unemployment that engulfed nearly one third of the labor force in involuntary idleness. In spite of this, the Depression did provide a boost in the use of leisure as a solution—this time for economic problems.

Under the leadership of President Franklin Roosevelt, the federal government responded to the depression by instituting a number of emergency work programs to reduce unemployment and stimulate the economy. This was labeled the *New Deal*, and many of these programs related to leisure. For example, workers were hired by the federal government to build concert halls and community theaters, develop outdoor recreation areas and camps, and help establish state park systems. Nationwide such federal work projects built or improved 12,700 playgrounds, 8,500 gymnasiums, 750 swimming pools, 1,000 ice skating rinks, and 64 ski-jumps (Knapp, 1973).

New Deal: federally sponsored programs to provide jobs and stimulate economic recovery created by President Franklin Roosevelt when he took office in 1933

The New Deal relieved some of the hardship of many Americans, but bad times dragged on until World War II military spending stimulated the economy out of its depression. The war also brought another emphasis by the federal government on leisure's utility. This time leisure was useful in relieving tension, increasing morale, and decreasing the psychological impact of being away from home and in combat. For example, approximately 40,000 officers and enlisted men and women of the Special Services Division of the U.S. Army provided recreation facilities and programs for units based around the world. Additionally, about 1,500 officers provided recreation services for the Navy, and nongovernmental organizations, such as the United Service Organizations (USO), offered recreation relief at airports, hospitals, hotels, lounges, and special clubs near combat areas and overseas rest centers.

When World War II ended in 1945, the United States entered the greatest period of economic growth in its history, resulting in a new lifestyle. Vast numbers of Americans moved out of cities to suburbs, where new housing was available. A rise in automobile ownership accompanied suburban growth. By 1960 over three-fourths of all American families owned a car, paving the way for a nationwide network of superhighways. These new roads enabled more people than ever to take vacation trips, and motels and fast-service restaurants sprang up to serve them.

Accordingly, outdoor recreation interests boomed in the 1950s and 1960s, which boosted the services of such federal agencies as the National Park Service and the U.S. Forest Service. The Land and Water Conservation Fund was created in 1965 to provide federal aid for outdoor recreation development to states and local communities.

The 1950s also witnessed new concerns for physical fitness because the effects of television and cars had already taken their toll. This led to the founding of such organizations as the National Collegiate Athletic Association and the President's Council on Physical Fitness and Sport.

Against the backdrop of the Civil Rights movement, integration of sports and recreation facilities was at last possible. First, the Brooklyn Dodgers brought Jackie Robinson up from their farm team in 1947. A series of legal test cases was also initiated, including one against the state of Maryland for racial segregation in its state parks. But, not until 1964 did the Civil Rights Act outlaw discrimination in public facilities.

This was also a growth period for the performing arts. The 1958 act of Congress that established the National Cultural Center for the Performing Arts (later named the John F. Kennedy Center for the Performing Arts) signaled their importance.

Box 10.7

In Your Own Experience

Community Inventory

Today organized leisure services are pervasive. There are several ways of proving this claim. For example, you could think about your own experiences. How many of the leisure organizations and services presented in this chapter have you belonged to or participated in?

Another way to demonstrate organized leisure's pervasiveness is to inventory your own community. Have some fun and try this: walk down to your nearest city bus stop. Get on (better pay the fare too). Ride the bus for its entire route, until you return to the stop where you originally boarded. While you ride and enjoy the passing scenery, keep a tally of the leisure organizations and services you see from the bus window. How many parks, playgrounds, community centers, public gardens, golf courses, art centers, museums, etc. do you count? Do you pass a YMCA, a Boy or Girl Scout office, a Boys or Girls club, a community arts agency, and country club? How about commercial leisure places, such as restaurants, bars, arcades, movie theatres, and bowling centers?

Bring your tally back to class and share with classmates. Discuss your reaction to what you observed. Point out legacies from the history of organized leisure still available today in terms of leisure's utilitarian role.

What We Understand About the History of Leisure's Utilitarian Role

As societies have become more complex, they have also become more reliant on leisure as a tool for creating public good. Although leisure is not a cure, it is certainly one of the most potent tools for solving social problems as it creates caring and vital communities. After studying this chapter on the history of leisure's utilitarian role in the United States, you should know that:

- During the colonial period leisure was useful in creating the new nation by providing rest and recovery from hardship and aiding in getting work done.
- The 1800s was a period of transition leading to the "birth" of organized leisure services.
- In the 1900s leisure became part of a social conscience movement striving for humanitarian goals.
- As use of leisure as a tool grew, services initially available to young children expanded to include services for all ages, and support shifted from the voluntary efforts of private citizens to governmental and community agency support.
- As a result, leisure is now highly organized, with specific agendas for solving particular social problems.

References

Borsay, P. (2006). *A history of leisure: The British experience since 1500*. New York: Palgrave – Macmillan.

Butler, G.D. (1965). *Pioneers in public recreation*. Minneapolis, MN: Burgess.

Carter, M.J., vanAndel, G.E., & Robb, G.M. (1985). *Therapeutic recreation: A practical approach*. St. Louis: Times Mirror/Mosby College.

Cross, G. (1990). *A social history of leisure since 1600*. State College, PA: Venture.

Daniels, B.C. (1995). *Puritans at play: Leisure and recreation in colonial New England*. New York: St. Martins.

Dieser, R.B., Harkema, R.P., Kowalski, C., Osuji, I.P., & Poppen, L.L. (September 2004). The portrait of a pioneer: A look back at 115 years of Jane Addams' work at Hull-House – her legacy still lives on. *Parks & Recreation*, 129-137.

Dustin, D.L., McAvoy, L.H., & Schultz, J.H. (1982). *Stewards of access, custodians of choice: A philosophical foundation for the park and recreation profession*. Minneapolis, MN: Burgess.

Fourastie, J. (June 1951). Productivity and economics. *Political Science Quarterly, 66*(2), 216-225.

Johnson, C.S. (1930). *The negro in American civilization*. New York: Henry Holt.

Knapp, R.F. (July 1973). Play for America: The New Deal and the NRA. *Parks and Recreation*, 23-27.

Kraus, R., & Bates, B. (1975). *Recreation leadership and supervision: Guidelines for professional development.* Philadelphia: W.B. Saunders.

MacLean, J.R., Peterson, J.A., & Martin, W.D. (1985). *Recreation and leisure: The changing scene.* New York: John Wiley & Sons.

McBride, P. (1989). Jane Addams. In H. Ibrahim (Ed.), *Pioneers in leisure and recreation* (pp. 35-37). Reston, VA: American Alliance for Health, Physical Education, Recreation, and Dance.

National Park Service. (2002). *Nicodemus.* Available from http://www.nps.gov/nico/. Retrieved 6/6/02.

National Resources Inventory (2008). *Fiscal Year 2007 Financial Report.* Available from www.nrcs.usda.gov/programs/fppa/. Retrieved 6/7/08.

O'Keefe, M. (November 20, 2002). The Puritans weren't so puritanical, scholars say. *Religion News Service.* Available from www.religionnews.com. Retrieved 6/7/08.

Sapora, A. (1989). Joseph Lee. In H. Ibrahim (Ed.), *Pioneers in leisure and recreation* (pp. 38-39). Reston, VA: American Alliance for Health, Physical Education, Recreation, and Dance.

Schultz, G.D., & Lawrence, D.G. (1958). *Lady of Savannah: The life of Juliette Low.* Philadelphia: J.B. Lippincott.

Sessoms, H.D. (October 1993). Quo vadis physical education and recreation. Paper presented at the Leisure Research Symposium, National Recreation and Park Association, San Jose, CA.

Smith, S. (August 7, 1890). Sophia Smith collection (SSC), Starr Family Papers, box 1, folder 3 [Newspaper clipping].

Towner, J. (1996). *An historical geography of recreation and tourism in the western world, 1540-1940.* New York: John Wiley & Sons.

World Association of Girl Guides and Girl Scouts (2008). *About Us.* Available from www.wagggsworld.org. Retrieved 6/7/08).

World Organization of the Scout Movement (2008). *Census.* Available from www.scout.org. Retrieved 6/7/08.

CHAPTER ELEVEN

LEISURE PAYS

PREVIEW

Is leisure of economic value?

Leisure is an economic balancing tool. For example, leisure mirrors a nation's level of economic development and its economic system. Leisure also drives an economy by fostering consumerism.

What is the positive economic impact of leisure?

Leisure makes good economic sense. It benefits, employment, taxes, and property values.

What is the negative economic impact of leisure?

Sometimes leisure results in undesirable costs. Examples are the negative economic impacts of leisure accidents and a nation's negative balance of payments.

KEY TERMS

Economics:

organizing resources for the efficient production and distribution of goods and services

Every society has a system for organizing the production and distribution of goods needed by its members. This system is called the economic system, and it differs from society to society. Individuals also have a system for organizing the acquisition of the goods and services they need or want. This, too, requires an economic system. Few persons or societies are prosperous enough to buy everything they want when they want it. Thus, economic systems are based on economizing—using resources wisely. This is the most essential task of *economics*.

Leisure is at the heart of economics. Increasingly, both private and public leisure goods and services are being produced, which means leisure is central to consumption and investment in an economy. Also, questions of how to distribute leisure goods and services have become central to concern for economic growth and economic decline. Further, changes in an economy create shifts in leisure, and shifts in leisure have an impact on the economy. In fact, a healthy economy depends on the relative stability of leisure. Leisure is, therefore, an economic balancing tool.

Figure 11.1

$177,000 – The amount of change Ohio's Cedar Point Amusement Park has collected under its 75 rides and donated to charity since 1988 (Midwest Living, June 2008, p. 82). (Microsoft, 2008)

In this chapter we tell this story by beginning with the intricacies of the balance between leisure and economics. Specifically, we consider the relationships between leisure and economic development, capitalism, and consumerism. Then, we contrast the positive and negative effects of leisure economics. The power of leisure to positively affect economic health through employment, taxes, and property values is compared with leisure's negative impact from the cost of accidents and export deficits.

Box 11.1

 *In Focus*

The Coming Leisure Economy

The Leisure Economy, a book published in 2007 by Linda Nazareth, claims we're in for profound economic changes. Due to the coming retirements of baby boomers and the pro-leisure attitudes of younger workers, the book predicts a new leisure economy. This will occur at the confluence of millions of baby boomers with new and large amounts of free time, replaced in the workforce by generations who

Box 11.1 (Cont.)

already understand the worth of free time. What does this "seismic shift" mean?

* Workers will make more demands on employers to accommodate special leisure-related requests—to bring the dog to work, or provide a fitness trail outside, or ride scooters down the corridors.
* Workers will use leisure as a source of status and a marker of success, rather than work, which will mean they'll never come into the office on weekends.
* Retirees who've not had much time previously to take up hobbies will make major expenditures in the leisure industries, particularly in the area of learning as leisure.
* Retirees will be tapping into the value of their homes and looking for more leisure-oriented places to live, at a quicker rate than their parents or grandparents did.
* Retirees and workers both will increasingly embrace the idea of volunteering, especially if they can use the skills they developed in professional fields and in school.
* Retirees and workers both will loiter more, so smart companies will follow the lead of Starbucks and create stores with comfortable spaces to hang out and things to do there.

Questions to Consider and Discuss

1. Do you agree with Nazareth that shifts in the leisure attitudes of retirees and workers can significantly affect the economy? Why? Why not?
2. If Nazareth's prediction is accurate, might there be other leisure impacts affecting the economy, such as more part-time work, sabbaticals, family-leave requests, and maybe even a labor shortage?
3. Why is adult education likely to be the biggest growth industry of the future? Which leisure industries do you predict will be the biggest winners (and losers) of the coming leisure economy?
4. More leisure time often means less income, whether we are talking about retired boomers or younger households. How might this affect consumer spending choices and the economy in general?

Balancing Leisure and Economics

The balance between leisure and economics is an elaborate, yet functional web. Leisure both helps shape an economy and is affected by changes in an economy. An examination of economic development, capitalism, and consumerism illustrates this function of leisure.

Economic Development

An economy must grow if its people want a higher *standard of living*. As an economy grows, it is able to satisfy more and more of its people's needs and wants, and thus increase their standard of living. Economists measure an economy's rate of growth by studying its *gross domestic product (GDP)* over time. For example, the GDP of the world in 2007 was about $54.62 trillion (USD) (International Monetary Fund, 2008). The fastest growing economy in the world is Azerbaijan, whose GDP grew in 2007 by 31 percent (*CIA World Factbook*, 2008).

Standard of living:
the degree of prosperity in an economy, measured by income levels, quality of housing and food, medical care, educational opportunities, etc.

Gross domestic product (GDP):
total market value of the goods and services produced in an economy

This increase in the GDP of Azerbaijan indicates there was a sizable increase in the value of all goods and services produced there that year, but does not take into account other indicators of economic development, such as inflation, purchasing power parity, and the human development index. For example, also in 2007 Azerbaijan ranked 77th in the world in total GDP, which was $31.32 billion, and its inflation rate was 16.6 percent. Its purchasing power parity ranked 89th and human development index ranked 101th in the world (*CIA World Factbook*, 2008).

What are these other measures of economic development? First, *purchasing power parity (PPP)* is a measurement of a currency's value based on the buying power within its own economy. PPP is derived from the logic that in an ideally efficient market, identical goods would have only one price, thus it equalizes the purchasing power of different currencies in their home economies. Using a PPP measure is more useful when comparing standards of living between economies because it takes into account the inflation rates and cost of living of different economies.

Purchasing power parity (PPP):
a ratio that compares the relative affordability of goods and services in different economies

A well-known example of PPP is the "Big Mac Index." *The Big Mac Index* is an informal way to measure purchasing power parity. It was introduced by *The Economist* in September 1986 as a humorous illustration and has been published by that paper annually since. The index is determined by dividing the price of a Big Mac sandwich in one country (in its currency) by the price of a Big Mac in another country (in its currency). This value is then compared with the actual exchange rate; if it is lower, then the first currency is under-valued and if it is higher the first currency is over-valued. For example, in 2007 the price of a Big Mac in the United States was $3.41 (table 11.1). Using this price for a Big Mac as the comparison standard, the most expensive Big Macs were in Iceland ($7.61) and Norway ($6.88), while the cheapest Big Macs were in China ($1.45) and Hong Kong ($1.54). This means the economies of Iceland and Norway are over-valued and the economies of China and Hong Kong are under-valued as compared to the United States.

Big Mac Index:
a demonstration of PPP based on the prices of the Big Mac sandwich in McDonald's restaurants around the world; published each spring by the *Economist*

In addition to the PPP, economies can be compared through the *human development index (HDI)*. The HDI, published annually by the United Nations, is an indicator of people's overall quality of life in a particular economy. It not only measures economic development, but also human development. The HDI combines measures of

Human development index (HDI):
a summary measure of livability in an economy

life expectancy at birth (an index of a population's health and longevity), adult literacy rate and school enrollments (a measure of knowledge and education), and the standard of living, as measured by gross domestic product per capita at purchasing power parity.

The HDI index ranges from 1.0 to 0, with a measure of 0.8 or more indicating high human development and below 0.5 indicating low human development. For example, the 2007 HDI for the United States was 0.951, while for Ethiopia it was 0.367. Table 11.1 compares the ranking of the top 10 national economies according to HDI, GDP and PPP. The point of the comparison is even though citizens of a particular economy may be able to buy more, living there might not always make them feel well off.

How is all this related to leisure? Economies develop when they increase the wealth and well-being of their inhabitants. Economic development implies, then, quality of leisure time, resources, and expression. Thus, in developing economies such as Sierra Leone, for example, free time and recreation resources are much more limited. Sierra Leone ranks last in the world in HDI, with about

Table 11.1

Comparison of Countries According to GDP, Big Mac Index (PPP), and HDI in 2007

The Wealthiest Countries (GDP) (in billions)	"Out of Whack" Economies (Big Mac Index, or PPP) (standard = $3.41 in US)	The Most Livable Countries (HDI) (highest = 1)
United States ($13,811)	Iceland ($7.61)	Iceland (0.968)
China ($7,055)	Norway ($6.88)	Norway (0.968)
Japan ($4,283)	China ($1.45)	Australia (0.962)
India ($3,092)	Hong Kong ($1.54)	Canada (0.961)
Germany ($2,751)	Switzerland ($5.20)	Ireland (0.959)
Russian Federation ($2,088)	Malaysia ($1.60)	Sweden (0.956)
United Kingdom ($2,081)	Egypt ($1.68)	Switzerland (0.955)
France ($2,053)	Denmark ($5.08)	Japan (0.953)
Brazil ($1,833)	Indonesia ($1.76)	Netherlands (0.953)
Italy ($1,780)	Thailand ($1.80)	France (0.952)

GDP statistics are from the *World Development Indicators database*, World Bank, July 1, 2008. Available from worldbank.org. Big Mac Index information is from *The Economist*, 2008. Available from economist.com/markets/rankings. HDI statistics are from the United Nations Development Program's *Human Development Report* 2007/2008. Available from hdr.undp.org.

Figure 11.2

Oslo, Norway has Old World charm with a highly developed economy. It has both a high 6DP per capita and a high DPI. The Norwegian economy is an example of a mixed economic system, featuring a combination of free market and government ownership. (© Ruth V. Russell, 2008)

two-thirds of the population engaged in subsistence agriculture. While the country has made economic progress since the civil war's end in 2002, unemployment is still close to 80 percent and poverty and corruption endemic. Improvements in daily life remain painfully slow.

In such developing economies, leisure is possible only for those who, because of their economic status, do not need to be directly involved in producing food or shelter. Often such a "leisure class" is supported by a working-class system. In Sierra Leone such leisure amenities as the cinema and sports are only available to the economically elite.

Thorstein Veblen's (1899) classic ideas about leisure and economics correspond here. Veblen was a late 19th century scholar who concluded that, as a nonproductive consumption of time, leisure is an aristocratic possession. To Veblen, leisure was a decadent economic exploitation because it was characterized by idleness and conspicuous consumption. Only the wealthy could afford to have nothing to do except play. Veblen's writings reflected his own time, for in the late 19th century the pastimes of the wealthy few in Europe and North America contrasted starkly with the poverty of the masses. Many have wondered whether today's economically developed societies still reflect Veblen's thesis.

Box 11.2

 *In Focus*

Are Veblen's Ideas Still True?

One hundred years ago economist Thorstein Veblen (1899) argued that leisure was the main way for the affluent to demonstrate their status. Is his claim still pertinent today? Does leisure still designate wealth? Which case are you prepared to make?

Yes, Leisure Remains a Status Symbol of Wealth

- Through our leisure consumption we make a clear statement about our place in society, or at least our intended place. Our "toys" are our social ID; our

■ **Box 11.2 (Cont.)**

"fun" is our social class.

- Our leisure consumption also designates our uniqueness. As advertising tells us, leisure is how we signal we are special.
- Our playmates appoint social status. We want to join the "right" clubs.
- Tourism itself is a symbol of wealth. For Americans a trip to Europe carries a higher status than a trip to Cleveland; a condo in Aspen is a far cry from visiting relatives in Illinois.

No, Leisure is No Longer a Status Symbol of Wealth

- Veblen's argument applied only to the "leisure class" and today most people have to work and even want to work. Nobody today lives a life of leisure.
- Leisure expressions are quite diverse. We do many things for many different reasons, which reflect our own unique personalities.
- Leisure expressions are also now more likely to be based on satisfaction. We stay involved in an activity because we enjoy it.
- Most of our leisure today is private and not on display. We read, watch television, and garden. We do many things that don't attract attention.

(based on Freysinger & Kelly, 2004, pp. 93-95)

Questions to Consider and Discuss

1. Which answer makes the most sense to you? Why?
2. Veblen's argument is based on the idea of conspicuous consumption. What is this concept, and can you name any leisure goods or experiences you've purchased lately that may carry a high status for you?
3. If leisure does remain a status symbol today, what implication does this have for the quality of leisure itself? If leisure is no longer a status symbol today, what implication does this have for the quality of leisure?

As industrialization reaches a successful level of output so that people have command over consumption, a developed economy is achieved. People's basic needs for food, shelter, and clothing are satisfied, and they can focus on such services as leisure. In mature economies, higher amounts of discretionary income abound, and leisure itself is an industry. Tourism is an excellent example of this. Tourism is an aggregate of many different businesses: attractions, transportation, lodging, restaurants, entertainment, and advertising. In Greece, for example, a majority of those working in the service sector of the economy, work in the tourist industries.

Figure 11.3

Figure 11.3. According to the Embassy of Greece (2007), twenty percent of the total labor force in modern-day Greece works in the tourism industry. (© Ruth V. Russell, 2008)

Economic system:

the organized way a society allocates its resources and apportions goods and services

Capitalism:

the system of privately possessing capital

Capitalism

Not only does the level of economic development affect the quality and expression of leisure, but also the economic system. An *economic system* is a particular set of social institutions that manage production, distribution and consumption of goods and services in a society. It is the systematic way in which economics are carried out. Although today no economic system is considered a "pure" version of its basic principles, examples of contemporary economic systems include capitalism, socialism, and mixed.

From some viewpoints, particular economic systems can be both harmful and enabling to leisure. We'll use the economic system of capitalism to illustrate this point. *Capitalism* is an economic system based on private ownership of the means of production and distribution of goods and services. It promotes a free market regulated by supply and demand, with the goal of making profits for private individuals or companies.

The central idea of the capitalistic free-enterprise system dates back to as early as 1656 when the philosopher Lee suggested "the advancement of private persons will be the advantage of the public" (quoted in Goodale & Godbey, 1988, p. 74). Scottish economist Adam Smith later expanded on this idea in his book *An Inquiry into the Nature and Causes of the Wealth of Nations* (1937). According to Smith the basic premises of economic order were (a) self-interest is a prime motivation, (b) individual striving and work will lead to a common good, and (c) no regulation of the economy is best. This argument serves as the basis of today's capitalist economic system.

How does leisure fare under capitalism? An early comment about this was made by Karl Marx in the 1800s. Marx, the father of socialism, criticized the suppression of leisure under capitalism. Because capitalism's idea of free enterprise is based on the labor of individuals, leisure was considered an obstruction. "In capitalist society ... leisure time for a privileged class is produced by converting the whole lifetime of the masses into labor time" (cited in Cunningham, 1980, p. 515). Even to Adam Smith the relationship was antagonistic: the more leisure, the less progress; the more progress, the less leisure (1937). Similarly, in more contemporary writings, the relationship between leisure and capitalism remains contrary. Based on the question of whether leisure meets individual or societal needs, Torkildsen (2005) maintains that under capitalism leisure is not an individual right, but rather something to be given as a reward or withheld as a punishment.

In contrast, many people believe capitalism has created more leisure for people. For example, in the United States in the 1960s economic progress through capitalism was projected to yield steady reductions in work time. Now, workers under capitalism have a 40-hour workweek, two weeks a year for a paid vacation, and extended years of schooling and retirement. With lots of discretionary income, people in capitalism are also able to buy more leisure goods and services.

Yet, some commentators consider this progress to be hollow. Economist Juliette Schor (1992), for example, argues capitalism tends to expand work to the detriment of leisure. Personal economic need and desire often requires workers to hold down more than one job or seek overtime above the 40-hour workweek standard. Plus, Schor maintains, almost all other nations have an average of twice the paid two-week vacation days as Americans (table 11.2). Schor's point is that capitalist economies contain biases toward "long hour jobs" (p. 7).

Table 11.2

Paid Time Off (with 10 Years' Tenure) and Paid Public Holidays

Country	Minimum Paid Vacation Days	Paid Public Holidays	Total
Finland	30	14	44
Israel	24	16	40
United Arab Emirates	30	9	39
Estonia	28	10	38
Greece	25	12	37
United States	15	10	25
Canada	10	10	20
Thailand	6	13	19

Mercer Human Resource Consulting, 2007. Available from http://money.cnn.com/2007/06/12pf/vacation_days_worldwide. Retrieved 7/8/08.

Other economic systems have also had roller-coaster relationships with leisure. For example, those within a socialist economic system have been able to acquire free time but are often unsuccessful in producing the goods and services people want for leisure. This might all mean that when leisure is defined as buying something, a capitalist economic system is effective.

Box 11.3

In Profile

Veblen, Smith, Marx, and Schor

Do economists consider the relationship between leisure and economics similarly? Separated by many years, is there still a common thread in the ideas of Adam Smith, Karl Marx, Thorstein Veblen, and Juliette Schor? Briefly, let's compare them.

	Adam Smith	**Karl Marx**	**Thorstein Veblen**	**Juliette Schor**
Time period	Late 1700s	Mid-1800s	Late 1800s	Late 1990s
Biography	Professor of moral philosophy at the University of Glasgow, Scotland. Generally considered the founder of the free enterprise economic system (capitalism).	From Prussia (now Germany). Working with colleague Friedrich Engels, is known as socialism's most zealous intellectual advocate. Spent much of his life exiled for radicalism.	From Wisconsin (of Norwegian immigrants). Professor at the University of Chicago. Coined the expression "conspicuous consumption."	Professor of sociology at Boston College. Focuses on trends in work & leisure, consumerism, & economic justice. Co-founder of the Center for a New American Dream to make North American lifestyles more ecologically & socially sustainable.
Economic premise	Individual self-interest with no regulation provides for a common good.	Exchanges of equal value for equal value, where value is determined by the amount of work put into whatever is being produced.	Economic behavior is socially rather than individually determined and driven by the human instincts of emulation, predation, and curiosity. His ideas are the basis of modern advertising.	Economics based on a consumerist mentality (spending for social meaning) harm people and communities.
Consequence for leisure	Leisure is an obstruction to progress.	Leisure is harmed when not equally available. To gain more leisure, the lower classes must overthrow the upper classes.	Leisure is the outward expression of the upper classes. To gain more leisure, the lower classes must climb up to the level of the upper classes.	Keeping up with the Joneses requires working more, which means less leisure time and energy.

Consumerism

Let's look at the idea of buying leisure a bit more. A fundamental part of any economic system is *consumption*. In most economies, it is the largest spending category. It includes purchases of nondurable goods, such as a bowling shirt, and durable goods, such as bowling balls. We also consume services, such as fitness classes. You can usually tell a lot about an individual's (and a society's) economic status by observing their consumption patterns. Do they drive a Hummer or an old VW bus? What do they eat? What do they wear? Although you sometimes come across people who live well below or above their means, consumption and income tend to be closely tied (table 11.3).

Consumption: all purchases of goods and services for personal use

Table 11.3

Average Per Capita Income and Personal Consumption Expenditures in the United States (in current dollars)

Year	Disposable Personal Income	Durable Goods Consumption	Nondurable Goods Consumption	Services Consumption	Total Personal Consumption
1950	$1,388	$203	$648	$420	$1,270
1970	$3,591	$414	$1,326	$1,424	$3,164
1990	$17,176	$1,871	$4,985	$8,472	$15,327
2000	$25,528	$2,976	$7,224	$14,230	$24,429

U.S. Department of Commerce, Bureau of Economic Analysis, July 2001. Available from http://www.bea.doc.gov. Retrieved 7/11/08.

Spending money for leisure is a common focus of consumption. Indeed, expenditures for leisure are at the center of some economies. People buy bowling balls, fishing licenses, amusement park admissions, gasoline for power boats, golf clubs, pets, DVDs, iPod downloads, flower seeds, and jogging shoes. According to the U.S. Census Bureau (2007) Americans in 2004 spent a total of $702.4 billion on durable recreation goods. The largest amount was for video and audio products, including computer equipment and musical instruments ($130.8 billion).

Economists also report expenditures for leisure goods have been increasing at a faster rate than other merchandise. For example, in the late 1800s in the United States, less than two percent of household expenditures were devoted to recreational goods, as compared to today's over 9 percent of all personal consumption. This means leisure is a growth industry. That is, buying these goods is good for the economy, but the web entangling leisure and consumption is quite dynamic, so there are problems in the relationship too. For example, for some people consumption is actually a form of leisure. Let's consider shopping as an illustration.

Although we have no clear estimates of how many of us spend time wandering around the stores, a number of research studies have pointed to the prevalence

Figure 11.4

Shopping for leisure goods, or shopping as leisure? (© Ruth V. Russell, 2008)

of shopping as a favorite pastime of North Americans. In fact, when people are given more free time, participating in shopping tends to increase. For example, in one study of the effects of converting to a four-day workweek and thus a three-day weekend, one third of the workers surveyed filled the extra time by spending more money on shopping (Maklan, 1977).

Visiting shopping malls is for many a preferred form of evening or weekend recreation. Shopping is fun—an experience—a fact not lost on retail marketing strategies today. As an example, take the Recreational Equipment Inc.'s (REI) flagship store in Seattle. With a simulated rain shower to test Gore-Tex jackets, a glass-encased climbing wall to test climbing gear, a rough-and-tumble path through a forest to test mountain bikes and boots, this outdoor equipment retailer reflects the growing trend of shopping as entertainment.

Yet, is shopping really leisure? If what we want are things, and things cost money, and money costs time (deGrazia, 1962), then are we experiencing leisure through shopping? This question leads us to the concept of the *harried leisure class*. First noticed by Staffan Linder in his 1970 book by the same title,

Harried leisure class: spending money for leisure and thus spoiling leisure by making us feel frantic

the relevance of this idea today is stunning. Linder was the first economist to understand and predict the frantic pace of leisure in modern life. In his little book he pointed out that consumption takes time, and with increased levels of products and services, time for consumption has to be sped up. Linder considered this the antithesis of leisure. We have to work more, to be able to buy more things, and thus get into a hectic, never satisfied, materialistic frenzy.

It is common wisdom that owning more and more material possessions will not necessarily bring happiness, particularly if working harder to have the money to buy, maintain and store them is required. Also, once an item of desire is purchased, it quickly converts to a need for a better purchase, so that first it's an iPod and then it's an iPod Touch that's needed.

Economists and psychologists have spent decades studying the relation between wealth and happiness, and they have generally concluded wealth increases human happiness when it lifts people out of abject poverty and into the middle class, but it does little to increase happiness thereafter (Gilbert, 2006). In one study of lottery winners, for example, even though the winners were

Box 11.4

 *In Profile*

Affluenza

Introduced in a Public Broadcasting Service documentary that first aired in 1997, and using the analogy of a disease, affluenza is defined as a "painful, contagious, socially transmitted condition of overload, debt, anxiety and waste resulting from the dogged pursuit of more" (deGraaf, Wann & Naylor, 2001, p. 2). Symptoms include compulsive shopping, high consumer debt, overwork, inability to delay gratification, a sense of entitlement, and an obsession for having it all. Affluenza is what Hamilton and Denniss (2005) label luxury fever.

British psychologist Oliver James (2007) asserts there is a correlation between affluenza and an increase in material inequality: the more monetarily unequal a society, the greater the unhappiness of its citizens. More specifically, James claims placing a high value on money and possessions is the rationale behind increasing mental illness where cultures encourage citizens to measure their worth by financial success and material possessions. He explains the greater incidence of affluenza in especially the United States is the result of selfish capitalism.

Here are some outcomes from affluenza:

- The average adult spends more time shopping each week than she or he spends with her or his children.
- On Sunday more Americans visit shopping malls than go to church.
- More Americans file for bankruptcy each year than graduate from college.
- The average American home is more than twice as large as it was in the 1950s, yet the average family is smaller.

much happier immediately after winning the lottery, one year later their average happiness had increased on a nine-point scale from 6.5 to only 6.8 as a result of winning (Sobel & Ornstein, 1987).

What if we were more conserving in our leisure consumption? Could we still have fun? What would happen if we didn't want faster jet skis, easy travel to unusual places, and hundreds of CDs? What would life be like if we engaged in only those activities that made a minimal demand on material goods, such as walking, yoga, reading, singing, and dancing? How would our health be affected if we chose cross-country skiing over downhill skiing, hiking over all-terrain motorbikes, or playing basketball at the park rather than at the club? Would recycling the medals won in sport competitions, repairing and passing on to others toys our children have outgrown, and taking our own cup to the refreshment stand at the ball game help the environment as well? These are examples of *conserver leisure*. Would we still have a good time?

Conserver leisure:
leisure goods and services that do not rely on consumption

Box 11.5

In Your Own Experience

Spending Nothing Day

Can you go for a day without spending any money? Try it. The day before, load up your refrigerator with the food you'll need for the next day, put in the gasoline for your car you'll need to get you to school and/or work, and acquire whatever other absolute necessities you'll need for the day.

Now, for 24 hours, live without consumption. Spend absolutely nothing. Of course, you won't need to spend anything anyway because you've already taken care of the necessities, right?

During the day keep a journal about your experience and feelings. Afterward ask yourself if you missed not spending any money. What was it like not to go to a movie, download a song, have a coffee with friends, or shop at the mall? Is spending money important to your leisure? Is spending money itself leisure to you? What leisure expressions that didn't cost anything did you substitute into your day? Take a moment to reflect about how much your quality of life is affected by the quantity of stuff.

So that you don't feel so unusual about this experiment, link onto the numerous "buy nothing" campaigns around the world available on the Internet. Just type "buy nothing day" into your browser.

Figure 11.5

Recycling children's toys and sports equipment would be a good place to begin practicing conserver leisure.
(© Ruth V. Russell, 2008)

How Leisure Benefits and Harms an Economy

In spite of the delicate balance between leisure and economics we just illustrated through the concepts of economic development, capitalism, and consumption, there is no doubt that leisure has economic power. The dollar and cents of leisure's economic worth can be both positive and negative. In this section of the chapter we explore both.

How Leisure Benefits an Economy

The presence of leisure facilities and programs attracts businesses and industries to particular locales. Cultural and sporting events are good public relations for the corporations that support them, ultimately increasing profits. Well-planned leisure services can help reduce the costs of crime. Therapeutic recreation treatments return injured workers to the job, thus contributing to their company's and nation's productivity. Leisure expenditures and investments provide a primary economic base for many cities, states, and countries. Although the list could go on and on, the specific positive economic benefits from leisure we'll review are employment, taxes, and property values.

Box 11.6

The Study Says

How to Spend $30,000

It costs about $30,000 to incarcerate a convicted youth offender for one year. According to research reported by the National Recreation and Park Association, if that money were available to the community recreation and parks department each year, the same youth offender could instead be taught good behavior through
- Swimming twice a week for 24 weeks
- Four tours of the zoo plus lunch
- Enrollment in 50 community center programs
- Visiting a nature center twice
- Playing league softball for a season
- Touring the public gardens twice
- Two weeks of tennis lessons
- Two weeks of day camp
- Three rounds of golf
- Acting in a play
- Participating in one fishing clinic
- Taking a four-week pottery class
- Playing basketball eight hours a week for 40 weeks

And still have $29,125 left over to spend on someone else.

National Recreation and Park Association. (2000). *Discover the Benefits of Parks and Recreation* (Brochure). Ashburn, VA: Author.

It is difficult to estimate the number of people whose job income is leisure-related, yet available statistics suggest many occupations have something to do with the provision of leisure goods and services for others. Those in the entertainment fields, supervisors in city recreation agencies, managers in parks and forests, employees of health and fitness facilities, workers in factories manufacturing recreational goods, recreation therapists in hospitals, employees of restaurants and hotels, wedding planners, bowling center managers, travel agents, and many more types of leisure-related employment provide benefits to an economy.

For example, U.S. state park systems employ close to 54,000 people (National Association of State Park Directors, 2004). Further, it is estimated that American full service restaurants employ over 3.9 million people, hotels over 1.3 million people, the motion picture industry about 300,000, casinos over 105,000, museums and historical sites over 123,000, and camps annually hire more than 20,000 people (U.S. Department of Commerce, 2005). As well, many other occupations, such as transportation system workers and child-care specialists, are indirectly or partially related to leisure and provide economic benefits as well. This represents billions of dollars in personal income, which is fed back into the economy as consumption.

There is another way to view the positive impact leisure has on employment. Substantial research data indicate participation in some leisure activities leads workers to be more productive. When this happens, the cost of production decreases, which means financial gain to employers. Particularly active leisure forms can help reduce health-care costs, lower absenteeism, and reduce on-the-job accidents (Ellis & Richardson, 1991). According to the Centers for Disease Control and Prevention, in 2007 the estimated cost of health care and lost productivity due to stroke in the U.S. was projected to be almost $63 billion for people who could have fought off at least a portion of the disease with even a little physical exercise.

Another category demonstrating leisure's positive impact on an economy is taxes and other governmental fees. Local, state or provincial, and federal revenues through taxes paid in connection with leisure contribute significantly to the economic health of a society. Each year, for example, the National Endowment for the Arts allocates millions of dollars in federal tax money to be used as matching funds by local arts organizations. The sources of these funds include sales taxes from the purchase of leisure goods and services, income taxes on wages earned in leisure-related jobs, property taxes from private and commercial properties that are partly or totally leisure oriented, gasoline taxes, and taxes on entertainment, restaurant meals, and hotel accommodations.

Also included here are the fees charged by governments for specific recreational services. For example, proceeds from the sale of licenses for hunting, trapping, and fishing benefit the upkeep of fish and wildlife habitats. Governments also require the payment of fees for travel visas and airports pass on government fees to passengers using the airport.

Of particular benefit to local and state governments are the revenues collected from legal gambling, such as lotteries and pari-mutuel betting. For example, in 2005 in the U.S., total consumer spending on lotteries surpassed $50 billion, with over $15 billion of this revenue transferred to state coffers (Hansen, 2007). Citing the state of Delaware, since 1975, more than $2.8 billion has been transferred to the general fund from lottery proceeds, making it the state's fourth-largest revenue generator. States and local entities typically use these proceeds to offset tax shortfalls to finance public and higher education, health and social services, public safety, judicial and correctional services, and environmental control.

Box 11.7

In Profile

CNL Lifestyle Properties, Inc.

CNL Lifestyle Properties is a real estate investment trust (REIT) that purchases income-producing properties based on leisure lifestyles, such as golf courses, ski and mountain resorts, and tourist attractions. Investors pay $10.00 per share for property that, according to demographic and lifestyle trends, is predicted to grow and produce a strong return. Assuming a baby boomer generation that wants active, fun, and new experiences, in the current CNL portfolio are such properties as the Brighton Ski Resort in Utah, the Gatlinburg Sky Lift in Tennessee, Great Wolf Lodge at Wisconsin Dells, Forest Park Golf Course in St. Louis, and the Sandusky Harbor Marina in Ohio. Leisure is a good investment.

CNL Lifestyle Properties Inc. (April 4, 2008). *Brochure.* Orlando, Florida.

Finally, we should mention leisure's positive contribution to property values. The value of land is often affected by the presence of leisure-related development. For example, large and well-maintained parks usually increase the value of adjacent property, such as the land near Central Park in New York City. In some locales, the highest priced residential property adjoins golf courses, developed lakes and reservoirs, resorts, wildlife refuges, and other leisure sites.

Perhaps the most visible example of the positive impact of leisure on property values is Palm Springs, California. Once barren desert land, today Palm Springs has a population of approximately 42,000 residents. Why? Sometimes the best economic use of an area is for leisure. Palm Springs has made itself into an adult playground. The Palm Springs industries are tennis, golf, cultural events, bicycling, lounging by the pool, pleasure walking, and eating fine foods. These industries bring in not only permanent residents, but also conventioneers and tourists. Two million visitors a year flock to this land of 354 days of sunshine. Based on an almost purely leisure-focused economy, where there was once nothing, median home prices in Palm Springs in 2008 are over $358,000.

How Leisure Harms an Economy

Sometimes leisure results in costs rather than benefits to both an individual's finances and a community's economy. For example, although businesses and local and state governments in Hawaii benefit financially from tourism, residents do not necessarily benefit. Hawaii's 6.4 million tourists a year also drive up inflation, and thus the cost of living for residents (Olson, 2001). There are many more examples, such as the decreased productivity of workers that often happens around holidays, such as the opening of baseball and hunting seasons, and the week between Christmas and New Years. In addition, leisure businesses are among the most susceptible to the whims of public taste. Fads come and go, and expensive leisure industries come and go with them. Financial headaches can also be caused by the seasonal nature of some forms of leisure, such as beach and ski resorts.

Frequently, members of society must pay high costs to solve problems resulting from leisure. For example, about 72 million dogs are kept as pets in the U.S., and the cost to taxpayers for dealing with strays and removing fecal waste from public places is about $500 million per year (American Veterinary Medical Association, 2007). Annually the U.S. Coast Guard spends $1 billion to rescue small pleasure boats. To understand more about how leisure harms an economy, we'll consider accidents and the negative balance of payments.

Unintentional injuries affect millions. In 2005, for instance, 33.2 million people (about one in nine) sought medical attention for an injury and 2.8 million people were hospitalized for injuries. Further, unintentional injuries are the fifth leading cause of death in the U.S. (National Safety Council, 2008). The economic impact of these nonfatal and fatal accidents—for lost wages, indirect work loss, medical expenses, insurance payments, rescue and emergency care, and lawsuits—amounted to $652 billion in 2006. This is equivalent to about $2,200 per person.

What proportion of these accidents and costs is leisure related? A comprehensive summary of all leisure induced accidents is not available, but The National Safety Council (2008) reports each year more than 200,000 children visit hospital emergency rooms because of playground injuries, more than 70,000 persons need emergency room treatment for injuries related to skateboarding, another 82,000 people suffer brain injuries while playing baseball and football, and drowning claims the lives of nearly 3,000—mostly children who've fallen into swimming pools.

Figure 11.6

Risks to bicyclists have increased, but according to the Bicycle Helmet Safety Institute, a bicycle helmet reduces the risk of serious head and brain injury by 85%. (© Ruth V. Russell, 2008)

Finally, an economy's balance of payments can represent a negative impact from leisure. *Balance of payments* is a measure of the payments that flow between any individual economy and all other economies. It is the comparison of imports against exports. In recent years several countries have experienced an imbalance. For example, in the first quarter of 2008 the U.S. deficit was about $176.2 billion (Bureau of Economic Analysis, 2008),

Balance of payment:

a comparison of all goods and services, as well as investments, that flows in and out of an economy

thus the economy was experiencing a negative balance of payments. This means Americans imported more than they exported.

How does this relate to leisure? You can answer this at the individual economic level. Inventory your own leisure-related equipment and clothing. Do you own athletic shoes, golf clubs, snow skis, a bicycle, a television, a CD player, a DVD player, or a musical instrument? Make a list of as much leisure stuff you own as you can think of. Now, indicate where each item was produced. Although this can sometimes be tricky with transnational manufacturers, you'll be able to make a pretty fair estimate of the proportion of your leisure possessions that were made in your own country. If you have more leisure equipment made outside your country than inside, then you just demonstrated a negative balance of payments accountable to leisure. Leisure imports and leisure exports are a major component in an economy's balance of payments.

The customary view (Sirgy, et al., 2007) is economic well-being is positively related to how much it is able to export. Exporting creates jobs and increases purchasing power. Likewise, the general assumption is there is a negative influence from an economy's imports, even though increased imports provide consumers with greater access to high quality and/or low priced products. This is because increased imports may result in decreased sales of comparable domestic products.

Box 11.8

 ## *In Your Own Experience*

The Freshman 15

The high cost of credit cards is hitting home for many people, including college students. Today, the average credit card debt at graduation for undergraduates is $3,000. The "freshman 15," which once referred to the typical college weight gain, now refers to credit card debt as many freshmen now easily rack up more than $15,000 of it. What about you? Answer the questions below to determine the role of leisure in your own credit card debt load.

1. Do you have more than one credit card? How many do you have?
2. Do you pay off your balance every month, or do you make only the minimum payments? That is, do you have a personal negative balance of payments?
3. If you make only the minimum payments, have you calculated how long it will take you to pay off your balance even if you charge nothing more? (See the various credit card debt pay-off calculators available on the Internet for help; for example try http://www.bankrate.com/brm/calc/creditcardpay.asp.)
4. Take a look at the most recent statement for your credit cards. About what proportion of your monthly charging on these cards is for things or experiences you'd label as recreational?
5. Would you say you are borrowing from future employment prospects to live the good life right now? Why or why not?

While it is certainly more complicated than this, and there are numerous counter arguments to this conclusion (consider, for example, the debate over NAFTA in recent years in the U.S.), leisure can generally impact an economy negatively if more leisure goods are imported than exported.

An example of these complications is tourism. In tourism one of the factors mixing up the balance of payments ledger is the extent to which tourist attractions are foreign owned. Disneyland Resort Paris is a good example. Walt Disney Company has a 51-percent interest in this 4,800-acre development located in Marne-la-Vallee, France (Rueters, 2008). Although the park is located in France, a majority of the income generated there goes to owners in the United States. This situation is called *foreign exchange leakage* and is a strong determinant of whether tourism really provides economic advantage for the locale hosting the attraction. In particular, for developing economies using tourism as an economic development tool, foreign exchange leakage caused by foreign ownership of the airlines, hotels, resorts, souvenirs, alcohol, and other tourist goods and services can be significant.

Foreign exchange leakage:
money generated in an economy that is removed because of foreign ownership of the goods and service sold there

So, in fact, leisure carries significant economic impact via both its power to benefit and harm an economy. There are many other examples, of course, such as the economic repercussions of people relocating to be close to recreation amenities. Such migrations can promote the economies of popular beach and mountain areas, for example, but also reduce the economies of the communities that lose population. It can also stress the economies of small communities receiving the influx of residents if they demand substantial infrastructure improvements to public facilities and services.

What We Understand About Leisure Economics

Leisure is a powerful economic balancing tool. Increasingly, both private and public leisure goods and services are being produced, which means leisure is central to consumption and investment in an economy. Also, questions of how to distribute leisure goods and services have become central to concern for economic growth and economic decline. Ultimately, changes in an economy create shifts in leisure, and shifts in leisure have an impact on the economy. A healthy economy depends on the relative stability of leisure. From studying this chapter you should know that

- Leisure is a mirror of a nation's level of economic development and its economic system.
- In economically developed countries (especially under capitalism), leisure drives the economy by fostering consumption.
- Sometimes consumption itself is viewed as a leisure experience.
- Leisure has both positive and negative economic impacts.
- On the one hand, leisure makes good economic sense; it benefits employment, taxes, and property values.
- On the other hand, leisure has monetary costs. Two examples are the costs of leisure-related injuries and a negative balance of payments.

References

American Veterinary Medical Association. (2007). *U.S. Pet Ownership & Demographics Sourcebook* Available from http://www.avma.org/reference/marketstats/sourcebook.asp. Retrieved 7/12/08

Bureau of Economic Analysis. (2008). *U.S. International Transactions*. Available fromhttp://www.bea.gov/newsreleases/international/transactions/trans newsrelease.htm. Retrieved 7/12/08.

CIA World Factbook. (2008). *GDP*. Available from https://www.cia.gov/library/publications/the-world-factbook/field/2195.thml. Retrieved 7/6/08.

Cunningham, H. (1980). *Leisure in the Industrial Revolution*. London: Croom Helm.

deGraaf, J., Wann, D., & Naylor, T.H. (2001). *Affluenza: The all-consuming epidemic*. San Francisco: Berrett-Koehler.

deGrazia, S. (1962). *Of time, work and leisure*. New York: The Twentieth Century Fund.

Ellis, T., & Richardson, G. (1991). Organizational wellness. In B.L. Driver, P.J. Brown, & G.L. Peterson (Eds.), *Benefits of leisure* (pp. 314-329). State College, PA: Venture.

Embassy of Greece. (April 18, 2007). World Tourism and Travel Council study predicts great increase in Greek tourism. *News Release*. Available from http://www.greekembassy.org/Embassy/content/en/Article.aspx?office=3&folder=361&article=20292. Retrieved 7/9/08.

Freysinger, V.J., & Kelly, J.R. (2004). *21st Century leisure: Current issues* (2nd Ed.). State College, PA: Venture.

Gilbert, D. (2006). *Stumbling on happiness*. New York: Vintage Books.

Goodale, T.L., & Godbey, G. (1988). *The evolution of leisure: Historical and philosophical perspectives*. State College, PA: Venture.

Hamilton, C., & Denniss, R. (2005). *Affluenza: When too much is never enough*. Sydney: Allen & Unwin.

Hansen, A. (July 3, 2007). Gambling with tax policy: States' growing reliance on lottery tax revenue. *Background Paper, The Tax Foundation*. Available from http://www.taxfoundation.org/research/show/22457.html. Retrieved 7/12/08.

International Monetary Fund. (2008). *World Economic Outlook Database, April 2008*. Available from http://www.imf.org/external/. Retrieved 7/6/08.

James, O. (2007). *Affluenza: How to be successful and stay sane*. New York: Vermilion.

Linder, S. (1970). *The harried leisure class*. New York: Columbia University Press.

Maklan, M. (1977). How blue-collar workers on a four-day workweek use their time. *Monthly Labor Review, 100*(8), 26.

National Association of State Park Directors. (2004). *State Park Facts*. Available from http://www.naspd.org/. Retrieved 7/11/08.

National Safety Council. (2008). *Report on Injuries in America*. Available from http://www.nsc.org/lrs/injuriesinamerica08.aspx. Retrieved 7/12/08.

Nazareth, L. (2007). *The leisure economy: How changing demographics, economics, and generational attitudes will reshape our lives and our industries.* New York: Wiley.

Olson, K. (July-August 2001). Please stay home. *UTNE Reader, 106,* 78.

Rueters. (2008). *Walt Disney Company: Profile.* Available from http://www. reuters.com/finance/stocks/companyProfile?symbol=DIS.Nrpc=66. Retrieved 7/12/08.

Schor, J.B. (1992). *The overworked American: The unexpected decline of leisure.* New York: Basic Books.

Sirgy, M.J., Lee, D.J., Miller, C., Littlefield, J.E., & Atay, E.G. (2007). The impact of imports and exports on a country's quality of life. *Social Indicators Research, 83,* 245-281.

Smith, A. (1937). *An inquiry into the nature and causes of the wealth of nations.* New York: The Modern Library. (Original work published 1776).

Sobel, J., & Ornstein, R. (1987). *Healthy pleasures.* Reading, MA: Addison-Wesley.

Torkildsen, G. (2005). *Leisure and recreation management* (5th Ed.). New York: Routledge.

U.S. Census Bureau (2007). Table 1218. Personal consumption expenditures for recreation: 1990 to 2004. *Statistical Abstract of the United States: 2007.* Washington, DC: Government Printing Office.

U.S. Department of Commerce. (2005). *American FactFinder.* Available from http://www.commerce.gov/. Retrieved 7/11/08.

Veblen, T. (1899). *The Theory of the Leisure Class.* New York: Macmillan.

CHAPTER TWELVE

OF TIME AND WORK

PREVIEW

How do we know what time it is?
People view time according to their history, biology, and culture.

How does leisure depend on time?
Leisure is shaped by many time factors, including personal perceptions of free time, the amount of time available, the time requirements of activities, and a culture's time sufficiency.

Is time ever a problem for leisure?
Time for leisure can be problematic in modern societies because of such time tyrannies as time urgency and time deepening.

Why do we work?
Work (like time) is a relatively recent phenomenon resulting from history and culture. It is necessary for human survival, yet it may or may not allow us to live well.

What is leisure's relationship to work?
There are conflicting answers to this question. Some argue work is a less desirable human condition and leisure is needed to overcome it. Others claim work and leisure are equally satisfying and necessary in life. There are also those who claim work and leisure are unrelated.

KEY TERMS

They lost a weekend. For the nearly 3,000 American military and civilian workers living on the remote Pacific atoll of Kwajalein, Marshall Islands, Saturday, August 21, 1993 didn't happen. They went to bed Friday night and woke up Sunday morning. That was because at midnight Friday, Kwajalein switched its system of time from one side of the international dateline to the other.

Kwajalein is west of the line, but for 40 years had synchronized with the United States mainland to the east in order to match its workday. They did this by pretending they were located east of the dateline. In 1993, however, The Republic of the Marshall Islands requested the change so all its islets would be on the same time. Since the residents of Kwajalein still wanted to match the U.S. work schedule, they switched their workweek to Tuesday through Saturday, which matches Monday through Friday in the U.S.

Much ado about nothing? People of many societies take the notions of time and work very seriously. In part, this seriousness is what distinguishes technological cultures from others. Also, the entanglement of our leisure within a utilitarian web of time and work is also responsible. That is, there is a symbiotic instrumentalism among time, work, and leisure. Each is used as a tool for the others.

Figure 12.1

Many pastimes are very time and work conscious. For example, football is played by the clock (60 minutes, out of which only 12-15 minutes contain actual playing), and is typically played at times when most potential spectators are not at their jobs. Also, football is itself considered a job to be done, with skills to work on, etc. (© Ruth V. Russell, 2008)

In this chapter we first consider leisure's relation to time, including types of time and time tyrannies. Then, we consider leisure's relation to work in terms of the purpose of work, worker rewards and dissatisfactions, and ways leisure actually depends on work. Throughout you'll notice that as with the citizens of Kwajalein, time, work, and leisure are functionally intertwined in contemporary society.

Time

Time is the most equally distributed of all our culture's resources—we all get exactly the same number of hours a day for days and weeks and months and years to do with as we choose. Yet, time is also considered the scarcest and most fragile of our culture's resources. None of us feel we have control over our time or that we even have enough time. What is this paradox? The answer has something to do with how time and leisure relate.

Time is a very complex phenomenon. Even Aristotle, in the book *Physics*, asked the question "In what sense, if any, can time be said to exist?" (as cited in Barnes, 1984, p. 369). Time has been a major subject of religion, philosophy, sociology, anthropology, and the physical sciences, but defining it in a non-controversial manner applicable to all fields of study has consistently eluded the greatest scholars.

Understanding time has nonetheless become important in contemporary life because time is the framework for all our behavior. To illustrate, in the English language the word is both noun and verb. And, notice how it has been applied to so many different actions: we save time, spend time, hoard time, make up time, speed up time, make good time, kill time, while away time, and of course, time flies!

Time for Leisure

Leisure certainly takes place in time, and although estimates vary, for the majority of adults in developed societies, about 40 hours each week are available for leisure, which amounts to over four months a year of free time. How do we experience all this free time? Time used for leisure is essentially shaped by four factors:

- Personal perceptions of free time
- Personal amounts of free time
- The time needs of leisure activities
- A culture's time sufficiency

First, people's perceptions of free time influence how they use it for leisure (table 12.1). If free time is regarded as a privilege, it is likely to be used wisely in pursuits perceived to be personally beneficial or socially constructive. Others may view free time as a chance for temporary escape from the physical and mental environment of work and daily routines. They regard it as an opportunity for getting away from it all. Still others see free time as neither a privilege nor an opportunity but as an empty space that, if left unfilled, becomes frightening. These are people who feel compelled from fear to keep busy, even in their free

Figure 12.2

Participating in a model railroad club. How do you choose to use your free time? (© Ruth V. Russell, 2008)

time. Finally, similar behaviors may arise from a perception of free time as a precious commodity. Stemming from feelings of guilt, every spare moment must be crammed with activity to be sure it is not wasted.

Quite related to perceptions of free time, leisure as experienced in time also depends on the amount of free time we actually possess. Whether the amount of free time people have is increasing or decreasing has been hotly debated recently

Table 12.1

Perceptions of Free Time

Free Time Perceived As:	Implication for Leisure	Example
Privilege	Seek personally beneficial or socially constructive pursuits.	Volunteer to coach a girl's soccer team.
Opportunity	A chance for temporary escape from work and daily routines.	Take a trip out of town for the weekend.
Empty Space	Feel compelled to be busy even in leisure.	Take a book with you to a musical concert.
Precious Commodity	Not wanting to waste free time.	Unable to spend the afternoon in a hammock.

Time famine:

having insufficient free time

because research findings on the question have conflicted. Yet, even without study findings, it is clear to us all that some people have more free time than others. For example, notorious deficits in free time are typically ascribed to specific sectors of the population, such as married women who are employed outside the home with children living at home. The expression *time famine* describes the condition of not having enough free time.

Box 12.1

 The Study Says

Is Free Time Increasing or Decreasing?

Study One

Juliet Schor, an economist, published a study in 1992 entitled *The Overworked American: The Unexpected Decline of Leisure.* Her argument was that Americans are working longer; she claimed the average employed person worked an additional 163 hours a year in 1987 compared with 1969 (p. 29). This amounts to a loss of nearly one month of free time per year. The reasons for such changes, Schor suggested, is the endless work-and-spend cycle. Her findings claim we are spending our way through life. This requires us to work harder to be able to have the money to buy more.

Box 12.1 (Cont.)

Study Two

Leisure scholars John Robinson and Geoffrey Godbey published a study in 1997, and again in 1999, that argued Americans actually have almost 265 hours more free time per year today than they did in the 1960s—that's five more hours per week. Their explanation was that we feel more rushed and stressed because we try to do many things all at once, having free time in only small segments rather than in a larger time period, such as a full weekend. Their findings also suggested we invest free time in activities that bring us minimal fulfillment, such as watching television, which also gives us a sense of time famine. Thus, the problem is not actually the amount of free time, but people's use of it.

Explaining the Contradiction

How might we explain the stark difference in the findings? Which study is true? One way to answer this is to compare the ways used to collect information. Schor's findings are based on estimates of time use from various government reports. These documents track the market hours of full-time and part-time employees. Robinson and Godbey's findings are based on individual time diaries. Every 10 years the project asks thousands of Americans to report their daily activities on an hour-by-hour basis. Since the two studies used different data sources, are the findings comparable? To help you make up your mind, see Schor's rebuttal to the debate at http://www.swt.org/putok.htm.

Robinson, J.P., & Godbey, G. (1997 and 1999). *Time for life: The surprising ways Americans use their time*. University Park: The Pennsylvania State University.
Schor, J. (1992). *The overworked American: The unexpected decline of leisure*. New York: Basic Books.

Leisure as experienced in time also depends on the amount of time an activity requires. For example, the game of *Monopoly* takes longer to play than *Dominos*, and tennis is a longer lasting sport than racquetball. One of the complications of contemporary society is that people are choosing shorter, less absorbing leisure activities to match shorter blocks of free time (Godbey, 2006). For example, the trend in vacations is multiple three-day excursions spread throughout the year rather than the traditional two-week trip in the summer.

Related, the concept of *temporal displacement* shows how people change the timing of leisure activities. Suppose boaters who in the past have frequented a lake become dissatisfied with something. This might be an increase in crowding on weekends. If the boaters decide to switch their boating at the lake from weekends to weekdays, they have demonstrated temporal displacement. Spatial displacement is another way to change an unsatisfying situation. This involves changing the location of the activity, such as to a different lake. Research has demonstrated, however, that temporal displacement is the more common way to avoid recreational conflicts (Hall & Shelby, 2000).

Temporal displacement: altering the timing of events as reaction to adverse changes at a recreation resource

Finally, the expression of leisure in time is a function of how much time a culture has. Referred to as a culture's *time sufficiency*, the amount of free time available affects the general welfare of people. First noted by Linder (1970), cultures can be categorized according to the amount of free time they have: they have either time surplus or time scarcity (table 12.2).

Table 12.2

Cultural Time Sufficiency and Leisure

Distinction	Time surplus	Time scarcity
Time	Time rich; much free or idle time	Time poor; no or little free time
Wealth	Poor	Rich
Production	Low	High
Work	Not dependent on mechanical time; no time-related work stress	Highly dependent on mechanical time; time stress causes illness
Leisure	Numerous holidays Popular recreation activities occupy large time blocks Much spontaneity Little consumption of special equipment	Few holidays Popular recreation activities occupy small time blocks Less spontaneity Much consumption of special equipment

While you might find it surprising, the least developed and poorest countries tend to have a free-time surplus. This is because production and income are low enough that large portions of time remain unused. In fact, in time-surplus cultures, rushing is considered a sign of rudeness and poverty of spirit (Robinson & Godbey, 1997). As a result, leisure tends to be more spontaneous, lengthy, relaxed, and frequent. Time-surplus cultures also tend to designate a larger number of days as holidays.

For wealthier cultures, on the other hand, there is a time famine. When the drive for time efficiency is dominant, free time is transferred to active use and becomes scarce. Punctuality becomes a virtue and rushing a sign of importance. For countries with time scarcity, leisure is less spontaneous and convenience becomes the rationale for choosing activities. In a study investigating time and cultural complexity, Chick and Shen (2007) concluded "our findings suggest that technological advancement and societal development do not necessarily and naturally lead to benefits when it comes to leisure" (p. 30).

Types of Time

Many other things affect leisure and time's instrumental relationship. One of them is the concept of time itself. Today clock time is measured as seconds, minutes, hours, days, weeks, months, years, decades, centuries, millennia, etc. Yet, this is not the only way to measure time. For example, there's universal time, international atomic time, sidereal time, and terrestrial time. Even clock time hasn't always been the measuring standard.

Our legacy of telling time perhaps began with *cyclical time*. Ancient cultures such as Incan, Mayan, Hopi, Babylonian and Greek understood time as a wheel. That is, early humans thought of time as part of the reoccurring and regular patterns of nature: the rising and setting of the sun, the tide coming in and going out, the passage of the seasons, the location of the moon in the sky (Green, 1968). Time recurred regularly.

Cyclical time:

time experienced as constant and returning

If we were able to experience cyclical time today it would mean we would sense that time is never lost or wasted, because, just like the cycles of life, time repeats itself. Likely we would have no concept of needing to get control over our time, we'd feel no responsibility for it. Life would not be thought of as a progression to an end.

The Balinese in Indonesia are often cited as coming closest to living with a cyclical perception of time today. While also affected by other notions of time, the Balinese still somewhat experience time as cyclical. Religious rituals and ceremonies, for example, are based on the constancy of the present. Recent scholarship has also explained a form of traditional Balinese music still played today, gamelan, as based on timing that is cyclical and not progressing to an end point (McGraw, 2008).

As best we know, about 5,000 years ago the great civilizations in the Middle East and North Africa began to perceive time differently. With emerging bureaucracies, these cultures apparently found a need to organize their time more efficiently. Instead of observing the stars, changes in seasons, and passing of day into night, devices were invented to measure the passage of time.

For example, the Egyptians were probably the first to divide their day into systematic parts. Obelisks (slender, tapering, four-sided monuments) were built as early as 3500 BC. Their moving shadows formed a kind of sundial, helping

Figure 12.3

Drawing of an early Egyptian water clock, which was among the earliest timekeepers not depending on observation of celestial bodies. (Source: http://physics.nist.gov/GenInt/Time/early.html, Retrieved 8/20/08)

Early water clock

people partition the day into morning and afternoon. A few hundred years later, the Egyptians are credited with the invention of the water clock. Called clepsydras (water thieves), these were stone vessels with sloping sides that allowed water to drip out a small hole near the bottom, making it possible to tell time at night.

From then, it wasn't until the 14th century that mechanical clocks were developed (Priestly, 1968). But, it took until the 17th century for Dutch scientist, Christiaan Huygens, to invent the balance wheel and spring assembly still found in some watches today. This improvement allowed portable watches to keep accurate time to within 10 minutes a day. Keeping accurate time was becoming more important, first for the daily prayer and work rituals of monks in medieval monasteries and later as a tool for industrialists to regulate the flow of production.

With the invention of the clock, people's perception of time changed. Now set to the rhythm of a machine, time became linear. This meant a period of time could pass, and when it passed, it could not be recovered. Time could now no longer be accumulated; it could only be spent and wasted. Referred to as the perception of *mechanical time*, which demands precision, punctuality, regularity, and reliability, time was now vital to furthering a work-focused civilization (Cross, 1990).

Mechanical time: time paced by machine, enabling the precise division of the day into equal parts and a linear perception of time

Time was now a resource to be used wisely. As the American statesman Benjamin Franklin recognized "Do not squander time, for that's the stuff of life" (*Poor Richard's Almanac*, 1733 to 1757). To this day, technology and the belief in the regularity of mechanical time have continued to sever our ties with nature. Lights, and heating and cooling systems that turn on and off according to timers, have eliminated the need for paying attention to natural daily and seasonal cycles. Digital alarm clocks wake us up in the morning, even if sunrise is still hours away. Wristwatches beep out the minutes it takes us to jog around the block. Today we live by completely artificial distinctions of time.

Box 12.2

 *In Profile*

Benjamin Franklin

Benjamin Franklin (1706-1790) believed that one must live an ordered daily life. This idea certainly seemed to pay off for him. Franklin's accomplishments as a printer, publisher, civic leader, statesman, and scientist seem astounding, even by today's inflated standards. How did he get it all done? Perhaps Franklin's greatest legacy was his system for how to organize the day. For example, here's how he did it.

The Morning Question: What good shall I do this day?		
	5	Rise, wash, contrive the day's
	6	business, and breakfast.
	7	
	8	
	9	Work.

Box 12.2 (Cont.)

	10	
	11	
Noon	12	Read, or overlook my accounts and dine.
	1	
	2	
	3	Work.
	4	
Evening	5	
Question: What good have	6	Put things in their places, supper,
I done this day?	7	music or diversion, or conversation.
	8	
	9	Examination of the day.
	10	
	11	
Night	12	Sleep.
	1	
	2	
	3	
	4	

Some predict our perception of time is switching to the rhythm of another machine—the computer. The computer works with the *nanosecond* as the basic time unit. At a billionth of a second, it is the measure of read or write access time to random access memory (RAM). Thus, a computer-driven concept of time speeds us up. As well, whereas the circle represented time for ancient peoples, and the straight line suggests society's experience of time since then, the double helix is considered the time-shape of the future (Rifkin, 1987). This spiral, with its feedback loops, suggests a computer-driven time experience is not only linear but also simultaneous (which may help explain multitasking).

Nanosecond: one billion of a second

These shifts in our perception of time are perhaps the most important changes in human life so far. Time now rules our lives. Although we still use the word "pastimes," for many of us it is almost impossible to think of simply letting time pass. Perhaps the first to call our attention to the implications of our time perceptions for leisure was Sebastian deGrazia in a classic study titled *Of Time, Work, and Leisure* (1962). "Clock time cannot be free," claimed deGrazia (p. 310), and because of this, few of us will ever experience the sublime state of leisure.

But, we experience other types of time, which perhaps are able to put us more in touch with freedom in our daily lives. For example, we also live according to *biological time*. Plants and animals have biologically based ways of knowing what time it is. One source, photoperiodism, is a plant's response to light. Another example is endogenous rhythms, which are common to many plants and animals, including humans.

Biological time: time controlled by biological processes

These *endogenous rhythms* are cyclical physiological functions. For example, the heart beats about 60 to 80 times per minute, and hunger occurs on about a 90-minute cycle. Endogenous rhythms predict and prepare our bodies for forthcoming events: increased sleepiness in the evening prepares us for sleep; increased deep body temperature in the morning heralds wake-up. However, because we have become so dependent on external factors of timekeeping, such as the clock, computer, and even television, we are not always able to experience time according to our endogenous rhythms.

Endogenous rhythms: timing generated within an organism

For example, one endogenous rhythm that is problematic in contemporary life is the daily rhythm of activity and rest. This relies on our *circadian clock*, a cluster of nerves located on the hypothalamus in the brain, which tells time according to environmental cues, primarily light from the day/night cycle. Although unique for each of us, a typical single circadian cycle of activity and rest ranges between 20 and 28 hours.

Circadian clock: daily rhythm of activity and rest

Many studies have demonstrated that when we live according to our circadian clock, we feel better. One reason is our natural circadian rhythm is experienced as comfort, even pleasure. This is why we particularly appreciate such rhythmic experiences as music and poetry. Paying attention to our internal clock also means we can be at our best. For example, elite athletes have used circadian rhythm charting to help predict peaks in performance.

This is also why abrupt changes in our circadian clock, such as jet lag resulting from air travel, have a detrimental effect on us. Additionally, season changes, which are accompanied by a decrease in the number of daylight hours, can negatively affect our circadian clock, primarily by increasing the secretion of melatonin to induce sleep. If these interruptions are strong and frequent enough they may lead to mood disorders, including seasonal affective disorder and mild depression.

Another type of time we live with is *cultural time*. That is, our social groups tell us what time it is. For example, in some families 6:00 p.m. is always dinnertime. In certain religious groups the week is formed around the idea of a Sabbath. On U.S. college campuses, if a professor is more than 10 minutes late for class, students begin to consider leaving. Cultural time is not the same in every culture or group. For example, in Brazil, university students define a professor's lateness as slightly over 30 minutes after the scheduled start of class (Levine & Wolff, 1985).

Cultural time: socially established perceptions of time

An example of cultural time differences with implications for leisure is waiting in line. Americans spend at least 37 billion hours a year waiting (Denny, 1993), and they do it by forming lines according to the order of arrival. But this is not universal. For example, in Israel, even though people wait for buses by stubbornly resisting forming lines, when the bus comes, they board according to the first-come principle as if they had been in line all along. Indeed, the fact that forming waiting lines is unknown or approached differently across cultures was a fact missed by the Walt Disney Company when it opened Disneyland Resort Paris in France and Hong Kong Disneyland.

Box 12.3

In Profile

Waiting in Line at the Disney Parks

There are cultural differences in how people behave while waiting in line. Understanding these have led to changes in how theme parks, such as those owned by the Walt Disney Company, organize queuing areas.

For example, Jay Rasulo, then chairman of Walt Disney Parks and Resorts, said in the first few weeks of the Hong Kong park's operation in 2005, officials noticed specific differences between Hong Kong visitors and those from mainland China. Since about 25 percent of Hong Kong residents had already visited a Disney theme park, they were better able to participate in the park's queuing system. Visitors from mainland China, where only 1 percent had previously visited a Disney park, were unsure about how lines work.

Meanwhile, at Disneyland Resort Paris, while British visitors were orderly, the French and Italians refused to adhere to line-waiting protocol. After the French park opened, Mr. Rasulo said, supervisors made the lines narrower by moving handrails closer together to try to prevent people from pushing ahead of others. Meanwhile, at Tokyo Disneyland it has been found that Japanese visitors are among the most patient and orderly in line waiting.

Fountain, 2005.

Time Tyrannies

Adherence to mechanical and computer time has disadvantages. Numerous polls have found a large majority of respondents say they are stressed because they don't have enough time to get everything done (cf. Barnette, 2004; Rueters, 2008). This is because of such time tyrannies as time urgency and time deepening.

A truly contemporary condition, *time urgency* is a quickened pace of life—feeling rushed. It is to approach the day with speed and impetuosity. Although not everyone or not every culture experiences time urgency, according to the time diary studies of Robinson and Godbey (1997), the "always feel rushed" response on questionnaires has shown a gradual increase since 1965. Today only about 25 percent of Americans declare they almost never feel rushed (Pew Research Center, 2006). Those who most typically report feeling time urgency are working women with children living at home.

Time urgency:
feeling rushed

What does this mean for our lives? As Rifkin worried in the book *Time Wars* (1987),

> *We have quickened the pace of life only to become less patient. We have become more organized but less spontaneous, less joyful. We are better prepared to act on the future but less able to enjoy the present and reflect on the past. (pp. 11-12)*

Box 12.4

In Your Own Experience

How Much Time Urgency Do You Experience?

Take a deep breath and ask yourself these questions:

- Do you dislike waiting?
- Do you typically feel impatient with the rate at which many things take place?
- Do you find it difficult to linger at the table after eating?
- Do you sometimes suffer from "racing mind?"
- Do you measure your self-worth by quantitative accomplishments?
- Do you feel anxious whenever you are idle?
- Do you feel you perform best when you have a lot to do?
- Do you often interrupt people when they are talking?
- Do you feel you are often racing against time?
- Does your schedule sometimes feel overwhelming?

If you answered yes to three or more of these questions you likely have time urgency. It's not a healthy condition to have.

Fast transportation, instantaneous communication, and "time-saving" technologies were supposed to free us from the tyranny of time. Instead, we rarely have a moment to spare.

Time urgency can be particularly problematic for leisure. The consequences include participating hurriedly in an activity (visiting a park without getting out of the car) or substituting an activity that can be done more quickly (jogging instead of walking so to complete the mileage faster). How much real pleasure and satisfaction can be attained from learning to play the guitar in three easy lessons, eating dinner in less than 10 minutes, or traveling through Europe in a week? Time urgency might mean condensing a birthday party into a meal at a restaurant, spending only a few seconds in front of a painting in a museum, or becoming irritated when previous players don't leave the squash court within a minute of your reserved time.

So, what's the tyranny in time urgency? Beyond losing the

Figure 12.4

People who say they always feel rushed also express being unsatisfied with life, including their leisure (Pew Research Center, 2006, p. 3). (Shutterstock©, 2008)

ability to savor the day, being in a hurry can kill you. Numerous medical studies confirm this. For example, a study conducted at the University of California at San Francisco looked at 32 patients with heart disease. Thirteen of the patients exhibited symptoms of time urgency, experiencing episodes of decreased supply of blood to the heart muscle. Beyond heart problems, the stress felt by people with time urgency can also cause muscle pains, headaches, high blood pressure, irritable bowels, insomnia, phobias, depression, and anxiety. Your immune system may be weakened as well (Krishna, 2008).

Box 12.5

 ## In Profile

The Slow Movements

Japan has a slow life movement. Italy has a slow cities movement. Spain has a network of siesta salons. Originating in Austria is the Society for the Deceleration of Time, which sets speed traps for pedestrians. Slow retail stores are opening worldwide. People are resurrecting the art of doing things more slowly.

For example, originating as a response to the arrival of the first McDonald's in Rome, the slow food movement is a fast-growing international organization with over 85,000 members in 132 countries. Slow Food is a non-profit, eco-gastronomic member-supported organization founded in 1989 to "counteract fast food and fast life, the disappearance of local food traditions and people's dwindling interest in the food they eat, where it comes from, how it tastes, and how our food choices affect the rest of the world" (Slow Food International, 2008). Honored are heirloom varieties of fruits and vegetables, handcrafted wine and beer, hand-parched wild rice, and farmhouse cheeses, and most of all cooking and eating that takes its time.

Another contemporary time tyranny is time deepening. Originally based on Stefan Linder's idea about the harried leisure class (see Chapter 11), *time deepening* means doing more than one thing at a time in order to crowd a greater number of activities into the same amount of time (Godbey, 1976; Godbey, 2003a). For example, do you ever eat dinner, watch television, leaf through a magazine, and play a computer game at the same time? According to the studies of Robinson and Godbey (1997), at least one-quarter of television viewing is combined with other activities. In the time-budget study of German sociologist Erwin Scheusch (1972), it was found "the more a person is part of an industrial society with a very high density of communication, the more educated a person, the more likely he (sic) is to do a number of things simultaneously" (p. 77).

Time deepening: doing multiple activities at the same time without fully experiencing any of them

So what's the harm? Although time deepening may have some advantages, there are also disadvantages, particularly for leisure. It can make us feel rushed, anxious, and unfulfilled. Our leisure becomes packed with activities that do not

Box 12.6

 *In Focus*

Multitasking

A special case of time deepening is multitasking. The term multitasking (and multiprocessing) was originally applied to a computer's ability to execute more than one task or program at the same time. In contemporary parlance it applies the concept of time deepening to work tasks. Multitasking typically involves juggling phone calls, e-mails, instant messages, and computer work all at once in order to be more productive.

Several research reports (Cf. Lohr, 2007), however, provide evidence that multitasking doesn't actually increase productivity. The findings of neuroscientists, psychologists and management professors suggest multitasking slows you down and increases the chances of mistakes. Doing more than one task at a time prohibits our ability to process information, and when done while moving can also be dangerous.

The young, according to conventional wisdom, are the most adept multitaskers: e-mailing, instant messaging, listening to iPods, and studying at the same time. Yet, in one recent study of young Microsoft workers (Lohr, 2007), it took them 15 minutes to be able to return to serious mental tasks, like writing reports or computer code, after responding to incoming e-mail or instant messages. It is estimated that the cost of such lost productivity to the U.S. economy is nearly $650 billion a year.

Questions to Consider and Discuss
1. Do you consider yourself to be a multitasker? If so, why? If not, why not?
2. Whereas time deepening prohibits our ability to enjoy leisure, multitasking is claimed to prohibit our work productivity. What might be the harm in these two conclusions? That is, why are enjoying leisure and working productively important for your quality of life?
3. A large part of the impetus for multitasking (and time deepening too) is the bombardment of constant technology-enabled communications. Some believe that at the very least all this is increasing our stress levels. With our increasing dependency on our tech devices and our seeming inability to separate work life from personal life, can we be happy?

provide pleasure or relaxation because no single activity is fully experienced. Perhaps it makes sense to say we have become "unleisurely" in our leisure (Godbey, 2003a, p. 75).

Work

In many contemporary societies there is an emphasis on work. Most of us understand from a very early age that work is a constant in life. We also know that work can be a curse and a burden, a benefit and release, boring and miserable, and fun and fulfilling.

What is work? Why do people work? Why do some people work harder than is required? Is there a work problem in society? Today there is tremendous debate about the worth of work—a debate also affecting the worth and experience of leisure. In this section of the chapter we continue our theme of instrumental connections—now between work and leisure.

Why Work?

Work, most simply, can be defined as the expenditure of effort. It is the use of energy—human, animal, mechanical, electrical, solar—to produce something. Answering the question of why people work is more complex than this, however.

One source of answer is based in the Latin expression *homo faber* ("Man the Maker"). Homo faber is considered the biological name for humans, suggesting work is what makes us human. Humans create, build, change, and control the world with tools. Work is for making possibilities—something that did not exist before. In contrast, there is also the idea of *homo ludens*, connoting that play also makes us human. Leisure is also for making possibilities.

Homo faber: human as worker

Homo ludens: human as player

Over the centuries, work has taken on many different meanings. For example, to the ancient Romans work was seen as a means to oversee a large empire. There were wars, taxes, barbarians, and millions of citizens to manage. Getting this work done often took precedence over individual freedoms and pursuits. Later, the powerful influence of early Christianity in medieval Europe elevated work to godliness. Work was self-denial in order to serve God. Over 1,000 years later the coming of Protestantism attached the idea of vocation to work.

Work ethic: belief in the virtues of hard work, including its ability to enhance character

Across several more centuries, industrialization and urbanization solidified the idea of a *work ethic*. The transition from a preindustrial to an industrial society during the late 1800s and early 1900s resulted in an even greater regard for work, and an increasing separation of work and leisure in everyday life. Driven by the voracious machines, work came to be associated with the values of speed and efficiency (Robinson & Godbey,

Figure 12.5

The Shakers were a religious group that came to the American colonies in 1774 to establish a utopian society based on a belief in hard work. Expressed in a common motto "Put your hands to work, and your heart to God," the Shaker heritage can be experienced today through an interpretation at Shakertown, Kentucky. (© Ruth V. Russell, 2008)

1997). And leisure was relegated to that time left over. Indeed, today one of the stereotypical distinctions between work and leisure is that work is economic and leisure is not.

Whether people work today because they have to or because they want to, work provides many rewards. An obvious reward is that workers exchange their time, energy, and talent for money to buy things. Yet, anyone who has ever worked, even for the necessity of earning money, knows work provides other rewards as well. For example, work activities often are creative, challenging, filled with opportunities for self-development, and sociable. Work can provide a sense of contributing. Sometimes work is even enjoyable, allowing for freedom of choice.

In fact, work often offers people their central identity. When we meet someone new, we typically introduce ourselves by what we do for work. "I am a lawyer," or "I am a professor." Even the retired are tempted to claim their identity through their former work, especially if they worked in a high status occupation. No society is without its status symbols, and in many contemporary societies, this status is provided by work—or at least those things that the money earned through work can purchase.

Box 12.7

 The Study Says

The Workaholic Elite

Being rich used to mean freedom from work. But, according to the research of Nobel prize-winning behavioral economist Daniel Kahneman and colleagues, "being wealthy is often a powerful predictor that people spend less time doing pleasurable things and more time doing compulsory things" (p. 1908).

The researchers have developed a tool to measure people's quality of daily life known as the Day Reconstruction Method (DRM), which asks people to record the previous day's activities in a short diary and describe their feelings about the activities. Surveys using DRM have been given to adults over several years, but the most recent focused on relations between income and respondents' feelings about their activities.

The findings broke with stereotypes. That is, people who made less than $20,000 a year spent more than a third of their time in passive leisure, like kicking back and watching TV. By contrast, those making more than $100,000 a year, spent less than a fifth of their time in passive leisure. In other words, the richer people spent nearly twice as much time as the poorer people in activities that were structured and often stressful, such as working, commuting, shopping, child care, and exercise.

Kahneman, D., Krueger, A.B., Schkade, D., Schwartz, N., & Stone, A.A. (June 30, 2006). Would you be happier if you were richer? A focusing illusion. *Science Magazine.* 1908 – 1915.

So work offers many rewards. But does all work provide these rewards, and is work satisfying to all workers? Clearly not, as according to a survey by the Opinion Research Corporation (2008), almost 100 percent of Americans feel at least some vacation time away from work is necessary to avoid burnout, with over half designating at least three weeks away.

It seems that a startling number of people feel unfulfilled and unhappy in their jobs. The tangible symptoms show up as tardiness, apathy, and complaining. The intangible symptoms are worse. According to one study, more than half of employees in the United States and Canada have negative feelings about their work (Patrick, 2003). Causes of the malaise included excessive workloads, concerns about management's ability to lead the company, anxieties about future incomes and retirements, lack of challenges, frustrations, and insufficient levels of recognition. What is it about work that might create such dissatisfaction? Often workers characterize their work as boring, stressful, unrewarding, and uninteresting—opposite the qualities of leisure.

Work for Leisure or Leisure for Work or None of the Above?

As you can tell, quite often leisure and work are compared. For example, leisure is often considered a solution for the dissatisfactions of work. As well, some people don't feel they deserve leisure if they don't have a job. Yet, just as often, other people love their jobs so much it seems like play to them. These are complex and contradictory views of the relationship between work and leisure.

For example, sometimes the same satisfactions (and dissatisfactions) we derive from our work can also be gained through our leisure. Let's consider the satisfaction from developing friendships. According to studies we are just as likely to develop good friends from our place of work as from our leisure activities. Yet studies also demonstrate work is more likely than leisure to create the dissatisfaction of stress (Reid, 1995).

Let's explore such work and leisure comparisons a bit more. There are basically three ways of comparing the intricacies between leisure and work. One view is rather pessimistic; it maintains work is a less desirable human condition and leisure is needed to control or even overcome its problematic effects. Another, and opposite, view is more optimistic. It suggests all is well with both work and leisure, and healthy people need the rewards and satisfactions from both. Life is only meaningful when both are in harmony. Finally, perhaps neither an optimistic nor pessimistic perspective is true, but rather the relationship is simply neutral. That is,

Figure 12.6

Today's newest entrants to the workforce are the least satisfied with their jobs. Less than 39 percent of workers under the age of 25 are satisfied with their employment situation (The Conference Board, 2007). (Shutterstock©, 2008)

work and leisure are two separate domains in life and not necessarily related to one another at all.

We'll start with the pessimistic view: leisure is needed to overcome work's inhuman consequences. One such consequence is *workaholism*. Workaholism has been described as an addiction to work—the pursuit of the work persona. It is working long hours in order to gain approval and success. Workaholics are unable to relax when not doing something considered productive. While there is no generally accepted medical definition, it is considered a serious social problem in many contemporary societies. For example, in Japan the condition has been dubbed karōshi, and is considered the cause of on-the-job deaths, such as the death "from working too many hours" by an engineer for Toyota Motor Corporation (Alabaster, 2008, p. A12).

Workaholism:
colloquially, compulsiveness about working

Not only does this condition affect the workaholic's health, but can also create marital and family discord, as well as stress for work colleagues. Ultimately, it reduces work efficiency and productivity. The prescription for workaholism, of course, is leisure: to return to health, the worker needs to incorporate more leisure into life. Common advice by counselors is to develop meaningful hobbies, get more outdoor exercise, and do enjoyable pursuits with friends and family.

Yet, what is particularly interesting is that the compulsive nature of workaholism can be applied to leisure as well. That is, we can engage in pastimes too in a work-like way. Many people today over commit themselves to recreational activities to the point where they take on the characteristics of work. They find their weekends are booked full with social obligations, shopping, gardening, youth sport schedules, and planned outings. No free time is left for spontaneity. Workaholism applied to leisure is called *play-aversion* (Dickens, 1991). Symptoms include placing a high value on always being busy in leisure, playing hard, over scheduling activities, and feeling anxious when nothing is scheduled.

Play-aversion:
applying the behaviors and performance standards of work to leisure

On the other hand, according to the optimistic view, work and leisure are not at battle with each other—both are desirable for their respective benefits. Meaning and satisfaction exist in both, and both are required for realizing life to its fullest. The secret, according to this view, is balance. How can this balance be achieved? People have implemented numerous ways to achieve a more leisurely work schedule, including downshifting.

The need for more freedom to choose when and how much to work is potentially more appropriate for people in contemporary societies. The ideas about downshifting in table 12.3 are for work schedules that achieve balance by adjusting the hours of the day or days of the week. What about freeing time for more leisure that is an adjustment to the entire lifetime schedule?

Most of us live on a lifetime schedule that follows a straight line. That is, life begins with play, is followed by a period of education, then a long term at work, and finally returns to a life of play again through retirement (figure 12.7). Such a traditional approach organizes life by strictly adhering to a single direction as preordained by society's custom. Is there another way?

As also shown in figure 12.7, an alternating life plan would redistribute some years of schooling from youth and some free time from retirement into the middle years of life. Work wouldn't need to be the dominant theme in middle age, nor

Table 12.3

Ways to Downshift

Like changing to a lower gear on your bicycle, downshifting is to shift your work life to a lower level of speed or intensity. It usually involves creating a simpler lifestyle, including living with less money by working fewer hours. By some estimates, millions of people around the world have chosen to downshift. How is this possible in today's society? Godbey (2003b, pp 131-132) offers these ideas:

Work Strategy	How it Works
Job sharing	Filling a single job with another person; both responsible for the same workload.
Flextime	Choosing the time to start and finish the work day.
Compressed workweeks	Taking time off on one day or week and making up that time by working longer later.
Four-day workweek	Working a 40-hour week job across four days – a specific form of compressed workweek.
Reduced work time	Working less than a 40-hour week, often with a proportionate reduction in pay.
Limited overtime	Not working over a set amount of over time.
Early retirement	Retiring from work sooner than legally required.
Phased retirement	Retiring gradually by cutting back on days, weeks, or months worked.

leisure in old age. Advantages of an alternating plan are a more even distribution of income over the life span and more people having the opportunity to realize personal goals, such as a college degree and child rearing. Foremost, it would also mean a more evenly distributed expression of leisure interests.

Figure 12.7

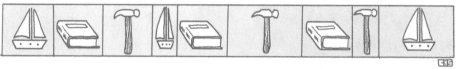

Figure 12.7. An alternating life plan redistributes schooling, work, and leisure throughout life. (© Christopher B. Stage, 2008)

Linear Life Plan

Cyclical Life Plan

Finally, the third view of the relationship between leisure and work is neutral. Unlike the pessimistic view, in which leisure cures us from work, and the optimistic view, in which we need both work and leisure in balance, this last view claims there is no relationship at all between work and leisure. For example, in a classic work by Huizinga (1955) leisure is envisioned as outside ordinary life, something special, and thus something that must remain separate from the rest of life. Leisure is spontaneous, mysterious, and a celebration, and thus to integrate leisure with work would destroy it.

One illustration of this neutral view is the concept of *central life interest*. Originally identified by sociologists in 1956, the concept usually cites work as playing the major role in people's lives. How about you? For example, suppose you won an obscene amount of money in the lottery. Would you still work if you never need to work again? If you answer yes, work is a central life interest for you.

Central life interest:
the primary focus of one's life

Actually, this is a fairly common interview question that assesses people's commitment to work, and according to polls taken across the years, most people would continue to work. Yet, there is a shift underway. Enjoying ample and meaningful leisure, and having a stable and thriving family and community are goals that are beginning to replace the centrality of work for some people.

Box 12.8

Ninety Percent Unemployment

Eve Smith heard herslf say, "Why not? Let's give it a try." The man from the Department of Creative Technology (DOCT) had left, leaving Eve in a somewhat skeptical frame of mind. Then again, it did sound reasonable.

Box 12.8 (Cont.)

Eve owns a shoe factory. One thousand workers are directly involved in the production of shoes at an average pay of $20,000 per year or a yearly payroll of $ 20 million. She produces one million pairs of shoes per year, which she sells for $60 million. The difference between total sales and payroll ($40 million) takes care of other expenses and profits.

The man from DOCT suggested that she install a computer-controlled robotic system that would enable Eve to lay off 90 percent of her workforce, that is, 900 workers. Output of shoes would remain the same: one million pairs per year. Eve would turn over the salary previously paid to the 900 workers (that is, $18 million) to the DOCT. It, in turn, would keep 10 percent ($1.8 million) of that amount to pay for the development of the robotic system and put 90 percent ($16.2 million) into a Guaranteed Income Fund (GIF).

The 900 laid off workers would be paid 90 percent of their previous salary from the GIF, either indefinitely or until they chose to seek other employment. In Eve's profit picture, nothing would change. She would have as many shoes to sell as before and, if anything, would have fewer labor and production problems.

Nine hundred workers, human beings, would be freed from the necessity of wasting their time making a living. They would be able to develop their capabilities, skills, and talent or, if they desired, work for the betterment of society.

Just then, Eve heard a faint ringing, as of a far away bell. Then it became more insistent. She opened her eyes, realizing that she had dozed off. Had it all been a dream?

Questions to Consider and Discuss

1. Is this truly a dream or can you see some real possibility in it? Why? Why not? What might be done to turn the dream into reality?
2. If you were given the opportunity to receive 90 percent of your salary and not work at a job, would you take it? Why? What about 75 percent of your salary or 50 percent of your salary? By the way, according to one survey (Hymwitz, 1991) almost 50 percent of the respondents said they would give up a day's pay each week for a day of free time.
3. Is leisure the ultimate good life, or is work? Read J.B. Nash's classic book Spectatoritis (1932) to form your own opinion.

Based on Neulinger, 1989, pp. 22-24; used with permission from the American Alliance for Health, Physical Education, Recreation and Dance.

What We Understand About Leisure, Time, and Work

Time, work, and leisure are instrumentally related. That is, each has an impact on the others. For example, although leisure is typically prescribed as a cure for the problems of time and work, it has also adopted many of the characteristics of time and work that make it problematic. From reading this chapter you should understand that:

- The expression of leisure in time is a function of personal perceptions of free time, personal amounts of free time, the time requirements of particular pastimes, and the amount of free time available in a society.
- Cyclical time is that pace set by the rhythms of nature. In developed societies it has been replaced by the concept of mechanical time, of life, and leisure paced to the machine.
- In the future, the computer may set an even faster and more artificial pace for life and leisure.
- Other types of time that affect our leisure are biological time and cultural time.
- There are unique tyrannies to leisure from time, including time urgency and time deepening.
- Although work offers the rewards of money, self-esteem, personal interactions, and the sense of making a contribution to society, some people are dissatisfied with work.
- How are work and leisure related? They are related in three ways: (a) work is a less desirable human condition and leisure is needed to overcome its negative by-products, (b) work and leisure can be in harmony by incorporating more leisure into the work sphere, and (c) leisure and work are two separate and unrelated domains of life.

References

Alabaster, J. (July 10, 2008). Toyota engineer killed by overwork. *The Herald Times*. Bloomington, Indiana, p. A12.

Barnes, J. (1984). *The complete works of Aristotle*. Princeton, NJ: Princeton University Press.

Barnette, M. (March 2004). The stressed-out American family. *Ladies' Home Journal*, 134-143.

Chick, G., & Shen, S.X. (2007). Time allocation & cultural complexity: Leisure time use across twelve cultures. *Proceedings of the 2007 Northeastern Recreation Research Symposium*. Gen. Tech. Rep. NRS-P-23, Newtown Square, PA: U.S. Department of Agriculture, Forest Service, Northern Research Station.

Conference Board (February 23, 2007). *U.S. Job Satisfaction Declines, The Conference Board Reports*. Available from http://www.conference-board.org/utilities/pressDetail.cfm?press_ID=3075. Retrieved 7/18/08.

Cross, G. (1990). *A social history of leisure since 1600*. State College, PA: Venture.

deGrazia, S. (1962). *Of time, work, and leisure*. New York: The Twentieth Century Fund.

Denny, D. (November 2, 1993). Waiting on down the line. *The Herald Times*. Bloomington, Indiana, p. E1.

Dickens, P. (March/April 1991). Playing hard or hardly playing? *Executive Female*, 46.

Fountain, H. (September 18, 2005). The ultimate body language: How you line up for Mickey. *The New York Times*. Available from http://www.nytimes.com/2005/09/18/weekinreview/18fountain.html. Retrieved 7/15/08.

Franklin, B. (1932). *The autobiography and selections from his other writing*. New York: The Modern Library.

Godbey, G. (September 1976). Time deepening and the future of leisure. *Leisure Today*. 12-13.

Godbey, G. (2003a). Book review (Stefan Linder's *The Harried Leisure Class*). *Journal of Leisure Research, 35*(4), p. 478.

Godbey, G. (2003b). *Leisure in your life: An exploration* (6th Ed.). State College, PA: Venture.

Godbey, G. (2006). *Leisure and leisure services in the 21st century: Toward mid-century*. State College, PA: Venture.

Green, T.F. (1968). *Work, leisure, and the American schools*. New York: Random House.

Hall, T., & Shelby, B. (2000). Temporal and spatial displacement: Evidence from a high-use reservoir and alternate sites. *Journal of Leisure Research, 32*, 435-456.

Huizinga, J. (1955). *Homo Ludens*. London: Paladin Books.

Krishna, R.M. (2008). Slow down, you move too fast. *Integris Center for Mind, Body and Spirit*. Available from http://www.integris-health.com/INTEGRIS/en-US/Specialties/MindBodySpirit/Newsroom/MindMatters/TimeUrgency.htm. Retrieved 7/15/08.

Levine, R., & Wolff, E. (1985). Social time: The heartbeat of culture. *Psychology Today, 19*, 28-30.

Linder, S. (1970). *The harried leisure class*. New York: Columbia University Press.

Lohr, S. (March 25, 2007). Slow down, brave multitasker, and don't read this in traffic. *The New York Times*. Available from http://www.nytimes.com/2007/03/25/business/25multi.html?_r=1. Retrieved 7/16/08.

McGraw, A.C. (2008). The perception and cognition of time in Balinese music. *Empirical Musicology Review, 3*(2), 1-17.

Opinion Research Corporation. (2008). *Results of Take Back Your Time's Right2Vacation Poll*. Available from http://www.timeday.org/right2vacation/poll_results.asp. Retrieved 7/17/08.

Patrick, S. (July 18, 2003). Employers face challenge of worker dissatisfaction. *Sacramento Business Journal*. Available from http://www.bizjournals.com/sacramento/stories/2003/07/21/smallb5.html. Retrieved 7/17/08.

Pew Research Center. (February 28, 2006). Who's feeling rushed? *A Social Trends Report*. Available from http://pewresearch.org/assets/social/pdf/Rushed.pdf. Retrieved 7/15/08.

Priestly, J.B. (1968). *Man and time*. New York: Dell.

Reid, D. (1995). *Work and leisure in the 21st century: From production to citizenship*. Toronto, OH: Wall and Emerson.

Rifkin, J. (1987). *Time wars: The primary conflict in human history*. New York: Henry Holt and Company.

Robinson, J., & Godbey, G. (1997). *Time for life: The surprising ways Americans use their time.* University Park: The Pennsylvania State University.

Rueters (2008). National Survey Reveals 90 Percent of Adults Want More Life Balance in 2008. Available from http://www.reuters.com/article/pressRelease/idUS113385+07-Jan-2008+BW20080107. Retrieved 7/15/08.

Scheusch, E. (1972). The time-budget interview. In A. Szalai (Ed.), *The use of time.* The Hague: Mouton.

Slow Food International. (2008). *Home Page.* Available from http://www.slowfood.com/. Retrieved 7/15/08.

CHAPTER THIRTEEN

IS LEISURE FAIR?

PREVIEW

Is there equity in leisure?

No. Barriers exist in contemporary societies to full fairness of opportunity in leisure.

What are some examples where inequity in leisure exists?

As illustration, there is discrimination in leisure for women, persons with disabilities, gays and lesbians, ethnic and racial minorities, and others.

Does leisure have the potential to enable equity?

Yes, indeed! Leisure is an important context for creating fair opportunities for a high quality of life for everyone.

KEY TERMS

The question of leisure's fairness derives from another question: is leisure a right or a privilege? This is simple to ask but much tougher to answer. Leisure is viewed by some as a privilege; something to be earned. On the other hand, leisure is also viewed as a right; something that is as essentially human and necessary as eating and sleeping. To illustrate, let's discuss the quandary a bit more.

Figure 13.1

Is it a right or a privilege for these young adults to participate in the drum and bugle corps? (© Ruth V. Russell, 2008)

As a privilege leisure is distributed unequally. When leisure is defined as free time or activity, for example, it is often viewed as a reward and thus a privilege for those who've earned it. As a privilege, leisure is a prize available only to qualifying people. Sometimes the qualifier is having enough money to pay for certain forms of leisure. Other times, it is the guilt-free sensation that, by the time the weekend is here, you have worked hard enough to take some hard-won time off.

As a right, on the other hand, leisure is supposed to be distributed equitably. Many cultures have a belief in natural or inalienable rights—rights that are impossible to surrender. These are often described as life, liberty, and the pursuit of happiness.

Box 13.1

 The Study Says

Winners and Losers

A number of high school extracurricular activities are selective, requiring students to apply and audition for membership. The experience of trying out for two such activities, cheerleading and the dance team, was explored in this study, and the reactions of girls who were admitted into membership were contrasted with those who were unsuccessful. Findings indicated significant differences in positive and negative emotions, classroom performance, school attendance/truancy, and feelings about self and about school. That is, the girls who were not admitted to these extracurricular activities demonstrated much more negative responses on all the assessments, except for drug and alcohol use. Further, these negative effects of being denied entry to the team lasted over a two-month time span.

Barnett, L.A. (2007). "Winners" and "Losers": The effects of being allowed or denied entry into competitive extracurricular activities. *Journal of Leisure Research, 39*(2), 316-344.

With these rights comes a commitment to equality—everyone has the same right to a good life. Accordingly, societies sponsor services considered vital to experiencing leisure. In fact, the very premise of recreation services provided by local, state or provincial, and federal governments is equitable distribution of leisure.

Regardless of your answer to the question of leisure as privilege or leisure as right, there is not *equity* of leisure in contemporary societies. For example, today there exists discrimination of opportunity according to gender, race, ability, income, age, and other distinctions. This is as it should be if leisure is a privilege. On the other hand, of all the tools available to societies to create equity of opportunity, leisure is perhaps one of the most vital. This is as it should be if leisure is a right.

> **Equity:** fairness

In this chapter we first discuss how leisure both restricts and enables equity. Then, we illustrate this through the examples of women, ethnic and racial minorities, gays and lesbians, and persons with disabilities.

Prohibitions and Permissions

In contemporary societies pastimes have been both a hurdle to equity and an enabler of equity. For example, women feel more constrained by fear than men to participate in solo hiking (Coble, Selin & Erickson, 2003). On the other hand, women are now resisting societal notions and entering the traditionally male area of computer gaming (Bryce & Rutter, 2003).

First, let's consider how leisure restricts equity. You are already well aware that, in general, certain pastimes are more likely to be pursued by people in certain ethnic, racial, age, gender, ability, and other social groups. Is this by choice or prohibition?

A way of demonstrating this as prohibition is to cite incidences against leisure participation for certain groups. For example, a study by Livengood and Stodolska (2004) evaluating the post 9/11 experiences of Muslim immigrants to the United States from Middle Eastern countries found that discrimination affected their leisure experiences by restricting the range of available leisure options and playmates. And, as another example, fully 9.7 million children in the U.S. in working families are alone with nothing to do every day after school (Afterschool Alliance, 2005).

There has been a great deal studied about and written on *discrimination* in leisure settings. One approach to this literature is by way of various theories attempting to explain it. For example, Stodolska (2005) proposed a model to explain individual discriminatory behavior. The model consists of three decision-making stages. First, an individual uses his or her own set of information to derive general beliefs about a group. Then, he or she combines these preexisting beliefs with any new information received to form an attitude signifying the degree of hostility toward the group at any particular point in time. Finally, he or she weighs the internal benefits of discrimination against external consequences of such an action and chooses to act accordingly.

> **Discrimination:** unfair treatment of a person or group

According to Stodolska's model, acting in a discriminatory way against others is an individual decision. Shaw (2005), on the other hand, proposed that discrimination is also a societal decision. Her point is that in addition to individual prejudices there are structural disadvantages experienced by certain groups. One source of societal structural disadvantages is power relations. Those who are discriminated against in leisure lack economic, social, and/or political power in the society. Shaw refers to this as a double discrimination. For those without societal power, leisure prohibitions pile on an additional disadvantage.

Constraints:

that which inhibits a leisure pursuit once an interest for it has been formed

Another way to think about prohibitions in leisure is through the concept of *constraints*. In fact, the investigation of leisure constraints has become a major focus in research over the past two decades. Essentially, the numerous studies start with the question, "Why do some people not participate in leisure in general or in particular activities for which they might have a desire?"

A model has also been developed to explain the concept of leisure constraints (Crawford & Godbey, 1987; Crawford, Jackson & Godbey, 1991). It suggests leisure participation is dependent on negotiating through a hierarchy of structural, intrapersonal, and interpersonal barriers.

Box 13.2

 ## In Your Own Experience

So Why Haven't You Taken A Cruise Lately?

Mark each statement according to how likely it is to keep you from taking a cruise. Use the scale SA = Strongly Agree; A = Agree; N = Neither Agree or Disagree; D = Disagree; SD = Strongly Disagree.

1. Taking a cruise would be too expensive for me.
    SA   A   N   D   SD

2. I have special needs that cannot be accommodated on a cruise ship.
    SA   A   N   D   SD

3. I'm not able to leave my school, work, and/or family.
    SA   A   N   D   SD

4. My friends and family members are not interested in taking a cruise
    SA   A   N   D   SD

5. I don't feel comfortable in a boat on the water.
    SA   A   N   D   SD

6. Ocean cruising is just not my thing.
    SA   A   N   D   SD

Scoring: items #1 and 2 represent structural constraints; items #3 and 4 represent interpersonal constraints; items #5 and 6 represent intrapersonal constrains.

Did you tend to agree more with any of these types of constraints?

Structural constraints are typically architectural barriers, such as a recreation center that is inaccessible to a person using a wheelchair, or economic barriers, such as high fees charged for a youth sport program that prohibits economically disadvantaged children from signing up. Intrapersonal constraints are personal psychological attributes that constrain leisure involvement. Perception of abilities, personality needs, and prior socialization typically are cited as intrapersonal leisure constraints. For example, if prior socialization suggests men do not participate in fitness classes, a particular man may feel constrained in participating even if he has an interest. Finally, interpersonal constraints are those barriers arising out of social interaction with friends, family, and others. In a family, for example, interpersonal constraints may occur when spouses or partners differ in their leisure preferences (Jackson & Scott, 1999).

In addition to constraints focused on participation versus nonparticipation, another aspect of constraints is inhibitions of frequency or intensity of involvement in leisure. For example, a study by Nadirova and Jackson (2000) found the single most constrained leisure situation was the inability to participate as often as one would like.

Indeed, leisure is a factor in prohibiting equitable individual and community lives. Yet leisure can also enable equity. In fact, leisure can be one of the most powerful forces for equity. For example, leisure can be a means by which people who are homeless, unemployed, or migrant are incorporated into mainstream society. As well, community festivals are able to unify a widely diverse population through a common spirit of cooperation. And, as demonstrated by the Olympic Games, leisure can call at least a temporary halt to international disagreements.

Inclusion:
valuing all people regardless of their differences

To harness leisure's equity powers, professionals in leisure services have focused on the concept of inclusion. *Inclusion* suggests that leisure service organizations provide mechanisms for people who have special life conditions, such as a physical disability, to participate according to typical circumstances and to help them become as independent as possible by joining the mainstream of society. Inclusion means the involvement and full acceptance of all people within the wide range of community settings. According to Schleien, Green and Stone (2003) inclusion involves three levels of acceptance ranging from a minimal physical level to an ultimate social level (table 13.1).

Ironically, another leisure concept that speaks to the ability to create equity—*diversity*—seems the antithesis of inclusion. A major

Diversity:
celebrating differences in people

Figure 13.2

For young immigrants, the inclusion role of leisure is likely to be particularly critical during the initial period in the new country. (© Ruth V. Russell, 2008)

Table 13.1

A Continuum of Leisure Inclusion

Level 1: Physical	Level 2: Functional	Level 3: Social
Access to buildings and programs.	Opportunities to be successful within buildings and programs.	Full and positive interactions with others through participation in activities.

conclusion from the most recent census of the population of the Unities States, for example, is that diversity has increased. Americans are more different from one another than ever before, becoming a mosaic of race, ethnicity, family type, household income, lifestyle, political beliefs, and other qualities.

As a result it is important to support and protect diversity, because by valuing the differences in individuals and groups, and by fostering a climate where mutual respect is intrinsic, a better society for everyone is created. Here is an illustration. In July 1996, the deciding game of the U.S. Cup soccer tournament was played in the Rose Bowl stadium in Pasadena, California. The contest matched the U.S. and Mexican national teams and featured important stars from both countries (Gramann & Allison, 1999). More than 98,000 spectators packed the stadium. In fact, the demand for tickets was so great that seats that had been held back because they offered poor viewing of the field were sold to fans waiting in lines outside the stadium even after the game began.

Was this a testimony to the rising popularity of soccer in a traditionally non-soccer-playing country? Probably yes, in part, but this is not all of the explanation, because most of the fans were cheering for Mexico. Mexican flags and banners of green, red, and white overwhelmed the red, white, and blue in the stands (Gramann & Allison, 1999). Because of a large Mexican American population living in southern California, it was a home game for Mexico. In other words, the sport of soccer was able to maintain and even strengthen group identity within a diverse society. Latino cultural traditions and pride were celebrated that day.

Examples

There are many more examples of how leisure is both a barrier to and an enabler of equity. To illustrate further the concepts of discrimination, constraints, inclusion, and diversity, we focus now on leisure and women, persons with disabilities, gays and lesbians, and racial and ethnic minorities.

Women

"The woman" has played many roles throughout history: mother, daughter, lover, and mate. She has also been prime minister, farmer, CEO, and scientist. Today women combine many of these roles, yet through the centuries, almost every society has developed definite ideas about what activities and behaviors are appropriate for women. Some of these ideas have disappeared or changed greatly over time, but others have changed little or not at all.

One way of considering leisure as both prohibition and enabler of equity for women is via the concept of feminism. *Feminism* is both an intellectual commitment and a political movement that seeks equity for women. There are many different interpretations of feminism and disagreements about what exactly ought to be done about it, but basically topics in feminism include the body, work, the family, popular culture, reproduction, and sex and sexuality.

Feminism:
the belief in and action toward political, economic, and social equality of the sexes

And, within the past 25 years a growing topic in feminism has also been leisure. What is the meaning of leisure for women? Is leisure equitable for women? For example, the U.S. Census Bureau (2007b) has reported that whereas 39 percent of men play sports, 23 percent of women do. Is this difference by choice or by prohibition?

The broad philosophical framework for questions such as these includes ideas of empowerment and social change. This is particularly poignant for leisure because both feminism and leisure are based on the qualities of choice and freedom. Yet,

Figure 13.3

A women's bicycle racing team at Indiana University's "Little 500." A shorter version of the men's race founded in 1951, women's teams have raced each other since 1988. Does this demonstrate equity for women's leisure? (© Ruth V. Russell, 2008)

in many contemporary societies, leisure for women has itself been constrained because of a lack of empowerment and social action. This conclusion can be demonstrated through a quarter-century of research.

Over this time our understanding about women's leisure has shown an evolution, progressively asking more and deeper critical questions. Earlier research (1980-1989) revealed several initial understandings in answer to these questions. According to an integrative review of research studies from that period (Henderson, 1990), leisure provided a common context for women and opportunity to share a common world. That is, leisure settings and activities helped women be with others who shared their concerns. Other research revealed these concerns to include: unstructured and fragmented leisure squeezed into brief time blocks around role and home obligations, fewer leisure opportunities for women when compared with men, and feelings of not deserving time off for themselves.

Later, another review of research studies on women and leisure (Henderson, 1996) published from 1990 through 1995 debunked the common world of leisure idea and revealed there are actually multiple meanings of leisure for women. That is, there is a wide diversity among women who live in western cultures about what leisure is and is not for them. This also broadened the feminist discussion to include what leisure can do for not only women, but men as well. In the later 1990s, studies broadened even further to include questions of race, social class, and age as related to gender.

According to the most recent review of research on women and leisure (Henderson & Hickerson, 2007), our understanding has transitioned from itemizing prohibitions on women's expression of leisure, to acknowledging what needs to be done about it. For the most part, studies carried out between 2000 and 2006 focused on how the benefits of leisure can overcome the constraints against it. For example, a study by Anderson, Bedini, and Moreland (2005) described the benefits of physical activity for girls with disabilities and how these benefits mitigated some of the constraints these girls faced because they were girls. In another study (Iwasaki, MacKay & Mactavish, 2005), leisure was confirmed to be a means for addressing stress through coping for women.

To conclude, although leisure is an important aspect in quality of life for people, women are unable to take full advantage of this potential. This must be corrected, because leisure provides the opportunity for maintaining personal choice and freedom often absent from other aspects of their lives.

Persons with Disabilities

The U.S. Census Bureau (2007a) has placed the number of noninstitutionalized Americans age five and over living with a disability at over 51 million. This is a ratio of nearly one-in-five U.S. residents, or 19 percent. Forty-six percent of these persons report living with more than one disability.

Box 13.3

 ## *In Profile*

Karla Henderson

Dr. Karla A. Henderson is a professor in the Department of Parks, Recreation, and Tourism Management at North Carolina State University. She teaches primarily graduate courses in leisure theory. Previously she was on the leisure studies faculties at University of North Carolina at Chapel Hill, University of Wisconsin, and Texas Woman's University. She has given presentations about leisure, including camping, throughout North America, Europe, Asia, and Australia, written over 250 scholarly articles, and authored several books. But, Dr. Henderson is no doubt best known for her ground breaking research and writing in the area of women and leisure. Most recently she conducted research on the physical activity patterns of African-American and American-Indian women, and studied women with disabilities.

A variety of *disabling conditions* are included in these statistics. The largest number (21.4 million) includes conditions limiting basic physical activities, such as walking, climbing stairs, reaching, lifting or carrying. Other conditions include sensory, involving sight or hearing, and cognitive and emotional that affects abilities to learn, concentrate, get along with others, and live independently. For example, about five million Americans are living with Alzheimer's disease, which is a progressive and fatal brain disease causing problems with memory, thinking, and behavior severe enough to affect work, lifelong hobbies, and social life (Alzheimer's Association, 2008).

Disabling conditions: a physical, sensory, or mental impairment that substantially limits one or more life activity

Disabling conditions cut across age, race, social class, gender, income, and educational backgrounds. What they have in common is people living with disabilities find it more difficult to attend school, pursue a career, live independently, and enjoy leisure.

In response, during the 1960s in North America, a movement developed emphasizing the rights of people with disabling conditions. A significant turning point in Canada was the amendment of the Human Rights Act in 1974, which prohibits discrimination for employment for reasons of physical or mental disability (Searle & Brayley, 2000). Such official notice of the rights of persons with disabilities did not occur in the United States until 1990, with the passage

Box 13.4

In Profile

Casey Martin

In February 1998, Casey Martin, a 25-year-old golfer and Stanford classmate of Tiger Woods, sued the Nike Tour for the right to use a golf cart. Martin has Klippel-Trenaunay-Webber Syndrome, a circulatory condition that limits his ability to walk. If he puts too much pressure on his legs, it could necessitate amputation.

His suit used the Americans with Disabilities Act (ADA) to defend three counts: discrimination in public accommodation, inhibition of professional advancement, and employment discrimination. Martin alleged the Tour was denying him the right to play, and as an employer of sorts, the right to work, based on his disability.

The Tour countered that the ADA didn't apply to professional-level sports and that walking is an essential part of the game. The Tour felt that if Martin could ride in a cart, he would have an unfair advantage over the other players who would be more tired from walking around the course.

The court ruled in Martin's favor, and even though the Tour quickly appealed, Martin was able to use a cart until his appeal was approved in 2000. This long, high-profile case gave the general public its first taste of the power of the ADA (Shklyanoy, 2000). Today Martin is the head coach of the University of Oregon's men's golf team.

Figure 13.4

FUSE, Families United for Support and Encouragement, provides information, resources and support to Indiana families raising children with special needs. (© FUSE, 2008, used with permission)

of the Americans with Disabilities Act (ADA), which required public institutions to provide fuller and more equitable opportunities for accessibility to buildings, programs, jobs, etc.

In applying the ADA to leisure facilities, programs and other services, the advocacy philosophy originally took the form of "separate but equal." Recreation programs in communities were instrumental in addressing the needs of persons with disabilities by establishing segregated programs (Bedini, 1990). These were often labeled as programs for special populations. Later it was realized that segregation sometimes invited others to view persons with disabilities as different and worthy of pity (Bedini, 1990). Now the focus is not simply on providing access to leisure resources through special programs, but also on enabling persons with disabilities to become full participants in community life. As an inclusive philosophy, the goal is to created options that optimize leisure equity.

At the core of such leisure service delivery concerns are several fundamental principles about leisure and disability, namely, self-determination, self-advocacy, normalization, and integration (Searle & Brayley, 2000).

Self-determination:
defining goals for oneself and taking the initiative to achieve them

First, one of the most significant ways persons with disabling conditions can be empowered through leisure is *self-determination* (Mahon & Bullock, 1992). Allowing people to make decisions for themselves, free from influence or interference, is important to everyone, and leisure settings and experiences are among the best sources. For persons with disabling conditions, it is especially important to have the right to choose leisure. Similarly, *self-advocacy* means individually and as a group persons with disabling conditions are allowed to speak for and on behalf of themselves. In the past 30 years, a great deal has been accomplished to facilitate equal rights for people with special needs, yet until recently, much of what was proposed was by people without disabilities. Self-advocacy gives persons with disabilities their own voice, and leisure settings and experiences are among the best sources.

Self-advocacy:
speaking on behalf of oneself

Normalization:
the availability of typical leisure experiences

The principle of *normalization* does not mean making persons with disabling conditions like "normal" people. Instead, it refers to the provision of typical experiences so that those with disabilities can maintain or develop leisure interests in accord with their own peers. One of the outcomes of normalization is *integration*. Integration requires both social interaction and social acceptance (Bullock & Howe, 1991) because it is based on the idea of integrity, meaning "to be yourself among others" (Fullwood, 1990, p. 3).

Integration:
enabling persons with and without disabilities to participate together

Box 13.5

In Focus

Nature Deficit Disorder

Nature Deficit Disorder is a term coined by Richard Louv in his 2005 book *Last Child in the Woods*. It refers to the trend that an entire generation of children is spending less time outdoors, resulting in a wide range of physical, emotional, cognitive and behavioral problems. Louv argues that sensationalist media coverage and paranoid parents have literally "scared children straight out of the woods and fields" (p.8). Fear of litigation, strangers, traffic, and wilderness itself, have led to a kind of generalized social anxiety; gone are the days of running in packs, building tree forts, hunting frogs, and playing hide-and-seek behind tall grasses. We've replaced these independent and imaginative outdoor play forms with indoor ones—the lure of the screen and the safe structure of adult-led activities. According to Louv, children's disconnect from nature is evident in the spiking increases in childhood obesity, attention deficit disorder, and depression.

Questions to Consider and Discuss

1. Do you agree with Louv's thesis? Are you aware of any anecdotal evidence either supporting or refuting the notion of nature deficit disorder?
2. Louv is not the first person to write about the effect of exposure to nature on the human psyche. His book builds on literature dating to over a century ago and the writings of Henry David Thoreau and Aldo Leopold. What do you think all these writings have in common?
3. Does Louv's use of the term disorder distort the intention of other physical and mental disability labels? For example, lately there has emerged some advocacy to consider obesity as a disabling condition covered by the ADA. What do you think?

To conclude, although leisure is an important aspect in quality of life for people, persons with disabilities are unable to take full advantage of this potential. This must be corrected, because leisure provides the opportunity for maintaining personal choice and freedom often absent from other aspects of their lives.

Gays and Lesbians

In the past, throughout much of the world, religious and governmental authorities have condemned gays and lesbians. Until more recently in the United States, for example, it was categorized as a form of mental illness by the psychiatric profession and as a crime by law enforcement agencies. Change began in the 1960s as civil rights movements began to remove many discriminatory laws.

Today, while the exact proportion of contemporary populations that is gay and lesbian has been difficult to estimate reliably (roughly 3-9%), an increasing visibility in many cultures means they are no longer thought of as counterculture. In particularly the last few decades there has been a trend toward increased recognition and legal rights, including marriage and civil unions, parenting rights, and equal access to health care. For example, today gay and lesbian marriage is legal in Canada, the Netherlands, Belgium, Spain, South Africa and in the states of California and Massachusetts in the United States.

As well, gays and lesbians have become an important consumer market in many economies, especially in tourism. For example, Gay Days at Walt Disney World in Orlando, Florida, annually draws some 135,000 visitors. While not officially sponsored by Walt Disney Company, the event is possible because of the park's official policy not to discriminate against anyone's right to visit the parks, and over the years has become more involved in working with the event coordinators.

This is because niche tourism marketed to people who want to travel to gay travel destinations is economically beneficial. As an industry it includes travel agents, tour companies, cruise lines, special events, travel advertising, and promotions campaigns. For example, the Illinois Bureau of Tourism (2006) estimated its sponsorship of Gay Games in Chicago would infuse between $50 and $80 million into the local economy.

Yet, due to discrimination, the lives of gays and lesbians continue to be stressful within the domains of family, employment, and social relationships (Miller, Forest & Jurik, 2003). Some leisure service organizations, for example, have explicitly refused participation by gay and lesbian individuals. These include recreation and social clubs sponsored by religious denominations, fraternities and sororities, and schools. For example, on February 6, 2002, the Boys Scouts of America adopted a resolution stating gays and atheists were unacceptable role models for scout youth (Scouting for All, 2008).

Researchers have only recently begun to give attention to the coping strategies used by gays and lesbians faced with such discrimination. Particularly, social support has been highlighted as an important stress-coping resource (Haas, 2002), and a growing body of literature emphasizes the significant role of leisure as social support.

For example, in a study on the lives of older lesbians, Jacobson and Samdahl (1998) found that despite their experiences of discrimination, these women actively created private safe spaces for themselves—an alternative community providing

Figure 13.5

The Boy Scouts of America represent a membership-based leisure services organization that discriminates against gays. Some argue that because it is a private club it has the right to do so. What do you think? (© Ruth V. Russell, 2008)

support and validation. Further, in a study on gay tourists, Pritchard et al. (2000) concluded the need for safety, to feel comfortable with like-minded people, and to escape to specifically gay spaces were key influences on their choice of vacation destination.

Box 13.6

The Study Says

Leisure as Coping Strategy

Given the prevalence and significance of stress in the lives of gays and lesbians, the study examined the role of leisure as a stress-coping strategy. A series of focus groups was conducted with 30 gays and lesbians living in a western Canadian city. The findings suggested that while gays and lesbians use a variety of coping strategies to deal with stress in their lives, leisure plays an important role in this process. One of the coping strategies found to be helpful is the creation of a gay-specific leisure space—an oasis for gays and lesbians to re-charge themselves physically, emotionally, and psychologically.

Iwasaki, Y., & Ristock, J. (2004). Coping with stress among gays and lesbians: Implications for human development over the lifespan. *World Leisure, 2*, 26-37.

To conclude, although leisure is an important aspect in quality of life for people, gays and lesbians are unable to take full advantage of this potential. This must be corrected, because leisure provides the opportunity for maintaining personal choice and freedom often absent from other aspects of their lives.

Racial and Ethnic Minorities

The increase in population diversity in North America is one of the most significant forces shaping these societies today. Diversity in ethnicity and race, for example, has been so dramatic that certain groups are on the verge of loosing their minority status. For example, in the state of Hawaii non-white ethnic groups account for about 75 percent of the population, with the largest being those of Asian decent at about 55 percent. Hawaii is one of four states along with the District of Columbia with majority minority populations, but the numbers are likely to grow until racial and ethnic minorities will make up the majority of the entire U.S. population in 2050 (*Star-Bulletin*, 2008).

Racial and ethnic minorities now account for more than one in three Americans, yet are not equally spread throughout the country. In fact, in all of North America, racial and ethnic groups are concentrated geographically. For example, the majority of French Canadians live in the province of Quebec. In the U.S., persons of Hispanic ethnicity are more likely to live in the west and south.

What do we mean by race and ethnicity? Definitions of what constitutes an ethnic or racial group are subject to much discussion, and the terminology used to describe them has changed significantly over time.

Let's consider *ethnicity* first. Membership in any ethnic group is something that is subjectively meaningful to the person concerned. For example, the ethnicity data collected by the United States Census Bureau is self-identified. Individuals respond to the survey according to the group with which they most closely identify. They may base this on any number of factors, including their nationality, country of birth, language spoken at home, parents' country of birth, geographical origin, religion, and/or even skin color.

Ethnicity:
a social contruction that indicates how a particular group defines common cultural traits

The U.S. Census Bureau also counts people according to *race* as self-identified. Residents choose one or more races with which they feel most closely connected. It is important to distinguish that the racial categories used do not reference particular biological, genetic, anthropological or even scientific characteristics. Race generally reflects a social definition. People of any ethnic group can identify themselves as members of any racial groups.

Race:
a self-defined distinction of people usually based on physical characteristics

As you might rightly conclude from all this, the increasing ethnic and racial diversity of North America also presents increasing challenges and opportunities in virtually every sphere of social life, including leisure. Accordingly, leisure has been a tool that both hinders and enables ethnic and racial diversity. For example, those who define themselves as Hispanic and Black are much less likely to read for leisure (U.S. Census Bureau, 2007c). Is this because of a prohibition, or is this by choice?

Over the past 35 years, scholars have produced a voluminous body of literature examining leisure meanings and differences according to racial and ethnic groups. For example, the focus of many studies has been on neighborhood/community-based leisure—how access to urban parks is affected by racial and ethnic identities. Similarly, ethnic and racial group use of the outdoors and forest-based recreation has been a common theme of studies, as has race and ethnicity in sports. For example, according to the research of Ogden & Hilt (2003), African American youth show a stronger preference for basketball, whereas white youth are more likely to be found participating in baseball and soccer.

There are several theoretical perspectives available attempting to make sense of the relationships among race, ethnicity, and leisure. For example, how leisure contributes to interracial interaction and race relations, as well as racial and ethnic identity in leisure have been theorized about. Other approaches suggest the distinctions are neither race nor ethnic based, but a matter of socioeconomic class.

One theoretical perspective that has been rather longstanding, but is still used today to explain ethnic/racial leisure distinctions is termed *marginality*. The term marginality was first introduced by Robert Park in 1928. This thesis suggests ethnic and racial differences are due to a group's marginal position in society. For example, over the years research has found differences between whites and blacks in their interests in outdoor recreation. In general, members of ethnic minority groups participate

Marginality:
being on the margins of the dominant culture

Box 13.7

The Study Says

A growing body of research evidence shows a widening gulf between baseball and African Americans. African Americans comprise less than three percent of the players at the highest competitive levels of youth baseball and three percent of NCAA Division I baseball players. African Americans also constitute less than five percent of spectators at major league parks, and the percentage of African American players in the major leagues has reached a 30-year low.

Why? According to studies, basketball has become the preeminent sport in African American culture. The studies contend this has been brought about by four factors: encouragement by authority figures to pursue basketball, the portrayal of basketball in the media as a form of empowerment, the abundance of black role models in basketball, and the perception of high and fast social mobility through basketball.

Ogden, D.C., & Hilt, M.L. (2003). Collective identity and basketball: An explanation for the decreasing number of African-Americans on America's baseball diamonds. *Journal of Leisure Research, 35*(2), 213-227.

less frequently (Gramann & Allison, 1999). Marginality would explain this difference as blacks feel more alienated from outdoor recreation because they feel alienated from the dominant culture that participates in it. Thus, they self-segregate from certain pastimes.

Some studies have argued that the marginal status of racial and ethnic groups in leisure is due to opportunity discrimination (Washburne, 1978). As applied to outdoor recreation participation, for example, this maintains the ethnic/racial differences are due to the cost of participation and the geographical location of resources—that historically the dominant groups have had a larger discretionary income and greater access to outdoor recreation sites. Others (cf. Floyd, 1998) have argued, on the other hand, the marginality theory fails to acknowledge socioeconomic differences within ethnic groups—not everyone who identifies themselves with a minority group lacks resources.

To conclude, although leisure is an important aspect in quality of life for people, members of ethnic and racial groups are unable to take full advantage of this potential. This must be corrected, because leisure provides the opportunity for maintaining personal choice and freedom often absent from other aspects of their lives.

Box 13.8

 *In Profile*

Healing Power of Play

Dateline February 25, 2008
Brookings, South Dakota

It is a painful truth of the Rosebud Reservation that some of its children born into grinding poverty and hopelessness decide that death is a better path than life. In reality, young Rosebud Sioux males between 10 and 24 years old kill themselves at a rate of 200 per 100,000 population. But now a group led by two South Dakota State University professors thinks it knows a way to change that. They believe a child who climbs out of bed each day with a baseball game to play, or a pond in which to float a bobber, or a golf club to swing, is going to choose life. In fact, they're so convinced of it, they've asked tribal officials and corporate America to join them in creating a sports emporium on the reservation. To build a ball diamond with lights, a soccer and flag football field, a path for walking, and maybe even a pier at a fishing pond, new basketball standards, and boxing equipment, Professors Russ Stubbles and Paul Fokken are trying to raise $2 million. (Young, 2008)

What We Understand About Leisure Equity

Our pastimes are a tool both for and against equity for people. For such groups as women, persons with disabilities, gays and lesbians, and ethnic and racial minorities the following major points can be made about leisure and equity:

- Leisure is not yet equitable; constraints to participation exist.
- Leisure has the potential of providing equality of opportunity.
- This can be accomplished through such principles as inclusion and celebration of diversity.

References

Afterschool Alliance. (March 24, 2005). News Release: New Survey Data: North Carolina Latchkey Kids from Working Families Vastly Outnumber Those in Afterschool Programs. Available from http://www.afterschoolalliance.org/press_archives/america_3pm/NC_NR2.pdf. Retrieved 7/19/08.

Alzheimer's Association. (2008). *What is Alzheimer's?* Available from http://www. alz.org/index.asp. Retrieved 7/21/08.

Anderson, D.A., Bedini, L.A., & Moreland, L. (2005). Getting all girls into the game: Physically active recreation for girls with disabilities. *Journal of Park and Recreation Administration, 23*(4), 78-103.

Bedini, L. (October 1990). Separate but equal? Segregated programming for people with disabilities. *Journal of Physical Education, Recreation and Dance, 40*, 40-44.

Bryce, J., & Rutter, J. (2003). Gender dynamics and the social and spatial organization of computer gaming. *Leisure Studies, 22*(1), 1-15.

Bullock, C.C., & Howe, C.Z. (1991). A model therapeutic recreation program for the reintegration of persons with disabilities into the community. *Therapeutic Recreation Journal, 25*(1), 7-17.

Coble, T.G., Selin, S.W., & Erickson, B.B. (2003). Hiking along: Understanding fear, negotiation strategies and leisure experience. *Journal of Leisure Research, 35*, 1-21.

Crawford, D.W., & Godbey, G. (1987). Reconceptualizing barriers to family leisure. *Leisure Sciences, 9*, 119-127.

Crawford, D.S., Jackson, E.L., & Godbey, G. (1991). A hierarchical model of leisure constraints. *Leisure Sciences, 13*, 309-320.

Floyd, M.F. (1998). Getting beyond marginality and ethnicity: The challenge for race and ethnic studies in leisure research. *Journal of Leisure Research, 30*, 3-22.

Fullwood, D. (1990). *Chances and choices: Making integration work.* Baltimore: Brookes.

Gramann, J.H., & Allison, M.T. (1999). Ethnicity, race, and leisure. In E.L. Jackson & T.L. Burton (Eds.), *Leisure studies: Prospects for the Twenty-first century* (pp. 283-298). State College, PA: Venture.

Haas, S.M. (2002). Social support as relationship maintenance in gay male couples coping with HIV or AIDS. *Journal of Social and Personal Relationships, 19*, 87-112.

Henderson, K.A. (1990). The meaning of leisure for women: An integrative review of the research. *Journal of Leisure Research, 22*, 228-243.

Henderson, K.A. (1996). One size doesn't fit all: The meanings of women's leisure. *Journal of Leisure Research, 28*, 139-154.

Henderson, K.A., & Hickerson, B. (2007). Women and leisure: Premises and performances uncovered in an integrative review. *Journal of Leisure Research, 39*(4), 591-610.

Illinois Bureau of Tourism. (March 3, 2006). Illinois Bureau of Tourism Announces $125,000 Grant to Help Promote and Attract More Visitors to 2006 Gay Games. *Press Release.* Available from http://www.sarafeigenholtz. com/Press%20Releases/03-03-06_ILTourismBureau_$125,000%20grant%20 for%20gay%20games.pdf. Retrieved 7/22/08.

Iwasaki, Y., MacKay, K., & Mactavish, J. (2005). Gender-based analyses of coping with stress among professional managers: Leisure coping and non-leisure coping. *Journal of Leisure Research, 37*, 1-27.

Jackson, E.L., & Scott, D. (1999). Constraints to leisure. In E.L. Jackson & T.L. Burton (Eds.), *Leisure studies: Prospects for the Twenty-first century* (pp. 299-322). State College, PA: Venture.

Jacobson, S., & Samdahl, D.M. (1998). Leisure in the lives of older lesbians: Experiences with and responses to discrimination. *Journal of Leisure Research, 30*, 233-255.

Livengood, J.S., & Stodolska, M. (2004). The effects of discrimination and constraints negotiation on leisure behavior of American Muslims in Post – September 11 America. *Journal of Leisure Research, 36*(2), 183-208.

Louv, R. (2005). *Last child in the woods: Saving our children from nature-deficit disorder.* Chapel Hill, NC: Algonquin Books.

Mahon, M.J., & Bullock, C.C. (1992). Teaching adolescents with mild mental retardation to make decisions in leisure through the use of self-control techniques. *Therapeutic Recreation Journal, 26*, 9-26.

Miller, S.L., Forest, K.B., & Jurik, N.C. (2003). Diversity in blue: Lesbian and gay police officers in a masculine occupation. *Men and Masculinities, 5*(4), 355-385.

Nadirova, A., & Jackson, E.L. (2000). Alternative criterion variables against which to assess the impacts of constraints to leisure. *Journal of Leisure Research, 32*(4), 396-405.

Ogden, D.C., & Hilt, M.L. (2003). Collective identity and basketball: An explanation for the decreasing number of African-Americans on America's baseball diamonds. *Journal of Leisure Research, 35*(2), 213-227.

Park, R.E. (1928). Human migration and the marginal man. *American Journal of Sociology, 33*, 6.

Pritchard, A., Morgan, N.J., Sedgley, D., Khan, E., & Jenkins, A. (2000). Sexuality and holiday choices: Conversations with gay and lesbian tourists. *Leisure Studies, 19*(4), 267-282.

Schleien, S.J., Green, F.P., & Stone, C.F. (2003). Making friends within inclusive community programs. *American Journal of Recreation Therapy, 2*(1), 7-16.

Scouting for All. (2008). *Policy Becomes the First in Organization's 92-Year History.* Available from http://www.scoutingforall.org/data/home.html. Retrieved 7/24/08.

Searle, M.S., & Brayley, R.E. (2000). *Leisure services in Canada: An introduction.* State College, PA: Venture.

Shaw, S. (2005). Discrimination is a societal issue too: Moving beyond individual behavior. *Leisure Sciences, 27*(1), 37-40.

Shklyanoy, P. (September/October 2000). Just how compliant are you? *Recreation Management.* 12-18.

Star-Bulletin Staff. (May 1, 2008). Hawaii's ethnic diversity still tops. *Star-Bulletin.* Available from http://starbulletin.com/2008/05/01/news/story10.html. Retrieved 7/23/08.

Stodolska, M. (2005). A conditioned attitude model of individual discriminatory behavior. *Leisure Sciences, 27*(1), 1-20.

U.S. Census Bureau. (May 26, 2007a). *Facts for Features.* Available from http://www.prnewswire.com/cgi-bin/stories.pl?ACCT=104&STORY=/www/story/05-29-2007/0004597318&EDATE. Retrieved 7/21/08.

U.S. Census Bureau. (2007b). Table 1222. Participation in various leisure activities: 2002. *Statistical Abstracts of the United States: 2007*. U.S. Government Printing Office.

U.S. Census Bureau. (2007c). Table 1217. Expenditures Per Consumer Unit for Entertainment and Reading: 1985 to 2004. *Statistical Abstracts of the United States: 2007*. U.S. Government Printing Office.

Washburne, R.F. (1978). Black underparticipation in wildland recreation: Alternative explanations. *Leisure Sciences, 1*, 175-189.

Young, S. (February 25, 2008). Group promotes healing power of play. *The Argus Leader*. Brookings, South Dakota.

CHAPTER FOURTEEN

LEISURE SYSTEMS

PREVIEW

Why are leisure systems important?

As you already know, having access to leisure resources is imperative to the lives of individuals, communities, and entire societies. Delivery systems for these resources assist with this access.

What are the types of organized leisure system resources?

Leisure resources are usually grouped into the categories of sports, cultural arts, outdoor recreation, travel, hobbies, social recreation, and others.

Who sponsors these leisure systems?

They are sponsored by public, private, and commercial agencies.

KEY TERMS

Where do places for leisure come from? How are they cared for so we may use them? Who manages our gymnasiums, playgrounds, art centers, concert halls, health clubs, campgrounds, and resorts? What makes it possible for us to have forests, gardens, parks, trails, reservoirs, and beaches? These and many other leisure resources are managed by a varied collection of agencies, organizations, and companies. Funds are generated, personnel hired, services offered, and people served by hundreds and thousands of these efforts, big and small—all focused on leisure. This is called a *leisure service delivery system*.

Leisure service delivery system:

a means for providing leisure products and services to the public

Of course, many pastimes are experienced in informal ways, such as reading a book, walking around the neighborhood, and socializing with friends. However, other pastimes require or are made better by a formal organization that provides facilities, equipment, leadership, instruction, schedules, and other support. Even such independently experienced activities as bicycling, picnicking, and swimming require the provision of safe, attractive, and accessible areas to be fully enjoyed.

Figure 14.1

Leisure resources come in many forms, including these park benches in London. (Shutterstock©, 2008)

Since leisure service delivery systems are broad, varied, and numerous, in our final chapter we explore only some of the typical ways systems for leisure resources are managed. We begin by exploring why leisure service delivery systems are important. Here we introduce the concept of cultural capital. Next, ways of structuring services according to type of leisure expression are presented. These include tourism, cultural arts, sports, and outdoor recreation. Then, ways of organizing leisure services according to type of sponsorship are discussed, including commercial, private, and public.

Why Leisure Systems are Important

Leisure resources are needed to enhance life's livability, and systems are necessary to insure people have access to the leisure resources they need and want. As we've discovered in previous chapters, leisure is of vital importance to our health and wealth, between birth and death, and in essence to our very meaning as human beings. Leisure is a major contributor to a society's quality of life, it helps define geography, and is at the center of the information technology revolution.

Cultural capital:

personal resources useful for achieving high-status

Another way of understanding the necessity of leisure resources, that we haven't discussed, is through the concept of cultural capital. *Cultural capital* is the knowledge, experience, and connections we acquire in life that enable us to succeed. This is our "life advantage" that comes from our families, education, and to the point—our leisure. Cultural capital is what gives us our status in society.

Box 14.1

In Your Own Experience

How to Find the World's Best Place to Live

Go to the website for the magazine *International Living* to determine where the best places to live are for this year:
http://www.internationalliving.com/internal_components/further_resources/quality_of_life08?id=115.

Using a Quality of Life Index, you'll notice this annual ranking places a good deal of emphasis on the role of leisure in its recommendation. For example, in 2008 it recommended France. According to the Quality of Life Index, not only does France have the world's best medical care, four seasons, three airports, and fast trains, but Paris "blooms with too-many-to-count museums, cafes, galleries, antiques shops, restaurants, boutiques, jazz clubs, theaters, bakeries, and cheese shops, as well as her multitude of parks and gardens, some growing and tended for hundreds of years."

Cultural capital is a sociological concept that has gained widespread popularity since it was first articulated by Pierre Bourdieu and Jean-Claude Passeron in their 1973 book *Cultural Reproduction and Social Reproduction*. They considered cultural capital to be the reason some children fail at school and some adults lack success in occupations. Their view was that people need to possess the behaviors and knowledge that are the most highly regarded in their society in order to succeed there. In other words, cultural capital is having the "currency" of a culture. This idea has been studied widely. For example, some studies (cf. Dumais, 2002; Kalmijn & Kraaykanp, 1996) suggest cultural capital includes a linguistic advantage; others (cf. Mohr & DiMaggio, 1995) have identified it as participating in the highbrow tastes and styles of the dominant in-power culture.

As well, many studies have investigated leisure's role in cultural capital. For example, Katsillis and Rubinson (1990) found high school students' attendance at lectures, the theater, museums, and galleries to be positively related to their success in school. In a study by Downey and Powell (1993), those eighth graders who were more successful in school participated in scouting, hobby clubs, boys and girls' clubs, non-school team sports, 4-H, and other recreation programs. As well, Rauscher (1994) found that listening to music helps the brain manage complex mental functions, such as understanding mathematics. In the area of sports, Stempel (2005) concluded from his data that the dominant social classes use strenuous aerobic sports, moderate levels of weight-training, and competitive sports that restrain violence to identify others as worthy of advancement in society.

Leisure Resource Types

What exactly are sources of cultural capital? We gain cultural capital in part from our pastimes. In fact, there are so many recreational activities that just listing them would take so many pages we'd call it a book. The variety is limited only by imagination, because leisure interests are as broad as humanity itself. People collect stamps, run marathons, fly airplanes, doodle, bake cookies, climb mountains, take photographs, join clubs, watch football games, sign up for classes, collect antiques, plant flowers, and roast marshmallows, just for the fun of it.

Figure 14.2

Susan Ogier and Abby (the horse) competing in barrel racing, ANB Boogies Bunny, Peoria, IL (© Barb Ray, used with permission)

Despite their wide variety, we can catalog pastimes. While even classifying experiences that offer leisure meaning and value is itself a difficult task, and the means of the classification are arbitrary, people's pastimes can be grouped by the activity types listed in table 14.1. The categories of sports and games, cultural arts, outdoor recreation, travel and tourism, hobbies, and social recreation are not all-inclusive, but they are useful for describing the common types of organized leisure services that are provided in modern societies. From this list, we now explore tourism, cultural arts, outdoor recreation, and sports a bit more. The question we ask is what are the resources for these pursuits?

Table 14.1

Types of Leisure Expressions

Category	Sub-Categories	Examples
Sports and Games	Individual Dual Team	gymnastics, ice skating, solitaire badminton, wrestling, chess volleyball, water polo, charades
Cultural Arts	Music Fine arts Dance Drama	guitar lessons, karaoke filmmaking, ceramics, painting ballroom dance, rhythm games mime, storytelling, stage shows
Outdoor Recreation	Camping Nature-oriented Conservation Adventure Outdoor Sports	backpacking, RVing stargazing, bird watching gardening, wildlife planting spelunking, extreme skiing fishing, horseback riding

Table 14.1 (Cont.)

Types of Leisure Expressions

Category	Sub-Categories	Examples
Travel and Tourism	Group tours Cruises Ecotourism Destination focused	bus tours, theater trips ocean liner, barefoot volunteering to count zebras cities, theme parks, resorts
Hobbies	Education Collecting	poetry writing, puzzles, reading autographs, dolls, coins, recipes
Social Recreation	Parties Clubs Eating events Visiting events	holiday, birthday, poker meetings, coffee houses, drop-in picnics, cookouts, potlucks coffee breaks, Web chat rooms

Tourism

Think about the last trip you took. In addition to commuting to school or work, driving to the grocery story, and other trips necessary for your ordinary life, what about recent trips for leisure? Most likely, your last leisure trip happened very recently. This is because traveling to leisure and traveling as leisure is a major category of leisure expression.

Tourism is travel for recreational purposes. It is the short-term movement of people to destinations outside where they ordinarily live and work. We travel to lose ourselves and we travel to find ourselves. While people have traveled from earliest times to find food and to escape danger, advances in transportation and communication have now made it possible for millions of people to travel for thousands of miles just for the fun of it.

Tourism:
the activities of people traveling to and staying in places outside their usual environment

Today people travel for many reasons, including for business and religious pilgrimage, but most of all they travel for and as leisure. According to the Travel Industry Association of America (2003), 82 percent of all trips by residents within the U.S. are for leisure (only 12% are for business/convention purposes); the most common form of transportation is auto, truck, or RV (78%); and the top activities during the trip are shopping (30%), family/social events (27%), and outdoor activities (11%).

The geographic spread of tourism continues to widen as all parts of the world are now accessible to tourists. While some destinations are not considered safe or are very expensive to get to, intrepid tourists still go. For example, while difficult to accurately count, in 2007 there were an estimated 346,000 tourists visiting Iraq, and the number of tourists in Antarctica has grown from a few hundred to more than 30,000 each year. Despite great uncertainties about the global economy, in the first four months of 2008, world tourism grew by about 5

Table 14.2

Top Ten International Tourist Arrivals by Country of Destination (2006)

Country	Arrivals (in millions)	% Change
France	79.1	2.2
Spain	58.5	1.3
United States	51.1	9.1
China	49.6	9.6
Italy	41.1	17.2
United Kingdom	30.1	2.6
Germany	23.6	8.8
Mexico	21.4	-1.1
Austria	20.3	-1.9
Russian Federation	20.2	7.7

World Tourism Organization (June 2007).

percent (World Tourism Organization, 2008). Top destinations for international tourists are France, Spain, and the United States (table 14.2).

Regardless of the destination or purpose of the trip, a complex network of agencies is required to support tourism. Since leisure travel involves a composite of activities, services, and industries including eating and drinking establishments, transportation, accommodations, entertainment, events and attractions, and others, the delivery of travel experiences must operate as a coordinated enterprise. For example, the success of the resort business on the island of Antigua depends not only on the marketing efforts of travel agents worldwide, the availability of transportation to and within the island, housing, and restaurants, but also retail shops, charter boats, diving and snorkeling guides, musicians, gardeners, and even weather forecasters. Taken together, these are referred to as the *tourism system*.

Tourism system:
an industry created for tourists

The exact mix of agencies and services within a tourism system for a locale depends, of course, on the type of tourism available there. An unqualified list of tourism types is not available, but most include mass tourism (large numbers traveling together to major sites), health tourism (spas), adventure tourism (remote destinations with active experiences), ecotourism (natural environment interactions), and even dark tourism, which features seeing battlegrounds, crime scenes, concentration camps, etc.

Another increasingly popular type is educational tourism, which focuses on learning through travel. For example, in the U.S., national park sites have interpretation centers and programs, and learning to cook excursions are a major source of tourist receipts in Italy. A famous example of educational tourism is Elderhostel. Founded in 1975, Elderhostel is an American educational travel company offering adults 55 years old and over more than 8,000 tours in all 50 states and 90 countries. The trips include in-depth and behind-the-scenes learning opportunities—from cultural tours and study cruises, to lectures and field trips (Elderhostel, 2008).

Box 14.2

 *In Profile*

New Resorts

One member of the tourism delivery system is lodging. To demonstrate the point that lodging accommodations not only support tourism, but also are often the very reason for the trip, here are the descriptions of some truly unusual hotels.

- *Kokopelli's Cave Bed and Breakfast* in New Mexico's Four Corners area is 70 feet below the surface. The entrance is located in a cliff face, reached by walking down a path, and onto a ladder at the bottom of the path that lands you on the flagstone porch. The accommodation has a bedroom, kitchen, and a bathroom with waterfall shower. (http://www.bbonline.com/nm/kokopelli/)
- *The Ice Hotel* (open in winter only) is located in Quebec, Canada. Made entirely of ice and snow, featuring 36 rooms and suites, an ice chapel, art exhibition rooms, and N'Ice Club, the hotel has 16-foot ceilings and furniture carved from blocks of ice. At night, you'll wrap yourself in a warm sleeping bag and enjoy the silence and pure air—all at around 23 degrees Fahrenheit. (http://www.icehotel-canada.com/en/)
- *Jules Undersea Lodge* in Key Largo, Florida claims to be the original undersea hotel, were qualified divers swim 21 feet below the surface to gain access to this two-roomed hotel that includes a hot shower, a well-stocked kitchen, books, music, and movies. Of course, guests can also snuggle up in the cozy beds to watch the fish. Entering through an opening at the bottom, the feeling is much like discovering a secret underwater clubhouse. (http://www.jul.com/)
- *Crane Hotel* in Harlingen, Netherlands features a dockside crane converted into a luxury hideaway for two. Replacing the external ladders with modern elevators to gain entry, the old machine room in the body of the crane has been transformed into a bedroom with observation windows, a flat screen television, double shower, and other amenities—all with an industrial feel. And, it is your own personal, working crane as you swirl around controlling it from the comfort of the driver's cabin. (http://www.uhotw.com/HotelDetails.aspx?HotelID=5597 &src=feedback&RatingID=)

Figure 14.3

Porpoise lagoon at the Hilton Waikoloa Village Resort on the big island of Hawaii. (© Ruth V. Russell, 2008)

Cultural Arts

The term art refers to a diverse range of activities that appeal to the senses. It most often refers to the visual arts, including painting and sculpture, but also is applied to other art forms that stimulate other senses, such as music, dance, and drama. Cultural art programs and facilities are an integral part of a community's quality of life. Indeed, summer day-camp programs for children are just as likely to include crafts and dance as swimming and games. Members of senior adult centers can sign up to learn to play the oboe. Haiku poetry is taught to youth offenders; football players take ballet classes; and executives join potter's cooperatives.

Communities everywhere have orchestras, dance companies, theater groups, and art fairs. Voluntary organizations sponsor photography clubs and crafts guilds. Army bases provide rap practice rooms, shopping malls feature art exhibits, and your university's string quartet perhaps performs weekly at noon on the campus lawn. To illustrate the pervasiveness of cultural arts services, Table 14.3 highlights some available in the U.S.

Community arts councils: umbrella agencies that support and promote cultural arts in a community

In fact, the options for cultural art resources are limitless, thus the challenge is to coordinate them to ensure their adequate distribution. One solution is *community arts councils*. In many

Table 14.3

A Sampling of Performing Arts Opportunities Annually in the U.S.(2004)

Opportunities	Number of
Broadway shows	39 new productions
Broadway road tours	1060 playing weeks
Professional theaters	169,000 performances
Opera companies	1,946 performances
Art museums	4,591 nonprofit institutions
Symphony orchestras	37,263 performances

U.S. Census Bureau (2007a).

communities, special interest organizations in the arts are coordinated or assisted by a comprehensive agency that helps promote their efforts to provide arts services. As a not-for-profit organization these community arts councils promote and support all forms of cultural arts for all ages. This means they often fund artists and art organizations, provide special programs and events, and sponsor art education sessions. For example, the Arts & Humanities Council of Tulsa, Oklahoma seeks to integrate art and culture into the everyday lives of its citizens. One of the ways it accomplishes this is through "The Write Place"—a forum for workshops showcasing the talents of local authors and writers.

A *cultural arts center* represents another way communities are able to promote and assist in the provision of arts services. These are multiple-purpose facilities often sponsoring dramatic, dance, and musical performances. In many communities, cultural arts

Cultural arts center:
a single facility supporting more than one art form

centers provide one or more stages, an art gallery, and rehearsal and workshop areas under one roof. One of the first multiple-purpose cultural arts centers was New York City's Lincoln Center for the Performing Arts. Founded in 1962, the Lincoln Center's buildings and auditoriums cover 16 acres. It supports 12 independent arts organizations including The Metropolitan Opera, the New York Philharmonic Orchestra, The Juilliard School of Music, The New York City Ballet, and the Film Society of Lincoln Center. In a typical year the center hosts over 5,000 performances featuring over 3,000 artists.

Sports

Even only casual observation of the average community demonstrates the priority of sport resources. Basketball hoops above garage doors, tennis courts behind apartment buildings, city swimming pools, private golf courses, and of course, softball diamonds can be found everywhere. In fact, you are hereby challenged to find even one town that does not have at least one softball facility. This is because according to the U.S. Census Bureau (2007a) about 27 million Americans play amateur softball.

Likewise each year, new highs are reached in attendance at sporting events, new teams and leagues in both amateur and professional sports are established, and new sports soar to popularity. For example, the new sport of bossaball, which mixes soccer, volleyball and gymnastics on trampolines and inflatables, can be set up in almost any location, including shopping malls, beaches, resorts, and summer camps. In Canada, curling has developed an immensely popular following, with an estimated 1.3 million active curlers (Weiting & Lamoureux, 2001). And, the New England Sports Academy was recently founded as the region's first multisport training facility designed

Figure 14.4

Softball for both youth and adults is one of the most commonly provided leisure services in the United States. (Shutterstock©, 2008)

to provide children the coaching, facilities, and training needed for excelling in sports.

Many agencies and organizations provide resources for sport participation and spectating. Athletic clubs, community centers, Boys' and Girls' clubs, YMCAs, commercial stadiums and tracks, hotels, camps, cities, schools and many others are examples. Governmental sponsors most likely provide programs in team sports, such as basketball, soccer, and softball; whereas, private sport and fitness clubs typically offer individual sports, such as jogging, weight lifting, golf, tennis, boating, and swimming. Commercial establishments cater to such sport interests as bowling.

Box 14.3

 *In Profile*

New Sports Center for Iraqi Youth

As residents of Baghdad hope for peace, some Iraqis are banking that sports can help find that peace. With the help of the U.S. Army, former Iraqi athletes have opened a sports center for the youth of the Adhamiya neighborhood as a means to keep young men out of violent extremist groups like Al Qaeda, which recruits heavily in the area. Opened in 2007, it offers programs in soccer, weight lifting, basketball, and wrestling—all free to participants. The only charge is for a three-hour pass to the swimming pool. Each week the center attracts between 700 and 1,000 young people. In the midst of Iraq's turmoil, investing in a sports complex may seem extravagant, but the Iraqi athletes know this is the power of sport. (Peter, 2008)

Even the home is an important sport resource. For example, exercise apparatus and portable swimming pools are common. Driveway basketball goals are also quite prevalent in many suburban and rural homes, and tennis courts at home are becoming more widely used. Perhaps the largest growth in sport participation at home now comes via the computer, in the form of sport video games and Internet-based fantasy sports. For example, according to the Fantasy Sports Trade Association (2008) 29 million people age 12 and above in the U.S. and Canada play fantasy sports.

Services in sports are offered not only in a wide range of facilities and programs, but to a broad range of participants as well. Communities offer sport services for the novice and the highly skilled, for the young and the old, for women and girls, as well as men and boys. For example, in St. Petersburg, Florida, a softball league has a minimum age requirement of 75 years. They call themselves Kids and Kubs, and they've been playing regular seasons since 1931. Sports for people with disabilities are also a major service provision with numerous organizations actively providing opportunities in a wide range of sports, including golf, skiing, tennis, and basketball.

The point of it all is that sport is everywhere. As a wildly popular activity to both play and watch, sport is an undeniably worthwhile leisure resource for communities. However, communities must also assume responsibility for issues associated with sport that are often not at all positive. Sports are plagued by questions of violence, racism and sexism (Freysinger & Kelly, 2004), as for example, boxing has been described as authorization to beat another person into unconsciousness, and sport in general has been accused of reinforcing gender stereotypes (Messner, 1992).

Perhaps the biggest concern in sport today comes from its potential for wielding power. While sport participation is central to the development of children and youth and provides opportunities for adults to stay active and healthy, and while sport spectating inspires social bonding and tension relief for a community's citizens, sport is also part of a large social system that is used for political and economic gain. As such, sport is a form of consumption supported by large investment and promotion enterprises. Some consider this to be a detriment to sport as leisure.

Outdoor Recreation

People join hiking clubs, go fishing, and make reservations months ahead to stay near the ocean. Normally sedentary and prosaic adults spend their weekends climbing rocks, exploring caves, or following soaring bald eagles. Caring for

Box 14.4

 The Study Says

Delivering on the Olympics

Cities that host the Olympic Games must commit to significant investments in elite sports venues and other infrastructure. It is commonly assumed that the scale of such preparations will create large and lasting economic benefits to the host city. In reviewing studies of host city costs and benefits after the Games, there appears no evidence of positive economic impacts from such mega-sporting events. In the case of the 2008 Summer Olympic Games in Beijing, it is predicted that organizers will only meet their expectations for long-term economic benefits if Olympics related investments on venues and infrastructure can be incorporated into the overall economy in the years following the Games.

Owen, J.G. (2005). Estimating the cost and benefit of hosting Olympic Games: What can Beijing expect from its 2008 Games? *The Industrial Geographer, 3*(1), 1-18.

plants provides therapy to patients in a convalescent center. Summer campers learn to overcome their fears of snakes and bugs.

The out-of-doors is a prime resource for leisure. Forests and soil, sunshine and rain, rivers and sky, the hills, prairies, and lakes are more than just pleasant places in which to play. In the outdoors, people participate more intimately in their own ecology. They go outdoors to repair what happens to them indoors.

A reason people seek nature in their pastimes is perhaps the surprise of the outdoors—it is where we can prove ourselves. Nothing exhilarates quite like racing a storm across the lake in a small sailboat. On the other hand, people may go to nature for leisure because of its beauty. They find strength in hearing the silence of the falling snow and smelling the sweetness of the pine forest.

Figure 14.5

Some outdoor recreation pursuits have become less reliant on nature and thus seem no longer to qualify as leisure pursued outdoors. (Shutterstock©, 2008)

Although the vast land and water holdings of federal and state/provincial governments constitute the major outdoor recreation resources in North America, local resources add considerably to our opportunities. These include parks, zoos, botanical gardens, camps, lakes and reservoirs, nature centers, forest preserves, resort ranches, marinas, ski slopes and trails, horse trails, campgrounds, rivers, and beaches.

To be more specific, in the United States, more than 200 million acres of federal land are available for our enjoyment; states offer another 42 million acres, and local governments about 10 million acres (Freysinger & Kelly, 2004). The National Park Service, for example, manages more than 79 million acres for an annual visitor count of about 63 million (U.S. Census Bureau, 2007b).

Box 14.5

 *In Focus*

Urban Sprawl

In the United States within the last decade 13.7 million acres of open land were converted to housing, industrial, and commercial development. This rate is 51 percent higher than in the decade before, even though the U.S. population grew by only 17 percent (U.S. Department of Agriculture, 2001). Developed acreage per person has nearly doubled in the past 20 years, and housing lots larger than 10 acres have

Box 14.5 (Cont.)

accounted for 55 percent of this (American Farmland Trust, 2007). When development is unplanned and uncontrolled, spreading urban development into rural areas, it is labeled urban sprawl. Sprawl spreads development out over larger amounts of land, and puts long distances between homes, stores, and job centers. It gobbles up more than two million acres of park, farm, and other open space land each year (National Resources Inventory, 2008).

Questions to Consider and Discuss

1. Opponents declare sprawl pollutes air and water since it typically requires reliance on cars, and as pavement for more roads increases, so does smog and pollution from water runoff. What do you think?
2. Some also emphasize the lack of pedestrian friendly neighborhoods within urban sprawl, which increases obesity since walking and bicycling are not viable options. What do you think?
3. Another concern about urban sprawl is for wildlife habitat and wildlife-based recreation. Opponents claim wild forests, meadows, and wetlands are replaced by pavement and buildings, making survival of certain wildlife species and outdoor pastimes difficult. What do you think?
4. Social fragmentation is another claim against urban sprawl. That is, neighborhoods with compact housing, front porches, a corner store, and a school two blocks away are more conducive to social interactions and feeling part of a community. Also, sprawl tends to replace public spaces such as parks with private spaces such as fenced-in yards. What do you think?
5. Finally, sprawl developments into the countryside are accused of damaging the tourism industry as the scenic qualities that attract tourists to a region are shrinking. Roads are straightened and widened, and there are fewer options for tourism and outdoor recreation. What do you think?
6. What might be some solutions to urban sprawl? Locate and read the article, "A New Perspective on Urban Sprawl, New Urbanism and the Role of the Park and Recreation Field," published in August 2005 by Don DeGraaf and others in *Parks & Recreation* magazine. Notice the proposed solutions of smart growth, livable communities, sustainable communities, and new urbanism. Do any of these seem viable? Why or why not?

Leisure Resource Sponsors

Leisure resources may also be classified according to the type of sponsor. For example, federal, state/provincial, and local governments provide leisure resources and so do nongovernmental, notprofit agencies. Private clubs and commercial for-profit businesses also provide for the pastime needs of people. Employers often offer facilities and programs for leisure as an employment benefit. Colleges and universities accommodate the sport, social, and arts interests of students. Recreation services are part of the treatment for residents of correctional settings and patients in hospitals. These and many other examples form the diverse members of the leisure service delivery system.

To help you grasp these numerous sponsors, we consider them according to three broad categories. First, public agencies are government sponsored and equitably available to all people. Private agencies, in contrast, offer facilities and programs for members, and commercial agencies provide leisure services as a business. Table 14.4 compares these categories of service sponsors in terms of purpose, typical services, and funding sources.

Table 14.4

Leisure Service Sponsor Types

Type of Agency	Example	Purpose	Services	Funding Source
Commercial	Blockbuster, Inc.	To sell leisure experiences in order to make a profit.	Wide variety, with focus on entertainment, sports, travel & cultural arts.	Paying customers.
Private	YMCA	To meet the leisure needs of members.	Wide variety, with focus on social recreation, sports, hobbies & voluntary service.	Member dues, donations & grants.
Public	City of Toronto Parks & Recreation Department	To see that all citizens are equitably able to experience a high quality of life.	Wide variety, with focus on outdoor recreation, cultural arts & sports.	Government taxes, user fees, gifts & grants.

Public Agencies

Of all the types of sponsors of leisure services, governmental agencies have the unique distinction of being:

- The first type of organization to be formally recognized as responsible for serving the public's leisure needs.
- The only type of organization that is responsible for providing services on an equal basis to the entire population of a locale.
- The only type of organization that has the power to secure, hold, protect, and open for use the natural resources upon which much of our leisure depends.

The primary function of government is to serve citizens' needs. Accordingly, government is the means by which people's leisure needs are met without regard to ability to pay, gender, race, occupational status, or any other distinction that can restrict access. This is perhaps best illustrated by the leisure services provided by local governments.

City, town, county, township, school district and other governmental agencies operating at the local level serve the broadest needs and largest clientele. Because they are that level of government closest to the citizens, they are better able to respond directly to the needs of the people. For example, in Ohio the city of Westerville Parks and Recreation Department is:

your community connection for sports, recreation, leisure classes, programs and entertainment. The Recreation Division seeks to provide professionally designed and supervised programs that benefit all ages—children, youth, teens, adults and seniors .... And that significantly contribute to the quality of life enjoyed by all Westerville residents. (Westerville Parks and Recreation Department, 2008, p. 1).

Because most North Americans now live in cities and towns, most depend on municipal governments to provide many important leisure services. In some areas, public school districts provide recreation and park facilities and programs, and in others, the county government operates these services. What are some of the primary functions of *municipal recreation* organizations?

Municipal recreation and park departments acquire, develop, and maintain facilities needed for the leisure participation of local citizens. As well, they provide the skilled leadership and program structure for the use of these facilities. For example, most cities provide softball and baseball diamonds, tennis courts, swimming facilities, basketball courts, playing fields, picnic areas, playgrounds, and community centers, as well as directors, supervisors, and other professional staff to plan programs for and manage these facilities.

Municipal recreation: leisure services sponsored by local government, such as a city

Medium to large communities also may have gymnasiums, golf courses, auditoriums, outdoor theaters, bike and walking trails, fitness centers, nature centers, skate parks, and cultural arts centers. Some also provide such special-interest leisure opportunities as museums, zoos, aquariums, arboretums, campgrounds, ice arenas, velodromes, and botanical gardens.

To avoid duplication of services, local government recreation and park services are sometimes coordinated among various community organizations. The local government leisure organizations also work closely with other branches of local government, such as the police department, to develop effective programs to solve social problems. They also cooperate with state and federal authorities to develop comprehensive long-range services plans.

Another level of government that serves as a leisure services sponsor is the state or provincial government. In the U.S., even though the Tenth Amendment to the Constitution gives states powers in such areas as public education, welfare, and health services, the idea that leisure services are a state responsibility didn't take hold until the 1960s and 1970s. Today, however, and even with recent cutbacks in budgets, states remain a viable leisure services sponsor.

Box 14.6

 *In Profile*

Leisure in Jail

In 1995, Michael Francis was looking for a new job. In the local paper he saw an opening for a recreation specialist at the Omaha (Nebraska) Correctional Center. Even though he had never heard of correctional recreation, he applied for the position, got the job, and from that point on, his view of leisure was changed forever.

I will never forget the first day I walked into the correctional center and heard the steel door close behind me. It startled me, and once inside, I knew I was in for a new and exciting experience (p. 27).

The correctional setting really resembles a small town, with educational opportunities, jobs, access to medical staff, and recreation services. The role of recreation services in corrections is also similar: a good recreation program seeks to promote safety, security and good order in the institution. Michael's program includes year-round services in athletics, music, hobbies, fitness and informal recreation. According to inmate interests, his goal is to provide experiences that are constructive, and help them learn how to get along with others. Life skills learned in the recreation programs are also considered important to rehabilitating the released inmate for life on the outside. (Francis, 2005)

This is because, states are able to function in ways not possible for local governments. For example, the functions of the state government in sponsoring leisure services can be summarized as (Maclean, Peterson & Martin, 1985):

- *Enactment of enabling legislation*. States give local governments the legal authority to operate recreation and park services. Such **enabling legislation** gives city, county, and other local authorities the power to acquire properties, employ personnel, and impose taxes to support leisure services.

- *Direct provision of leisure services*. States operate a network of parks, forests, and recreation areas. These resources typically include nature preserves, historical monuments, beaches, campgrounds, rest areas, and parks.

- *Education*. States also provide educational services related to leisure, including publications, traveling exhibits, workshops, conventions, and outreach programs in schools. State-affiliated colleges and universities also offer professional curriculums that prepare students for careers in leisure services.

Enabling legislation:
state or federal legislation that grants authority to local government to enact ordinances and regulations to control local activities

- *Promotion of tourism*. State departments of commerce, planning, highways, natural resources, and tourism typically make special efforts to attract visitors to the state. They conduct marketing research and promotions campaigns focused on getting their share of the tourist dollar.
- *Regulations*. State standards affecting leisure are of two types: those protecting participants and those protecting leisure resources. Those protecting participants include regulations for safety, cleanliness, and health in camps, resorts, swimming pools, and restaurants. Regulations protecting leisure resources pertain to water pollution, fire dangers, and soil conservation.

Federal governments, in turn, manage leisure resources of even greater significance than those managed at state and local government levels. In the United States, for example, the federal government provides a broad assortment of services. While difficult to count from election to election, there are more than 90 departments, bureaus, commissions, councils, divisions, and authorities at the federal level having at least some responsibility for leisure provisions. As you can imagine, coordination among these many agencies has been difficult. Overall, the complexity of federal level efforts to support leisure services can be summarized into six functions (Maclean, Peterson, & Martin, 1985):

- *Ownership and management of land, water, and wildlife for leisure*. Approximately 270 million acres of land used primarily for parks, forests, and recreation areas are managed by federal agencies. An example is the U.S. Forest Service.
- *Grants to state and local governments*. Several federal agencies make financial grants to lower level governments for purchasing land, facilities, training and programs in leisure. For example, the federal government awards grants of up to $50,000 for developing services in correctional institutions.
- *Direct program operation*. While this function is more likely the responsibility of local governments, some federal agencies operate leisure services directly for participants, such as in *military recreation*.

Military recreation: sponsored by the Department of Defense, community recreation and sport for military personnel and their families living on military bases

Figure 14.6

The USS Arizona Memorial in Hawaii. Managed by the National Park Service, the location is the final resting place for many of the battleship's 1,117 crew members who lost their lives on December 7, 1941. The Memorial commemorates this as the site where World War II began for the United States. (© Ruth V. Russell, 2008)

- *Research*. The federal government supports a broad spectrum of research about leisure ranging from outdoor recreation trends, to the status of urban recreation. For example, monies are available to collect and analyze data leading to increasing the integration and inclusion of persons with developmental disabilities into the community.
- *Regulation*. Federal regulations affecting leisure systems include standards regulating hunting and fishing, boating safety, the impact of leisure activities on the environment, and architectural accessibility for persons with disabilities.
- *Advisory services*. More than 30 federal organizations offer technical assistance for local agencies. For example, The President's Council on Physical Fitness and Sports provides consultation and publications to schools, recreation and park departments, and youth organizations who wish to introduce or improve physical activity or sports programs.

Box 14.7

In Profile

Armed Forces Recreation Systems

Within the U.S. armed forces, the system of leisure services is labeled Morale, Welfare, and Recreation (MWR). Supported by Congress, as well as by user fees, the Navy, Army, Air Force, and Marine Corps assign thousands of both uniformed and civilian employees to recreation responsibilities at installations around the world. Programs in sport, outdoor recreation, hobbies, travel, entertainment, and special events are designed to make such a positive contribution to the military life of soldiers and sailors that they will be combat ready as well as want to reenlist (Russell & Jamieson, 2008).

For example, civilian MWR employees of the U.S. Army work closely with deployed soldiers to support physical fitness centers, recreation centers, cyber cafes, and other activities in the Iraq and Afghanistan theaters. Then, *Warrior Adventure Quest* is a program developed to support the needs of returning soldiers with high-adrenaline experiences to help them transition to non-war life and decrease high-risk behavior (Department of the Army, 2008).

Private Agencies

Government sponsored leisure systems are just one slice of the resource pie. Another type of leisure services organizations is private. These are the social, civic, religious, political, fraternal, labor, conservation, special interest, and youth-serving agencies that provide for the pastime interests and needs of members. Almost all of us have been touched at some point in life by this type of leisure service agency. Have you ever been a Boy or Girl Scout, a Big Brother or Big Sister? Have you been a member of the YMCA, or 4-H, a country club, or fraternity or sorority? Did you play baseball in Little League? Does anyone you know belong to Kiwanis, the Nature Conservancy, the Catholic Youth Organization, or Bass Unlimited?

Private leisure organizations are defined as those providing recreation opportunities for their members. These range from small groups of people gathered to express a particular leisure interest, such as your grandfather's poker club, to complex organizations with thousands of members, such as Girls Inc. A tidy system of categorizing this range does not exist, but it may be useful to consider them according to those that are private leisure dominant organizations, private secondary leisure organizations, and quasi-private organizations.

First, private leisure dominant organizations exist primarily to serve the leisure interests of their members. For example, social clubs, country clubs, college alumni clubs, and poker clubs provide for members' social needs. Clubs promoting drama, music, the fine arts, and hobbies are also extensively available. Some of these organizations own extensive facilities, such as retreat centers, clubhouses, dining rooms, libraries, studios, practice rooms, and game rooms.

Other examples include organizations focused on sports. Thousands of private sporting clubs were formed in the late 1800s, and there remains many golf, tennis, cricket, bowling, swimming, sailing, skiing, and track and field clubs today. While some sports clubs have no facilities of their own and use public facilities, others control extensive properties, including marinas and playing fields.

Further, outdoor recreation expressions are often the feature of private leisure-dominant organizations, including hiking, bicycling, mountaineering, and camping clubs. For example, the Appalachian Trail Conservancy (http://www.appalachiantrail.org) is an 80-year-old private organization made up of members dedicated to the conservation of the 2,175-mile Appalachian National Scenic Trail—a 250,000 acre greenway extending from Maine to Georgia.

Another category of privately sponsored agencies is the secondary leisure organization. These organizations contribute to the supply of leisure opportunities, even though their primary purpose is something else. For example, residential management associations, composed of owners of houses or condominiums, exist primarily to maintain and manage shared residential facilities, such as roads, parking, trees, lawns, etc, but also frequently manage shared recreation resources, such as swimming pools, tennis courts, and party rooms. Religious organizations are another example of private secondary leisure sponsors. Some religious groups provide gymnasiums and swimming pools, own land and buildings in resort locations, and offer campgrounds and cabins.

A final example of the private secondary leisure category is that of corporations and industries. *Employee recreation* services provide facilities and programs ranging from holiday events, sports leagues, and summer camps to charter travel arrangements, stores, fitness centers, and even stress management and weight control classes—all aimed at building a sense of camaraderie and loyalty among company employees. The payoff for the company, of course, is healthier employees, which both increases work productivity and decreases insurance costs (Russell & Jamieson, 2008).

Employee recreation: leisure services sponsored by companies as an employee benefit

Finally, a large collection of private organizations can be grouped under the heading of quasi-private organizations. These represent a special kind of private leisure resource, because while they exist to serve the needs and interests of their members, they also receive support from the public at-large or a governmental agency. For example, such organizations as 4-H clubs and YMCAs may receive government grants or public donations, and although they may have membership policies, participation cannot be denied on account of race, religion, ethnicity, sexual orientation, or income level. For example, there are 4-H clubs for urban residents and people of any or no religious affiliation are welcome to join the YMCA.

Perhaps we can cite *campus recreation* as another example. Regardless of whether a college or university is privately or state supported, the leisure services offered on campuses are open not only to students but often also to faculty, staff, and the broader community. For example, the University of Nebraska at Lincoln boasts one of the largest collegiate recreation programs in the United States, serving over 25,000 student, campus, and community facility members annually. Services in fitness, outdoor adventures, and intramural sports seek primarily to help current students cope with academic pressures as well as recruit new students, but these services also provide for a more vibrant campus community all around, thus everyone can belong.

Campus recreation: leisure services sponsored by colleges and universities for students, as well as the campus and town communities

Commercial Agencies

As we noted in Chapter 11, in contemporary societies, people are willing (and often eager) to pay for leisure services. In fact, commercial sponsorship of leisure is one of the largest and fastest growing areas of the leisure resource system. Commercial leisure service organizations sell leisure experiences to make a profit. Expenditures for commercially sponsored pastimes far exceed those for services offered by public and private agencies.

Leisure resources operated for commercial purposes include ski resorts, water parks, campgrounds, bowling centers, riding stables, health spas, hotels, restaurants, theaters, casinos, theme parks, sport stadiums, and music halls. In some cities, regions, states, and even nations, commercial leisure organizations are the principal industry.

In spite of this variety, certain types of pastimes are regarded the domain of mainly commercial sponsorship. For example, commercial agencies are more likely to be associated with entertainment, popular culture, spectator sport, theme park, food and drink, and shopping facilities and programs. As a frequently glamorous resource for leisure, commercial services provide a magnitude of opportunities that round out the services offered by public and private sponsors. This is because commercial enterprises are able to offer activities that are too expensive for public and private sponsors, and that offer unique experiences not a part of people's everyday leisure expressions.

As well, commercial leisure organizations are able to respond quickly to current trends and often more willing to take speculative risks, thus creating demands for new leisure resources. A good illustration of this is the wave pool. Commercial developers introduced the idea into the United States and demonstrated its ability to entice patrons to stay longer, return more often, and pay higher admission charges than conventional swimming pools (Chubb & Chubb, 1981). As a result, public agencies such as cities, now offer wave pools as standard services.

In spite of the many benefits of commercial recreation, there are also criticisms. A prime complaint is the profit motive itself. Commercial establishments have been blamed for being too tempted by making money and thus disregarding the overall welfare of people. By actively advertising, they can create demands were none previously existed. Such facilities as adult bookstores have also been blamed for the demise of a positive moral order in society.

Those criticisms that ring true are, however, controlled. Such regulations as legal and trade boundaries, competition, and public opinion indicate what is appreciated from what is not tolerated in commercial recreation. For example, a dishonest operation is likely to have to close up when a responsible competitor opens for business.

Figure 14.7

Commercial leisure enterprises are often trendsetters in delivery of services to people. (© Ruth V. Russell, 2008)

To conclude the chapter, there is one more form of leisure resources that combines everything we've discussed. *Therapeutic recreation (TR)* services seek to restore or rehabilitate in order to improve the well being of persons with illnesses or living with disabling conditions. Using travel, cultural arts, sports, and outdoor recreation, as well as social activities and hobbies, as part of a treatment regime, TR services are sponsored by public, private and commercial agencies. For example, commercial hospitals, private rehabilitation centers, nonprofit extended-care services, public recreation and park departments, colleges and universities, and many other different kinds of sponsors use a wide range of leisure expressions as a tool for curing, improving, or accommodating conditions.

Therapeutic recreation (TR): the provision of recreation services as treatment for persons with illness or disabling conditions

What We Understand About Leisure Service Systems

Leisure is a significant institution in contemporary societies. It includes a wide range of leisure expressions and social structures. Once chiefly the responsibility of the family, leisure services have become the responsibility of a number of organizations, loosely formed into a leisure services system. From reading this chapter you know that:

- Leisure is sponsored by numerous public, private, and commercial organizations.

- These include cities, hospitals, schools, correctional institutions, the armed forces, universities, retail businesses, clubs, and thousands of others.
- The leisure experiences provided by these sponsors primarily include outdoor recreation, cultural arts, travel, and sports.

References

American Farmland Trust. (2007). Farming on the edge report. *Resources.* Available from http://www.farmland.org/. Retrieved 8/7/08.

Bourdieu, P., & Passeron, J-C. (1973). Cultural reproduction and social reproduction. In R.K. Brown (Ed.), *Knowledge, education and cultural change.* London: Tavistock.

Chubb, M., & Chubb, H.R. (1981). *One third of our time? An introduction to recreation behavior and resources.* New York: John Wiley & Sons.

Department of the Army. (2008). Morale, Welfare, and Recreation. *2008 Army Posture Statement.* Available from http://www.army.mil/aps/08/information_papers/sustain/Morale_Welfare_and_Recreation.html. Retrieved 8/18/08.

Downey, D., & Powell, B. (1993). Do children in single-parent households fare better living with same-sex parents? *Journal of Marriage and the Family, 55,* 55-71.

Dumais, S.A. (2002). Cultural capital, gender, and school success: The role of habitus. *Sociology of Education, 75*(1), 44-68.

Elderhostel. (2008). *Home page.* Available from http://www.elderhostel.org/. Retrieved 8/5/08.

Fantasy Sports Trade Association. (July 25, 2008). Fantasy sports industry grows to a $800 million industry with 29.9 million players. *eMediaWire.* Available from http://www.emediawire.com/releases/2008/7/emw1084994.htm. Retrieved 8/5/08.

Francis, M. (September 2005). Free to change: In a correctional facility setting, recreation has the power to bring inmates into a social setting. *Parks & Recreation Magazine,* 27-31.

Freysinger, V.J., & Kelly, J.R. (2004). *21st Century leisure: current issues* (2nd Ed.). State College, PA: Venture.

Kalmijn, M., & Kraaykamp, G. (1996). Race, cultural capital, and schooling: An analysis of trends in the United States. *Sociology of Education, 69*(1), 22-34.

Katsillis, J., & Rubinson, R. (1990). Cultural capital, student achievement, and educational reproduction: The case of Greece. *American Sociological Review, 55*(2), 270-279.

Maclean, J.R., Peterson, J.A., & Martin, W.D. (1985). *Recreation and leisure: The changing scene.* New York: John Wiley & Son.

Messner, M. (1992). *Power at play.* Boston, MA: Beacon Press.

Mohr, J.W., & DiMaggio, P. (1995). The intergenerational transmission of cultural capital. *Research in Social Stratification and Mobility, 14,* 169-200.

National Resources Inventory (2008). *Fiscal Year 2007 Financial Report*. Available from www.nrcs.usda.gov/programs/fppa/. Retrieved 6/7/08.

Peter, T.A. (August 1, 2008). New sports center helps Iraqi youths opt out of insurgency. *The Christian Science Monitor*. Available from http://www. csmonitor.com/2008/0801/p12s01-wome.html. Retrieved 8/5/08.

Rauscher, F. (1994). *Music and spatial task performance: A causal relationship*. Irvine, CA: Center for the Neurobiology of Learning and Memory.

Russell, R.V., & Jamieson, L.M. (2008). *Leisure program planning and delivery*. Champaign, IL: Human Kinetics.

Stempel, C. (2005). Adult participation sports as cultural capital: A test of Bourdieu's theory of the field of sports. *International Review for the Sociology of Sport, 40*(4), 411-432.

Travel Industry Association of America. (2003). *Travel Statistics & Trends: US Travel Market Overview*. Available from http://www.tia.org/Travel/tvt.asp. Retrieved 8/4/08.

U.S. Department of Agriculture. (August 2001). Development at & beyond the urban fringe: Impacts on agriculture. *Agricultural Outlook*. Available from http://www.ers.usda.gov/publications/AgOutlook/aug2001/AO283f.pdf. Retrieved 8/7/08.

U.S. Census Bureau. (2007a). Table 1219. *Statistical Abstract of the United States: 2007*. Washington, D.C.: Government Printing Office.

U.S. Census Bureau. (2007b). Table 1239. *Statistical Abstract of the United States: 2007*. Washington, D.C.: Government Printing Office.

Weiting, S.G., & Lamoureux, D. (2001). Curling in Canada. *Sport in Society, 4*(2), 140-156.

Westerville Parks and Recreation Department. (2008). *Home page*. Available from http://www.westerville.org/Default.aspx?tabid=121. Retrieved 8/11/08.

World Tourism Organization. (June 2007). *UNWTO World Tourism Barometer, 5*(2). Available from http://www.tourismroi.com/Content_ Attachments/27670/File_633513750035785076.pdf. Retrieved 8/4/08.

World Tourism Organization. (June 2008). *UNWTO World Tourism Barometer, 6*(2). Available from http://www.tourismroi.com/Content_ Attachments/27670/File_633513750035785076.pdf. Retrieved 8/4/08.

INDEX

H

I